# Propriety and Permissiveness in Bourbon Mexico

This book was donated
in honor of

*LESLIE KIM*

*HISTORY TEACHER*

*by*

*BEVERLY ABRAHAM*

*MARCH 2001*

DATE

D0150284

# Propriety and Permissiveness in Bourbon Mexico

Juan Pedro Viqueira Albán

Translated by
Sonya Lipsett-Rivera
and Sergio Rivera Ayala

A Scholarly Resources Inc. Imprint
Wilmington, Delaware

Scholarly Resources Inc.
104 Greenhill Avenue
Wilmington, DE  19805-1897

www.scholarly.com

**Library of Congress Cataloging-in-Publication Data**

Viqueira Albán, Juan Pedro.
    [Relajados o reprimidos?  English]
    Propriety and permissiveness in Bourbon Mexico / Juan
Pedro Viqueira Albán ; translated by  Sonya Lipsett-Rivera and
Sergio Rivera Ayala.
       p.   cm. — (Latin American silhouettes)
    Includes bibliographical references (p.    ).
    ISBN 0-8420-2466-2 (cloth : alk. paper). — ISBN  0-8420-
2467-0  (pbk. : alk. paper)
    1. Mexico City (Mexico)—Social life and customs.
2. Mexico—Civilization—French influences. 3. Elite (Social
sciences)—Mexico—Mexico City—History—18th century.
4. Popular culture—Mexico—Mexico City.  I. Lipsett-Rivera,
Sonya, 1961–  . II. Rivera Ayala, Sergio, 1961–  . III. Series.
F1386.2.V5713   1999
972'.53—dc21                            99-19888
                                            CIP

*A book which attempted to chronicle*

*the history of public entertainments*

*in Mexico would be curious indeed.*

—Enrique de Olavarría y Ferrari

# About the Translators

SONYA LIPSETT-RIVERA earned her Ph.D. at Tulane University in 1988. She is an Associate Professor of History at Carleton University. For her articles she won the Tibesar Award in 1992 and received Honorable Mention in the Conference on Latin American History Prize in 1999. She is the author of *To Defend Our Water with the Blood of Our Veins: The Struggle for Resources in Colonial Puebla* (1999) and the coeditor of *The Faces of Honor: Sex, Violence, and Shame in Colonial Latin America* (1998).

SERGIO RIVERA-AYALA, an Instructor in the School of Extension of the Universidad Autónoma de México in Canada, received his Ph.D. in Latin American Literature from Syracuse University in 1998. His research focuses on the strategies of power in colonial Mexican literature. He published an article about street dance and songs in eighteenth-century Mexico in William H. Beezley et al., *Rituals of Rule, Rituals of Resistance* (1994) and co-authored another about film and history in Donald F. Stevens, ed., *Based on a True Story* (1997). Dr. Rivera-Ayala is currently working on a series of articles about the conceptions of colonial urban landscape as well as reworking his dissertation, "Space, Body and Power: Strategies of Colonial Discourse in Some Texts of New Spain" as a monograph.

# Contents

# Acknowledgments

I owe a great deal to the Colegio de Michoacán. My most important debts are to my training as a historian and the institution's constant support for this project. I began this venture under the guidance of Andrés Lira, who inspired me in his class on historical theory. He became the supervisor of my Master's thesis, which I presented in 1984. It was the seed from which this book sprouted. Thanks to his wise advice and observations—in general and in detail—I was able to correct, complete, and improve it substantially.

My interest in the study of the eighteenth century in colonial Mexico emerged in the fascinating seminar on the period of the Enlightenment given by Roberto Moreno y de los Arcos in the Universidad Nacional Autónoma de México. When I moved to Zamora in Michoacán, I lost the benefit of his sound advice. The counsels of Jean Pierre Berthe, an old teacher of mine, were of great utility. Luis González and Heriberto Moreno also made important suggestions for its improvement. Guillermo Bonfil read part of the first draft and encouraged me to finish. Without the discussions with Luis María Gatti, the stylistic corrections of my mother, Anne Marie Albán, and the support of my wife, Graciela Alcalá, I would never have been able to finish it. Alberto Cue edited the final version and improved it. Patricia Lagos and Gloria Valero deciphered my horrible handwriting and typed the original manuscript.

The Consejo Nacional de Ciencia y Tecnología, the Colegio de Michoacán, the Escuela Nacional de Antropología e Historia, and the Centro de Investigaciones y Estudios Superiores en Antropología Social all provided financial support, which made the Spanish version possible. Despite the backing of such prestigious institutions and the kind advice of so many eminent historians, I am responsible for the final product. I thank these researchers for their interest, and their assistance. I do not hope to use the prestige of their names to protect myself from deserved criticism.

The thinker who inspired this apprehension regarding enlightened despotism, the notion of progress and knowledge as mediums to achieve happiness, is only explicitly mentioned in this book when I discuss those who wished to introduce the theater into the city of his birth and those who wished to trick his contemporaries by supposedly turning a jug of water into wine. I refer, of course, to Jean-Jacques Rousseau. I had to keep a special place in my acknowledgments to honor him and his defiant clearheadedness.

*J.P.V.A.*

# Preface

Many readers might wonder if this work is not really a study of the breakdown of customs in the eighteenth century but rather a clear example of the breakdown of academic customs in the present. Undoubtedly, such a belief would not be without some basis. It is not uncommon for the present to influence the study of the past. These days, presentism does reach such extremes.

In such a context, it should come as no surprise that when the moral values and the norms of conduct change drastically from one generation to the next, an interest in the phenomenon of the breakdown of customs in the century of the Enlightenment piqued someone's interest.

In fact, I began the research that led to this study by looking at eighteenth-century New Spain for a mirror in which to examine the present. I wanted to know how a period and a society had invented a more unfettered manner of daily existence. But, in my search for this liberation within sociability, I stumbled onto something quite different: enlightened despotism. This monstrous creation was born of the coupling of Absolute Power with Knowledge. This discovery is at the same time a reflection and a mirror of the present day.

Over the course of my work, it became evident that the problem of the breakdown of customs was too vast for the time I had and also for my capacities. It was too large a subject to be taken on in its totality. So I decided to limit myself to the study of some of its aspects that I believed would shed light on the whole. Popular diversions or, more precisely, the bullfights, the theater, street entertainments, and the game of pelota formed the core of my study. For this same reason, my investigation centered on Mexico City, the urban center par excellence of the colony that held the greatest concentration of public diversions.

As for the chronological limits, I did not restrict myself to the traditional boundaries that demark the period of the Enlightenment. I looked at documents from the eighteenth century but some from the seventeenth century, too. But, actually, the documentation on popular diversion only began to be abundant in the latter half of the eighteenth century. I also decided to include the period of the Wars for Independence with the belief that some of the alterations to the social order that this conflict provoked might shed light on some of the hidden mechanisms of colonial society. The outer limit of my chronological reach was the consummation of Independence. This boundary, I believe, marked an abrupt change in the development of the public diversions that had been under the protection of the viceregal governments.

Despite this restriction on the area of my investigation, I did not consult many archival documents and did not extend the consultation of secondary works any further. Erudite historians will, no doubt, notice the numerous omissions. If, despite all these weaknesses, this book entertains readers, its goal will have been reached in good measure.

*J.P.V.A.*

# Abbreviations and Equivalencies

| | |
|---|---|
| ABMNAH | Archivo de la Biblioteca del Museo Nacional de Antropología e Historia |
| AGN | Archivo General de la Nación |
| AHA | Archivo Histórico del Ayuntamiento de la Ciudad de México |

| | |
|---|---|
| 1 peso | 8 reales of silver |
| 1 real of silver | 1 *tomín* or 12 *granos* |
| 1 *carga* of pulque | 18 *arrobas* or 450 *cuartillos* of pulque |
| 1 *cuartillo* of pulque | .396 gallon of pulque |
| 1 *fanega* of corn | 1.5 bushels of corn |
| 1 *vara* | 1 yard |
| 1 *legua* | 2.6 miles |

# Introduction

# The Decline of Propriety

A historian is not one who knows, he is one who seeks. And
therefore calls into question answers that have been given
and retires old cases when he has to.

When he has to. Doesn't that mean always? Let us not
pretend that the conclusions of historians are not of necessity marked by contingency. . . . History is the daughter of
time. I say this not, surely, to disparage her. Philosophy is
the daughter of time. Even physics is the daughter of her
own time; the physics of Langevin was not that of Galileo,
and Galileo's was no longer that of Aristotle. Was there
progress from one to the other? . . . But, as historians, let us
speak of adaptations to the times, . . . every period mentally
constructs its own maps of its historical past. . . . How? Out
of the materials at its disposal. . . . But not only materials are
involved. . . . Above all, there are also interests and areas of
concern which are so quick to change and which direct the
attention of men of a certain period to aspects of the past
that were long hidden in obscurity and will soon recede into
the shadows again. Let us not say that this is human but
rather that it is the law of human knowledge.

—Lucien Febvre

By the end of the eighteenth century, New Spain's economy, society, and culture had all been transformed radically. In his book
*Humboldt y México*, the historian José Miranda emphasizes, among
other changes, the imitation of French manners and customs by
the Mexican elites. Miranda states that the spread of the ideas of
the Enlightenment in the eighteenth century was accompanied by
this trend towards gallicization.[1] According to this author, the adoption of French ways by the elites marked an abrupt departure from
the monotonous and austere social life of the seventeenth century.
By the end of the eighteenth century, New Spain's social life was

rich, agitated, and varied. Public diversions expanded to include cafés, paseos (promenades), and dances. The upper echelons of Mexican society were not the only group affected by this transformation; in fact, it extended to the entire population. While the elites embraced French ways they indulged in an appetite for popular diversions, and so the contact among social classes encouraged the spread of ideas and manners from one group to another. In many of these amusements, such as the dances, "people of all social classes" mixed. As a result, a "decline of propriety" at all levels of society took place during the second half of the eighteenth century.[2]

This generalized "decline" of customs is part of a positive portrayal of the economic, social, and cultural situation of eighteenth-century New Spain. The enormous increase in mining production caused an "explosion of prosperity." It was accompanied and sustained by the penetration of Enlightenment thought, modern philosophy and science, and by the many reforms that had the "goal of promoting the spiritual and material progress of the kingdom of New Spain." Included were administrative reforms, philanthropic measures, and projects of social welfare promoted by the state as well.[3]

When confronted with this vision of the "decline of propriety," it seems obvious that it was really composed of two related phenomena: a gallicization of the elite and a restructuring and strengthening of plebeian culture in the cities. Although these two processes were apparently related, they were characterized by different and opposing logics. If two currents of change existed at the same time, then the idea of a diffusion of "decline" from the top down within Mexican society must be rejected. On the one hand, the upper classes adopted French manners; and, on the other, demographic growth and the economic transformations of the period caused a restructuring and strengthening of urban popular culture. But what exactly was the transformation that affected the lower classes? Recent studies question the optimistic view of the eighteenth century and show that behind a facade of mining wealth the majority of the population lived in very harsh conditions. The eighteenth century was a period of "growth without development."[4]

The numerous epidemics and famines that the lower classes suffered indicate that their living standards had fallen. The increase in banditry and begging is another, clearer sign of the impoverishment of groups at the bottom of society. The historian Enrique Florescano shows the devastating effect that agricultural crises had upon these classes and, in particular, upon the indigenous population. Famines and epidemics were simply another factor that contributed to the process of disintegration of the indigenous communities. At the same time, the owners of haciendas, who were eager to absorb more lands, caused another series of pressures upon indigenous communities. All these social and natural calamities provoked an exodus from the countryside to the city. Displaced Indians enlarged the plebeian classes of the cities.[5] Some industries (workshops, mines) appeared in these urban centers and thus concentrated large contingents of workers in the same place. There are two examples that represent this phenomenon at its extreme: the mine of Valenciana, which in 1809 employed three thousand workers, and the tobacco factory in Mexico City, which employed six thousand workers.[6]

Would these new economic and social conditions have changed the way of life of the urban popular classes in any radical way? Was it this transformation that awakened a preoccupation in the church and the viceregal authorities to end the "disorders" and the "decline of propriety" within these social groups? A writer of the period expressed these concerns: "In these factories, a multitude of people of both sexes work and despite all the vigilance exerted . . . who can hinder perverse and harmful conversations of licentious people there?" He went on to lament, "Who can stop the pernicious harm occasioned to young men and women who, although they leave by distinct and separate doors, meet around the corner?"[7] Besides, much to the despair of the authorities, many of these centers were the starting point for strong movements of protest.[8]

It is very tempting to make a connection between this phenomenon and Edward Shorter's analysis in *The Making of the Modern Family*.[9] In late eighteenth-century Europe, the advances in the market economy and industrialization undermined the traditional base of agrarian communities, which provoked a migration to cities and the proletarianization of male and female workers. As they broke their ties with their villages, both men and women also escaped the control exerted by these communities and adopted new and more liberated patterns of behavior (including sexual conduct). Shorter calls this trend the "first sexual revolution." Was this transformation the European equivalent to the "decline of propriety in New Spain"? But such European models cannot be adopted without a few warnings. New Spain was not in the process of becoming an industrial society in the eighteenth century. An uprooted Indian was not the equivalent of a proletarianized French peasant. The fact that these two processes occurred at the same time does not mean that the contexts of each phenomenon can be ignored.

What, then, does the "decline of propriety" of New Spain mean? The documents of the period can help explain this question. After 1750 rules and regulations proliferated. Therefore, decrees, royal patents, edicts, inquisitorial proclamations, and pastoral letters provide the most obvious starting point in the documentary trail of information. Much of this regulation—civil and ecclesiastical prohibitions—reiterate and lament the perversion and breakdown of customs and, therefore, the need to solve this serious problem. The officials who wrote these documents described in some detail the excesses that they hoped to combat. Lascivious dances, public drunkenness, fights in *pulquerías*, women of ill repute, disorders in the theater, and insults at games of pelota are all described repeatedly. As a result, scholars have concluded that another well-documented phenomenon—the gallicization of the elites—was transformed into pure "depravity" as it spread into the lower classes.

In order to understand the real significance of this increased regulation of private and public customs and styles, however, these rules must be placed in the context of the Bourbon reforms. In the second half of the eighteenth century, the Spanish state undertook major reforms that profoundly altered life in New Spain: reorganization of the financial system, boosting of mining production, creation of the intendancy system, expulsion of the Jesuits, alienation of the goods of the church, free trade, suppression of the *alcaldes mayores*, creation of a regular army, the multiplication of obstacles to the industries in New Spain, and the rest.[10] The Spanish Crown thus attempted, through the establishment of a modern state apparatus, to subject and exploit colonial Mexico more systematically. But was this proliferation of rules really a reaction to the new social mores? In other words, does the multiplication of laws and decrees to stop certain public entertainments confirm a transformation in New Spain? Was it the society itself that had altered? Had the decline of propriety really occurred? Or was it a shift in the state that meant that the officials no longer tolerated traditional social practices? Perhaps both the Spanish state and society in New Spain changed in important ways during this period.

Clearly, both the Spanish state and the elites of colonial Mexico underwent a radical transformation as they modernized, but what is less obvious is whether the popular classes followed their lead or found their own way along the path of change. Did the urban popular classes change their lifestyles and their view of the world? Did they shed their traditional nature while becoming a kind of proletariat? Did they follow the perilous path of "social degeneration"? In short, did the urban popular classes stray from the behavior prescribed by the dominant elites or were they already very far from this ideal of public morality?

There is no simple, clear-cut answer to these questions. Historians have examined similar questions for eighteenth-century Europe, and they have offered only very cautious explanations. The situation in New Spain was much more complex. There, the diversity of population—indigenous and, to some extent, African peoples as well as racially mixed men and women of diverse ethnicities and social provenance—affected the urban masses. Finally, when was eighteenth-century urban culture the result of change and when was it simply the continuation of previous patterns? Until now, most historians have insisted that the change detected in these social groups was a "decline," but perhaps this interpretation neglects the attitude of the state in its new enlightened intolerance toward traditional forms of conduct among those not considered "decent folk."

Not all commentators of the period mention the social disorder, the perversion of customs, and the agitation of public life; on the contrary, apparently some observers perceived the opposite. Let me cite three witnesses; the first is none other than that enlightened Viceroy Juan Vicente de Güemes Pacheco y Padilla, the second count of Revillagigedo, who noted, "Nor are there cafés in this city where people read gazettes, where the shiftless get together to discuss the news, nor are there houses where influential foreigners gather, nor meetings where subversion is sown and encouraged." He also states that "even in the houses of Spaniards, there are hardly any social gatherings."[11] Obviously, the viceroy refers only to social activities at the level of the elite. But the usual supposition is that the "decline" began in the *tertulias* (regular gatherings of intellectuals) and cafés of the upper echelons of society.

Another observer, a journalist, wrote in 1806: "The principal spectacle is that of the theater; its decorations are good; the actors are not bad, and among these, there are some who could shine even in Madrid or in Naples, the house is comfortable and well regulated by the judges." But, he objected, "I have only one query. Why do the more educated members of the audience applaud the short farces presented only to please the vile plebeian classes?" In an attempt to explain such puzzling behavior he asked, "Perchance, do they ignore that, with their intemperate applause, they encourage this depraved appetite that stimulates representations that should disappear from an enlightened country and a century like ours?" But finally he concluded that "otherwise, to be truthful, it must be noted that European theaters do not display the same type of moderation and decency that ours does in its interior, particularly for the boxes and stalls," and that "our theater could be improved by exerting more modern taste in the selection of works to present, better trained actors, less use of the prompters, not smoking while on the stage," and "finally, the pressure of opinion so that people can sit in the patio without preoccupation for their dress and without any worry about the diversion, that is not harmful in itself. This will make our theater more agreeable and its attendance more useful." All in all, although this observer noted room for improvement in the Mexican theater, he did not find it inferior to those of Europe, nor did he note this supposed "decline of propriety."

This journalist, however, went on to describe and comment upon other areas of social life in New Spain. The game of pelota, a forerunner of jai alai, he states "is open to all and offers a pleasant diversion for the spectator and healthy exercise for the participants." Gambling was allowed, but "bets on the contestants should not surpass a few pesos. The person who wagers more than an *onza* of gold seeks a ruinous game and not an honest pastime." He found that the same conditions applied to cockfights. They were held in an adequate building that "would seem perfect if the bookies who manage the gambling would not take on so many bets at one time and would acknowledge more promptly the need for more personnel to take the wagers." Apart from such diversions as the theater, pelota, and cockfights, colonial Mexicans also gathered at cafés. But "cafés in Mexico only serve as a place to eat and to discuss matters in a *tertulia* for a while; literary discussions are just starting to take place in such spots." But people in New Spain did read the newspapers *El Diario*, *La Gaceta*, and the *Jornal Económico Mercantil*, which "provide so much food for thought." Still, according to this author, these newspapers did not disturb the social peace of the colony: "Luckily, because of the criticisms in these papers, our cafés are kept free of murmuring and plots, which are generally hatched and protected in the cafés of most other parts!"

For the elite, the paseo, or promenade, was another important diversion. It consisted of a regular walk along a prescribed route around a square or along the banks of a river, at which time, men and women discreetly greeted and observed each other. For this author, "the most popular and important paseo takes place in the Alameda on Sundays." At that time and place, "The multitude of carriages of all colors and structures, the fastidiousness of dress, the distinguished people who attend, the exquisiteness of the ladies who grace the event, all these factors contribute to make this the most agreeable of public spectacles." But he had one reservation: "Only one caprice spoils this custom: the habit of those who sit in the coaches facing each other and the custom of not being able to arrive on foot without provoking disapproval." He objected to these conventions because they "are insufferable for those who have no carriage," but also stated that "these prejudices are being recognized and perhaps soon will be eliminated."

The beauty of the surroundings made the paseo a particularly pleasant diversion for the elites. During the period of Lent, the paseo took place at La Viga. This paseo lasted until Assumption Sunday at the end of the Easter period. The author describes the area around La Viga as particularly appealing for "the luxuriance of the trees that line the avenue provide an agreeable shade, the *chinampas* [raised fields] nearby, and the beautiful canal on which many people navigate in canoes and small boats, the nearby country houses." Such natural beauty was complemented by "the beautiful architecture and gardens of these residences," which "not only provide a pleasing sight but also inspire a sweet enthusiasm and elevation of the spirit in meditation on the Supreme Creator of Nature."[12]

These are rather extensive passages to cite, but the descriptions indicate an orderly society, in contrast to the prevailing view presented by historians, and as such are rather surprising. According to this observer, a definite supporter of orderly diversions, only a few vices and excesses needed to be eliminated—more mannerly behavior in the theater, moderation of bets at the game of pelota and cockfights, walking during the paseos—and a perfect tranquillity would reign in public places.

Finally, the last word goes to the eminent members of the Royal Audiencia of Mexico who, in 1784, wrote the "Informe sobre pulquerías y tabernas" (Report on pulque shops and taverns). Their goal in writing this report was to put an end to the excesses caused by public drunkenness. They commented that "those who have come to these parts, especially in the last twenty years, assure that those who knew Mexico before are aware that every day there is less and less laxity in the customs of people of every class and rank including the regular and secular clergy." According to members of the Audiencia, the explanation for this improvement comprised

many factors. They could not "enumerate all the secondary reasons that explain why Mexico is less morally lax and its population
no longer so naked as they were twenty years ago," but they provided a list of some factors:

> the arrival of veteran troops, establishments like the Maritime
> Mail, the Monte de Piedad, and the Hospice [for the poor], the
> administration of royal income, less self-serving use of position
> by officials, especially in their own jurisdictions, the increase in
> positions in this Audiencia and the creation of the post of regent
> to facilitate the administration of justice, having qualified subal-
> terns in the positions of *alcaldes del crimen* and judge of the
> Acordada, the zeal with which those who carried prohibited arms
> have been caught and prosecuted, the creation of eight districts
> within the city with thirty-two alcaldes from the different
> neighborhoods.[13]

Contrary to the views of many historians, these local officials
thought that the Bourbon reforms had not been accompanied by a
breakdown of customs, but rather that these measures created a
more orderly society by instituting new mechanisms of education,
control, and the repression of the popular classes of Mexico City.
In other words, in these twenty years, the government had succeeded in more efficiently curbing those customs of the populace
that the enlightened officials considered depraved.

Such testimonies should not be overrated; they prove nothing
in isolation. Certainly, it would be easy to find other passages that
indicate the opposite. These excerpts are useful, however, to reopen the historical discussion regarding the decline of propriety in
late colonial Mexico. This question needs to be examined again with
a healthy degree of skepticism.

# 1

# From the Don Juans to the Patriots

The Spanish Crown's preoccupation with the breakdown of Mexican customs did not begin in the eighteenth century. As early as 1633, Philip IV had written to Viceroy Marquis of Cerralvo that he had "heard by means of accounts and notices of this province, from dutiful and loyal people who have been there and have informed me, that the decline of customs and licentious lifestyle is common to all types of people."[1] The king had good reason to worry about the situation in colonial Mexico. In 1624, Viceroy Marquis of Gelves and Archbishop Pérez de la Serna were involved in a rancorous conflict. The residents of Mexico City supported the archbishop and they rioted, forcing the removal of the viceroy. By 1633, people in the capital were still by no means pacified. The king named both a new viceroy and a new archbishop—the Marquis of Cerralvo and the priest Francisco de Manso y Zúñiga respectively—but the rivalry between the civil and religious branches of government continued to threaten social peace in New Spain.

Apart from these political conflicts, the Crown's power in the colonies was also weakened by the long-standing and deeply rooted corruption of bureaucrats. Even at the level of viceroy—the highest office in the land—widespread corruption was a problem.[2] Then, as if in divine retribution, a devastating flood engulfed the city of Mexico in 1629. In fact, the dilemma of moral decay was a critical problem in the entire empire and not just in Mexico. Spanish decadence had already begun. The shipments of silver bullion from the Americas had started to taper off considerably; the population of the Iberian Peninsula was diminished; industry and pastoralism there were undergoing a severe crisis; other nations constantly breached the commercial monopoly with the colonies; and other European powers challenged the supremacy of Spain.

Faced with such a desperate situation, Philip IV, who was at the same time pious and libertine, interpreted these reverses as divine punishment for the moral dissipation of the empire. The situation in New Spain seemed particularly deplorable. The king reasoned that political reverses were linked to the decline of propriety among his subjects; his logic is obvious in the letter he wrote in 1633 asking Viceroy Marquis of Cerralvo to put an end to the moral dissolution prevailing in the colony. The king stated his belief "that Our Lord sends us the hardships that we suffer every day because of these and other great sins of Christians, which transgressions prevent Him from being compassionate," and thus Philip IV understood why God punished him through defeats and political reverses. The penalties suffered by the king and his empire included "the events that reduced the remittances from these provinces; as a result of our nation's decadence, we lost these riches, and other income was lost because of adverse weather and the unfortunate defeats of the armies who fight for us." Many others agreed with the king's judgment that "Our Lord is angry and that He allowed these continual disasters in castigation for our sins." Therefore, it seemed only logical to instruct the viceroy to "punish public sins with much diligence and care and to prevent those scandals that may cause some distress to the republic, and in all this, to procure the correction of those customs without making exceptions for anyone."[3]

In the years that followed, however, the situation in Spain worsened. France's intervention in the Thirty Years' War in 1635 seriously threatened the predominance of the Spanish armies. As a result, in 1637, Philip IV once again ordered the viceroy of New Spain to combat moral laxity in an attempt to regain divine grace. He stated that "with the threat of the violence of our enemies on all sides . . . I have deemed it appropriate to tell you that in order to achieve some successes, I am counting entirely on the goodness and compassion of Our Lord and to prevail, I entrust you . . . to punish all the vices and scandals."[4] These supplications and entreaties to divine power did not prevent the increasingly rapid crumbling away of Spanish power. After the Dutch defeated the Spanish army in 1639 at the Battle of Dunas, the Netherlands began to dominate the Atlantic. By almost totally cutting off communication between Spain and its colonies, the Dutch prevented the transmission of bullion to the Iberian Peninsula. In 1640, Portugal became independent and Catalonia rebelled, and so the political reverses were much closer at hand.

In a royal decree of 1646, the king once again asked the viceroy of New Spain to arrange prayers and to prevent public sins in the colony in order to recover divine compassion.[5] Charles II, the son and heir of Philip IV, adopted the same policy as his father; he tried to delay the ruin of Spain by appealing for divine assistance. In 1677, he sent a royal decree to Archbishop-Viceroy Brother Payo Enríquez de Rivera that entrusted him with the correction of sins. The king stated that "the most secure method to ensure the common good is to appeal to Our Lord, imploring Him for divine assistance." He believed that, in these difficult times, "the most assured route is to prevent public scandals and sins using the righteousness of justice to reward and punish, cultivating virtues with the institution of good customs." It was vital to reject vices and to repair the "prejudicial abuses which had been introduced into this society." Therefore, the king "resolved to make this task a priority of the archbishops and bishops . . . who, with the help of my viceroy and presidents [of Audiencias], . . . will find a remedy for this public defect, by taking charge of the correction of sins by all means possible."[6] The king renewed this order in 1679 because the troubles that afflicted Spain had not ceased.[7]

During most of the seventeenth century, Spanish kings were preoccupied with the decline of propriety. Moral and religious concerns were at the heart of this fixation. The campaign to combat the breakdown of customs in this period was undertaken not because of a threat to the social order—such concerns were never even mentioned—but rather because God had withdrawn his protection from the empire.

Then, what did the decline of propriety mean in the seventeenth century? The royal decree of 1646 provides a rough answer; it lists the public sins that were to be eliminated. These sins included those "of sensuality, oaths that should be avoided as well as all illicit dealings which have been introduced into the kingdom, particularly by greedy judicial and government officials." The king also urged officials to "be particularly vigilant that no layperson may enter a convent." Finally, he stated that "you must severely punish the most minor impropriety committed in the visiting room of convents since the news of such behavior has reached us even here."[8] These violations of the moral and religious order can be categorized under three headings: the corruption of bureaucrats in New Spain, the abuses of the clergy, and sexual licentiousness.

Philip IV knew this problem intimately because his court was one of the best examples of sexual abandon. Even the king was widely credited with sexual adventures and extramarital love affairs. When the king censured colonial subjects for their public immorality, his royal decrees were an expression of his periodic repentance for his own dissolute conduct.

The seventeenth century in Spain was the century of *donjuan-ismo* (womanizing), when the legend of the mythical figure of Don Juan first emerged and when the first account of Don Juan's amorous adventures of seduction and betrayal of virgins was written.[9] The intransigence of church rules regarding marriage and sexual morality had not curbed people's passions. On the contrary, as the church reiterated and reinforced these principles, more and more people disobeyed them. The seduction of women became a source of prestige for the Spanish nobility; the greater the difficulty and the risks of a sexual conquest, the more distinguished the seducer became. Thus, the seduction of nuns was the ultimate gallant adventure. Not only did the authorities object to such practices but divine law also proscribed it. The moralists of the period believed that the defilement of nuns was the worst sin imaginable. Nevertheless, men frequently committed such transgressions. Rumor had it that Philip IV himself had engaged in a love affair with a nun. Most historians, however, categorically deny this report. The king was a rake but, most scholars agree, his faith and pious devotion stopped him from committing such a sacrilegious act.[10]

As womanizing and the seduction of nuns became common in the seventeenth century, the trend revealed both the strength and the weakness of the traditional moral order. Those who engaged in such conduct rebelled against the morality espoused by both church and state, but they did not attack it outright. They recognized it as a hierarchy of values. *Donjuanismo* did not represent a substitution of new moral principles for the old ones, but rather an inversion of their order. The worst sin became the greatest virtue. Contemporaries perceived romantic adventures inside the convent walls as an attack upon the foundation of society: its religious infrastructure. The seduction of nuns represented the theft of God's most precious possessions; it was an assault on the divine order; it was the union of lechery and sacrilege. Over the course of the century, the Crown attempted many times to root out *donjuanismo*. The king strictly forbade the communication of laymen with nuns several times in an attempt to cut off opportunities for seductions. A royal decree of 1682 prohibited "the frequent conversations of laymen and nuns in the convents" of New Spain that, "with the cover of devotion," soon passed to "illicit" matters and led to "sins and scandals."[11]

Even the mention of such transgressions was frowned upon. In 1612 and in 1660, the Inquisition vetoed the presentation of two plays that mentioned sexual liaisons with nuns. The main reason for the censorship of these plays, however, was not that they alluded to the seduction of nuns. In fact, in one instance, the Inquisition objected to the attribution to Saint Joan of the Cross of miracles that had not been officially recognized. In the other instance, the inquisitors opposed the author's discussion of predestination. But, in both examples, the inquisitors cited the dangerous references to nuns and love as an aggravating factor; these secondary faults also deserved censure.[12]

Apart from *donjuanismo*, the king worried about control over the morality of priests and monks who were also caught up with the uncontrolled sensuality of the period. Many priests took advantage of the power granted them as nuns' confessors, soliciting sexual favors from the women in return for absolution of their sins. Quite a few clerics succumbed to this sin of solicitation. Jesuit Gaspar de Villenas, for example, tried to seduce ninety-six women in the confessional, although he was successful in only thirty instances. Among those whom he solicited, women of all races and positions in society were represented and, of course, among these, there were some nuns. Both the priest's trial in 1621 and the practice of solicitation were kept secret because officials believed that public knowledge of the clergy's exploits was inadvisable.[13]

The third sign of the breakdown of customs in New Spain that worried the Crown was the corruption of local administrators. The bureaucrats in charge of the Royal Treasury were a particular concern. In this case, financial reasons joined the traditional moral worries.

When the Spanish Crown ordered an end to the decline of customs, the aim of such measures was always directed exclusively at the elite of society. Members of the nobility, it seems, were the most likely to fall into the traps of immorality, because it was usually within this group that *donjuanes*, the clergy, and of course, colonial bureaucrats were found.

These royal orders focused on the elite. The conduct of the lower classes, however, was not always above reproach, and government officials made some attempts to keep the plebeians on the straight and narrow. For example, in 1650, the Crown renewed previous prohibitions against alcoholic drinks. These bans focused in particular on pulque that had been fortified by roots and herbs. The colonial officials also limited the number of *pulquerías*; with these orders, they hoped to end the public disorders caused by drunkenness.[14] The campaign against the consumption of pulque continued in 1671.

The Crown began to impose taxes on pulque and created a branch of the Royal Treasury to regulate its sale and consumption.[15]

In 1688, after the archbishop of Mexico had failed several times to eliminate cockfights, he bought the right to license this diversion and then simply withheld permission to hold them. The archbishop objected to cockfights because he believed that they were the reason for both "secular and spiritual ruin" in the city. He also thought that cockfights caused the "breakup of marriages, thefts, and disgraces." When the king found out how the archbishop had eliminated cockfights, he was delighted. He not only congratulated the archbishop but ordered financial compensation for the cleric. Then the king banned cockfights.[16]

Some viceroys came to believe that the people were, in reality, the source of society's moral dissolution. When in 1663 the Marquis of Mancera advised his successor, the Duke of Veraguas, he wrote that "it is the nature of plebeians that they need too much maintenance." He accused them of "laziness, liberty, and drunkenness" that "precipitate them into all sorts of dissipation and vice."[17]

Most Spanish officials did not, however, share the attitude reflected in this passage. Members of the colonial government differentiated between the shiftless and the dangerous classes from the working population. They categorized mestizos, blacks, mulattoes, and other castes as lazy and dangerous, while they defined the Indians as workers. The second group was worthy of compassion and support. When the king believed that his empire was threatened on all sides and invoked divine assistance, he always remembered his traditional duty to protect the destitute and spoke of the people in terms of paternalistic protection.

When in 1633, 1637, 1646, 1677, and 1679, the king ordered that the lax customs in New Spain be eradicated, he always ended with the directive that the poor be treated justly and be protected from abuses. He stated that "I have resolved . . . that you should be extremely careful . . . that justice is administered in all the districts of your bishoprics, without exception, protecting the poor from the oppression of the powerful, to secure the effects of divine compassion."[18] Over the course of the seventeenth century, even as the king worried more and more about the decline of propriety, he was also concerned about the blurring of social distinctions among the various ranks in society.

Since the first days of the colony, the Spanish rulers had imposed a utopian system of social and political estates that was highly anachronistic. The process of race mixture meant that the real social structure was very different from its representation in laws and social thought. Thus, mestizos, mulattoes, and other castes, who embodied an ever-larger segment of the population, were actually absent from the legislation and also the estate system of the colony. By the seventeenth century, the old order was already much eroded. Individual wealth more than birth determined power within colonial society. But the Spanish state as well as the Mexican elites worried about these changes. Because it was actually impossible to stop these transformations or eliminate their fundamental causes, the only possible remedy was to try to control the results that were considered the most pernicious.

King Philip II's 1611 order provides an example of the Crown's obsession with the maintenance of the traditional system of hierarchy. He commanded that, when addressing a person either orally or in writing, correct titles, distinctions, and courtesies according to rank must be respected in order to put an end to "the disorder, excess, and inequality" that had been introduced into social mores. Philip IV reiterated this order in 1623.[19] In the same way, the sovereign often intervened in conflicts over precedence that arose in public ceremonies where the honor of civil and religious authorities was given a concrete physical manifestation. Thus, in the seventeenth century, there are many royal decrees on such matters. The Crown, for example, gave orders regarding the way *oidores* (judges) could travel in a carriage with the viceroy, the use of pillows during a religious ceremony, the positioning of the viceroy's pages during the procession of Corpus Christi, and more. In the vast majority of such orders, the king's message was the same: avoid innovation and follow tradition.[20]

The king's constant desire to maintain a clear differentiation of the estates was another aspect of this campaign. It was also illustrated in the dispositions that prohibited wearing clothes associated with another social group. In the same tone, in 1679, the bishop of Michoacán denounced "the notable disorder . . . in the clothes, as well as their lack of honesty because without any distinction, both nobles and plebes dress with silks and precious cloths, wear jewels of gold and pearls, and silver."[21]

The king's desire to return to a traditional social order that would make racial mixing impossible was also apparent in the many royal orders. The efforts in Mexico City to segregate the Indians in their neighborhoods and to keep Spaniards living inside the city boundaries was another way that officials tried to prevent cross-racial contact.[22] The commissioner general of the Franciscans,

Brother Hernando de la Rosa, wrote in 1670 that this cohabitation of Indians with Spaniards, blacks, mulattoes, and mestizos was one of the worst evils, because it meant that the Indians no longer received even the most elemental religious instruction. The Indians adopted perversions from the example set by other castes who stooped so low as to rob "even the convents of nuns."[23]

These examples clearly demonstrate that the breakdown of customs that so preoccupied the Crown in the seventeenth century was, in reality, simply social change. In effect, the decline of propriety was a sign of the breakdown of the old social order. All these elements—the sacrilegious *donjuanismo* of the nobility, the immorality of the clergy, the corruption of bureaucrats, the jockeying for social prestige within the governing elite, and the weakening of the distinctions among castes—were unequivocal signs of this society's profound transformation. In the seventeenth century, faced with this evidence, the Crown set itself up as the guardian of tradition.

In quite a contradictory manner, throughout the eighteenth century, the Spanish monarchs converted themselves into the most determined promoters of the modernization of their empire and, of course, of New Spain. The preoccupation with the decline of customs took on a very different meaning from the one it had had in the previous century. An event in Mexico City at the end of the seventeenth century precipitated this change.

In 1692, Indians and other castes rioted against the Spanish government because of a shortage of wheat and corn. The mob stoned and later burned the viceregal palace, while they screamed: "Kill the Spanish and the Gachupines who are eating our corn! We go to war happily since God wants us to finish off the Spanish, we do not care if we die without confession! Is this not our land? Well, what do the Spanish want of it?"[24] Although the city returned to its normal tranquillity the next day, the Spaniards did not recover for a long time from the fear and shock that these events provoked. Since the Conquest, no rebellion had threatened to end Spanish domination in the very capital of the colony. The viceregal government and the elites' confidence in the supposed submissive character of the Indians ended on that day. They began to perceive their subjects as potential enemies.[25]

To prevent any recurrence of these events, the government ordered that all Indians should leave the center of the city within twenty days. This order, like all those that had been emitted over the course of the seventeenth century, was useless. But this order was still different from the preceding ones, and the distinction was highly significant. The Crown commanded the isolation of Indians from the other city residents not the better to indoctrinate them into Christianity, nor to preserve them from bad examples that might lead them to poor conduct, but rather to protect the Spaniards.[26]

That same year, at the request of the viceroy, Carlos de Sigüenza y Góngora wrote the report that determined the places within the city where the Indians could not live. He states that "because the Indians have mingled with the Spaniards, they have tried, with the help of the blacks, to cause an uprising in the city in the year 1537, and if the plot had not been miraculously discovered, they would have been successful (because of the large numbers they represented at that time)." Sigüenza y Góngora found many examples of mutinous Indians: "Among the Indians who resided within the city limits, Juan Román, a hosier, was conspiring, in 1549, to control the city. It was also Indians who formed the bulk of the sedition of January 15, 1624, which children started." But, the general tenor of life among the indigenous population led to a rebellious nature: "The Indians, who live in the houses of Spaniards, in the very plaza, as well as in stables that are there, who day and night frequent the *pulquerías* in the hundreds, are those responsible for the havoc that we are confronted with today, and that we shall lament forever."[27]

The rebellion of 1692 so unsettled the Spanish that they began to examine the past in a new way. They discovered that they had been living in terrible danger without knowing it. They could not believe that they had lived for such a long time surrounded by such dangerous rebels without noticing the risk. In Sigüenza y Góngora's account of the rebellion, he comments upon the "most culpable negligence in which we lived among such an enormous plebeian class."[28]

The colonial government announced new measures to prevent further uprisings. These orders revealed a change in the government's policy and reflected the character of the eighteenth century. From then on, the authorities and the elites perceived the dissipated customs of the people as potential seeds of social subversion that needed to be weeded out. This new attitude led to a paradoxical decision. At the same time that the government tried to reform society and to bring the ideas of the Enlightenment to Mexico, it also tried to preserve the social peace by the perpetuation and even reinforcement of rigid legal divisions among the various social castes of New Spain. The progressive policy of enlightened despotism stimulated a reaction in favor of the traditional order of estates. This response was not in opposition to official policy but was rather actually one of its basic parts.

## The Festival of the Estates

The hierarchical model—the system of estates that supposedly governed social relations in New Spain—was expressed in a more formal and tangible manner in various ceremonies and festivals. The bullfight was the most important of these ceremonial occasions.[29] Since the turn of the eleventh century, the Spanish celebrated important events with bullfights, and they became known as the quintessentially national festival. The various estates took part in the celebration in symbolically differentiated roles. Nobles on horseback participated in the fight supposedly to protect the peons of plebeian origin.[30] Don Luis de Trexo affirmed that the aristocrats who normally entered to kill bulls "professed taking on this task principally to save peons, and apparently nonparticipation would represent a dereliction of their duties." But, the bullfights were also considered "a pastime appropriate for any blueblood, given that the principal objective of nobles is to risk their lives to help someone in need of assistance."[31] In one sense, the bullfight exemplifies the hierarchical order that had to reign among the various estates. The domination of the nobles over the other estates was justified in the festival as the former were the protectors of the latter.

The bullfight was also considered to be an "exercise of horsemanship" and, since its beginnings, it was linked with an aristocratic and military view of the world.[32] During the Middle Ages, because of this conception, it was considered ignoble to fight the bulls for money.[33] In the eighteenth century, people debated whether those bullfighters who did not recover after being gored by the bull died in mortal sin. Doctor Don José Ortiz Cantero, a priest, defended the purity of the corrida by claiming that the bulls "[were] permitted by the republic to train in courage and be ready for war."[34]

When the critics of the Enlightenment attacked the bullfight, one of its defenders, Juan Pablo Forner, wrote, "The bullfights are the product of military times, they are characteristic of a nation which since the twelfth century has not laid down arms, nor has known any other type of honor, other nobility, other merit than marshaling its forces and the distress of hard conflicts of the militia." He further vindicated bullfights as an institution of social cohesion by affirming that "there is, among us, no other spectacle more suitable to the upholding of laws, more useful to the public good, or less pernicious to customs."[35]

As a ceremony, the bullfight represented the order of estates not only in the Iberian Peninsula but also in all the Spanish empire. Since its inception in Spain, the bullfight legitimized the right of warriors to rule over peons; in New Spain, the corrida illustrated the right of Spanish conquerors to dominate the indigenous peoples. It was not coincidental that the first bullfight celebrated in New Spain was held on August 13, 1529, to commemorate the anniversary of the fall of México-Tenochtitlan to the Spaniards. From this day, it was established that "every year, to honor the feast of Saint Hipólito, on whose day the city was won, seven bulls will be fought."[36] Likewise, the day of Saint James (the epitome of warrior saints) was marked with bullfights as were the celebrations for taking the oath of allegiance to the new monarchs, the celebrations for the queens' successfully giving birth, and on the saint days of the kings and princes.[37]

These festivals were also considered indispensable when the viceroy ceremonially entered Mexico City. The occasion was used not only to welcome the viceroy in royal style but to affirm and legitimize his power over the capital's residents. In 1800, the Ayuntamiento stated that "it is important that the representative of His Majesty be welcomed with rejoicing and receive the honor and precedence due to the Sovereign he represents." The celebrations made the viceroy's authority more concrete; through them "the people form this concept of authority by seeing the public demonstrations, and develop the respect and recognition which the viceroy deserves." In addition, they believed that "above all other functions, the bullfights are the most important because of the decorum and courtesies that are dedicated to the Supreme Chief of the Kingdom, it is also very appropriate that the public recognizes him and knows to whom they owe respect and obedience."[38] After 1586, it became customary to stage bullfights for royal festivals and for the entry of the viceroy. These celebrations took place in an enclosure that was erected for their duration and were the only ones held in the Plaza del Volador, located next to the viceregal palace.

For the audience, the bullfights were a visual representation of the hierarchical order at the highest levels of colonial society. Therefore, because the viceroy was the supreme authority in attendance, he presided over the bullfight from a special box that was constructed inside the enclosure. Many other civil authorities, such as *oidores* (judges of the Audiencia), *regidores* (councilmen), royal officials, alcaldes, and members of the nobility, also had the right to occupy sumptuous boxes. Similarly, the troops in charge of maintaining order at these events also were given the right to reserved seats.[39]

But the bullfight would not have been an authentic festival of the estates if the clergy had not participated. At first, the Vatican disapproved of this dangerous diversion. Pope Pius V ordered the kings to disallow bullfights with a threat of excommunication, *latae sententiae*. But subsequently Pope Gregory XIII revoked this order, although he maintained the prohibition against the attendance of ordained clergy. In the eighteenth century, highly placed ecclesiastical officials had to remind Mexican clerics of this ban. In 1640, Bishop Palafox y Mendoza used this regulation as an excuse for his absence at the bullfights in honor of the entry of Viceroy Duke of Escalona. The *visitador* (inspector) of the Augustinians used this same reasoning to refuse permission to members of his order to frequent bullfights and the theater.[40]

Despite these stipulations, some high church officials attended most bullfights. When the enclosures for the bullfights on the occasion of royal events were built, special boxes were always included for the archbishop, the Metropolitan Cathedral chapter, the tribunal of the Inquisition, the Collegiate Church of Guadalupe, and the Royal and Pontifical University. In addition, before the festivities began, mass was celebrated inside the ring. Using the excuse of a petition for divine protection for the toreadors, the church openly displayed its backing of the festival and emphasized the central role it played within the ceremonies.[41]

The provision of free boxes to important officials, ecclesiastics, and corporate groups reflected the position that these groups occupied on the social scale of power and prestige. When Viceroy Marquina vetoed the organization of bullfights for his entry in 1800, the bureaucrats, who traditionally were given free boxes, felt that his suppression of tradition deprived them of an occasion to display their position of honor. They believed that, as a result, their social prestige was reduced and that they were being placed on the same level as the common folk of the capital. At least, this was the argument that the Ayuntamiento used when it tried to convince Viceroy Marquina to reverse his decision. They claimed that "you should equally consider that in this most Noble of Cities, the Ministers of the Royal Audiencia, members of the Ayuntamiento, tribunals, and offices of His Royal Majesty, as well as many other subjects, enjoy the privilege of having a box at the bullfights." Therefore, in the absence of the traditional corrida, "These men would be deprived of a bonus that is associated with their positions, which, although it may seem worth very little, is appreciable when judging the decorum and distinction conferred upon them."[42]

For the elites in New Spain whether they had a box for the bullfights associated with royal festivals was vital to the preservation of their social prestige. For this reason, invitations to the bullfights were always sent early to the important civil and ecclesiastical officials and groups.[43] Invariably, bureaucrats, employees, and corporate groups who had not been invited to the festivities protested that their absence from the list was an oversight of their positions and their importance. They usually pointed to other persons of equal or lesser social standing who had been given free boxes. In 1761, the deputy *alcalde mayor* of the *tribunal de cuentas* (Exchequer), who wrote to the Ayuntamiento demanding a box for the others in this office, contended that, "as a deputy I have enjoyed all the honors, privileges, emoluments and prerogatives that the *alguacil mayor* had, and one of these was that whenever bullfights were held, along with all the other professional and honorary regents and bookkeepers [I] was given a box." He asserted a right to ceremonial parity with his counterpart, stating that "it seems appropriate that I should be accorded the same honor and on the day of the Purification, I should also be given the same candle as the *alguacil mayor* and the aforementioned gentlemen. Your Lordship's justness and prudence will, I am certain, ensure that the proper provisions will be made and that I will not be left out of these prerogatives."[44]

Also, because there was a clear gradation within the various boxes, the status of individuals and corporate groups was measured according to the type of box that they received. Accordingly, people who felt belittled by the method of distribution of boxes also lodged protests. In 1774, the Protomedicato wrote a curt note to the Ayuntamiento to denounce the box that had been assigned to them. First they express their dismay when "[a]s the bullfight arena is being erected for the festivities that Your Lordship has ordered for the new Viceroy, we cannot but look upon the tribunes except with great sadness because of the assignation of boxes." Their "allotted place is in a much poorer and more contemptible location than in other years and it is not at all suitable for distinguished persons." But "to make matters worse, it will be exposed to the sun at its height." The members were in a quandary because they had an obligation to be present, which they described as "a grave responsibility," and they concluded "that the individual members of our guild will attend the festivities. Otherwise, they would have to abstain in order to avoid the aforementioned annoyances." But they believed that these objections justified an intervention from the Ayuntamiento to correct these wrongs and "to assign our guild a better position in the shade and on the same level as the other seats, so that it will be obvious that the Royal Protomedicato enjoys the same or even higher honor than others, that the notorious high rank and merits of its members is shown."[45]

Conflicts over rank and precedence grew in the second half of the eighteenth century. In an attempt to strengthen the state, the Bourbon reforms created a multitude of new posts within the viceregal government. It became impossible to provide boxes for all the important officials. Bureaucrats as well as civil and religious corporate bodies wrote to the Ayuntamiento to demand that they be assigned a box or that theirs be changed to a more prestigious one so as to reflect the honor owed to them. A great variety of persons petitioned to be admitted without charge to the bullfights; these ranged from the attorney of the Royal Audiencia and of the state and Marquesado del Valle (1716), to the Royal University (1720), the chaplain of the city (1746), the coachmen of the *regidores*, who only requested to be able to look through a small window (1746), the notary of the police (1747), the colleges of San Juan de Letrán—the principal saint—(1747), the *corregidor*'s deputy (1747), the superior treasurer and bookkeeper of the Casa de Moneda (1755), the *contador del viento* (1761), the deputy of the *alguacil mayor* of the *tribunal de cuentas* (1761), the Royal Collegiate Church of Our Lady of Guadalupe (1767), the bookkeeper and treasurer of the *monte de ministros* (1780), the accountant general of *propios y arbitrios* (municipal properties and taxation) (1780), the chief clerk of the General Indian Court (1783), a judge of the Acordada (police courts) (1783), the alcaldes de barrio and *alcaldes ordinarios* (1783), the general bookkeeper of *temporalidades* (1785), the *ayundantes de plaza* (1794), the regent of the Audiencia (1794), and the *ensayador mayor* of the kingdom (official responsible for assaying metals) (1798).[46] The Ayuntamiento depicts the new situation very clearly in its letter of refusal to one of these candidates: "If we were to distribute the balconies by parity of status, there would not be enough balconies even if the bullring extended half a league."[47]

Faced with this avalanche of requests, the Ayuntamiento decided to assign boxes only to those officials and organizations that had always had this privilege and to give less weight to the hierar-

chical importance of the various petitioners. Of course, their solution did not satisfy persons who occupied recently created high
offices and so some exceptions were made to the rule. Some, such
as the adviser of the tribunal of the Acordada and of prohibited
drinks, tried to fool the Ayuntamiento with an invented precedent.
He stated that those who had occupied the post before him had
always enjoyed this privilege just to secure himself a position of
honor in the bullfights.[48]

The controversies over the allocation of boxes reflected the way
eighteenth-century Mexico had been transformed. These conflicts
reveal that the bullfight no longer reflected and reproduced the
social order. In fact, for those who followed the ideas of the Enlightenment, bullfights were just a barbarous and bloody diversion
that only those who opposed progress and civilization could enjoy.

The bullfights were thus a major political event and, as a result, had always been linked to social hierarchy. Logically, as the
estates began to unravel and their social importance diminish, the
bullfights lost favor in the eyes of the kings and the viceroys. Significantly, in 1692, when rioters threatened to destroy social order
in Mexico City, colonial officials canceled the bullfights for more
than three years.[49] From that point forward, the organization by
estate and the bullfights ceased to reflect the essence of colonial
Mexican society. In fact, the bullfights were transformed into a re-
actionary symbol.

## The Enlightened Spoilsports

During the eighteenth century, the internal organization of the bullfights changed significantly. They also lost their function of political legitimation of the hierarchical order to become just one
spectacle among many. Hipólito de Villarroel had censured the
custom of granting free boxes to the dependents of the various tribunals, arguing: "Because the bullfights are a popular and profane
function, there is no reason to observe this singular custom for the
members of the tribunals in the same way as for events of a sacred,
religious, or political nature."[50] The manner in which the transformation occurred is revealing. At the beginning of the eighteenth
century, no bullfights occurred on the day of San Hipólito.[51] Therefore, the original meaning of the bullfight in New Spain and its
link to the Spanish domination of the indigenous population was
lost; the bullfights ceased to form part of those ceremonies that

legitimized the Conquest and, also as a result of this change, to a great extent they lost their militaristic character.

In both Spain and New Spain, nobles no longer confronted the bull from horseback. This encounter had been the central event of the bullfights, but with its demise the bullfights were left in the hands of the plebeians. Henceforth, it began to be considered dishonorable for the highborn to fight the bulls. In New Spain, those nobles who continued to engage in this anachronistic hobby did so either hidden away on their country estates or wore masks to conceal their faces. During the reign of Viceroy Bernardo de Gálvez, particularly in the years 1785 and 1786, a large group known as the *tapados y preparados* (hidden and ready) represented this trend. This viceroy encouraged the colonial Mexican taste for the bullfight.[52]

Both in Spain and in the colonies, as the nobility retreated from the bullring and left it in the hands of the people, the central interest of the actual bullfight also was displaced. The man on horseback was no longer the principal protagonist of the festival, and his place was taken by the former peon. As a result of this transformation, the centerpiece of the drama now took place on the ground. At the same time, the whole bullfight was restructured so that each of its parts contributed to increasing the excitement of the audience and leading them to the moment of apotheosis: the death of the bull.[53]

Bullfights were no longer organized exclusively for political or religious festivities but now served to collect funds for the state treasury. At first, these series of bullfights were simply an extension of the official season, which took place in association with the royal festivals. They were designed to allow the contractors who had built the ring to recoup their investments and perhaps show a profit. But, after 1753, seasons of bullfights were arranged in Mexico City independently of any political event.[54]

Because royal edicts had specified that bullfights in the Plaza del Volador could only be held on the occasion of the entry of the viceroy and as part of royal ceremonies, the enclosures for corridas not associated with royal occasions were set up in a variety of locations: the Plaza Mayor, Chapultepec, the Paseo Nuevo, the Paseo de Jamaica, the public squares of Don Toribio, San Diego, San Sebastián, Santa Isabel, Santiago Tlaltelolco, San Lucas, Tarasquillo, Lagunilla, Hornillo, San Antonio Abad, and, finally, the Plaza de San Pablo.[55] Tickets for the bullfights varied widely in price according to how much these contractors speculated. At times, the admission price reached such a high level that, despite their fondness for this entertainment, the common people stopped attending the bullfights.[56] In order to make the bullfights more attractive, the contractors began to add a multitude of little diversions. These completely altered the traditional character of the bullfights as an exercise of horsemanship. For example, the public really enjoyed women bullfighters who appeared frequently, but their presence definitely was incompatible with the bellicose nature of the sport. The crowds also appreciated a diversion called "the crazy man of the bulls," in which a bullfighter, dressed like one of the inmates from the asylum of San Hipólito, provoked the animal and hid in an empty barrel, which the bull then attacked. Clearly, these diversions demonstrated a total loss of respect for the values and principles of bygone days. On other occasions, the organizers let dogs loose in the ring to fight the bull. In the intermissions, dog and hare races took place, and spectators bet heavily on cockfights. Other times, hydrogen balloons and grandiose fireworks formed the entertainment. Sometimes the organizers even placed a carnival display of goods in the center of the ring, which consisted of one big pile of clothes, small livestock, and food. At first, soldiers protected these goods but, at a signal from the viceroy, the soldiers made way and the spectators threw themselves on the heap to grab what they could while fighting each other. A variant on this "diversion" was the greased pole, or *cucaña*. Nobles and officials enjoyed displays in which plebeians, because of their poverty, fought among themselves over a hen or some stockings.[57]

Once the popular diversions became simply an entertainment, their characteristic disorder invaded the bullfight. The crowd would go down into the ring while the bullfight took place and try to enrage the animal by pricking it with swords, spears, and spikes, while the rest of the crowd insulted the bullfighters to inspire them to more dangerous performances. Beggars as well as vendors of water, fruit, sweets, and cakes filled the stands. Below the front rows, in various vacant spots and the surrounding area, merchants set up fry stands and drinks booths. After the show was over, and well into the night, the plebeians brought food and drink into the ring and danced in a scandalous manner to the accompaniment of live musicians. The authorities tried to end these "abuses" with the promulgation of edicts in 1769, 1787, and 1794.[58]

In 1792, an unusual outburst occurred during a bullfight when the crowd threw aniseed and other objects into the ring to protest the poor quality of the bull. The contractor had probably bought cheap stock in order to reduce his costs.[59] This incident reveals that the bullfight had become—for the spectators and for the contractor—a simple diversion that was regulated by the logic of profits and consumption. And, according to this reasoning, it began to seem absurd to build and tear down a stadium for the bullfights every season. While the bullfights remained a unique event that made the meeting of the various estates possible at crucial moments of the colony's political life, the ring could not be permanent, because its profound social significance would be worn away by its daily presence in the city. In the eighteenth century, however, when the bullfight became nothing more than a source of entertainment and profit, the custom of seasons only made the contractors' costs that much more exorbitant and left them a very narrow profit margin. In fact, by the end of the eighteenth century, the contractors began to lose money on the venture. When the Ayuntamiento (town council) tendered for bids on the construction of the bullring, it became more and more difficult to find someone who wanted to risk capital in such a low-yielding enterprise. Finally, in 1790, when no one was willing to bid, the city government decided to administer the bullfights directly.

The viceroy then put the ministers of the treasury in charge of an investigation into the causes of the decadence of the bullfights and possible solutions. In a lengthy report, they responded that the answer was to build a permanent ring "with high quality wood firmly joined by nails" that "would last undamaged for more than ten years." Once it had been built, it would be sold to the highest bidder. In order to cover the costs of such a large-scale project, they would have to hold about forty bullfights a year. They also considered the possibility of erecting a ring made of masonry and had even decided that the area around the Acordada and the Paseo Nuevo was an ideal location for such a project.

There were many potential economic spin-offs from this project. Not only would it be much easier to find contractors willing to bid higher amounts for the right to present the bullfights, but because the stadium would be located near the new tobacco factory, living quarters for the factory workers could be built on its exterior, a market could be set up nearby, and, during holidays, acrobats could perform there in the afternoons. Despite these advantages, the viceroy rejected the idea.[60] It was only in 1815 that the viceregal government decided to construct a permanent bullring on the Plaza de San Pablo.[61]

Apart from all these transformations in the eighteenth century, enlightened thinkers also assaulted the bullfighters. In the eyes of these intellectuals, a cultivated nation should not dignify such a cruel and bloodthirsty sport. What would others think of a people who enjoyed watching the sacrifice of an animal that was doing no more than defending itself and seeing that, moreover, a man risked his life and sometimes lost it without reason? Lizardi, like many intellectuals of his time, expressed such views: "They say that the bullfights are a barbaric spectacle and a residue of paganism. . . . That it is an extension of the gladiators of Rome and a bloodthirsty diversion fit for making hearts fierce and denuding simpletons of all notions of sensibility by accustoming them to watch the shedding of blood of brutes and, at times, of men."[62]

Not satisfied with this criticism of the bloodthirsty aspect of the sport, these enlightened intellectuals also blamed it for many of the ills of society. In 1788, the *síndico del común* (official receiver of the *común* [community goods]) received an inquiry as to the most suitable location for the season's bullring. He took the opportunity to openly express his disgust with the spectacle and to detail all the problems it caused. Government offices shut down on these days; fathers spent exorbitant sums to attend and deprived their families of sustenance; workers extorted the price of admission from their employers with threats to abandon their posts. In short, this diversion impoverished the population of Mexico City, already exhausted from its recent epidemics and famines.[63]

In Spain, the representatives of enlightened thinking also opposed the corrida. Father Benito Feijóo, José Clavijo y Fajardo, and José Cadalso declared themselves in opposition to the sport. The Count of Campomanes considered it ruinous for the economy. Gaspar Melchor de Jovellanos y Ramírez even denied that it was popular among the common people and thus disavowed it as a national festivity. He stated that "bullfights have never been a diversion, nor a daily event, nor very popular, nor represented in all the villages of Spain, nor generally sought out and applauded." Far from being widespread, "in many provinces they were never known; in others they were found only in the capitals, and where they were celebrated, this was only intermittent and only when the residents of the capitals and some nearby villages were the spectators." Finally, Jovellanos concluded that "probably only one-hundredth of the total Spanish population has ever seen such an event. How is it, then, that some give it the title of national diversion?"[64]

The Bourbon kings shared the horror of the bullfights expressed by Enlightenment intellectuals. Philip V, the first Bourbon, was a great foe of bullfights. In the period from 1767 to 1768, under Charles II, the government began to take measures to stop bull-fights in Spain.[65] After this, it was rare that a viceroy showed any inclination for the bullfights while in New Spain.

In February 1779, as a result of Viceroy Antonio María de Bucareli's decison not to allow the construction of a stadium for bullfight season, the theater contractor began to present bullfights during the intermissions of plays. Needless to say, the viceroy pro-hibited these functions without delay. Viceroy Mayorga only per-mitted one very short period of bullfights during his years in office.

When Don Matías de Gálvez arrived for his term of office, the city council organized impressive festivities, including bullfights, to welcome the new viceroy. Despite the fact that all the prepara-tions were complete, because it was Lent, Gálvez ordered that these festivities be postponed until after Easter. Don Bernardo de Gálvez was the only viceroy who had been an avowed fan of the bulls and he sponsored lavish seasons during his short tenure in office. In contrast, his successor, Don Alonso Núñez de Haro y Peralta, did not allow them. For the reception of the next viceroy, Don Manuel Antonio Flores, the city councillors decided to mount a really splen-did show. They contracted the best bullfighter of New Spain and they secured the bravest bulls for the occasion. But the viceroy showed little interest in the spectacle and attended only the after-noon presentation.[66]

The fact that bullfights were not banned entirely can probably be explained by the officials' discovery that they were an impor-tant source of income for the Royal Treasury. In New Spain, the bullfights financed various public works in the capital. Thus, Vice-roy de Croix organized long periods of bullfights in 1769 and 1770, which were held in the Plaza del Volador even though they were not royal festivities. The financial benefits, however, were plenti-ful; the take for the first season was 25,000 pesos, and for the sec-ond, it was more than 16,000 pesos. These profits paid for the expansion of the Alameda.[67] So the barbarous spectacle that so dis-gusted the enlightened thinkers subsidized their promenades in the Alameda. Paseos were much more to the liking of the intellec-tuals and the colonial authorities of the time.

Bullfights, organized for the entry of the viceroy into Mexico City, also served to pay for the lavish ceremonies and festivities for his reception.[68] After Don Bernardo de Gálvez left office, the Crown ordered annual bullfights to restore the huge sums that this vice-roy had taken from the Royal Treasury to begin the construction of

Chapultepec Castle.[69] The very financial interests of the Crown were an obstacle to the total abolition of bullfighting. By the beginning of the nineteenth century, however, the antibullfight faction grew stronger within the Spanish state. In fact, as early as 1785, a pragmatic sanction prohibited "the festivities of bullfights to the death in the towns of the kingdom," and in 1790, a Royal Act prohibited "in general the abuse of running bullocks and bulls in the streets in a herd, both by day and by night." These dispositions were not applied in New Spain.[70]

The winds of change were only felt in the colony in 1800 when Viceroy Marquina arrived. He canceled the bullfights that the Ayuntamiento had organized for his grand entry. When the town councillors protested that these activities were needed to pay for the festivities, he ended the discussion by paying for the ceremonies himself.[71] From this moment, it became clear that economic considerations would not stop the will of enlightened despotism to put an end to the bullfights.

The final blow came in 1805. A royal decree prohibited "absolutely, in all the kingdom, and without exception of the Court, to hold festivities of bullfights and *novillos* [a bullfight in which young bulls are used] to the death." The *Novísima recopilación* (1805 legal code) explained the rationale of this decree as follows: "The abolition of these spectacles is necessary, because they do not enhance the humaneness so characteristic of the Spanish, they prejudice agriculture because they are an impediment to the orderly cultivation of cattle and horses, and they retard the development of industry because of the unfortunate waste of time devoted to these labors."[72] Ironically, the financial reasoning that previously had saved the bullfights from elimination was turned against these festivities to argue for their demise. The decree of 1805, unlike previous orders of this nature, apparently was actually carried out in Mexico City and so, from then until 1809, when the reign of Charles IV ended, there were no bullfights at all.[73]

The Enlightenment was a period of bold attacks against the festival of the estates. The state did not reason that the display of the hierarchical order that governed the people was no longer needed. Rather, it argued that, because the bullfights were out of step with the times, they no longer provided the appropriate place for such a demonstration.

In contrast, the theater, as we shall see, became the vehicle of progress as it was conceived by the thinkers of the Enlightenment. It conquered the approval of the powerful. In fact, an old rivalry existed between the theater and the bullfights. Since the seventeenth century, these two spectacles were generally considered the antithesis of one another. Bishop Palafox y Mendoza, for example, stated in 1644 that the theater was "a seminary for passions where cruelty was provoked," but he believed that the *cañas* (a form of jousting)[74] and the bullfight were the most benign public entertainments.[75] In contrast, the Marquis of Mancera, who governed New Spain from 1664 to 1673, and was no enthusiast of the bulls, bolstered the theater by organizing plays in the very viceregal palace.[76]

By the end of the colonial period, after a long struggle, the theater triumphed over the bullfights. The defeat of the latter was complete. It was not only degraded to a simple bloodthirsty spectacle, but it also went from being the setting for a parade of the cream of society to a dire fate. In 1807, according to the president of the Royal Academy of History in Spain, Vargas Ponce, it was accepted only among "a scatterbrained youth, lacking in education as well as enlightenment and experience, those preoccupied in aging without use of the faculty of thinking, those with habitual vices, hungry always for disorder, and in a word, the dregs of all levels of society."[77]

## The Precarious Restoration

Charles IV's 1805 prohibition of bullfights was strictly enforced in Mexico City until the Napoleonic armies invaded Spain. The armies obliged the king to abdicate in favor of his son—Ferdinand VII—who then left the throne to Napoleon's brother, Joseph Bonaparte. But the political vacuum in the metropolis as well as the rise in insurgent movements in New Spain caused confusion that allowed the decree of 1805 to be ignored and led to a restoration of bullfights.

Even so, there were few bullfights in Mexico City before 1815. In fact, only two seasons are recorded; they took place in the Plaza de Jamaica at the beginning of 1813 and in November of the same year. The Royalist government—which fought the insurrection begun in 1810—gave the necessary authorizations and argued that in these tempestuous times it would be dangerous to forbid the bullfights. On the contrary, they served to entertain the people and lure them away from the subversive ideas of the insurgents. In 1813, the attorney of the Royal Treasury expressed his support for the November season. He stated that previously the granting of a license at the beginning of the year for the whole season was not a problem, but "in the present state of things, it is not an impediment, since these days it is advantageous to grant permission for these public spectacles in order to draw away the people's attention to subjects of little concern and prevent them from imagining corrupt ideas."[78] Another equally important reason to authorize the season was that the Royalist government's treasury was empty, and the contract for the bullfights was a potential source of abundant compensation.

Nevertheless, bullfights were not held to celebrate the liberal and progressive reforms of the Cádiz Parliament (which attacked the powers of the monarchy). So in 1810, when the Mexico City town council elected a deputy to sit in the Cádiz Parliament, various festivities were organized including three days of illuminations, a ball, and special performances in the theater, but no bullfights. The authorities followed the same pattern when the Constitution of Cádiz was announced in September of 1812. The celebration was lavish; the people collectively swore an oath of loyalty in all the city parishes, and the *cabildo* (town council) organized a free show in the theater but the bulls were not invited to the party.[79] Clearly, it would not do to celebrate the political accomplishments of the enlightened Spanish Liberals and the advances of progress with the festivity that had previously served to reaffirm the hierarchical order of society.

It was the expulsion of the French invaders from Spain and the consequent return of Ferdinand VII to the throne in 1814 that destroyed the reforms promoted by the Cádiz Parliament. The king had barely verified his popularity among the people and the army when he abolished the Constitution of 1812 and restored absolute monarchy. News of the king's return and the suppression of the Cádiz Constitution reached New Spain at the same time. Viceroy Calleja, who had always opposed the application of the constitution, received the tidings on August 5, 1814, with "unspeakable joy." To spread the word in the city, he ordered the celebration of a grandiose Te Deum in the cathedral.[80] The viceroy also ordered that the celebration of these events would be marked with a huge season of bullfights; this was, of course, the most appropriate spectacle for the occasion. The Liberals, for whom the suppression of the constitution was a grave defeat, perceived these bullfights as a clear symbol of the return of the old order.

Lizardi used the same symbol to show his opposition to the restoration of absolutism in a veiled manner in the newspapers. In 1815, after the festivities were over, he published two articles, "La conferencia de un toro y un caballo" (The conference of a bull and a horse) and "Sobre la diversión de toros" (On the diversion of the bulls), in which he carefully attacked the bullfights by inferring that they were an entertainment suitable only for barbarous, ignorant, and fierce people. Although he was not so blunt in his writings, it was understood that those who celebrated their victories with such diversions deserved the same epithets.[81]

Viceroy Calleja entrusted the *cabildo* of the Ayuntamiento with the preparation of the festivities. Although this body had always been responsible for this task, on this occasion, the viceroy's assignment had a particular political significance. It became a form of humiliation for those who had supported the liberal reforms.

Even though they could not say so openly, the *cabildo* members had nothing to celebrate. They were all Creole Liberals who were elected in 1813 under the auspices of the Constitution of Cádiz. They knew that, with the abolition of the constitution, sooner or later, they would necessarily lose their positions and would be replaced by the previous alcaldes, *regidores*, and *síndicos*. Viceroy Calleja must surely have delighted in the fact that this elected body—the very people who had defended the constitution against all his efforts to limit its application—had to organize the festivities to mark its suppression. Cursing their fate, the alcaldes, *regidores*, and *síndicos* reluctantly took up their task until a viceregal decree of September 15, 1814, announced the disappearance of the elected town council and the reinstallation of the former one. The council members were thus liberated from their despised burden.[82]

Before the reprieve, however, the members of the constitutional Ayuntamiento were confronted with the task of inviting and assigning free boxes to the prominent personalities of the colonial civil and religious society who would attend the bullfights in honor of the restoration of Ferdinand VII. Bullfights were proposed in order to celebrate the return of the monarch with great pomp and circumstance, but the choice also demonstrated that the old hierarchy and absolutism had survived the attacks of their enemies unscathed. The highest ranks of society, who in theory presided over the fate of New Spain, had to occupy boxes that materially represented their place within the hierarchy of power. After all the social and political commotions of the previous years, however, it was extremely difficult to know which officials did or did not have the right to the boxes, and the assignation of these boxes according to rank was nearly impossible.

To make matters worse, at first the viceroy ordered that there should be no innovation in the assignment of boxes. His order seemed contradictory to the members of the *cabildo*. They wrote to the viceroy to explain that it was impossible to be guided by tradition because no conventions existed at all. Not only had the method of assignment of the boxes varied constantly over the years, but so many abuses had been introduced over time that a reform was sorely needed. Also, and more important, the officials could not proceed in the same way as the earlier *regidores*, because "in those days, the nobles and employees of the first order could be counted by units or tens, but today they are numbered in the thousands." In the interim, many new offices had been created and consequently the bureaucracy was larger. Apart from employees in offices, "there is a multitude of military leaders, . . . there are brigadiers, marshals, army intendants, judges, all respected persons within the republic who would resent the implication that their standing and services were considered lower than that of a clerk of the Royal Treasury." To deprive any of these persons of a box for the bullfights would be insulting, but "what stadium would allow a division of boxes to satisfy all these people even if it was double or more in size than the usual one?"

The problem of seat assignments obliged the elected *cabildo* to ponder on which principles the allocation of boxes should be based. They concluded that "in the question of who should receive the boxes, this *obligation* should originate only in a written title or a legitimate custom or at least legitimated." After demonstrating that these conditions did not exist, however, the *cabildo* asked once more: "On what should we base our distribution of the boxes? Without rules or precedents from which to proceed, how can the Ayuntamiento formulate a rational and uniform system? Up to now, the committee has not been able to find this rule."[83]

Beyond the immediate objectives of the Ayuntamiento, their questions can be read as a genuine contemplation on the lack of legitimacy of the old order and the previous hierarchy that absolutism was trying to restore. The tradition, that is to say, the idea that monarchy had a divine origin, had lost all credibility after the events of 1808. The Constitution of Cádiz—a written code—could have been the basis of a "rational" legitimacy,[84] but Ferdinand VII abolished it. Henceforth, Spanish domination was only maintained by the power of arms.[85]

Despite the difficulties that the Ayuntamiento confronted, the allocation of the boxes was finally accomplished, and the highest members of the colonial power made a public appearance when the bullfights were held in the Plaza del Volador at the beginning of 1815. Of course, the portrait of His Majesty Ferdinand VII occupied a position of honor in the front row. The Holy Office, which had been suppressed by the Cádiz Parliament and reestablished by the king, was allocated three rows even though there was only one inquisitor left in New Spain.[86]

The festivities were barely over when the viceroy ordered another season of bullfights in order to raise funds for the Royalist armies. At the end of that season, workers carried the wood of the bullring to the Plaza de San Pablo to be used in the construction of a permanent site for the bullfights. From this moment until 1821, there were several seasons of bullfights every year in Mexico City. They paid for the purchase of uniforms for the Royalist soldiers. In effect, the bullfights financed the military campaign of the backlash.[87]

At the beginning of 1821, a few months before Mexican Independence, the bullring in the Plaza de San Pablo was burned to the ground. The monument that the forces of conservatism had erected during their precarious restoration disappeared in the flames.[88]

# 2

# Progress or the Theater

Everyone loves it when a show really works
And the audience shouts "Bravo!"
Human life is nothing but acting, so
Let Heaven sit in the best seats
To watch a play on your stage, World.

—Pedro Calderón de la Barca

During the period of the Enlightenment, both officials and intellectuals protected and championed the theater more than any other public diversion. Unlike the bullfights, which seemed only to propagate brutality among the lower classes, they believed that the theater was an efficient medium for the refinement and edification of the common people. The fact that the theater had a long tradition in New Spain and was well established in lower-class tastes made it the ideal spectacle to promote the sentiments, attitudes, values, and ideas of the Enlightenment among Mexico City's population. For this reason, the viceroys never skimped in their efforts to protect the theater from its competitors. They intervened to reform the theater; they interceded in conflicts between actors and administrators, or among the actors themselves. They even gave advice on the production of comedies to correct really obvious faults.

The eighteenth-century theater was a microcosm of the larger society. On the stage, the "freedom" of artistic creation and the "spontaneity" of public reactions reflected the lively reality of Mexican society. The theater revealed the limitations and strengths of Mexicans. Within the theater, contradictory forces coexisted, although rarely harmoniously: the ideas and beliefs of colonial Mexican society, its myths and hopes, the common people and the elite, the power of capital, the traditional hierarchies, the desire to enlighten and the need for physical coercion, morality and impudence, order and "mayhem," legitimacy and rebellion, with and without norms.

Several centuries from now, if a historian wished to describe the life of the residents of an industrial city of our time in one concentrated paragraph, a summary of a night at the movies would provide an obvious common experience. How would this future historian portray such an evening?

Imagine a dark room. It is more or less comfortable according to the level of development of the nation. A large number of people occupy it; they are all anonymous, seated close together in a uniform, well-defined pattern and in a designated space. Their arrangement seems to correspond to the rows of seats, all equal one to another, but in reality, they are clustered in groups of family or friends, with the women placed on the interior and men to the outside. This grouping creates the illusion of a protected, possessed space. All are seated; they are absorbed in an entertainment that was previously programmed and that inevitably runs its course. No spectator can alter it even to the slightest degree. There is no sense in applauding or jeering but inevitably people do become emotional or indignant. "Freedom of choice" is only exercised with the purchase of candy or other treats in the intermissions set aside for this purpose. After the break, each individual returns to his or her seat, each cut off from the next in an individual place, to witness the common spectacle that none can control. This is the way that these people amused themselves; this is the way that they lived.

The eighteenth-century theater was like the cinema of today: a privileged spectacle that represented the way people really lived. It represented the substance of the imaginary representations of the society—its myths and stereotypes. It expressed societal anxieties and its ideals of justice during the brief time of a performance. The imaginary representations of society have always dominated the theater. What we define as "imaginary" was very real for people of bygone eras and it shaped their world. Gods, virgins, saints, devils, and evil forces controlled fate; they infiltrated people's passions, rewarded and punished their actions; priests and bishops, even those who were libertines and social climbers, were but more or less faithful products of this imaginary entity. The theater portrayed clerics and political officials as righteous administrators of justice and earnest defenders of the poor; these were but pale copies of the church and viceroys and other political officials' power as well as their corruption and despotism. The theater gave form to these "authentic truths"; it made them visible to a public that no longer found it so easy to recognize them in the ordinary course of events. The theater put people in contact with the great beyond that dominated the world. Its power was gigantic.

A crucial battle between the world of "magic" and the "rational" world took place in the eighteenth century. Apparently, people began to recognize those things that were visible and had a material presence as the real.[1] Inevitably, the theater was the setting for this struggle between magic and logic. It was a highly theatrical society that placed the theater in the center of this process. Entries of the viceroys, coronations, anniversaries of the royal family, religious festivities, and processions were all nothing more than carefully staged montages. In a period when conventions and social rules were not so well internalized as they are today, the roles played by the high officials were to a great extent simply good acting.[2]

In fact, the theater is so useful as a window onto this period because it was so intertwined with society. Every society needs to explain itself, to create a self-representation that goes beyond daily realities. These interpretations provide coherence and a self-justification that make its elusive structure visible. Theater portrays the invisible social organization that exists just below the surface of daily events but is present every day in individual actions. Theater and theatricality were unique media in a world where visual representations were more important than intellectual concepts.

Theater was also synonymous with a common shared experience, even if a fleeting one.[3] The "imaginary" was presented to all spectators alike with the seal of truth. The fantasies, myths, and desires were made visible and undeniable; they imposed themselves upon the public. Therefore, the theater easily provoked scandal. The subversive, the immoral, and the impious ceased to be only simple possibilities within the mind of an individual and took shape, took over the stage; they invoked violent passions and confrontations among the audience; this was none other than the reverse of a common shared experience. The power of the theater was such that the authorities tried to make use of it as much as they tried to control it. It was because of this contradictory relationship that the theater in colonial Mexico suffered so many ups and downs over the course of its history.

When the first missionaries arrived in New Spain in the sixteenth century, they considered the theater an important medium for the Indians' religious conversion. Even as they made use of it,

however, they always considered it a concession to vulgarity, a
necessary adaptation to the low intellectual level of the popula-
tions that they wished to proselytize. Despite this reticence, the
missionaries were won over by the apparent objectivity of the staging of Catholic dogma. The transformation of religious teachings
into visible manifestations made these appear to be universal truths,
whereas when they were translated into languages whose logic was
foreign to Western discourse they seemed questionable.[4] At the same
time, however, as part of its educational mission, the church
launched furious attacks against the secular plays, which it considered "schools where wickedness is taught."[5]

The civil authorities of New Spain used the theater but also
tried to regulate it. Great political festivities were always marked
by plays, and in moments of crisis, theater's power of legitimation
was resolutely summoned. Although the theater was useful to the
authorities, they nevertheless insisted on strict censorship of the
plays, and the viceroy constantly interfered in theatrical affairs.
During the period of the Enlightenment, the theater also served as
a privileged laboratory in which enlightened despotism tried to
spread the "rational" formulas of progress to the rest of society.

## From the *Corrales* to the New Coliseum

Traditionally, historians have portrayed the religious theater of
evangelization as the origin of scenic representations in New Spain.
In reality, in sixteenth-century New Spain the separation between
religious and secular theater was already quite pronounced. These
two genres of theater really had totally independent and parallel
histories. For the purposes of this study, only the history of the
secular theater is relevant.

Although the indigenous peoples of Mesoamerica mounted
various lavish spectacles, the Spanish Conquest destroyed this tradition to such an extent that it is almost impossible to detect any
pre-Hispanic influence in the urban theater of colonial Mexico.[6] The
conquerors were the precursors of the secular Western theater in
New Spain. They liked to celebrate and commemorate their victories with the representation of small theatrical works.[7]

Over the course of the sixteenth century, theater rapidly became an integral part of urban life in Mexico City. The dignity of
all civil or religious festivals was enhanced by the performance of
one or more plays. Theatrical works were indispensable on the day

of San Hipólito and on the first and the eighth day of the festival of Corpus Christi when processions were held.[8]

The small number of acting companies was scarcely sufficient to satisfy the demand for theatrical representations in New Spain. Their services were therefore very much in demand in the Mexican cities. Theatrical companies took advantage of this shortage and obtained an official monopoly on theatrical representations. In return, they guaranteed the performance of the plays needed for every festivity. In 1595, the Bachelor Arias de Villalobos's company received this privilege for the feasts of San Hipólito and the first and eighth days of Corpus Christi, but they lost the concession nearly immediately because they did not fulfill the contract.[9]

Apparently, these performances took place in several locations. Some dramas were mounted next to the cathedral. Others took place in the cemetery (cohabitation with the dead was part of daily life). Despite a strict prohibition against theatrical perfomances in churches, this was a common practice. And, finally, although it was rather unusual, others were acted in carts. Apart from these public presentations, in the seventeenth and early eighteenth centuries, the viceroy and the court enjoyed other performances inside the viceregal palace.[10]

By 1597 at least, individually owned private playhouses or *corrales*, which were similar to "la Pacheca" or "la Cruz" so popular in Madrid, were common in the city. These *corrales* were located in the patios of open tenements and were very rudimentary. The back of the slightly elevated seating—the loges and the gallery— was covered by a roof of straw, whereas the front part—the front row and *mosquete* [rowdy section]—were protected from the rain by Anjou cloth.[11]

For a long time, historians believed that these *corrales* were the first permanent theaters in Mexico City, but, at present, most scholars consider the theater of the Royal Indian Hospital to be the first such theater. The royal edict that authorized the hospital to put on public performances to support its work dates from 1553, but it certainly did not begin to use this licence until at least 1563.[12]

Although the Royal Indian Hospital theater occupied many different locations, as an institution it had the most permanence during the colonial period. The *corrales* soon disappear from the documentation, while clearly, at some point, the hospital's theater obtained a monopoly on theatrical representations, which it maintained until 1822.

The theater belonging to Lima's Royal Hospital of San Andrés—
built in 1601—was modeled on the one in Mexico City. For the period, the Lima theater was particularly sumptuous. It was shaped
like a trapezoid, had a depth of thirty-three *varas* and a base of
forty-two and fifty-one *varas*, and was completely roofed. The first
theater of the Royal Hospital was remodeled and improved extensively in the period from 1638 to 1640 and then again in 1665, but it
was totally destroyed by fire in 1722.

The theater was rebuilt in the same location but remained there
only a few years, for "experience showed that the poor patients
suffered greatly because of the noise of the audience who only
thought of their amusement and diversion, so it was resolved to
make another using the same materials, which was accomplished
in 1725 on a site belonging to the hospital between the alleyway
called the Holy Spirit and Acequia Street, near where the principal
entry of the city was located." This new theater, which was known
as the Coliseo Viejo (Old Coliseum), turned out to be rather ugly,
inconvenient, and dangerous in that it was built with the charred
timbers from the first theater.

Partly because of these problems but also in order to imitate
the elegant theaters of Madrid, in 1752, Viceroy Francisco de
Güemes y Horcasitas, first Count of Revillagigedo, ordered the construction of a new modern theater, to be built of stone rather than
wood. The new theater was erected in the area around the Old
Coliseum, on Colegio de las Niñas Street, and the viceroy inaugurated it in 1753. The building was called the Coliseo Nuevo (New
Coliseum), and it lasted with a few changes of names after Independence until 1931, when it too was destroyed by fire.[13]

Depending upon the situation, the Royal Hospital's administrator managed the New Coliseum directly when such an arrangement was financially beneficial to the hospital, and on other
occasions, contractors rented it.[14] The profits generated from the
theater were added to the hospital's other sources of revenue such
as the rental of houses, the printing of books, and a tribute of half a
real yearly that the indigenous population of New Spain paid. These
profits covered the costs of the hospital, which attended to the needs
of all Indian patients who arrived at its doors.[15]

Despite the backing of the viceroys, the New Coliseum was
never a very prosperous business. In the papers of the theater's
administrators a litany of lamentations occurs, about the high cost
of the salaries of personnel, the costumes and the scenery, and the
maintenance of the building. To make matters worse, over the

course of the eighteenth century, the Royal Hospital was forced to dispense large sums of money to the victims of the numerous and serious epidemics and famines that afflicted the indigenous population in this period.[16] The hospital's substantial economic needs, combined with the weak financial balance of the Coliseo, obliged the administrators to be constantly on the watch that attendance in the theater did not decline; they had to program entertainments that reflected the taste of the public even if they did not conform to the aesthetic ideals of the Enlightenment.

Within the long tradition of drama in Mexico City, the people, the elites, and the principal civil officials of New Spain all met at the theater whether it was in the *corrales* or in the theater of the Royal Hospital. From its very beginnings, theater, whether out in the open, in the plazas, or in closed quarters, was a diversion that broad sectors of the population shared. Even though the civil authorities at times had private performances, they continued to attend the spirited public representations regularly. They also held the right to enter without tickets and had reserved places.[17]

The long tradition of theatrical representations during the colonial period does not mean that the theater in New Spain had an unbroken and unproblematic history. In reality, the development of the theater was continually subject to the church's changing policy. During the course of Western history, a dual movement of attraction and rejection has characterized the relationship of the church and the dramatic arts. New Spain was no exception to this rule. After the initial use of theatrical representations to convert the indigenous population, toward 1545, the church severely limited theater during religious festivals, and from 1574, the Inquisition began to censor both religious and secular plays in New Spain. Attacks by the Mexican church on the theater increased in the seventeenth century, as they had in the rest of the Western world.[18]

Generally, the civil authorities favored the theatrical arts much more than the church did. Despite the fact that in the last part of the sixteenth century and during the entire seventeenth century, Spanish theater underwent alternate periods of support and repression on the part of the Crown, in New Spain the viceroys constantly protected and fostered it. For example, Viceroys Luis de Velasco II (1590–1595) and Gaspar de Zúñiga y Acevedo, the Count of Monterrey (1595–1603), exerted their authority to ensure that plays would form a part of the festivities for Corpus Christi despite the costs. Viceroy Cerralvo (1624–1635) made sure that Mexico City was never deprived of a company of actors. During the reign of Philip IV, it was not uncommon for private performances of plays to be held in the viceregal palace, and this custom was still in place at the beginning of the eighteenth century.[19]

The period of the Enlightenment was a golden age for theater; not only did the civil authorities constantly support it but the church also abandoned its previous animosity. In New Spain, 1753 marked the start of a new epoch for the dramatic arts when Viceroy Revillagigedo, the first Count, inaugurated the New Coliseum, which had been built on his orders. In addition, ecclesiastical authorities allowed the burial of Diego de Arias, the leading man of a theatrical company, in the aristocratic convent of San Bernardo. This gesture confirmed that a radical transformation in the attitude of the church toward the theatrical world had taken place. The theater was no longer considered a marginal form of entertainment. [20] These alterations, however, did not mean an end to the denunciation and repression of "excesses."

The problems that the writer José Antonio Alzate y Ramírez ran into when his newspaper commented upon the theater are highly instructive. In May of 1768, the *Diario de México* dedicated the entire edition to a reader's letter on the subject of the theater's improvement. The viceroy prevented the circulation of that particular issue without providing any clear rationale. Apparently, it was not so much the contents of the letter—which were quite inoffensive—but rather the format that angered the viceroy. Five years later, with the appearance of the first number of *Asuntos varios sobre ciencias y artes* (Various themes on science and the arts) in October 1772, Alzate defended contemporary theater decisively. But, perhaps because of the disturbances in the Coliseum—rather common disorders in this period—and the precedent of the previous censorship, in December 1772, he opted for a toned-down version of his opinions. He began almost apologetically: "I don't want my use of the word theater to be understood as that place where people assemble to watch comedies or tragedies but rather those excellent plays that are presented or are read." And he continued with more caveats: "Nor was it my intention to imply that all plays that have been written in the last few years benefit from all these advantages." Alzate compared Spanish-language theater to others: "I have seen the critiques of some that are in foreign languages whose authors seem to have no other goal but to corrupt society, to undermine virtues and form a school of libertines, effects of some blind souls who enjoy the title of philosophers (not Christians) or who are strong spirits who do not recognize any other authority than their unflinching and particular mode of thought." He defended good plays "in which the intention is to correct the vices of men, those in which the recognized rule of morality are demonstrated, those in which the morality that corresponds to a Christian people is respected." Such plays, he believed, "should be accorded the status of real plays of a reformed theater and would serve either as a diversion or a corrective."[21] Under the control of civil authorities, the theater emerged victorious in these many struggles and made its triumphant entry onto the stage of the Enlightenment.

## The Enlightenment and the Theater

Enlightened thinkers believed that the theater, if developed with skill and wisdom, had the potential to become a powerful medium for the moral regeneration of society. Eighteenth-century intellectuals called this period the age of philosophy. During these years, the efforts of scholars of the two previous centuries to make Reason the privileged instrument of Knowledge prospered and bore fruit. The success of physics and mathematics—as most dramatically represented by Newton's laws—encouraged enlightened thinkers to apply these methods of analysis to other spheres of knowledge. They hoped that these sciences would provide universal laws that governed not only nature but also economics, society, politics, and morality. The intellectuals abandoned the seventeenth-century claim that philosophical systems were based on abstract premises. Instead, they sought to understand the concrete aspects of reality by simple deduction and began to exalt observation and scientific experimentation as the way to prove the relationship between cause and effect.

Knowledge and examination were the primordial principles of the Enlightenment. These axioms were closely tied to empirical advances in the sciences, but they were applied to a critical inquiry regarding philosophy, religion, and society. Science advanced through a critical examination of prejudice and other false idols that got in the way of Reason and Truth. By building upon the concrete advances of the sciences, logic was gradually freed from the chains that had limited it for centuries. Subordination neither to tradition nor to the revealed truths of religion was accepted. The possibilities and aspirations of the proponents of this view were unlimited. In addition, the advocates of logic were not satisfied with a simple conquest of autonomy. Rather, they soon contended that these forms of knowledge and methodologies were immutable, that they were valid universally because they were part of human nature. If real people did not immediately begin to act in accordance with their dictates, it was only because of the false interests and prejudices that sidetracked them from the path of truth.

The proponents of logic, self-elected as purveyors of the only valid form of knowledge, began to repay their former jailers. Religion, metaphysics, art, politics, the law, traditions and customs, the economy, and more were all called to account. The Enlightenment's fundamental task was to elevate logic, and so science became the supreme judge of the universe.[22]

Following this logic, the enlightened thinker is not necessarily a great intellectual who reveals the secrets of Nature. Rather, he can also be a simple dilettante who observes phenomena superficially and comes to mistaken conclusions as long as he accepts that reality can be explained correctly by science. As long as he believes that reason can distinguish between real and false miracles, the enlightened thinker is not necessarily or frequently an atheist or even a deist. In fact, as Max Weber observes with such foresight, the science that the adherents of the Enlightenment promoted did not increase the knowledge that particular individuals had of the world around them. Only a few specialists understood the majority of the advances of this period. At the same time, the effects of this progress increased the complexity of the devices used by humans and also the social mechanisms that governed them. The "accomplishment" of the enlightened was to convince people that hidden and unpredictable powers do not exist in the universe and that any phenomenon can be explained.[23]

Brandishing reason, which they considered to be all-powerful, the enlightened thinkers wished to reform society, to clear out its abasement, and to lead it along the road to progress. To do so, these intellectuals proposed to study the ills that society suffered as well as their causes. They could then dictate the most efficient remedies. Studies of social and economic problems began to proliferate; in these inquiries, the authors proposed practical and concrete measures to resolve social problems. They hoped that the government would implement their ideas. The Spanish intellectual Antonio Capmany wrote about agriculture, commerce, and industry. He stated: "Who would not delight in the well-founded hope that the works that a multitude of writers have penned, inspired by the same spirit, and that reflect the same zeal, must soon confirm the famous

*Republic* of Plato, and see a population of philosophers governed by philosophers?"[24] For these audacious intellectuals, the most efficient measure to improve the lot of the people was to win over the king and governors to the new philosophical principles, in other words, to enlighten the despots. Francisco, Count of Cabarrús, expressed these desires in the following manner: "If an entire generation could be informed, a time would come when the governments would be just because they would be enlightened."[25]

At the same time, those in power also sought to ally themselves with the enlightened thinkers. In Spain, the Bourbon monarchs were convinced that the Spanish empire could not play an important role in global politics if it did not redress its characteristic state of social and economic backwardness. In order to address these problems and discover the origins of the decadence, it was necessary to have a profound understanding of the situation both on the Peninsula and in the colonies. Then, they could take measures for the reestablishment of imperial glory. The Crown implemented all types of practical inquiries in New Spain. These investigations included many explorations of the coastlines (1774, 1775, 1779, and 1790, as well as two in 1792), the mapping of the seaboard, travelers' accounts from the northern regions, the inception of botanical and mineral collections, the gathering of reliable statistics and geographical relations as well as descriptions of the provinces by the intendants. The state apparatus also had to be modernized and rationalized. It had to be able to formulate precise plans and put them into practice efficiently. To do so, a large professional bureaucracy had to be formed that understood the technical and scientific information of the day.[26]

The thinkers of the Enlightenment were developing a type of knowledge that was useful to the state in its implementation of economic, political, and social reforms. But it also served to create a new form of legitimation. In fact, it superseded the religious ideas that were then falling from grace. Faced with the complexities of the modern world, many believed that only experts imbued with the wisdom of the Enlightenment could lead society through the dangers that lurked on all sides and choose the most appropriate options for all. The Spanish enlightened thinker Juan Menéndez Valdez justified this belief in the following manner: "The ignorant person hesitates and stops at the rough exterior, but the contemplative politician casts his penetrating gaze into the future and can see the indispensable consequences of the challenges undetectable to the vulgar eyes of the former."[27]

Clearly, the uneducated did not possess the necessary capacity to understand public affairs and therefore had no reason to participate in them. In addition, all decisions were taken with the greater good of all in mind. José Moñino, Count of Floridablanca, condensed this policy in the well-known if rather blunt phrase, "All for the people, but without the people."[28] Marquis Carlos Francisco de Croix, the first enlightened viceroy of New Spain, published a decree on the occasion of the disturbances caused by the expulsion of the Jesuits. It was a reminder to the people of their obligations: "Once and for all, the subjects of the great monarch who occupies the throne in Spain must realize that they were born to silently obey and not to discuss nor voice their opinions on the lofty matters of government."[29]

Plebeians could contribute most to the greater good of society and their own, by maintaining themselves in the social position that fate had decreed for them and, within that position, training themselves to support actively the monarch's plans. In his discourse on the development of popular industry, Pedro Rodríguez, Count of Campomanes, wrote: "Men of letters have the same standing in the republic as officials in the army. Moreover, why pay these men if they do not use their experience and military proficiency to discipline the troops?"[30]

Miguel Pacheco Solís, the *corregidor* (royal district governor) of Tlancalán, states in his *Proyecto sobre la forma de remediar la decadencia de la industria minera* (Project on the manner to remedy the mining industry): "Every vassal is a portion of the moral body of which society is composed: logically, they all occupy their respective position, but they should also undertake to be as active and flexible as possible: the monarch, as the head, cannot influence some parts without suppleness."[31] In order to accomplish the reforms needed by society, reason sought to influence force and force took on the cloak of reason. Enlightened despotism emerged from this alliance.

The thinkers of the Enlightenment recognized that it was not sufficient simply to have an enlightened monarch to reach their dream of a just society governed by reason. Rather, the people had to be enlightened, knowledgeable, and obedient to the moral, natural, and rational principles. How could the people be educated? How could the new learning be spread among them? To the thinkers of the Enlightenment, the theater seemed like one of the most efficient media for this task. In New Spain, the intellectuals considered it practically the only instrument available. In various European nations, such as France, a variety of lampoons, newspapers, and political writings allowed sectors of the common people to come into contact with the literary world.[32] In New Spain, however, the economic, social, and cultural chasm that separated the elite from the common people as well as the very high level of illiteracy made the use of writings for the spread of modern ideas infeasible. The lower classes' attraction to the theater made its use for the realization of this project possible as well as for the refinement of the insolent plebeians of the city.

In reality, the intellectuals' use of the theater was not a novelty. Their goals and their methods did not differ much from those of the sixteenth-century missionaries. Just as the monks taught the indigenous population the "true religion" and "how to live properly" through religious dramas, the intellectuals wanted to instruct the people on the "moral virtues of reason" and the "good customs of civilization" with bourgeois plays. In both cases, the idea was to make these new behaviors and values visible through their dramatic representation, so that the members of the audience would adopt them in their daily lives. Both the missionaries and the intellectuals hoped to capture the minds of the people through their eyes.

When viceregal officials and colonial Mexican intellectuals wrote about the theater, they began to refer to this goal more frequently. In 1786, Viceroy Bernardo de Gálvez had some verses inscribed on the curtain of the New Coliseum. These lines pointed out that the "duty" of drama was to "correct mankind" and make of the people "a friend of virtue" and "an enemy of vice."[33] The censor of the Coliseum's plays, Father Rincón, an adherent of the ideas of the Enlightenment, thought that the theater should be "an entertaining school of private and social virtues."[34] In 1821, a journalist stated that the theater should be "a school of good conduct, of education, and of delicacy."[35] Spanish and European thinkers, in general, were in complete agreement with the ideas expressed by these Mexican intellectuals.

Gaspar Melchor de Jovellanos y Ramírez stated in his report on public entertainments and diversions that the theater was "the first and most recommended of all spectacles." He argued that "it offers a more general, more rational, more profitable, and, by the same token, the most appropriate diversion for the attention and concerns of the government." For this reason, he believed that "the government should consider the theater not as a public diversion but as a spectacle that can instruct or pervert the spirit; it can perfect or corrupt the heart of citizens."[36]

In the article "Geneva" in the *Encyclopédie*, Jean Le Rond D'Alembert wrote the words that provoked the first confrontation between Jean-Jacques Rousseau and his old friends, the *philosophes*: "Theatrical representations could form the taste of the citizens [of Geneva], and give them a fine touch, a delicacy of sentiments that is difficult to achieve without assistance."[37] Paradoxically, the *philosophes* hoped to transform dramas into models of morality by making them more realistic and by constructing them around more plausible plots. The most didactic works would be those that faithfully reflected reality with only an artistic embellishment. The thinkers of the eighteenth century embraced the notion that moral values were objective. They believed that an observation of reality freed from prejudices and passion would lead to a discovery of the real norms of private and public behavior. They believed that the stage should be a privileged space where the world would finally see unadorned reality without the interference of economic and political interests, which usually impeded its clear appreciation. The spectator would be distanced from the action. Devoid of selfish interests, the public would no longer feel involved in the plot as it would in the real world. This supposed "objectivity" would force the manifestation of "natural" sentiments and oblige the viewer to take the side of "justice" and "virtue."

At the midpoint of the eighteenth century, the impresario of the Coliseum announced the debut of a new play with these words: "A wise man called the Theater the mirror of life (and with reason). Just as imperfections or defects are revealed in the looking glass, the same mechanism is, however, not true for the theater. There, the actions of men are not represented just as they are, but adulation covers their faults and injustice hides their qualities."[38]

For the spectators, the theater was supposed to provide a catharsis and to "purge them" of wicked emotions by showing them the terrible results of such passions. As such, the theater contributed to the creation of a new secular morality. With great discretion, the plays unconsciously excised divine caution from values. God no longer rewarded or punished human actions in the other world. These actions were punished through the consequences of acts that were committed in this world. Nature, in its wisdom, protected virtue and stopped the triumph of evil. The Marquis de Sade wasted his time mocking this morality, which, in spite of its weak "rational" grounds, prevailed in the following centuries.[39]

The motivation behind the theater reform was not solely a desire to educate the people and to teach them new values but also to provide Mexico City with a playhouse on the level of those in the great European capitals. The progress of the arts in New Spain depended upon a worthy theater to which men and women of culture could flock to amuse and to instruct themselves without having to suffer the discomfort and disorder that were customary in the Coliseum. According to the intellectuals of New Spain, the prestige of New Spain in the eyes of "civilized" nations depended to a great extent upon the quality of its theater. A reader wrote to the *Diario de México* on this subject in 1768. With obvious patriotism, he began: "Apart from the very obvious usefulness [of theater reform], which is worthy in itself, this cause also has implications for the honor of America and her sons, who love the fatherland, and who cannot turn their backs on this quest." Yet he worried that "many [people], little instructed in the advantages of this philosophy, will fearfully exclaim: Goodness! The honor of an entire Empire hangs on one little play! Yes, gentlemen, if you are willing to listen I will tell you: glory and honor for both Americas, for the entire nation, rests on the composition of a dramatic work, . . . would it be such a small feat . . . to show that there are minds capable of the sublime?"[40]

It was in the same tone that some of the improvements to the theater were announced in 1824. The Ayuntamiento named a commission to be responsible for theatrical affairs in general. The commissioners undertook some improvements to the theater because "they were convinced of the usefulness of the theater for a cultivated people and that it serves as a barometer on which the culture of nations can be measured." The members of the commission worked tirelessly: "They rooted out the abuses on stage, they improved the theater until it was as close to perfection as it can be, such are the demands of the Mexican Enlightenment." Their efforts gained them admiration and respect.[41]

Apart from these noble goals, the authorities hoped that the theater reforms would fulfill some other less lofty, but no less important, objectives. With a show of a rather modern and utilitarian way of thinking, Viceroy Bernardo de Gálvez saw the economic benefits in New Spain of a well-ordered theater: "I have resolved to . . . arrange the diversions in such a way that they interrupt the work of the public, entertain them for a short while in a blameless idleness so as to then make them more ready and diligent for the ordeals of their destiny."[42] Also, an educational, enlightened, and moralizing theater of good quality would distract the residents of Mexico City who, dragged down by laziness, succumbed to "gravely prejudicial" pastimes.[43] Finally, with the advent of the French Revolution, the viceroys began to think that a people occupied and entertained in healthy diversions would be less susceptible to rebellions.[44]

In reality, Mexico City's theater was a far cry from the ideals of education to which the enlightened thinkers and government officials in New Spain aspired. Let us imagine what a night at the New Coliseum would have been like in the 1780s.

## A Night at the Coliseum for Javier Orozco Rivadeneyra

The New Coliseum presented shows every night of the week except Saturdays. Normally, the show started fifteen minutes after the evening prayer. The schedule allowed the people to attend functions after the completion of their daily chores. The performances ended in the wee hours of the night—between 10 and 11 P.M.![45]

The New Coliseum was located on Colegio de las Niñas Street. Whenever a show was really popular, it was no simple matter to reach its doors. If you went on foot, which was not fashionable at the time, you had to walk along Acequia Street, which was perpetually under repairs so that it was a real obstacle course. Mexico City had been built on the site of a drained lake. In the rainy season, the lake reemerged to take revenge on the population; it temporarily returned to its old bed and flooded the street where the Coliseum stood. In this case, if you did not want to arrive wet and muddy, you could contract the services of an Indian who, carrying you on his shoulders, would take you across the street, safe and dry.

If you went by carriage, as all respectable people did, an inevitable traffic jam awaited you at the approach to the New Coliseum. At the end of the performance, the traffic problems were even worse. These problems inspired Viceroy Bernardo de Gálvez to institute one-way streets and no-parking zones in the city. From then on, it became vital to instruct your coachman clearly to leave the carriage in a permitted zone. If not, an unpleasant surprise often awaited spectators when they left the performance. Often, coachmen who parked illegally ran into trouble with the troops who very often treated the humble with undue harshness. After a heated exchange over whether it was permissible to leave the coach in a certain space, the soldiers would hit the mules with their musket butts, which infuriated the coachman who finally ended the night in prison. For those who found such a situation when the show was over, the only solution was to get the coachman out of jail.

When you arrived at the Coliseum, a handsome and agreeable building of masonry was your first sight. A portal of three arches formed the entrance. Tickets had been purchased ahead of time; if you were poor you had done so in person. If you belonged to the upper classes, you had sent a servant. Ticket prices were relatively cheap, starting at half a real, the lowest denomination. The prices doubled for special performances.

A strange and not particularly pleasant smell pervaded the Coliseum. It was caused by the odor of the burning oil in the lamps mixed with the smoke of cigars enjoyed by men and women alike. Actually, this smoke covered up the more offensive stench of black waters that did not drain well, as they were progressively blocked by the public's littering: glass, fruit peels, cigar butts, and other debris.

Once accustomed to the smoke and poor lighting, you would notice the motley crowd of men and women. They came from every social group, from the highest bureaucrats—it was not unusual to see the viceroy and his wife there—to rich Creoles dressed in their best finery, fops and dandies, mestizo artisans, and day laborers clothed in their Sunday best who came to divert themselves raucously at the play. The only component missing was the Indians, who lived in barrios and towns outside the city.

Beneath the appearance of anarchy exuded by this mass of people, individuals knew their place. In the patio, right next to the stage, there were four rows of seats called the *luneta*; there and in the lateral boxes nearest the front were the best-dressed people. These were the places of greatest distinction. Just behind the *luneta*, the *mosquete* was the cheapest area, where the common people jostled together in standing room only.

The upper part of the theater had three floors, each with eighteen boxes. These were constructed of masonry and each had an ironwork balcony covered with a painted canvas. The boxes were entered by wooden doors with iron locks and keys and had wooden seats like those in the rest of the theater. The balconies on the first and second floors were rented for the season or for holidays. It was in these boxes that the habitués of the theater met. The boxes on the third floor, however, were rented for one show, and it was more common to encounter people of the lower classes there.

The gallery was located above the boxes in the *cazuela*. It was divided into two parts to avoid scandals. One section of 236 seats was reserved for women; the usher for this section had to be a mature man—never a young one. Another section with 159 seats was reserved for men. Disorder usually originated in the *cazuela* and the *mosquete*, which were the exclusive territory of the common people.

Without counting the numerous members of both sexes who climbed up onto the roof and watched from the skylights, the theater could hold 800 people. In fact, it was a mistake to trust the roof. There were numerous drips, and the beams that supported the structure had deteriorated over time. In 1806, during a performance, part of the roof collapsed, injuring several members of the audience.[46]

Concentration on the show was by no means an easy task. Everyone talked. There were few public places where people could get together (the first café, the Café Tacuba, opened in 1785, and in 1790, according to Viceroy Revillagigedo the second, such places were still rare), so the Coliseum was the ideal place to chat and discuss the latest events,[47] criticize the lifestyles of others, examine the people in the balconies with opera glasses, grumble, gossip about a thousand foolishnesses, and seduce women. All these conversations caused a constant buzzing that distracted viewers from the action on stage. In addition, the spectators, especially the women, came and went constantly, disturbing their neighbors. Gentlemen liked to keep their hats on, and calling this breach of good manners to their attention entailed definite risks, given that some responded with insolence or violence. Itinerant vendors shouted their wares during the performance: sweets, ices, cold cuts, and flavored waters.

Some of the spectators in the upper balconies and the *cazuela* carelessly tossed lit cigar butts and fruit peels onto the people below. Others indulged in spitting, which led to fights among the assemblage. If the performance took place during Carnaval (the pre-Lenten festival, like Mardi Gras), the unfortunate people in the *luneta* and *mosquete* were covered with a thick shower of aniseeds, coated almonds, barley, *alverjones* [peas], and even, at times, small stones. In spite of all these incidents, the show did go on.

The favorite themes of the plays were either the intrigues caused by love, jealousy, and the vagaries of unreciprocated love or they were based on sight gags, using complicated stage machinery and dense, implausible plots. Between each act, musical interludes of *sainetes* (short plays or farces), *tonadillas*, and various types of dances were presented. If, in the eyes of the cultivated public, the plays were rather frivolous, these interludes verged on the indecent. The interludes were even more implausible and involved more buffoonery than the dramas. The *tonadillas* erred in an excess of licentiousness and bordered on profligacy if the titles are any indication: "La resaladota" (The vivacious one), "Los celos infundados" (The undeserved jealousy), "Las mañas de una casada" (The tricks of a wife), "La confiada" (The trusting one), "El novio simple" (The innocent fiancé), "El encuentro nocturno" (The nighttime assignation), "La aguardientera" (The female brandy seller), and many others.[48] Also, the words of these songs were replete with double entendres, which usually involved ridicule and social satire much to the delight of those present. The *tonadillas* and their interpreters were very popular in the *mosquete* and *cazuela*.

Women performed the dances with a sensuality that scandalized the authorities, enlightened thinkers, and fathers concerned with the morality of their daughters. These dances were considered dissolute, impure, lascivious, and lewd. The common people, in contrast, enjoyed these dances and shouted "My soul! God preserve you!" at the performers. The dances provoked such a stir in the theater that the actors, their assistants, the musicians, and the stagehands came out on stage to enjoy them as well. According to a cultivated member of the public, they turned the stage into a pigsty.

Even according to the norms of the day, the actors' work left a lot to be desired. With more or less discretion, they signaled from the stage to their friends and acquaintances in the audience. When they had no lines, they took the opportunity to gossip and joke among themselves, and their absorption and distraction caused many missed cues. In the wings, the actors had a good time. Some brought snacks, drinks, and even alcohol. All chatted merrily and collectively, causing a cheerful uproar.

All this not only distracted the actors, but made hearing the prompter almost impossible. Such situations could seriously throw off the performance, because regular rehearsals were well-nigh unknown and thought to be unnecessary for most actors. The repertoire of the day was extremely vast, hence the role of the prompter was vital. If the actors could not hear the prompter, they became infuriated, much to the amazement and amusement of the spectators. If the prompter did not show up at the Coliseum, putting on the show took an almost superhuman effort. For example, in 1729, the prompter was ill and could not be properly replaced. Rapidly, the "little or no preparation of some of the principal actors, the little care and polish of their performance despite the shouts of another prompter were such that the man responsible for the plays had to go out and ask the public if the performance could be replaced with a *zalla* [theatrical piece], to which the audience did not consent. They demanded that the play should continue, more to mock the confusion than to applaud the quality of interpretation of the play."[49]

The spectators, especially those in the *mosquete*, did not rein in their reactions to the performances. They applauded and shouted raucously and brazenly in response to plays, rejoinders, and acting that was to their taste. In loud voices, they demanded the presentation of certain *tonadillas*, dances, and the presence of certain of the more popular actors. Most of all, they whistled, booed, mocked, and ridiculed the errors and gaffes that occurred during the show. Faced with this onslaught, the actors did not remain impassive but responded to the public's attacks with insults, thus igniting a generalized chaos in the theater.

Finally, in the midst of this anarchy, the curtain fell. The public could then, once more, read the lines that Viceroy Bernardo de Gálvez had ordered inscribed there:

> Drama is my name
> and my duty is to correct mankind
> in the exercise of my profession,
> friend of virtue, enemy of vice.

## Through Repression to Enlightenment

Perhaps this description of the performances in the Coliseo in Mexico City was a little exaggerated, with too much emphasis on the improvisation and disorder that reigned there. In all likelihood, however, this image is not too far from the perception of the period's enlightened thinkers of the events that took place every night inside the Coliseum. In 1768, a reader of the *Diario Literario de México* (Literary journal of Mexico) wrote that many persons cringed "with horror at only the word play" and that, for them, it was unthinkable that "honorable families" and "the maidens" who lived "in fear of God and jealous of their reputation" could attend such spectacles.[50]

In the eyes of the enlightened thinkers, the situation had become intolerable. A thorough reform of the theater was the only solution. In 1786, Viceroy Bernardo de Gálvez launched the first attempt to transform the theater into an effective mode of diffusion of the new ideas and a diversion that corresponded to the norms of decency, decorum, and order.

Early that year, the viceroy formed a society of subscribers to the theater composed of prominent citizens. Their directors were two members of the Royal Audiencia, the *corregidor*, the general adviser of the viceroyalty, the superintendent of the Royal Customs of Mexico City, and the Marquis of San Miguel de Aguayo. The object of the society was to collect funds to renovate the theater and to take over the administration of the Coliseum when the current rental contract ended. The viceroy hoped that this society could end the abuses, vices, and defects of the shows simply by the authority of their personages and also because, unlike the private contractors, these august men would not be guided solely by the incentive of profit. Despite all these good intentions, the society folded after only three years.

At the beginning of 1786, the viceroy also ordered Silvestre Díaz de la Vega, the accountant general of the Royal Tobacco Monopoly, to draft the rules of the society. Later, the viceroy requested Díaz de la Vega to write a discussion of the various types of drama, their classes, and the reason to maintain these shows. This text was added as a memorandum to the document. The viceroy contributed his advice, suggestions, and corrections to the document. The directors of the subscribers' society approved the document on March 28, 1786. On the same day, the viceroy gave it his approval and then ordered it printed.[51]

The significance of the regulations outlined by Silvestre Díaz de la Vega was not in the various legal dispositions designed to do away with the most notorious disorders, for in previous years, other administrations had undertaken similar efforts. Rather, the Reglamento's importance lay in the attempt to create a systematic and comprehensive body of dispositions that touched upon all aspects of the operation of the Coliseum. It marked the passing from a series of haphazard dispositions to a rational type of regulation. Although the rules were part of a compilation and classification of previous dispositions, with the addition of a few new ones, the innovation can be seen in the fact that these rules were not tacked onto the previous ordinances but rather replaced them. The various royal decrees and orders collected in this document were all— with the exception of one dated 1725—relatively recent. They were originally published in 1763, 1765, 1779, and 1781.[52]

The Theater Regulations of 1786 began with a reminder regarding the resolution of June 9, 1765, which prohibited the presentation of plays of a religious character. This ban corresponded to a desire to ensure that the proper respect was accorded to such serious subjects as religion. In fact, it was a serious blow to the church, because it meant the loss of an effective means of disseminating its principles to the lower classes of the colony. In 1768, New Spain's Inquisition explained that the ban extended to the performance of pastorals in public places at Christmas and during Lent.[53] It seems likely that the church endorsed this prohibition with an eye to the purification of the faith and to end the almost sacrilegious abuses that occurred in these representations.

Also, in an attempt at total control, the Theater Regulations of 1786 not only renewed the previous censorship of all dramas to be presented at the Coliseum but also canceled all prior permissions granted before its promulgation. It also made clear that not only the texts of plays would have to be cleared with the censors but also that the staging would be scrutinized. For a more efficient censorship, a month ahead of scheduled presentations, the theater's directors had to send in a complete list of all plays, *sainetes*, *tonadillas*, and dances that they planned to present.

The regulations also proposed the elimination of certain forms of conduct on the part of actors while they were on stage. These rules were more directly aimed at actresses, however, whom the authorities considered immoral and indecent. Just as in previous provisions, while on stage, actors were to maintain "the proper modesty, circumspection, and composure in their actions and words, and show the proper respect for the public; they must avoid all indecency and provocation that might cause the most minor scandal especially during the dances . . . characteristic of this country . . . which are hereby prohibited in the strictest form, as are any invented supplement to the dances such as the one called the *cuchillada*, any jumps or other provocative movements."

In order to enforce obedience to this article, those who disobeyed were threatened with the following punishment: "The actor or actress who engages in such disorders will be arrested on the spot and will be jailed for one month. The culprit will be taken from the stage where the transgression occurred in full view of the public and the members of the company in order to serve as a lesson and example."[54] With such a tone, it comes as no surprise that the regulations also kept a rather prudish stipulation from 1725 that a board should be attached to the front of the stage. This barrier was supposed to be "the height of a *tercia* [a third of a yard]" and was designed to block the libidinous glances of spectators at the feet of the actresses.

The regulations collected previous ordinances and amplified and specified precise penalties for those who provoked disorders. The goal was to impose a certain type of conduct on the public. In line with the sexual puritanism of the rules, the Regulations of 1786 reiterated a strict separation of the sexes in the *cazuelas* and third-level balconies, which were rented by the seat.

Raucous acts on the part of the audience were also forbidden. If members of the public wished to show their appreciation for a certain aspect of the work of one of the actors, a restrained clapping would be "tolerated" at the end of the actor's speeches. Disapproval could only be manifested "with silence and in no other manner." Individuals who did not comply with these rules of good conduct and who mocked the actors or talked with "unruly voices" would be punished with eight days of imprisonment if they were "not persons of distinction, and if they were (which should not be the case—says the viceroy), will be conducted to my presence where I will assign their discipline."[55] Rowdy and degenerate students were no longer tolerated in the school of virtue; spare the rod and spoil the child.

The discipline and professionalization of the actors was the really radical innovation of the regulations. Actors were prohibited from talking, making signals, laughing, or distracting one another while on stage. They were further forbidden from any show of anger when the prompter or the musicians missed their cues, nor could they show themselves to the public before the curtain rose or bring alcohol backstage. Finally, they were enjoined to arrive on time for the beginning of every performance.

Actors, dancers, and musicians were to attend regular rehearsals daily; the excuse that they already knew their lines was no longer considered valid. Such an imposition was quite a novelty. The regulation stated "that the appropriate measures would be taken, these would be far-reaching and would culminate in a prison term for those who missed rehearsals. No exceptions or discrimination of any kind would be allowed so that this stipulation would achieve a due compliance."[56] As if this measure did not suffice, there was an addendum: "All those who do not know their lines, the words of the *tonadillas*, or the steps of the dances when the time comes to perform are warned that their salaries will be docked to the amount that corresponds to that day for a first offense; the second time the penalty will be doubled; and the third time, after being conducted publicly from the theater, the culprit will be jailed for an appropriate sentence."[57] The viceroy probably did not believe that he would have to impose such severe punishments frequently. Rather, he obviously hoped to do away with the improvisation and disorder that reigned in the theater. To do so, half-measures would not suffice.

The Regulations of 1786 dealt with many other details that touched upon diverse subjects, but all related to the imposition of good order in the theater. The apparel of actresses, the functioning of dressing rooms, the actors' assistants, the cleanliness of the hall, the hawkers of sweets and flavored waters, the traffic congestion on streets surrounding the Coliseum, the reserved seating, and the pricing and sale of tickets were just some of the other topics that were subjects of the regulations.

The Regulations of 1786, boldly modern and markedly repressive, were the appropriate means for the creation of a theater that corresponded to the ideals of the Enlightenment. This relationship can be confirmed by the long duration of these ordinances. During the colonial period, a few rules were added to the Regulations of 1786. The first addenda were crafted in the very year of its printing and by the very same viceroy, Bernardo de Gálvez. These concerned only some very secondary issues. Later, in a royal decree of 1792, various sections, already in the regulations, were reiterated. In 1794, Viceroy Revillagigedo the second generated a new regulation that apparently was almost a carbon copy of the previous one. With the declaration of the Constitution of Cádiz in 1813, a similar process was followed.[58]

After Independence, the rules that governed the theater continued to be based on the 1786 regulations. For example, the rules declared in 1846, after the tumultuous years of multiple and changing governments, maintained, with a slightly muted tone, the 1786 stipulations on censorship and the fines to be imposed on actors who flubbed their lines. Even the ordinances on the parking of carriages outside the theater were cribbed from those of Viceroy Bernardo de Gálvez.

It was not until 1894 that a theater regulation radically distinct from the 1786 one was issued. By this time, the state had adopted a fundamentally different attitude toward the theater. The training of the actors became the responsibility of the impresario, not the civil authorities. The behavior of the public needed only to conform to current and generally accepted legal norms. Thus, the Regulations of 1894 were not concerned with hygiene and security in the hall. In this new regulation, the theater became a capitalistic enterprise just like any other. As for censorship, the impresario had to submit a list of plays to be presented for each month five days before the first performance in order to receive the necessary license.[59]

The rules implemented by Viceroy Bernardo de Gálvez were only abandoned a century after their promulgation. Of course, it would be a mistake to overestimate the impact of the Regulations of 1786 and to identify them as the root of all the changes in the theatrical world of Mexico City in the last decades of the colonial period. It is much more likely that these transformations were due to insignificant but regular decisions reached on a daily basis. They were the result of a profound change in the mentality not only of the viceregal officials but also of the contractors and actors. These alterations were reflected in the Regulations of 1786 but the rules were only one expression of the changes.

The actual influence of the ideas of the Enlightenment on the theater and the significance of the changes that followed can be appreciated through an examination of the transformations in particular sectors of the theatrical world. The actors, the shows, censorship, and the relationship between the theater and officials will illuminate the changes in the dramatic arts. At the same time, using the prism of the tempestuous life of the theater, it will be possible to decipher some of the modifications in practices and customs in eighteenth-century Mexican society.

## The Life of Actors

In New Spain, actors were actually "rather scarce." It was not an easy task to secure their services and to make sure that they continued in their jobs. The methods used by the viceregal authorities to procure the services of actors, however, were a far cry from free wage labor. Although these techniques never reached the level of compulsion that was regularly used to force Indians to work in Spanish sectors of the economy when labor was scarce, the manner of acquisition of the services of actors was by no means free of force and coercion.

Actors and other workers within the theater were conscious of how difficult it was to replace them and tried without much success to take advantage of the situation. With a tinge of despair, the judge of hospitals, Don Francisco Valenzuela, clearly describes the problems caused by the scarcity of actors: "Because [the Coliseum company] is composed of people who can only work for this institution, every day there are disagreements and hostilities among them. None of the precautions and warnings nor admonitions seems enough. Although as a company they sign a contract for the whole year, they break it and lapse in their observance of these agreements very easily. And the next year they want the salaries that they think they deserve." The *mayordomo* of the Royal Indian Hospital did not resist these salary demands, so the actors "get whatever they want and the specified punishment is never applied to them, since when the poor chap wishes to take some remedial action, they have fled, or he himself comes to their aid because their services are so needed. So it always comes down to the fact that there are no others in the same profession who have any talent in this city and who could replace the culprits."[60] The authorities who were concerned with the maintenance and development of the theater—*mayordomos* of the hospital, contractors, judges, and viceroys—dealt with this continual shortage by various practices.

One tactic was to arrange for the transfer of resources from other institutions. Musicians were frequently secured in this way. At the end of the eighteenth century, the army kept a good number of musicians in its ranks to perform for its functions. The theater contractors therefore petitioned the viceroy to commission some of them for service in the Coliseum. The viceroy always acceded to these requests. In 1790, Pablo Buisin, the commandant of the Company of Dragoons of Spain, was ordered to Mexico City so that he could play in the Coliseum's orchestra. In 1791, the viceroy ordered Manuel Flores of the Regiment of Dragoons to remain in Mexico City. In 1789, Flores had been the contractor of the theater. By preventing his transfer, the viceroy ensured that Flores and his wife, María Martínez, could continue to work in the Coliseum as musician and singer, respectively.[61]

For exceptional functions, the viceroy did not hesitate to order retired actresses to return to the stage. Viceroy Mayorga did so with the actress Madame Olivares, who then played a part in the comedy *Mujer, llora y vencerás* (Woman, cry and you will conquer), which was presented to celebrate the birthday of the Princess of Asturias.[62] When actresses did not respond to entreaties, the viceroy did not balk at using threats. In 1789, when the return to the stage of Antonia de San Martín displaced Bárbara Josefa from her starring role and she consequently stopped acting at the Coliseum, various pressures were exerted to make her change her mind. Faced with this coercion, La Josefa argued that she was leaving the stage to devote her attention entirely to her four children. Within colonial Mexican society, imbued as it was with Catholic morality, it was hard to object to her reasoning. The authorities accepted her resignation but not without threatening her with five years in the Recogidas (a closed institution for women) if she acted in any other theater. They also warned that they would be observing her private life and would not hesitate to punish her for the most minor scandal. Luckily for her, a few months later, Viceroy Revillagigedo the second took office and canceled these dispositions.[63]

Within the year, Antonia de San Martín herself began to miss performances, alleging illness. Despite certification from four doctors who confirmed her delicate state, everyone believed that her ailments were contrived. In order to oblige her to perform in the Coliseum with some regularity, the viceroy instructed that another doctor, named by the judge of the theater, should examine the actress. This specialist declared that San Martín's infirmities were not so serious as to prevent her from acting. Rather maliciously, he added that if, despite this diagnosis, she continued to feel incapable of returning to the stage, he would order the administration of strong preparations of mercury to speed up her cure. Faced with this treatment, which was really a veiled threat of poisoning, the actress declared herself ready to perform.[64]

The methods used to ensure the fulfillment of actors' obligations were not always so subtle and legalistic as those just reviewed. On some occasions, the methods were openly coercive. In 1664, for example, various actors of the company of the Royal Indian Hospital had dispersed to find work in provincial cities where they probably hoped for better labor conditions. They failed to satisfy the obligations they had contracted in the capital's theater. At the request of the mayordomo of the hospital, the viceroy tried to solve the problem by edict: "By the present authority, I order you, the justices of His Majesty, in any part of this government wherever these actors might be and reside, do not allow nor permit them to act and with all rigor oblige and compel them as is best suited to return to this city." In 1687, the viceroy gave a similar order.[65] In desperate cases of shortages of actors, even more unusual methods were used and actors were sought in the most peculiar places. In 1794, when the theater was in ruins because of the lack of talented performers, the administrator of the Royal Indian Hospital, Don José del Rincón, asked the viceroy for permission to contract the actress María Bárbara Ordóñez, who at that time was locked up in the Recogidas de Puebla. Also administrator of the Coliseum, Rincón, reasoned that the petition would "conform to various dispositions of justice and the laws that warn that if a person who is a supreme expert in an art commits some crime, the execution of the penalty should be suspended so that the prince might be consulted about its revocation and the substitution of a lighter sentence so that this person might continue to exercise professionally and to be useful to the Republic."[66] His arguments won over the viceroy who ordered that "the prisoner Bárbara Ordóñez, presently in the Recogidas of Santa María Egipciaca of the city of Puebla, should be transferred, as a prisoner, to this court under the responsibility and care of the said administrator, Don José del Rincón, who will put her in a house that meets his requirements." Furthermore, the viceroy stated: "She must complete the period of her sentence not leaving except to go to mass on days of obligation and to act in the theater. She will go out only with a responsible person. The people of the house where she will live are advised that they must scrutinize her conduct and [need] report only the slightest defects of conduct for her to be taken to the Recogidas and severely punished."[67]

This curious case is reminiscent of one of the dispositions of the Regulations of 1786. It threatened to imprison actors who froze during performances. Because of the chronic shortage of even dismal players, the administrator could not indulge in the luxury of losing even one who was disastrous on stage. The regulations went on to say that the actor who was imprisoned would be escorted to the Coliseum for each function so that he could fulfill his obligations.[68]

In the 1790s, when the attempts to reform the theater were at their zenith, the scarcity of actors became alarming. To make matters worse, if this anonymous satire of the period is representative, those who were available were terrible:

They want to force us
to enjoy the howls of the Güero,
the bellows of Nicolás,
the sham of Tules:
and even though a glance
does adjust his unhappiness,
lukewarm passion, he wants,
who thus plots it,
with strange novelties,
that represent a spider
in the role of leading actress.

What unseemly thought made
a pigmy the understudy
the public has to observe
through a microscope?
The very largest microscope
cannot distinguish his figure
and only by the guesses
of those two strange and first-class scrap dealers
give him this stature.[69]

In 1792, faced with this disastrous situation, the administrator of the Royal Indian Hospital contemplated resorting to the importation of a better sort of actors. The viceroy even approved this project enthusiastically. They believed that the high costs incurred by bringing in such luxury goods would be offset by a higher sale of tickets that "the attraction of good and new talents" would undoubtedly attract.[70] The exact outcome of this project is not clear, but there is no evidence of the arrival of foreign actors in New Spain. Perhaps, despite the increased exports of silver, problems of cash flow prevented contracting them.

By 1814, with the country sunk in a serious crisis, someone had the idea of applying the principle of import substitution to actors and thus, in other words, to instruct and prepare professional thespians. A former actor, Don Ignacio Miranda, prepared the project and submitted it to the city's intendant who gave him the necessary license to begin operations.

Along with the authorization to open the first acting school in Mexico City, Don Ignacio Miranda asked for permission to launch a puppet theater on the same premises. It does not seem too much of a leap to suppose that the proposed school was just a facade used to obtain the needed permit to start a marionette theater, which promised to be a prosperous business. In any case, three months after the opening, trouble began to brew between the partners in this scheme. Don Ignacio Miranda withdrew from the newly founded school, which was left in the hands of Don Mariano Aguirre, who retained the license. Even so, it does not seem very likely that this center lived up to the goals of the original establishment.[71]

Despite the permanent dearth of adequate actors, performers were not able to use this shortage to obtain higher salaries, in direct contradiction to the laws of supply and demand. Only those who played the most important roles were well paid and the rest received a pittance. Most actors, however, both well remunerated and otherwise, insisted on living above their means. For this reason, the documents related to the theater of the period continuously mention players who owed considerable debts to merchants.[72]

Their labor situation appears even more dismal when we consider that they were responsible for a much wider range of roles than an actor is today. They were required to learn an extremely large repertory. Every week, they played in four different shows, and, at times, they opened a new show weekly. Clearly, the pace of openings and performances made the prompter—who freed the players from the requirement of learning their lines—the cornerstone to every performance.[73]

The paltry salary that most actors received, however, made it necessary for them to seek other sources of revenue as a supplement. When they were not acting in the Coliseum or even after the conclusion of their night's performance, it was not at all unusual for them to moonlight in puppet theaters. During the Wars for Independence, their situation worsened; several petitioned to be allowed to mount marionette shows or *pastorales* during Lent. This period was critical for actors because the Coliseum staged no plays then and they got no salary.[74] Because of this situation, the "professional" theater of the Coliseum was always connected to the "popular" theater. No clear or precise division existed between them as does today. In fact, the pair represented two facets of one reality. The same actors who trod the boards at the Coliseum later went to outbuildings to manipulate puppets late into the night for the diversion of those who congregated there. Retired actors used their extensive experience in these merry functions, while young newcomers and second-rank actors acquired experience in an atmosphere freer than that of the Coliseum. In fact, Don Ignacio Miranda's idea to combine a drama school with a puppet theater was not a bad one. He simply recognized the prevailing but spontaneous practice and shaped it into an explicit arrangement.[75]

The poorly paid and debt-ridden actors became quite combative when contractors or the hospital administrators tried to impose obligations that were not customary. Labor conflicts were not uncommon, and the theater officials often reacted to these complaints in a violent and repressive manner in order to quash them. In 1777, for example, the actors clashed with the contractor when he tried to force them to perform in more works than they had agreed upon at the beginning of the season. The contractor's request contradicted the usual practices at the Coliseum. The players refused to accede to the new conditions, arguing that these "free" productions were "amusing" but not of "rigorous justice." In this case, the actors were able to impose their own conditions. The contractor agreed to supplementary pay for those who acted in the "complimentary" functions.[76]

The conflict of 1793–1794, however, was much more serious and was not resolved on such favorable terms for the actors. Viceroy Revillagigedo the second, concerned about the poor quality of theater, decided to take this opportunity to introduce various reforms in actors' salaries as well as to demand punctual and regular attendance at all rehearsals. The actors categorically rejected the imposition of these new conditions. The 1792 proposal to import foreign actors, which the viceroy had approved, may have contributed to the unease in the theatrical world. It only came to the surface on the occasion of these reforms. The actors took a stand and threatened to resign rather than accept the new conditions. They said that the salaries would be too low and that the rehearsals, as one actress stated, "are most annoying and useless. They consist solely in the representative giving instructions on who must exit and by what door. For this, the whole morning is wasted, women must absent themselves from their household duties, and no progress is made; this instruction would be better taken in one's own room, without being exposed to the unpleasantness of the idle."[77]

The viceroy did not flinch in his repression of this actors' revolt. He warned the actors who threatened to resign that henceforth they were prohibited from acting in any theater in New Spain. He further mandated that if they had not found employment in three days, they would be treated as vagabonds, loafers, and vagrants. Any foreigners would have to leave the territory of New Spain immediately, and Don Mariano Flores, the musician from the army, was sent back to his regiment. As for the actress Teresa de Aconda, "Her conduct was to be scrutinized with great compunction and if she reverted to her past disorders, she would be treated appropriately."[78] Faced with such intimidation, the actors capitulated and implored the viceroy for clemency. The viceroy forgave them and they returned to work at the Coliseum. Only a few stood firm; one of these was the musician from the Regiment of Dragoons who returned to the army along with his songstress wife; another was a comedian who set off for Puebla in search of a job.[79] The viceroy explained the reason for implementing such severe measures to end the insubordination of the actors to the judge of theaters: "This type of person must be governed with much skill and prudence, and it is fitting to treat them affably; but occasionally it is critical to impress them with superiority and the respect that they must hold."[80]

The protest of the actors was not the only such movement to be quashed in the period of the Enlightenment. The actresses also suffered the blows of new enlightened concepts. The acting of women was perceived as questionable at the beginning of the colonial period and was prohibited in religious plays.[81] Gradually, however, actresses consolidated and increased their presence in the theatrical world to such a degree that, in the documentation of the end of the seventeenth century, it is not unusual to find mentions of women who directed stage companies. Ana María, whom the viceroy ordered to come from Puebla to Mexico City along with her company to give some performances, is one of the first examples of such women. Later, in 1687, the viceroy named María de Celis, a famous actress, directress of the company of the Royal Indian Hospital, although the post was accorded "because there is no man who is a director."[82]

Unlike these instances from the seventeenth century, in the eighteenth century women in the world of theater lost much ground. In 1736, at the death of the celebrated playwright Eusebio Vela, the actress Ana María de Castro assumed the directorship of the theater, but only after a struggle with the widow of the author, who expected to succeed her husband in the post. The reign of Ana María de Castro as directress was brief, however, because a few years later, influenced by the sermons of Father Matías Conchoso, she left the stage. The priest, inspired by such an edifying decision, composed a poem entitled "The Farewell."[83] The other directress, María Bárbara Ordoñez, assumed the position in 1748 but, as we have seen previously, she ended up jailed in various *recogimientos*.[84]

This is a melancholy end to the list of directresses. It seems that during the second half of the eighteenth century, actresses lost many of the advances they had achieved in the seventeenth century. Probably, the power of women within the theater and their demonstration of their capability frightened the authorities. Like Molière in his plays, they believed that it was time to draw a line in the sand for these educated women who crossed the boundaries of their assigned roles. Some scholars affirm that the period of the Enlightment in New Spain was characterized by liberalization and dissolution; this is not accurate.

The precise social milieu from which the actors of New Spain were recruited is hard to determine. The question is not specifically whether they were enlisted from the ranks of the *gente de razón*—that is to say, Spaniards, *castizos*, and sometimes whitened mestizos—because this is the most probable source, but rather whether they were "decent," that is, from the moneyed class. Interestingly enough, the songstress "Inesita," who was wildly popular toward the beginning of the War of Independence, did not know how to sign her name. Was she from a poor family?[85]

What is certain is that when these people entered the theatrical world they became part of a group that was socially "declassed"; they had an ambiguous and even contradictory social status. On the one hand, they were applauded and admired by the whole city, from the day laborers and the artisans to the enlightened mine owners and *hacendados* (landed class). The viceroy held them in high esteem and intervened on their behalf to resolve professional, economic, and legal problems, and even on occasion, certain private matters. On the other hand, however, they were not able to dispel the condemnation with which the church had marked them in an earlier period. The persistent rumors about dissolute private lives prevented them from ever being considered "decent" persons. In 1786, Silvestre Díaz de la Vega continued to think that actors did not feel the call of a vocation but rather, that those who embraced this career did so "because of their ineptitude for other destinies or because of their indigence."[86]

Their relations with other sectors of society must have been quite limited except for other marginalized groups. They lived enclosed in a little world of fame and rejection, in a daily rhythm unsynchronized with the norm—they worked when others partied, and partied when others slept. Their experiences were unusual for the period; they suffered from a type of collective madness that the general public questioned avidly and apprehensively.

The 1727 lawsuit between the celebrated playwright Eusebio Vela and a merchant reveals the ambiguous status of actors in this period. As was usual among actors, Vela owed money to a merchant. One day, when he paid one of the installments, the merchant gave him a receipt that refered to the author only as Eusebio Vela without giving him the honorific "Don." In New Spain, in a society in which people jealously guarded deferential treatment, distinctions, honor, and respect and obstinately clung to the ideology of estates, the merchant's conduct was certainly not innocent.

A complete system of values and hierarchies was at stake between two individuals whose social standing was far from clearly defined. A "storekeeper," an upstart who tried to buy prestige with money that no one was sure was acquired legally, was opposed to an actor, celebrated by the public but suspect in the eyes of the church. The conflict occurred on the margins of the system, in the chasms in which modernity and the new rules filtered into the society at large. It was through the daily hidden confrontations, these little slights in service, that the new hierarchy was sketched. What was the place of the most prestigious actor of the period vis-à-vis an unknown but wealthy creditor? Social definition took place in these incidents.

After reading the receipt, Eusebio Vela charged into the store and with "discomposed and injurious" words demanded to know if the merchant knew his name. The tradesman answered that, yes, he was called Eusebio Vela. The author replied that he was Don Eusebio Vela, and the storeowner was Francisquillo the Shit. In court, the merchant alleged that he did not write Don Eusebio Vela on the receipt because "he is so common that no other treatment should be given in writing. . . ." The judge ordered Eusebio Vela imprisoned.[87] Undoubtedly, the merchant commented on this incident for a long time to all his clients, emphasizing the actor's lack of solvency, attributable to his dissolute life, and the unseemliness of the actor's—someone said to be so famous—reaction, and the indignity to which he was victim, and, finally, the just and proper resolution offered by the judge.

Let us not be too amazed at the emotional instability that was so frequent among actors. Torn between fame and discredit, between contradictory and disproportionate "role" and status, on the margin of public life, without any social moorings, to their eyes, the world could seem savage, without rules, and without order. The cohesive spirit that created social conventions could suddenly lose its apparently necessary character, its illusory substance. The treatment of others as similar or different that daily sustained institutional existence could be abandoned spontaneously and internalized. Tearing themselves away, for a fleeting moment, they were one step away from madness and rejection of the daily grind of legitimacy. They were exposed to the ultimate reason, the invisible but omnipresent constraint: physical force.[88] It was in these moments that actors, fleeing from derisory debt, left everything (work, family), furiously insulting the administrator or knifing a friend at the luncheon counter.[89] An objection could be raised that these were isolated cases among actors, and this would be quite true, but all the same, the lives of most actors were remote from the times' moral norms.

Bishop Palafox's accusation that actresses destroyed marriages among those who attended the theater was not altogether without basis. In 1816, Doña Dolores Valdivielso y Valdivielso, the fourth Countess of San Pedro de Alamo, asked for a divorce. She accused her husband, Don Francisco Xavier Valdivielso y Vidal Lorca, of having an affair with two actresses at the Coliseum, Isabel Munguía and Ignacia Aguilar. The husband could not deny the charge and the divorce was granted.[90]

In fact, it seems that conjugal fidelity was not much practiced in the world of theater. Deception and scandal were commonplace on a daily basis. Jealousy, whether founded or not, was a current running constantly through the life of the theater and had to be taken into account. In 1777, the wife of the general administrator of the Coliseum sued for divorce. She accused her husband, Don Juan Manuel de Vicente, of adulterous relations with María Ortega. It seems that one day when the wife visited the theater, the actresses insinuated that her husband was unfaithful. The public scenes of jealousy, insults, and hair-pulling between the legitimate wife and the actresses were followed by a formal accusation of adultery before the judges. These charges disturbed life in the theater sufficiently to force the husband, who evidently had denied all the accusations, to sign an extremely curious document in which he promised to maintain a distance from the second lady and to do everything possible so that his wife and the other actresses would not have the chance to meet.[91]

Another sensational case of jealousy occurred in 1815. More unusual than the former episode, it resulted from the suspicions of the actor Teodoro Borja, who believed that his wife, the premier actress, Agustina Montenegro, was cheating on him with another woman. The matter ended violently; in a fit of fury, the husband beat his wife's supposed lover and wounded her seriously. Despite the legal action taken against him, the actor continued to terrorize his wife unimpeded for several months afterward.[92]

Undoubtedly, the actresses' life was pretty licentious and scandalous by the norms of the time. It was not in vain that the most usual and effective threat used against them was that their private life was to be watched very strictly. One more example will conclude this survey of the dissolute life of the theatrical crowd. In 1783, the leading actress, Antonia de San Martín, asked the viceroy for a separation from her husband, also an actor. She accused him of drunkenness, gambling, being spendthrift and jealous, of beating her, and also of trying to force her to commit carnal sins "against nature." If this were not enough, the actress also stated that he "wants me to follow only his ideas. These are of the worst infamy, because without paying attention to the purity that must be conserved in a marriage, he has allowed and has suggested dishonest solicitations that should never be admitted in violation of the faith of the spousal contract. And, after these words had their effect, with great contempt he left me, taking the fruit of my labors." In the end, the husband had fled with some of her money to Guanajuato, where he formed an acting company and lived in a state of "drunkenness, gambling, and illicit relationships." It was his threat to return to Mexico City, however, that prompted the actress to petition the viceroy for protection from her husband. The viceroy gave San Martín her wish; he categorically prohibited her husband from reentering the city because he was a "vagrant and a loafer."[93] It is entirely possible that in order to secure the desired separation, the actress exaggerated the vices and perversions of her husband. For our purposes, however, it is sufficient to note that the viceroy found the description by the wife, a fellow actor, to be plausible.

The life of actors seemed enormously similar to those of the characters whom they represented on the stage. Jealousy, betrayal, mutual adultery, unleashed passions, and violence; none was unknown to the members of players' companies, nor were great actions, redemptions by faith, and last-minute repentance. The public laughed, applauded, and asked for these love stories, while at the same time, the church saw in them a school for depravity.

A conclusive demonstration is only a step away. Licentious plays ending with a moral lesson, represented by actors whose private lives were scandalous, applauded by a public who recognized themselves in all of this—this was the most damning proof of the decline of propriety. Was the theater a mirror, a microcosm of society? Can we go so far? Shall we accept this supposed demonstration without any hesitations? To say yes would imply that today the audience for television police series are all members of the repressive forces and not passive employees and professionals, that people who watch pornography are all sexual acrobats and not poor repressed souls. Doesn't the public seek in entertainment, more or less, what is missing from their daily lives, yet of which they are conscious? Is the theater, like other arts, the expression not of the norm but rather of the exception, not of the social order but rather of the disjunctions that accompany and negatively define it? Are the members of the audience just seeking a place where their repressed thoughts, their anxieties, can be manifested openly?[94]

The theater reveals the exceptions, the fears, those who are marginalized, the anachronisms of a society. What is a play but the presentation of the ridiculous, the mise-en-scène of unacceptable attitudes—sometimes because they are antiquated and traditional, and other times, because they are too modern. Ultimately, does the play not reaffirm the systems of exclusion? Does it not point out those who must be rejected: the miser, the scholarly woman, the bourgeois gentleman, the betrayed husband? In fact, the fundamental characteristic of the Enlightenment period plays (which originated in the French neoclassic theater of the second half of the seventeenth century) was not that they were the antithesis of the sixteenth- and seventeenth-century Spanish traditions. Indeed, those plays elevated and aggrandized the tragic, the irregular, the atypical, and they trivialized the abnormal, stereotyped it, and ridiculed it.[95]

In this, the enlightened thinkers were much more perceptive than the church. The plays were not schools of licentiousness but, on the contrary, they were tribunals in which these archetypes were judged by society—as represented by the audience—who condemned by their laughter and absolved by their clapping. Clearly, the verdict was almost totally established by the playwright/prosecutor who provided all the proofs. Generally, the public only concurred. Alzate y Ramírez demonstrated the moral and social virtues of plays like Molière's *L'Avare* with the following words: "And he who is afflicted with miserliness, would he not be cured by the fear of being pointed out?"[96] In reality, are not comedies of love, jealousy, and betrayal providing lessons about the disasters that result from the shameful and ridiculous choice not to live peacefully and reasonably in the bosom of a well-ordered family?

In the theater, the middle classes gave and received lessons of *savoir-vivre*, of fine manners; they polished themselves and created a self-image of respectability. Gradually they learned to correct or at least to hide their vices, their pettiness, and their absurdities, and to exalt their strengths and their virtues. In 1790, the censor of the New Coliseum said that the goal of the theater was "to imitate the ridiculous actions of *personalities of medium condition* in order to correct them by the means of derision."[97] Whether the theater was the norm or the exception, evidently the decline of customs on stage at the New Coliseum as well as behind the scenes was a problem that obsessed the enlightened society of New Spain.

## Pure Theater, Theater of Purity

**I.** To carry out this much desired reform of the theater and thus make it a center for the diffusion of the ideas and attitudes of the Enlightenment, it was necessary before anything else to transform radically the entertainments that were presented in the New Coliseum. The authorities and Enlightenment critics considered the shows excessively vulgar—that is to say, they appealed to the mob. They had to be replaced by others that would show passions and sentiments in accordance with the authentic moral virtues of men. Great dramatic works were required to enlighten the public in the capital of New Spain.

The officials and Enlightenment thinkers had very high hopes. The efforts to achieve these changes would have to be gigantic, if one judged by the spectacles that, in actuality, were being presented in the Coliseum. Plays with titles such as *El diablo predicador* (The devil preacher), *El negro valiente en Flandes* (The brave black man in Flanders), *La gitana de Menfis* (The gypsy woman of Memphis), *Hados y lados* (Fates and sides), *El falso nuncio de Portugal* (The false nuncio of Portugal), and *El mágico de Salerno* (The magician of Salerno) were certainly not those of which the enlightened thinkers dreamed. To make matters worse, the plays were divided into acts, and during the intermissions, artists presented interludes of *tonadillas* and dances. In the opinion of modern and cultured critics, these entertainments did not promote higher culture among the people but rather contributed to dragging their tastes farther into the gutter.[98]

In the last quarter of the eighteenth century, to attract larger audiences to the Coliseum and improve their feeble earnings, the contractors began to present spectacles inappropriate for a school of virtue. During Lent, a period in which there was no theater, the contractors put on shows of *colloquia* (playlets on religious themes), Chinese shadows, hand games, "acrobatic stunts, tightrope artists with a balancing pole and without, on ropes de voltear, a flexible wire," and balance artists, horseback exercises and jumping in the Coliseum. Even though all these activities were not particularly conducive to reflections suitable for Lent, they were acceptable. It was also tolerable to lend the Coliseum to such personages as Señor Falconi, "celebrated physicist, engineer and mathematician," who, in 1786, presented a spectacle that was composed "of physical pieces, automatic and mathematic," a show fitting for a century so imbued with a love for the sciences, even though it turned out that

Señor Falconi was a total fraud. The presentation of tightrope walkers or, even worse, cockfights, greyhounds chasing rabbits, and bullfights during the intermissions of plays had become unbearable.[99] What was the Coliseum to become? Fortunately, the authorities intervened rapidly to halt these abuses.

Apparently, a contractor dared to implement these novelties in 1779. The first day, he presented a bullfight in the intermission. Heartened by his success, he repeated the bulls the next day and added the diversion of greyhounds chasing after rabbits. On the third day, as the public became more and more excited, besides the bullfights there were two cockfights on which members of the audience bet heavily. The same entertainments were repeated for the following two days. The contractor was salivating over the handsome profits he was reaping from increased attendance when the viceroy published a decree that categorically prohibited these types of diversions in the Coliseum. The catcalls from the balconies must have been unending that night.[100]

In 1798, a new contractor decided to resurrect the idea of his predecessor but, aware of the previous disaster, prudently asked for a license from the viceroy first. He alleged to the viceroy that, because of "the present catastrophic season, . . . it is vital to excite the public to attend the diversion of the theater . . . with a few novelties acceptable to the tastes of the common people," for which he asked permission to mount a "function named *fallas*, some fights between turkeys and cocks, . . . but without any formal wagers." The viceroy gave the license, but on the night in question, the theater judge would not permit the birds to fight with spurs and ordered the arrest of the contractor and also the administrator. The contractor, most incensed, wrote to the viceroy to explain the events and to clarify that it was impossible to engage turkeys and cocks in fights without spurs: "This would not be a diversion for the public but rather an annoyance and a nuisance because the fight would last more than an hour." Although the viceroy confirmed the license, the outcome is not so clear nor do we know whether the contractor was able to put it to use shortly thereafter.[101]

In any case, the enlightened thinkers judged that the status quo was unacceptable and they initiated a campaign of purification of the theater to eradicate such vulgar spectacles from its hallowed halls. Their sights were set on the interludes, the *sainetes*, the *tonadillas*, and the dances. In 1786, Silvestre Díaz de la Vega had criticized the *sainetes* and interludes severely: "Commonly these are just impertinent and ridiculous representations that in general are of little or no worth."[102] A journalist argued the case even more forcefully in 1806, when he wrote: "Why do the sensible members of the audience join in the applause for such interludes, which are presented only to please the lowest people? Do they ignore that such an impetuous ovation will strengthen the depraved taste of those who extol such representations, which should be banished in a century and a country of such enlightenment as ours?"[103] Nor did dances escape the critiques of the capital's newspapers. Another commentator wrote: "I also took the liberty of recommending that he speak out against the dissolute ways of certain dancers. Well, in order to demonstrate to us their agility and dexterity, it is not necessary for them to also lapse into impurity."[104] In fact, it was the lascivious and impure dances that most disgusted this refined sector of the public. In 1786, Viceroy Bernardo de Gálvez allowed a glimpse of the possibility that he would prohibit all dances, but especially the local ones, if they continued to give rise to provocative movements.[105]

In 1794, the authorities resolutely began an offensive to eradicate such vulgar entertainments. The viceroy then consulted Father Rincón about the possibility of banning them from the Coliseum. The priest apparently supported the idea, arguing that the expense to sustain the dancers was a burden to the theater. Also, he added that the dancers were a recent addition to the repertoire of the Coliseum. If dancers had not always been a part of the program, why was it necessary to continue to present them? Father Rincón did not refer to the moral difficulties the dances presented, probably because that was old ground. In fact, the economic argument was not too solid. The same priest admitted that it was possible that "some" spectators would stop attending the theater, but even so, this loss would be more than counterbalanced by not paying any dancers. The viceroy banned dances from the Coliseum.

The indignation and discontent of the public must have been of considerable magnitude. Many spectators, not just a few as Father Rincón had predicted, stopped attending the Coliseum. The perpetually delicate economic situation of the Royal Hospital could not withstand such a decline in its earnings. Three days after the publication of the order, the officials backtracked, "so that the public was able to enjoy a popular diversion and the interests of the hospital were not irremediably prejudiced, as they would be as experience had shown."[106] The viceroy acknowledged defeat.

In 1806 another, more cautious blow was aimed at the dances. When the New Coliseum was reinaugurated after a remodeling, an announcement was made that, since the goal of the theater was to "teach while amusing" and dances were "only a diversion of the senses and not of understanding," and furthermore, since they required excessive costs of "a laudable charitable institution" such as the hospital, which could not afford such expeditures, therefore the grand dances were suspended "for now," while the small ones like the *minuet congo* and the *morenita* would continue to be presented.[107]

Was this suppression of grand dances really inspired by economic necessity on this occasion? If so, why were the references to the educational mission of the theater required? It seems much more probable that this ban represented the first salvo in a campaign to eradicate all such entertainments. The onset of the Wars for Independence soon after turned the colonial world upside down and cut short the theatrical reform campaign, and the ultimate goal of this unfinished crusade is therefore impossible to determine.

In any case, the precedent of the noisy failure of 1794 makes it seem unlikely that the total suppression of dances from the theater would have been possible at this time. The dismal finances of the hospital formed an unsurmountable obstacle on the road to theater reform. As one cultivated regular at the Coliseum, who was concerned with the theater's situation, noted: "In this capital, it is necessary to accommodate the depraved taste of the people."[108]

The persecution of "vulgar" entertainments was not limited to those that took place inside the Coliseum. The monopoly on theatrical representations that had been accorded to this theater did not guarantee it the economic strength that would seem to follow. The administrators of the hospital and the contractors of the Coliseum started to blame the popular buskers for stealing their public. Already, in 1727, Eusebio Vela, the playwright, actor, and contractor of the Old Coliseum, had complained of the sad state of affairs in the theater. For the previous two years, ticket sales had been severely reduced, and a recent measles epidemic had pushed the theater even closer to the brink of disaster. He added: "No plays were presented on many days because of the lack of funds for the basic costs; and on some feast days, the playwrights had to contribute some of their own money in order to prevent a closure." What was the principal reason for this disaster: "The licensing of cockfights has been the cause of the ruin of the said Coliseum; since the start of the cockfights, plays are presented on Sundays only."[109] The solution was to end the licensing of cockfights.

By 1760, street entertainments were forbidden "because of the prejudice" that they caused the Coliseum. The victims of this measure were, first of all, the puppet theaters, and then also, the tightrope walkers and the acrobats. For this same reason, bullfights in the market could be mounted only with a special permission from the viceroy.[110] This ban did not last long; it was rapidly replaced with more flexible measures. Street entertainers were to be licensed and pay a "pension" to the Coliseum, which would also determine the conditions in which these street shows could be mounted.[111]

The change in rules did not, however, put an end to the problems facing popular diversions. In 1786 the Coliseum's actors were strictly forbidden to moonlight in puppet theaters, because "staying up until all hours of the night, they do not have the time to learn their lines the next day, a duty of theirs, to which is added the disorder and drunkenness with which it is understood that they behave; they contract illnesses and indispositions that cause them to miss work in the theater to the grave prejudice of the interests of the theater." Following this prohibition, inspectors visited these houses of entertainment to review their licenses and when they discovered irregularities, the puppets were confiscated.[112]

The growing monopoly of the theater was verging on tyrannny. In the world of entertainment, the theater, as an enlightened despot, ruled arbitrarily, observing, controlling, and even banning inferior diversions. Its absolutism expanded every day with no apparent limits.

**II**. The battle of the forces of enlightenment against "vulgar" entertainments did not take place only between the theater and plebeian diversions but also within the theater itself. To reform the dramatic arts, it was not enough to separate the plays from the interludes, *sainetes*, dances, and other such unedifying spectacles. In addition, clear divisions had to be delineated within the repertoire of plays. In fact, this distinction was made in the introduction to the Theater Regulations of 1786.[113]

The most important difference was drawn between comedy and tragedy. The latter provided the highest degree of theatrical perfection; it expressed only noble thoughts and sublime virtues. Its characters were taken only from the highest spheres. Clowns and lackeys were excluded. Comedies, in contrast, aimed to ridicule the vices of men by inspiring repulsion from and derision of these flaws. Their characters tended to be, at best, from very middle-class origins.[114]

Although enlightened thinkers held tragedy in much higher esteem than comedy, they could not propose the presentation of only the former, because such a ploy would signify a massive abandonment of the Coliseum. Their objective, therefore, was to preserve the comedies but to isolate the good ones from the bad and eradicate the latter. The cultivated thinkers of this period envisaged this second criterion of differentiation among theatrical works as a simple question of quality. In reality, it represented something much more profound.

The enlightened thinkers had very precise ideas regarding what made a quality play and what differentiated such works from vulgar ones. Those plays in tune with "the depraved taste of the people," those that attracted the people to the Coliseum, were "comedies of heroes, magicians, and flights with other such similar vulgarities"; they were all "displays and stage machinery," "extravagant," and "implausible."[115] This last characteristic, which summarized many of the former explanations, was the principal defect. Quality plays were distinguished by precisely the contrary property: by their authenticity, that is to say, their realism.

The highest aspiration of the theater should be to present works so similar to reality that, at times, the audience might confuse them with actuality. The theater should create the illusion of reality on stage. Viceroy Revillagigedo the second reinforced the desirability of theatrical realism in 1794, when he defined the effect of illusion as a "quality particular to the theater without which it would be reduced to nothing more than representation."[116]

At first, this objective did not contradict the theater's goal of education and edification of the people. On the contrary, dramas had to demonstrate that, just as in life, the virtuous triumphed while the enemies of good received their just desserts. In these works, it had be crystal clear that those afflicted with vices succumbed to the natural and social consequences of their perversions.

Realism, as understood by the enlightened thinkers, was in fact an apology for the real. It could only be promoted by those who planned to conquer and to dominate the material world and were on the verge of doing so. The theater of realism, which likened success to virtue, legitimized them in the eyes of society and in their own. The bourgeoisie thus provided itself with an art suited its members. A whole new vision of the world was expressed in the search for the "effect of illusion," the ultimate goal of the theater of the Enlightenment.[117]

The intentions of the enlightened thinkers to make the theater a mirror of reality should not be taken too seriously. Realism in the dramatic arts, as in any other art form, is only a convention. Reality represented as it is on stage would immediately cease being realistic. A staging is always a creation, a selection, and an interpretation of reality. To seem authentic, an actor must use makeup, must talk in an artificial manner—loud and clear; "realism is no more than images and trickery."[118]

For example, how could the private thoughts of a character be shown? The monologue, a much-used convention until then, seemed false to the enlightened thinkers. Juan Cristóbal Gottached, a German critic and great defender of French neoclassicism, affirmed with reason that "intelligent people do not talk aloud when they are alone."[119] French drama found another solution to this dilemma; they used servants as confidants of the principal characters. Apart from its lacking authenticity, this practice had some rather disturbing social implications. Conscious of these undertones, the author of a letter on the subject of the theater was indignant that, on stage, "a lackey, a man of the vilest social extraction, should be familiar with a prince and be the keeper of all the most serious secrets and consulted on the most momentous affairs." He called for all such episodes to be erased from all the tragedies.[120]

Realism was in fact just another theatrical convention but, unlike previous styles, its adherents pretended that it was not merely another form, rather they presented it as the *only* valid method of representation. With great despotism, they denied other visions of the world the right to be expressed. Realism, like scientific objectivity, concealed its totalitarian intentions behind a facade of humility and modesty. Realism in drama proposed "just simply" to show things as they had been: what Ranke later considered as the "limited" objective of history. Realism did not aspire to show, to point out another invisible world just beyond the supposedly palpable and quotidian experience. The "effect of illusion exalted appearances and opposed all speculation on the hereafter." It was also in this denial of other worlds that its novel character was located.[121]

It would be erroneous to present the theater as an art that has aspired, since its beginning, to imitate reality and has achieved this objective little by little as it found the means to do so. On the contrary, before the Enlightenment, all theater had intentions radically different from these. The creation of flashy spectacles was one of its aims. Another was to make visible the spiritual—all that was fundamental and gave meaning in this vain and fleeting world.

In 1538, Motolinía made clear the first goal of the pre-Enlightenment theater in his description of a drama presented by some Indians for the feast of Corpus Christi: "Because they did not have rich jewels or brocade cloth, they had to do with other embellishments *worthy to see*, especially the flowers and roses, which God raises in the trees and in the countryside, so *that our eyes would have pleasant sights.*"[122]

The second proposition of the theater is evident in the spiritual colloquia of González de Eslava, a Mexican author of the second half of the sixteenth century. In his writings, González de Eslava represented characters as the embodiment of virtues, sins, and various supernatural forces either divine or diabolic. Take, for example, this passage: "The pages Rectitude and Purity, Faith with his clothing, Hope with the Cross, Charity with the hyacinths, Moderation with the mitre, Rectitude with the crozier, and the World, the Flesh, and the Devil dressed as Chichimecs with bows and arrows."[123]

Occasionally, "special effects" were used to facilitate the leap from the visual to the spiritual, from the natural to the supernatural, to establish the necessary communication between these two realms. These effects obliged the spectator to recognize the presence of the invisible within the dramatic symbols. In a sixteenth-century religious play, for example, indigenous actors playing the part of sinners were led into a small room, and before the audience caught on that they had exited by a false door, it was incinerated—much to the dismay of the public.[124] In the same manner, in 1599 in Lima, the Jesuits enacted the work *Historia alegórica del Anticristo y el Juicio Final* (Allegorical history of the antichrist and the last judgment). They sought a strong edifying impact among the spectators. They removed many bones and even cadavers of Indians from graves. Some of these were still complete but dessicated; the Jesuits placed these human remains on the stage.[125]

Over the course of the seventeenth century, because of the development of many new techniques, the theater in New Spain became more and more geared to the use of special effects. The increased emphasis on these effects culminated at the beginning of the eighteenth century with the works of Eusebio Vela, who wrote scenographic notations to his plays, such as, "as flashy as possible," and who included violent storms, capsizing ships, creatures of the sea, flying gods, and more on stage. One play started thus: "With a tremendous roar of thunder, the hill opens and Pluto is uncovered in the midst of flames; and in the air, there are various nocturnal birds and the Furies on the sides."[126] Paradoxically, this type of dramatic montage used the scientific techniques that were doing away with magic in the real world to make the mystical real in the theater. This other world disappeared with the introduction of the methods used to make it apparent on the stage.[127]

The Enlightenment thinkers believed that this type of theater sacrificed content to form or, as Father Rincón stated, it had "no substance."[128] Despite these objections, the flashy theatrical style still prevailed at the end of the eighteenth century because it continued to please the public. The enlightened thinkers fought it in their attempt to impose their realistic conception on the dramatic arts by doing away with the "reliance on visual effects" and replacing it with a true "effect of illusion." The madness of baroque illusionism had to be stopped. The theater had to accept its "natural" limits and to cease representing the fantastic by the "unreal"; it had to acquiesce in the reproduction of what already existed and, within these limitations, only that which was controlled by human agency.

What was necessary to reform the theater and to create the effect of illusion? First, the relationship between the actors and the public had to be concealed. Catcalls, jeering, and expressions of appreciation that were overly effusive broke the spell and destroyed the illusion and thus had to be banned, as the Regulations of 1786 had done. The show had to go on without audience interference. The public had to be transformed into silent spectators: invisible, clandestine observers of an action supposedly out of their sight. Spectators had to become objective scientists spying on the hidden secrets of human nature.[129]

For the same reason, a precise and insurmountable separation had to be established between the space of the stage and the seating. The baroque theater sought to create a continuity between these two spaces. The decoration was the same in both and stairs united the two. Actors mingled with the public. Above all, the scenery had multiple surfaces in the manner of *Las Meninas* of Velázquez. These were layered from the most real to the least, making the spectator one extreme of this continuum and situating the actor in an intermediate zone. This effect brought the player closer to the audience and to the real during monologues.[130] The theater of the Enlightenment did away with the stairs that united the two spaces and in the process of purging the scenery, the reformers sacrificed the diverse surfaces that had maintained the illusion of continuity.

   Apart from the creation of the "effect of illusion," on stage the actors had to disappear into the characters that they portrayed. In order to achieve this end, the Theater Regulations of 1786 established various precise norms. Actors no longer were allowed to greet or signal to the audience, to laugh privately among themselves, or to get mad when they missed a cue or the music. No longer could actors lounge against the scenery, or make noises behind the wings, or commit other such abuses. At the same time, the authorities expected the actors to "professionalize," to remember their lines, and in order to reach this level of competence, they required the actors to attend all rehearsals. If they did not fulfill these requirements and they did not perform their parts correctly on stage, the actors were subject to strict punishments.[131]

   To achieve "realism" in acting, other smaller but more particular defects also had to be eliminated from the mise-en-scène. In 1784, Viceroy Revillagigedo the second did not hesitate to intervene in theater affairs by indicating to the director of the Coliseum certain "defects and improprieties." According to the viceroy, actors should remove their hats in places where it was customary to do so and they should not apologize for their mistakes at the end of the play.[132] The elimination of interludes, *sainetes*, and dances from the theater was not only to purify it but also to preserve the effect of illusion in the plays, as was stated clearly in 1806 by a journalist: "The *tonadillas* and *sainetes*, which serve as intermissions, should be exiled forever because, apart from being composed of impudence and dishonesties, they are set to a music so outlandish that it dishonors the taste of the spectators. Short pieces alternating with dances and a few well-chosen arias could serve, not as an intermission because this would destroy the whole effect of illusion of the principal drama, but rather as a finale to the functions."[133]

   Theatrical realism also required a greater psychological depth to the characters. These could no longer simply be the symbols of some virtue, vice, or social group, but rather took on certain traits supposedly essential to humans: an inner being and coherence. To achieve this, the author of the letter on theater reform recommended to playwrights that they should "inviolably maintain the decorum of the people represented, observe the character of each one, and conserve it without weakening throughout the whole drama."[134] The search for realism had precise limits. In 1823, the chronicler of *El Aguila Mexicana* would record them thus: "In reality, the theater should be a mirror for nature, but an adorned nature such as a painter seeks out or a sculptor desires as the most beautiful and perfect model."[135]

In fact, the enlightened thinkers had delimited their understanding of realism a long time ago. For example, the Theater Regulations of 1786 ordered the following: "Actresses should present themselves with decent and proper clothing not on pure ceremony but rather as it corresponds to a real modesty, to serve as a good example, not as a fall. Everything that should be conveyed about a role or a character strictly and without recourse to fashion or other pretexts, even in the personage of a gypsy or a *maja* [woman of the people], should be done with circumspection and reserve."[136]

In the same manner, Viceroy Revillagigedo the second wrote to the director of the Coliseum in 1794 to give him advice on the improvement of the shows presented there: "The representations are characterized by certain defects and improprieties that should be avoided and are easily corrected. Such is the practice . . . of those who play the part of the poor and vilest plebeians coming on stage dressed in tatters. This custom borders on the indecent and shows a serious lack of decorum and the respect owed to the public. This defect approaches the degree of an unsupportable excess when it is accompanied by brazen actions."[137] To the affirmation that the theater should copy reality in its entirety, an addendum was slipped in that this should be done by showing its best side, its "more true" face.

Society should appear in the theater always dressed in its Sunday best, just as the enlightened thinkers and the officials envisioned the society once it had been reformed by the action of intelligence. In this desire to impose realism on the dramatic arts, in fact, the reformers hoped to give a concrete form to the ideal society on stage as imagined by enlightened despotism, to unfold this social utopia before the audience. Theater reform was nothing other than the expression of enlightened despotism's reforms in the realm of the imaginary. Moreover, it was a general rehearsal of these reforms in anticipation of those that were to be achieved in reality.

This analysis of theater reform reveals nothing less than the implementation of new principles of ordering and exclusion that insisted upon the differentiation and strict separation of the plays from the "indecent" interludes, the tragedies from the comedies, the spectators from the actors, and the actors from their roles. This effort represented the attempt by an elite to take over the stage, to transform its image and likeness, to eradicate from it the entertainments that pleased the people in order to impose the elite culture despotically.

## From the Dogma of the Holy Trinity to That of the Three Unities

The crusade for the "effect of illusion" and for realism on stage inevitably brought with it the establishment of the famous rule of the three unities: space, time, and action. Enlightened critics believed that for a play to be staged, it had to obey this formal rule. How, for instance, could the same scenery depict various places? How could actions that the audience saw unfold before them, in a couple of hours at the most, take place over more than one day? How could various simultaneous or parallel intrigues be presented to the public without breaking the unity of space or the linearity of time? As such, the three principles were reduced to only one: verisimilitude. A notice, posted in the Coliseum, which invited participation in a contest to create a play, summarized this creed with great clarity: "The general [rule] of the three unities in action, time, and space follows precisely from the desire for verisimilitude, but [does] not [mean] that these or other regulations must be arbitrary, as some believe, but rather [that they are] derived from reason and in conformity with nature, according to the most exact observation of Aristotle's and other very wise philosphers who dealt in this delicate science."[138]

The success of the theater reform depended upon a selection of dramatic works according to this formal criteria. Who had more means to pressure and more power to impose this selection than the censor? To make the censorship of the theater part of an institution that aimed at the defense of the neoclassic style of theater against the depredations of the baroque style, however, was to effect a revolution of unpredictable consequences within this agency of political and religious control. By making the censors the caretakers of literary form, was there not a risk of relaxation of control over the content of the plays?

Despite this risk, at the end of the eighteenth century, the censors had become the guardians of enlightened good taste. In 1790, Father Ramón Fernández del Rincón, the theatrical censor, considered that, according to the viceroy, one of the goals of his work was to ensure "that the theaters of this city present plays that are worthy of the attention of a civilized gathering, in which there are many individuals who, because of their fine education and discrete knowledge of the world, know how to judge correctly the entertainments that are offered to them."[139]

In New Spain, censorship had originally been in the hands of the church. Although at first it was the bishop who watched over the content of dramatic works, later this duty devolved upon the Inquisition. The aim of control over the theater was principally to ensure that the works that were presented to the public conformed to Catholic dogma.[140] A few examples will suffice to demonstrate the way in which this function was acquitted. In 1612, the Inquisition forbade the presentation of the play *Santa Juana de la Cruz* (Saint Joan of the Cross), because the way in which it presented her life was much too profane. It showed certain "vices of nuns that were not appropriate for depiction to the vulgar masses" and also made mention of certain miracles that had not received institutional recognition.[141] In 1660, Luis Zapata's play *Lo que es ser predestinado* (What it is to be predestined), which was tendered to the censors for approval, provoked differing opinions among the members of the Holy Office. To begin with, the title was most unfortunate because in this century of religious wars, it conjured up the notion of predestination. At this time, the concept of predestination was causing major confrontations between Catholics and Protestants and in France even among the Catholics, between the Jesuits and the Jansenists. At least on the topic of the title of this play, the inquisitors were in agreement; it would be better to change it to something less controversial, such as *Los triumfos de la gracia* (The triumphs of grace) or *Lo que es el favor divino* (What divine favor is). The censors disagreed, however, over the content of the drama. The first censor believed that while such a delicate point of religion was too hazardous to present in a play for the masses, this particular work also had a suspiciously high number of references to black magic and other sacrileges, and so he recommended a total ban. The second censor, however, asserted that with a few corrections of detail, there was no impediment to its staging. To resolve this impasse, a third cleric was consulted. With the wisdom of Solomon, he decided that, because the great masters had advised not to speak on it from the pulpit, the topic of predestination was suited for clerics only. Therefore, this particular play should not be staged. Given that it did not contain anything that would harm the dogma, "persons of talent and learning" could read it.[142] In 1682, the Inquisition banned the drama entitled *El valor perseguido y traición vengada* (Persecuted valor and betrayal avenged), because of its treatment of "immoral subjects" but, most of all, because the author did so with allusions to passages from the Scriptures and expressions derived from the religious vocabulary.[143] In the same vein, in 1684, it prohibited the presentation of the comedy *El peregrino de Dios y patriarca de los pobres* (The pilgrim of God and patriarch of the poor) for providing an overly mundane vision of the life of Saint Francis.[144]

An additional layer of censorship, derived from civil power, was overlaid on this ecclesiastical censorship; the former partially but never totally displaced the latter. From 1765, when the presentation of religious plays was formally proscribed, the Inquisition no longer could justify its judgment of theatrical works. Henceforth, in fact, the individuals named by the viceroy managed the task of censorship. The promulgation of the Theater Regulations of 1786 cemented the arrival of a civil censorship, as did the cancellation of all licenses for the presentation of dramatic works. The repeal obliged all interested parties to submit plays to be examined by censors once again.[145]

During the 1790s, the civil and enlightened censorship was under the direction of a cleric, Father Rincón, but followed criteria radically distinct from those of the Inquisition. Father Rincón openly stated that his role was to be the watchdog of good taste for the cultivated public: "Because we do not have enough good plays to convert the theater into an entertaining school of private and social virtues, at least the presentation of monstrous plays that not only do not improve mores, but only serve to bring taste into the gutters can be stopped." Following this maxim, the enlightened censor barred certain works whose principal sins were that they were not realistic and did not follow the rule of the three unities. For example, he recommended that a comedy called *El más honrado más loco* (The most honored, most crazy) be "proscribed and exiled from the theater," because it was "a monstrous hodgepodge in which *all the rules of art are defied*, . . . two considerable plots are presented during its course, of which *one takes place in Naples and the other in the kingdom of Aragón*, . . . the whole play is a mixture of ineptitude and nonsense that is not worthy of the attention of any man who makes use of reason." The play *Astucias por heredar un sobrino a su tío* (Tricks for a nephew to inherit from his uncle) suffered the same fate; it had various defects, among which the most striking was "the unlikeliness that the events of the plot could take place in the space of two and a half hours, when in this interval it can only be read superficially." It seems that the author overcompensated in his aim to maintain the unity of time that caused "the muddle and confusion that is observed in the third day." *Lucinda y*

*Velardo* was rejected because it was "a potboiler that broke all the rules, it did not have a recognizable arrangement, or plausibility, or meter, or anything to recommend it." To make matters worse, the work touched upon such religious themes as martyrdom. Finally, the tragicomedy *Troya abrasada* (Troy in flames) was banned because it contained "the great folly of trying to reduce into the time of a theatrical representation a war that lasted ten years, and this does not justify occupying the public with similar stupidities."

If these stylistic principles had been applied strictly, the entire repertoire of the Coliseum would have been excluded. According to these criteria, none of the works of the great Spanish playwrights would have been allowed on stage. Only the creations of the French neoclassic theater would have received the censor's approval. Fortunately, in the case of already hallowed plays, Father Rincón was condescendingly tolerant: "Certainly, in the productions of Calderón, Moreto, Solís, Cándamo, and other highly esteemed comic poets, and principally in the tragedies and heroic plays, the rules of uniformity are violated and irregularities abound; but the fluidity of the meter, the beauty of the thoughts, the gravity of many opportune maxims, the happy connection of various incidents, and other things *make the other defects tolerable and even hide them from the eyes of the less intelligent.*"[146]

During an absence, Father Rincón entrusted the examination of dramatic works to Don Silvestre Díaz de la Vega, the accountant general of the tobacco monopoly. In 1790, with these exquisite principles in mind, Don Silvestre authorized the presentation of a play originally called *México rebelado* (Mexico in rebellion). The substitute censor considered that a change of title to the much less problematic *México segunda vez conquistado* (Mexico conquered a second time) to be sufficient in order for the play to be acceptable. The work in question dealt with no less a topic than the capture, torture, and execution of Cuauhtémoc (Guatimotzin) and, it seems, Cortés was not presented in a heroic light. On opening night, the Coliseum was full to the rafters. As the play unfolded, tempers heated up, and the spectators began to take sides with the various characters and thus formed two opposing camps. At the end of the show, while most of the audience applauded enthusiastically, the Spaniards left in a huff, much bothered and disgusted. It was the last performance. Although it was supposed to run for two nights after the opening, "It was suspended because the play presented untruths about events; these were uncertain and contrary to the character of the nation."

Responsibility for the demonstration caused by the play fell to the censor, Don Silvestre Díaz de la Vega, because he had authorized its performance. He defended himself by saying that he had acted correctly, that the play contained no untruths, everything had been taken from Don Ignacio de Salazar y Olarte's *La Historia de México*, and he did not see why Cortés' errors and injustices should sully the honor of the Spanish nation.

As soon as Father Rincón returned from his trip, he was asked to judge this particular work and to review the authorization for its presentation. After a perusal, Father Rincón defended his substitute, justified the performance of the play, and expanded the arguments that his replacement had presented. The events narrated in the drama could be read about not only in the work of Salazar y Olarte but also in that of the chroniclers Bernal Díaz del Castillo, Antonio de Herrera, and Brother Juan de Torquemada. The censor did not understand—or at least he feigned ignorance of—the reasons for the public's indignation. His opinion was that the play was not only believable, it was much more: it re-created real events. What more could one ask? Did they not want realistic plays in the theater? Also, it was not an insult to the honor of Spain to show the errors of Cortés, "because the failing of one individual should not devolve upon Spain, particularly when his very companions disapproved." Consistent with his principles, Father Rincón recognized that the work suffered from certain defects: "Unfortunately, the subject [of the play] was taken up by an amateur, who without knowing even the unity of space, as is obvious at the end of the third day, wove a long-winded potboiler, which instead of inciting compassion, which is the goal of tragedy, provoked anger and the fury of onlookers." With apparent candor bordering on recklessness, he added: "And they, also in ignorance of the laws of the theater, did not guess the reason for their nightmare, but to relieve it, they took as a pretext the honor of the nation." In short, the work did not fail in its respect for Spain but rather with respect to the stylistic rules of the theater.[147]

It is not particularly likely that these arguments swayed either the theater judge or the viceroy. In any case, his rationale did not even convince the other censors, who probably had recognized the political risks of the drama. What is important about his argument is the fact that they decided that the verisimilitude, or more precisely the truthfulness, of the play and Father Rincón's critique of its departure from the rules of theater were the best defense against the complaints of the authorities. Most certainly, the play *México segunda vez conquistado,* we can be sure, was not performed a second time.

Enlightened censorship, formalistic and preoccupied by style and the rules of the theater, turned out to be inadequate to deal with the new problems facing New Spain. After the English colonies in North America gained independence and one year after the beginning of the French Revolution, such political errors were no longer acceptable. After these events, the civil and religious authorities began to distance themselves from the very ideas of the Enlightenment, which they had introduced into New Spain. The Enlightenment began to slide from reform into revolution.

The authorities reestablished a strict ideological censorship over the theater that conformed to the new political circumstances. In fact, this strengthening of theatrical censorship began in Spain. From there, in 1801, the ban on the following works arrived: "*La fianza satisfecha* (The redeemed bond) of Lope de Vega Carpio . . . for prejudice to proper conduct; *El sitio de Solís* (The siege of Solís) . . . for giving information about suicide and fanaticism; *Lo que pasa en un torno de monjas* (What happens in a convent's interview room), an anonymous drama printed in Córdoba at the Colegio de la Asunción, without a date . . . for ridiculing the religious state and people devoted to our Lord."[148] In New Spain, 1809 was a year of great tensions. Once more the Inquisition began to intervene in theatrical questions. It totally prohibited the plays *El falso nuncio de Portugal, El diablo predicador,* and finally *El negro sensible* (The sensitive black man), which was extremely popular. According to the Holy Office, however, it inspired rebellion of slaves against their masters.[149]

With the outbreak of the Wars for Independence in Mexico and the establishment of the Cádiz Parliament, the censorship of the theater and the press in Mexico City was confused and constantly changing. When the parliament in Spain abolished the Inquisition, the administrator of the Royal Indian Hospital quickly petitioned for a license to put on the plays that the Holy Office had banned in 1809. The new Supreme Council of Censorship, one of the members of which was José Mariano Beristáin y Souza, gave its approval. Only a few months later, however, the archbishop of Mexico issued an edict warning that, despite the elimination of the Inquisition, all the interdictions it had decreed remained in force. Facing the financial difficulties of the hospital and the decadence of the Coliseum, the administrator wrote to the archbishop on November 30, 1813, to ask that licenses for works prohibited by the Inquisition should not be revoked: "If I could proceed as I wished in this matter, please believe me, Your Illustrious Lordship, that I would not disturb you with such an impertinent consultation because, indeed, these plays are rife with implausible and extravagant situations that assault good taste and are foreign to any cultivated person." But, he continued, "These are precisely the plays that attract the public and to some degree sustain the theater, on which the hospital in my charge depends almost entirely for funds in these calamitous times." Taking into account the needs of the hospital, the archbishop deigned to authorize the performance of the plays in question.[150]

The whole problem of censorship was quite muddled in New Spain because, although the Cádiz Parliament had decreed freedom of the press, Viceroys Francisco Javier de Venegas and Calleja tried to block any attempt to put this freedom into practice.[151] This period of uncertainty ended in August 1814 when news of the restoration of Ferdinand VII to the throne and the abolition of the Consitution of Cádiz reached New Spain. Viceroy Calleja, bolstered in his authoritarian policies by the Mother Country, could impose an iron control over the press without any impediment and, in passing, also the theater. On November 23, 1814, he wrote to the administrator of the hospital to announce the reinstitution of censorship: "Every new play or performance, whether of verse, song, or dance that has not until now been presented and all those that were presented or printed since the establishment of freedom of expression that so corrupted our customs, must be submitted to the censor and approved by this superior authority if they are to be performed."[152] Thus, this most brief period of freedom of expression came to an end.

Theatrical censorship in New Spain had gone from the defense of Catholic dogma—such as the Holy Trinity, for example—in the first centuries of colonialism to preserving the stylistic dogma of the three unities, but very rapidly, social and political conditions caused the abandonment of such exquisite and cultivated principles in order to rush to the defense of a new dogma: the security of the state.

## The Theater of Power

In 1799, a very curious description of Mexico City was published in the collection *El Viajero Universal* (The universal traveler) in Madrid. It started with a list of the most important religious buildings: the cathedral, the parish churches, the convents, and the monasteries. Then it passed on to an enumeration of buildings associated with civil powers: the viceroy's palace, the Royal Audiencia, the court and audiencia de cuentas (accounting department), the administration of the mercury monopoly [mercury was used in the refining of silver], the town council, and many more. It continued with the university, the guilds, the *parcialidades* (outlying jurisdictions) [Indian rather than Spanish neighborhoods]. Finally, the list got to the Parián, the Coliseum, the lottery, and the *colegios*. It ended with the paseos.

The text's order was not quite so linear as this description might imply. The author backtracked to some buildings already mentioned and deepened his description. He sometimes mixed religious structures with the civil and constructions with the institutions. In any case, it is clear that he wished to demonstrate the social organization of Mexico City, the institutions that governed it, through a portrait of the buildings in which these organizations were lodged and which were their physical manifestation. The inclusion of the *parcialidades* and the guilds—which were integral parts of the judicial and social systems but did not have a material headquarters, that is to say, a building that lodged them—in the inventory of prominent buildings of the city was in this respect extremely meaningful. In fact, the author continually slipped from the description of buildings to an explanation of the functions of those institutions that resided there.

The author began by showing the physical structure, the institutional framework, of the Mexican capital. To this material description of society, he added a summary of its spiritual counterpart, its imagination, the aspects that completed the stone and marble: the depiction of the major civil and religious festivals of Mexico City.[153] These festivals constituted the self-portrait of this society. In them, society reordered its elements in a hierarchical fashion; it created a communion in which all participated although from different positions, and thus it reinforced social cohesion. These ceremonies were genuine social dramatizations; they were the theater in which society was both an actor and a spectator, carrying out a rigidly preestablished action and provoking a catharsis that confirmed and consolidated its collective existence.[154]

What were these festivals that formed this spiritual substratum of Mexico City? First, the procession of Corpus Christi was the most grandiose, the most showy of all.[155] This festival celebrated the rite of the Eucharist, the miracle of the real presence of the body and blood of Christ through the bread and wine. In the procession, all believers had a place, none was excluded. The civil and religious authorities, the guilds and *cofradías* (fraternal associations), the Indians and the *castas*, all participated. In its splendor, Corpus Christi was the ceremony of self-representation of the city. On this day, there was no excuse for the absence of theatrical representations of religious dramas because, just as the festival of Corpus Christi was the celebration of the transubstantiation of the bread and wine into the body and blood of Christ, the procession was also the society and its lives were represented on stage in the bodies of the actors. Corpus was the theatrical festival par excellence; in it, the spiritual, the infinite, the invisible were materialized, were manifested physically, in the finite and the visible.[156]

The viceroy's entry was the second most important celebration. It was the festival of power. While Corpus was all inclusive of the society, this celebration involved only its head, its leaders. The viceroy's entry strictly ritualized and dramatized the functions of social leadership by presenting the new actor who would have the role of viceroy and who became the repository of a power that transcended him. The ceremony brought society to a standstill, everyone suspended activities, preoccupations, and problems, thus muffling the social tumult that all changes of government implied and avoiding any momentary appearance of a power vacuum. The new viceroy went through the streets of the capital where he was acclaimed by the people. The various organized groups within society honored him in the proper way. The public acceptance of the symbols of power and the demonstrations of obedience and loyalty legitimated the power entrusted to this bureaucrat by the king. In this gigantic representation of power and submission, which lasted several days, the recitation of praises, and plays, either in public plazas, or as exclusive performances for the elite in the viceregal palace, or as gala shows in the Coliseum, were all important elements. Theater played its role in this political dramatization.[157]

The festival of San Hipólito was the third of these celebrations; it was the festival of colonial submission. In it, the surrender of México–Tenochtitlan to the Spanish conquerors was commemorated in theater and symbolically revived. In solemn procession, a standard, copied from the one carried by Hernán Cortés, was carried through the city as a sign of the subjection of the city to the Spanish Crown. On the eve of the festival, the standard, or banner, was taken from the chapter house to the viceregal palace, where the mounted viceroy, in the company of other officials, took it to the Church of San Hipólito. This particular church was built on a spot where many Spaniards had died during the Night of Sorrows. After a solemn mass, the viceroy retraced his route and returned the banner to the chapter house. The whole ceremony, the date of its celebration, its homage to fallen conquerors, the religious rites, all contributed to the reliving of the historical events that shaped and legitimized the subjection of Mexico City to Spain. The festival of San Hipólito was a theatrical representation of history at the service of colonial domination. Nor was there a shortage of dramas that surely dealt with themes alluding to the Conquest.[158]

These three festivals provided a venue for the dramatization of power within society and thus allowed it to renew and consolidate itself. The theater intervened in these dramatizations to represent to the public the invisible reality, which was incarnated at that very moment. It was theater within the theater, a never-ending game of mirrors in which the social dramatization was reinforced and achieved a greater presence.

Just as the powers legitimated themselves in certain preordained and cyclical moments through these theatrical gestures, in times of crisis they depended even more upon the theater to achieve this same goal. The viceregal government's use of the theater in this manner became more common after 1808, when the Napoleonic invasion of the Iberian Peninsula kindled desires for national independence in New Spain. Plays then had to abandon their previous function as schools for virtue in order to become political catechism. In 1809, a show of horsemanship exercises and jumping in the Coliseum included various numbers performed by a monkey dressed as a French general. This incident marked the beginning of this open politicization of the theater.[159] On May 30, 1810, on the anniversary of the "beloved sovereign Ferdinand VII," the Coliseum mounted a show to revive loyalty to Spain and love for the king—still a prisoner of the French. The entertainment included a new drama, *La fineza de Inglaterra y embarque al norte de las tropas al mando del excelentísimo señor marqués de la Romana* (The excellence of England and the northern military expedition under the command of the most excellent señor Marqués de la Romana), and a duet that sang "Los sentimientos de los leales habitantes de América por su rey cautivo" (The sentiments of loyal inhabitants of America for their captive king). On June 25 of that same year, the Coliseum staged a gala performance to celebrate the election of the first Mexican deputy to the Cádiz Parliament. It included a march accompanied by song and dance entitled: "Españoles la patria oprimida" (Spaniards of the oppressed homeland). Finally, to celebrate the arrival of Viceroy Venegas, three theatrical performances were held in his honor.[160] The elegance and tenacity with which the Coliseum tried to cultivate the allegiance of the residents of Mexico City to the Spanish Crown could in no way detain the movement for independence. While the second performance in honor of the new viceroy took place in the Coliseum, Father Hidalgo was ringing the church bells in the town of Dolores, inciting the residents to rebellion.

With the start of military conflicts, the theater took on the defense of the Royalist cause with even more fervor. That same year, in December, on the occasion of the viceroy's birthday, the Coliseum organized a gala performance of *tonadillas*, songs that exalted the figure of the governing official and predicted the rapid defeat of the insurgents.[161] From then on, the Mexico City Coliseum celebrated every Royalist victory with great fanfare. In 1812, General Calleja's victory over the rebels was the occasion of a theater performance of magnificent luxury and splendor. The presentation's ostentation, which seemed like a plebiscite rather than a celebration, apparently bothered the viceroy, who saw the victorious general as a powerful rival.[162] Also in 1812, the Ayuntamiento provided free entry to the theater to mark the announcement of the Constitution of Cádiz in Mexico City.[163]

In 1813, a performance was given in the Coliseum to benefit the very popular *tonadilla* singer "Inesita," who, according to the historian Manuel Mañón, "was a beautiful woman with whom our great-grandfathers were head over heels in love." The singer dedicated her performance to Viceroy Calleja. At the end of the show, the viceroy ordered that one hundred *onzas* (ounces of gold) be placed at the feet of the star and the vicereine sent her one of her best diamonds. The people also showed their appreciation by showering her with large sums of money, literally throwing it onto the stage. The conduct of the viceroy and his wife was sufficient to launch persistent rumors across the city that "Inesita" was the viceroy's lover and that the vicereine sent the diamond as a cover-up for her husband's suspicious generosity. It is hard to determine whether this gossip was accurate, but it certainly reflected the degree to which the theater had prostituted itself to political power.[164]

In 1817, theatrical performances with a political character were once again organized to applaud the capture of the rebel Francisco Javier Mina.[165]

Independence did not in any way end the politicization of theater; rather, this pattern became even more pronounced. The first independent governments in Mexico made use of the same theater and probably the identical actors as the previous viceregal government to legitimize and disseminate their political ideas. When Agustín de Iturbide entered Mexico City at the head of the Ejército Trigarante (Army of the Three Guarantees), the Coliseum arranged three shows in his honor. The drama *México libre* stood out on the program.[166]

The increased use of the theater for political purposes was at the root of conflicts within the Coliseum; those who had supported national independence divided into opposing camps. During the performances, Centralists and Federalists, Liberals and Conservatives insulted and attacked one another. For many years the factions that characterized the divisions within the nation had also existed in the theater. Now the freethinkers got their revenge for the persecution they had suffered in the colonial period. In 1824, they staged works attacking monarchs and religious fanaticism that did not fail to inflame controversy among the public.[167] In 1829, the governor of Mexico City named an enlightened censor, "charging him most particularly that no kings should appear on stage, if it is not to recommend their death or punishment when they violated the sacred laws of society and Nature. In this way, laughter will heal customs and the theater will be a school for virtue."[168]

The politicization of the theater in no way contradicted the ideals of the Enlightenment. On the contrary, it was no more than the logical continuation of its principles. Independence meant a change in control over civil authority, but the theater continued to be used for the same ends: the legitimation of the state and the inculcation of the moral and political values of the elite among the common people.

## The Denouement of the Theater

The Mexican Enlightenment fought to reform the theater and to transform it into a diversion that would contribute to the "improvement" of the common people's conduct by teaching them the new moral values. Another aspect of this campaign was an effort to modernize the performances and bring them in line with the demands of the elite's artistic preferences. To do so, they imposed realism as the only valid aesthetic form and they also fought the disorder of the seating, the lack of professionalism among actors, and the presentation of vulgar shows. The viceroys did everything possible to ensure the success of the reforms, using every means they had at their disposal: decrees and regulations, threats and penalties for the audience and the actors, and the transformation and later the strengthening of censorship. What were the results of this battle to reform the theater? What were its achievements?

The year 1806 provides a good benchmark. The Theater Regulations of 1786, introduced by Viceroy Bernardo de Gálvez, had been in place for twenty years. The major convulsions that tore apart the life of the nation—and by extension, the theater—for more than a decade and ended Spanish rule had not yet begun. It seems an appropriate moment to gauge the result of such a significant effort to reform the dramatic arts in Mexico. That year, a journalist described the general situation of public diversions in the capital. I cited his account extensively in my introductory chapter.[169] The opinions of the theater critic merit further analysis with reference to other sources.

The tone of the text is optimistic, even bantering. Except for a few details, the city provided the best diversions imaginable. Plays—the "principal spectacle"—headed the list. The author devoted the most space to this diversion. The state of drama was as satisfactory as the other diversions, although this section of the text contains more "buts" than any other. First of all, "good order prevails in it." Does this mean that the authorities were finally able to school the public, to inculcate proper conduct in them? Did the theater achieve its goal of propagating moral virtues among the people? Not totally. Good order prevailed "because of the vigilance of the judges," and, in fact, their task must have been very difficult. The common people clung to their bad habits. After the first publication of the Theater Regulations of 1786, it was necessary to repeat the prohibition of certain diversions, to make addenda, to imprison certain troublemakers who, hidden among the crowd, flirted with the dancers and committed other such abuses.[170] Also, this journalist recognized that members of the audience continued to throw fruit peels and other garbage from the uppermost balconies. In any case, if the behavior of the common people left much to be desired, the conduct of the more cultivated public seated in the lower boxes and balconies, in contrast, would be the envy of any European nation.

As for the rest, the panorama was even more sobering. To what degree had the actors embraced professionalism and how often did they attend rehearsals and learn their lines? To what extent had the rules and stern warnings of the viceroy, as well as the increased scrutiny of the puppet theaters, impeded the actors who habitually moonlighted in these establishments? Definitely, these areas left much to be desired, and there was a continued need for "more preparation among the actors" and "less dependence on the prompters." The professionalism of the actors had improved at least. It was no longer common to hear mayhem and laughter behind the wings.

The public's depraved taste had not, however, changed much if at all. Even "the sensible among the public" gave thunderous applause to some interludes that were fit only for "the lowest plebs." The dances and *sainetes* continued to be considerably indecent but, nonetheless, remained favorites of those who attended the Coliseum. Clearly, their exile from the theater was nearly impossible; the precarious financial situation of the Royal Hospital would not allow such a course of action.

As for the plays, a lack of criteria continued to be the rule. Inexplicably, the public continued to demand the most implausible plays full of heroes, magic, flights, and other absurd fantasies, such as *El mágico de Salerno,* in which the most elementary rules of dramatic composition were ignored, without even mentioning the extravagant melodramas such as the acclaimed *El negro sensible* or, even worse, others such as *El diablo predicador* or *El falso nuncio de Portugal,* which were nothing more than bold mockeries of religion. Fortunately, if works in such poor taste could not be eliminated, others of better quality were imported from Europe, among which were several classic seventeenth-century comedies by Molière such as *Le Mariage forcé* (Marriage by force) and *Le Misantrope* (The misanthrope). In any case, it was clear that "a little modern taste was missing in the process of selection of plays."[171]

In short, it was possible to control the abuses of the public but not to transform its taste. The reformers would have been able to achieve more if not for the permanent shortage of funds at the Coliseum. This situation made them so dependent on the plebeian spectators who, by means of boycotts, were able to impose their criteria. Indeed, although the progress was substantial, it was also fragile. Its consolidation was possible through more education, more policing, more authority, more threats, and more exemplary punishments. The insurgency made the continuation of the reformers' efforts impossible and halted the reform of the theater. The economic status of the Royal Hospital, and by extension the Coliseum, worsened with the disturbances caused by the war. The Constitution of Cádiz contained an order to bring theaters under municipal authority and to use their earnings for works of charity. In Mexico City, however, this measure apparently was never fully implemented and simply contributed to an increasing confusion within the Coliseum. In January 1814, the administrator of the Royal Hospital was uncertain whether to submit the list of plays for the season for the approval of Viceroy Calleja or of the political chief of the city, Ramón del Mazo, with whom he was at loggerheads.[172]

In April 1814, the serious financial situation of the Coliseum caused the administrator to raise the price of tickets. The price hike caused a serious drop in attendance, however, and so in the end, the administrator was obliged to lower the charge for the cheapest seats and offer a discount to those who paid for their tickets in advance. To make matters worse, the flip-flop of prices embroiled the Royal Hospital in a conflict with the Ayuntamiento.[173] By 1817, the theater had descended into total chaos. Because no one wanted to rent the Coliseum, the actors took over its administration to guarantee their jobs.[174]

Disorder reigned with a renewed vigor in the hall. In 1811, Viceroy Venegas had to prohibit "with severity whistling and all demonstrations of derision with which the actors insulted the public." By 1819, mayhem prevailed as much among the spectators as on stage, and it had definitely escalated. What occurred night after night in the Coliseum was no longer "in line with public decorum or moderation." The public mocked, whistled at, and insulted the actors. The players were not intimidated and they responded with "injurious words." Soon, various factions formed within the audiences that were for or against the actors under siege, thus broadening the uproar. The spirits of the spectators were also boosted by the appearance on stage of women dressed as men, "with stockings, pants, and a short jacket, so that the audience was not left guessing as to the irregularity of their shapes." The *alcaldes del crimen* wanted to put an end to such abuses but their plan did not prosper, so they launched a jurisdictional struggle with the *alcaldes del ordinario*.[175] To avoid losing its public, the Coliseum had to set aside the plays of the Enlightenment, which reflected good taste, and scheduled plays that appealed to the common people.[176]

At the end of the War of Independence, the theater was in sad shape. Hardly any of the reforms initiated by the viceregal

governments were still in effect. According to a journalist of the
*Semanario Político y Literario* (Political and Literary Weekly), the
building that housed the New Coliseum was in bad shape, scenery
was meager, and so the same backdrops, poorly painted, old, and
in bad taste, reappeared in many different plays. All this meant
that the dramas presented at the Coliseum seemed more like "neighborhood farces" than works of a professional theater company.
The lighting was a disaster; often the center of the stage was dark,
and even from close up the public could not see the characters on
stage. On top of all this, the critic added: "Everyone talked out loud,
everyone smoked . . . everyone bothered whoever wanted a moment of peace, and in the end no relief was possible because those
who attended the theater and held themselves to be enlightened
were the first to impede it, because it seems that all they desire is
to pester the rest." In the words of another critic, "There is hardly
a night in which [the public] does not manifest its disgust with
whistling."

The quality of the actors had also worsened considerably. In
1825, there were still actors who did not learn their parts and simply amused themselves on stage. The prompter held all the plays
together. Actors, servants, and stagehands peeked out from behind
the wings to see the dances. Also, according to a journalist of the
*Semanario Político y Literario*: "The majority of the players do not
even attempt to amend the licentiousness and misconduct in which
they engage, and it happens that the person playing the role of
Lucretia had the rest of the night divided among a portion of the
admirers of virtue, as a celebrated writer has stated."

As for the show, it was far from the ideal of the Enlightenment.
*Tonadillas*, *sainetes*, and dances, all more or less "dishonest," were
still used for the intermissions, thus destroying the "effect of illusion" of the plays. Also, the most implausible and vulgar, "immoral
and scandalous" dramas were presented. And as if to push the
nation's cultivated elite to desperation, romanticism was taking
hold in Europe, whereas in New Spain the common people still
resisted developing a taste for the neoclassic style. Another journalist summarized the situation by saying: "In effect, nothing has
been reformed in the theater."[177]

During the War for Independence, it became clear that none of
the theater reforms had substantively changed the attitudes of the
actors or those of the spectators. Rather, it was, in truth, only the
repressive force of the viceregal governments that had sustained
the reforms. When the power of the state was overturned, the Coli-

seum returned to its previous condition. In contrast to events in France, in New Spain the Enlightenment did not trickle down to the people. Its influence was felt only in a small sector of the population. The economic, social, and cultural gap that existed between the elite and the people in New Spain made such a broad diffusion of ideas impossible.

The transformation of the theater that took place in Mexico after Independence was not the result of a conscious policy, but instead was quietly developed in accordance with the daily practices imposed by the new economic and political situation. Those who lived through these changes did not take note of the innovations in the Mexican theater straightaway. The new conditions that changed the dramatic arts in post-Independence Mexico were shaped in the last years of Spanish colonialism, when public performances of *colloquia* and *pastorales* were presented during Lent. Apparently, the first season of such shows took place in 1814. That year, the following notice was printed in the *Diario de México*: "Although it is personally repugnant to him that theatrical performances be held during Lent, the Most Excellent Viceroy has condescended to permit them, moved as he is by the shortages experienced by the Royal Indian Hospital." Accordingly, in these days, *colloquia*, sacramental acts, Chinese shadows, hand tricks, and acrobats were shown at the Coliseum.[178]

During the Lenten season of 1817, these performances no longer took place in the New Coliseum but rather in the Plaza de Gallos, where plays about saints were performed. The organizers of these occasions were probably Coliseum actors who wanted to supplement their meager salaries. Their performances unleashed the fury of the Inquisition, because to make the show more agreeable the pious dramas alternated with "indecent dances with impure and scandalous touching."[179] The Holy Office's accusation did not seem to have had the desired result, however, because the next year, Don Juan de Villela asked for a license to present *pastorales* in the Coliseum during Holy Week, offering nineteen pesos to the Royal Hospital for each day of performances.[180]

In 1821, a group of actors from the Coliseum requested permission from the viceroy "to present twelve performances of *pastorales* and *colloquia* in the Plaza de Gallos on the Sundays and Mondays of Lent," because their salaries during this period had been "most inadequate." They were granted a licence without difficulty in the month of April. The shows took place in Mexico City where fevered excitement and open anxieties were the norm. Iturbide's army

was gaining in strength and popularity and had started to advance
on the capital. The shows took place in an atmosphere of disorder,
confirming that the government no longer controlled the population. At the first performance, a "type of wine bar" was installed
near the entrance, and so alcoholic drinks were plentiful among
the spectators. Under the influence of the alcohol, a woman danced
a *jarabe* with particular brazenness and unleashed the spirits of the
audience, who let fly "a considerable excess of obscene comments."
The tumult grew easily, given that the army officer in charge of
maintaining order "was otherwise entertained independently of his
duty." The show only ended at the incredible hour of 1 A.M. All
these excesses led the authorities to police the following performance much more strictly. Although the assistance of troops controlled many of the worst disorders, it was not possible to suppress
all of them. For this reason, an official who had been present proposed that no more such shows should be allowed, but if they were
permitted, he added that "the authorities should stop . . . the mixing of the *colloquia* with the *jarabe*, that most indecent dance, particularly in the intermission, and not allow any such others in this
style nor ridiculous interludes, which at the very least diminish
the morality of such acts." A few months after Mexican Independence, no one paid any more attention to this official, who had been
the guardian of good conduct. At the next Lenten season, the new
authorities granted a license to the same group of actors to organize a show of *pastorales* in the Plaza de Gallos.[181]

The production of these *pastorales* was proof of the great appetite on the part of the public for such light dramatic works. The
Coliseum could not satisfy this demand without abandoning its
enlightened moralizing urge. In any case, the monopoly that the
New Coliseum held over all theatrical performances was clearly
anachronistic. Actually, the *pastorales* that were presented in the
Plaza de Gallos were a first crack in this monopoly. It paved the
way for the transformation of this plaza into a permanent theater,
which was inaugurated on October 9, 1822. It was called the Teatro
Provisional.[182] The official protection that the New Coliseum had
enjoyed under colonialism came to an end with Independence.
Within one year, a competing theater appeared on the scene. To
use an unpolished metaphor taken from economics, it was at this
moment that the theater passed from its mercantilist monopolist
stage into liberal capitalism.

The end of the theatrical monopoly not only led to a proliferation of theatrical spaces in Mexico City after 1840, but also to their

differentiation by the type of show presented and the social origins of the spectators. The theater, which during the colonial period had been a diversion that a broad range of urban social groups shared in common, split into a "cultivated" theater for the elite and another, more popular version.[183] One of the new houses was the Teatro del Unión, which was inaugurated in 1841 with the performance of two plays: *Quiero ser cómico* (I want to be an actor) and *La vieja y los dos calaveras* (The old woman and the two ruffians). In the intermission, dancers performed. The program also included a lavish overture. In the words of a critic of the period, the hall "was not decorated decently so to speak . . . the carpets that covered the ground were *petates* [rush mats]." The noise and disorder of the public was simply indescribable, to such an extent that the critic proposed changing the name from Theater of the Union to Liberty. Everything that the enlightened thinkers had conceived of as abuses was allowed there.[184]

The common people fled the enlightened theater, with its judges and soldiers charged with the maintenance of order, its ever more moralist and edifying shows, and the rigidity of bourgeois customs that prevailed in the hall. The flavor of the popular theater was reminiscent of a reclaimed liberty. The enlightened thinkers had not been able to create a new theater that corresponded to the cultural needs of the people. Their failure thrust the dramatic arts into the waiting arms of the unscrupulous merchants and market forces.[185]

The high-culture theater had to survive and develop within a market economy in the same way as the popular drama. It had to become a profitable business at a moment when the majority of the population turned its back on this diversion. Two factors favored the financial renewal of the theater in Mexico City. First, its separation from the hospital meant that its earnings no longer had to finance charitable activities. This allowed a larger profit margin for the impresarios. Second, the cultivated theater raised the price of its tickets. During the colonial period, such a measure had never been contemplated without serious consideration of the possible consequences. Any price hike would have deprived the people of the only reasonably acceptable diversion they had and condemned them to sink further into the morass of vice. This measure would have left the Coliseum without an audience, as had occurred in 1814, forcing the contractor to reduce the price of low-end tickets. In post-Independence Mexico, the logic and the need for such a measure imposed themselves upon the impresarios. In 1827, the

Teatro Principal, the new name of the Coliseum, raised its prices. The Ayuntamiento, which had not yet conceded that the theater was just one more commercial activity, intervened and fixed the prices. This act provoked much indignation among the impresarios and the drama critics. One of the critics wrote: "How is it possible that the Ayuntamiento has meddled with the impresarios of the great opera by making them, against their will, offer these diversions at a certain price, denying them their judgment to regulate prices according to their interests by the force of authority?"[186]

Paradoxically, this excision of the theater improved the chances that many of the ideals of the Enlightenment would be realized. In a theater from which the "common people" had been expelled, it was possible to end the disorder of the audiences and to professionalize the actors by giving them a more precise status and a more stable financial situation. Finally, with the exile of vulgar diversions from the stage, the theater returned to simpler fare. With this withdrawal, however, the goal of making the dramatic arts a school of social, civic, and moral virtues moved further out of reach. Of course, such a laudable ambition did not disappear, if only remaining in the form of discourse.

The division of the theater was also irksome in that it allowed the common people their own space where they were free to indulge in their "dissolution." It became necessary to double the vigilance and control of the show halls that the people attended in order to prevent the spread of disorder. The scrutiny of the government became selective; it was useless to watch over the high-culture performaces at which the public had already assimilated the new rules of behavior. It was essential to do so, however, in the popular theater, where only threats and coercion could guarantee order. In the Theater Regulations of 1859, while the first-class theaters were governed by a precise series of dispositions, the others were subject to a fluctuating and often arbitrary criterion that the officials could impose within a permanent state of emergency:

> Art. 66. Regarding the theaters of the inferior category cited in article 35 [El Nacional, Iturbide, and the so-called Principal], the inspector's council has extremely ample capacities; consequently, and keeping in mind the particular circumstances of each of these theaters, they can subject them or not to all or part of this regulation, giving them a dispensation if it is suitable, of the obligations which are herein established or imposing these rules if it is judged necessary, being guided always by the principal object of the improvement of these theaters.[187]

During the entire colonial period, theater reform had been attempted despite the financial exigencies of the New Coliseum. With a monopoly over theater, an artificial market for drama was created, but it could not reconcile the divisions within the public. The new theatrical values of the Enlightenment could not be implemented without sacrificing the financial well-being of the theater and vice versa. The solution to this dilemma pointed to the development of two separate markets. Because of these conditions, it was inevitable that a split would occur between the theater of the elite and that of the common people in post-Independence Mexico.

# 3

# Disorder or Street Diversions

Come all, singing joyous tunes,
Leave the plains and the mountains
To dance to the sound of tambourines.
Later Lent, fasting, and weakness
Will rain upon the city.

—Emile Deschamps

A t the end of the colonial period, 137,000 people lived in Mexico City. Contemporaries considered four-fifths of the population—110,000—as members of the "pleb" or popular classes. This group was divided more or less equally between Indians, *castas* (which included the mestizos), and Creoles. Only one-third of the total population had more or less stable employment. Some 6,700 were artisans, 7,500 worked in the Royal workshops—principally manufacturing cigars and cigarettes—3,000 worked at home, 14,000 were domestic servants, and 5,000 were in the ranks of the military. The rest either operated small stands in the market or worked as porters, water vendors, gardeners, and day laborers. Finally, some 15,000 lived from begging or from activities of dubious legality. Many of the members of the popular classes supplemented their incomes by raising livestock, and some of the more fortunate had small orchards or fields. All of these people lived under the shadow of hunger and the devastating epidemics that overwhelmed the city in the eighteenth century.

The elite of the city was composed of mine owners, merchants, the proprietors of large landed estates, bureaucrats, and priests. Except for a Spanish minority of 10 percent who generally occupied the highest posts and enjoyed the largest fortunes, these people were Creoles with a few mestizos who had managed to enrich themselves.[1]

All these people, rich and poor, white and Indian, roamed the streets of the city among grandiose convents and churches, imposing government buildings, sumptuous palaces, and modest—if not miserable—tenements. The streets did not serve solely for the circulation of persons and merchandise. They were also the very center of sociability; they were the privileged space for social interaction. In the streets, city residents worked, made purchases, ate, took part in civil and religious ceremonies, paraded themselves, amused themselves, and got drunk. Sex and death were also present in the streets on a daily basis.[2]

The street invaded other social spaces: the shops, wineries, workshops of artisans, government buildings, and even homes. Privacy, as we conceive of it today, did not exist. The majority of the population lived in tenements: these buildings afforded no privacy. Moreover, the residents spent most of their time on the communal patio rather than inside the small, dark, and unhealthy rooms of their homes. Certainly, outside the *traza* (city core), where the population was mostly indigenous and *casta*, the houses tended to be small constructions of adobe. There too, however, the life of the barrio, with all its licentiousness, infiltrated the houses through the activities of the street or patios and *solares* (plots of land). To hide away in the interior of one's home was unthinkable. To go into the street, that is, to go from a semipublic space to one that was entirely public, was to enter into a colorful and boisterous world. The "pleb" dominated the public spaces of the streets. Groups of paupers, beggars, the mutilated, and the blind wandered the city permanently.

In the period before Viceroy Revillagigedo the second's reforms (1789 and 1794) were applied, the streets were extremely dirty, muddy, and poorly cobbled. During the rainy season, they were frequently flooded. In addition, the common people did not hesitate to perform natural functions in full view of all passersby. After a few glasses of pulque or some other alcoholic beverage, the little modesty the plebeians had disappeared entirely.

By day, the streets were animated. Apart from the crowds of plebeians on foot, the elite circulated on horseback or in fine carriages. Numerous carts transported food or construction materials. The grid of streets was also crisscrossed by a reduced, but still active, network of canals or channels. Residents of the nearby villages whose *chinampas* produced vegetables used these waterways to supply the city with these edibles and other provisions.

The urban space was not divided according to specialized activities. The most diverse endeavors coexisted side by side and often intermingled. Even the boundary between city and countryside was not clear-cut. Little *solares,* which were used for agriculture, infiltrated residential spaces. In many of the dwellings on the edges of the city, the occupants raised poultry and pigs on their patios. Some of the residents of the capital even had cows, which were let loose on the streets at night to graze.

The streets were also the scene of multiple and varied occupations. The *aguadores* (water carriers) hauled water from the public fountains to private houses; porters transported heavy loads at a steady pace; the artisans, carpenters, painters, and leather workers, because their shops were narrow and small, spilled out onto the street where they performed many of their tasks. All types of merchandise and services could be procured in the streets as well. There hundreds of street vendors shouted their various wares. Many of the stands in the markets were open or simply covered by a *petate* or a heavy cloth. The prosperous stands were nothing more than a sort of wooden "box" or installations in the arches of nearby buildings, but even so, they disgorged into the street and never lost contact with it.

The Plaza Mayor was always bursting with stalls, some in the open, others in the arches. There merchants sold candies, toys, serapes, rebozos (shawls), hats, real and paper flowers, files, knives, hammers, machetes, and all sorts of secondhand and sometimes stolen merchandise. Of course, numerous food stands also populated the square; they provided *atole* (gruel) and tamales (corn-based foods), *buñuelos* (fried pastry), hot chocolate, and other foods fried, dried, or pickled. The *pulquerías* that jutted out into the street were often simply small booths nestled against some wall and protected from the weather by a roof of shingles. There, a multitude of Indians, *castas,* and poor Creoles got drunk in the midst of the flow of people coming and going. Notaries public also operated in the squares; they wrote letters and petitions for licenses.

Isolation from the street was a rare commodity for public places and work spaces. The annexes (outbuildings) where most artisans worked and sold their goods, where lunch counters and wineries were located, always had their doors open to the street and maintained a constant communication with it. For a long time, even the viceregal palace allowed the intrusion of the street. Inside its walls, individuals sold produce and operated small restaurants. The hustle and bustle of people was constant.

The only places that were in some way isolated from the presence of the street were those dedicated to diversions such as bullfighting, the theater, and pelota. Inside these specialized buildings, however, the atmosphere differed little from that of the street. At this time the most selective and isolated places were the few and expensive *mesones* (inns), as well as the cafés, which appeared only at the very end of the eighteenth century.

The street was the privileged space of the popular classes, but it was also the ideal place for single men and women to meet. It was in the open spaces that they exchanged first glances, smiles, and then salutations. The next steps of the courtship took place in the same venue. Sexuality also made an appearance in the street. "Young women of bad morals" lurked in doorways and on corners close to wineries. Other women "who did not prostitute themselves entirely, hung around hoping for invitations for a drink or joined groups passing by or going in for a drink."[3] At night, those streets surrounding such buildings as convents and monasteries, which were less populated and usually darker, became the ideal spots to commit "obscenities," that is, sexual acts.

Death was another regular passerby. Sometimes, funeral processions on their way to the cemetery reminded people of death's presence. Another such reminder was the small but solemn procession of people carrying lit candles and intoning funeral songs and prayers who accompanied monks on their way to give extreme unction to some unfortunate on a deathbed. Between the Plaza Mayor and the Plaza del Volador, it was also not unusual to see some poor soul—clearly intoxicated—standing next to the corpse of a family member, asking for donations to pay for the funeral.

Faced with a society that lived permanently in the streets, the religious and civil authorities—if they wanted to have any effect—could not remain isolated within their buildings. During the entire colonial period, many of the church's activities took place in the open. Processions through the streets and squares were the most frequent of such exercises. Sometimes they were enlivened with dance and music. Apart from these eye-catching endeavors, the many crosses and chapels scattered around the city were also the focus of religious devotions in their immediate vicinity. At the same time, all of the most important civic ceremonies (the entry or death of the viceroy, feasts for the coronation of a new king, the birthdays or marriages of members of the royal family) took place in public on the streets.

The exaggerated importance of the street in the population's social life was actually reinforced by the viceregal authorities. The officials believed that the public nature and constant mutual contact among individuals in the street made surveillance of the plebeians easier and thus control over them more effective. Privacy was considered an obstacle to the power of the state and thus an enemy of social peace. In 1821, a syndic of the Ayuntamiento expressed this concern in the following manner: "All civilized [peoples] keep this principle foremost: the man who enjoys himself publicly takes care to do so with decorum even if he is bad and immoral. Private diversions are the source of limitless evil and their repercussions, in general, are more significant."[4]

To control the artisans, for example, a series of ordinances decreed that these persons had to work and sell their products in the same location. Their workspace had to be an *accesoria* (annex) whose only access was directly on the street. Eventually, they were also required to live in their workshops. Inspections were therefore easier, but it was also hoped that because these artisans worked under the scrutiny of passersby, they would take greater care in their craft.[5]

A similar principle was at the heart of the ordinances governing wineries and *pulquerías*. The rules ordered wineries to keep their doors open and to place the counters near these doors. The *pulquerías* had to be set up in the street and open to it on three sides. The vigilance of the judges was simplified, and because the "modesty" of drinkers was in full view of passersby, the authors of these rules hoped to avoid or limit disorders.

The author of the "Discurso sobre la policía de México" (Discourse on the police of Mexico City) agreed with these legislative strategies. Despite the repugnance he felt toward the numerous food stands on streets and squares, he considered them to be the lesser of two evils. He could not imagine the mischief in store if these same people ate in enclosed spaces, such as restaurants in which "diverse grave disorders might possibly originate from the mixing [of the sexes] or simply their concealment."[6]

Because the street was central in the social life of the Mexican capital, it could not be ignored in a study such as this one, which deals with diversions. An omission of street diversions would mean overlooking the most numerous and varied as well as the best

attended and enjoyed of all amusements of the period. The viceregal authorities, however, were divided in their opinions on the subject of these entertainments and, indeed, they had formed many
policies on this matter. A hierarchy of diversions came about; some
were considered totally noxious, while others were considered beneficial to society. Not surprisingly, the ranking reflected that of the
social groups who most enjoyed those activities. Because Indians
from outside the city generally dominated Carnaval, the viceregal
authorities tenaciously hindered it. On the other hand, the officials
constantly encouraged paseos, or promenades, which appealed to
the elite and the enlightened thinkers.

In fact, the policy of protection for certain street entertainments
and the attempts to oust others, or at least to watch over and regulate them strictly, hid a social struggle in which the authorities tried
to impose a precise order on the privileged space: the street. By the
mid-eighteenth century, the urban popular classes still set the tone
that dominated the public throughways. The artisans, water carriers, and itinerant merchants as well as the numerous paupers and
beggars formed not only the majority of those found on the streets
but also of those who occupied these spaces in the most permanent
fashion. The enlightened critics, travelers, and various officials constantly complained about the presence of veritable armies of sup-
plicants who swarmed around the rich; they showed their
mutilations and asked for charity. To make matters worse, these
paupers shouted vulgarities at passing women. When they gathered in large groups in *pulquerías*, they got drunk and engaged in
brawls. Finally, they harassed people who passed nearby.

During the eighteenth century, the elite in New Spain did not
feel comfortable in the capital's streets. When they left their houses,
all they saw were the intolerable excesses of the plebs and, even
worse, a continuous state of disorder. The custom of circulating in
the streets on horseback or in carriages, which most members of
the upper classes owned, was not solely motivated by an inexpli-
cable snobbery; more to the point, it was only by putting themselves above the anarchy of the streets, and thus avoiding the
multiple disturbances, that they could maintain a social distance
from the popular disorder.[7]

Because the social life of the lower classes took place mostly in
the streets, the reforms that enlightened despots hoped to accomplish in Mexico City's society could not be achieved without a far-
reaching transformation of these spaces. For this reason, the
authorities began a campaign to end the disorder that prevailed in

the streets and to make them into agreeable and welcoming places for the colonial elite. In addition, the viceroys believed that if they could restore real and effective control over the streets, they would also be able to dominate the activities that occurred there and all that this implied.

During the period of the Enlightenment, the state and the common people clashed over the control of the streets. An examination of the various entertainments that took place on the streets— Carnaval, the religious festivals, the *colloquia, posadas* (Christmas parties), and *jamaicas* (charity sales), the *pulquerías*, and finally, the street shows and paseos—provides the setting for an explanation of this struggle.

## Don Carnal and Doña Cuaresma

For centuries, just before Lent, Europeans threw themselves into an unbridled enjoyment of the pleasures that they would deny themselves during the forty-day period of fasts, penances, and restrictions. While they were at it, they also savored some pleasures that were not allowed during the year. Year after year, the festival of Carnaval took place in the days of *Carnestolendas* (Shrovetide). Pagan values dominated during these days until Christian morals gained the upper hand and were imposed rigorously once again. Carnaval is one of the paradoxes of Christianity; without Doña Cuaresma (Mrs. Lent), we would not know her mortal enemy, Don Carnal (Mr. Appetite). The latter epitomizes the human needs that were repressed by the church's morality.

The imposition of Catholicism in New Spain led inevitably to a period when the inhabitants let loose their appetites just before Lent. They did so that the imposed abstinence afterward would be more bearable. The actual date when the festivities of Carnaval were introduced into Mexico is not known nor whether religious or laypersons were responsible. For a long time, civil and religious authorities tolerated these festivities. As with so many historical phenomena, the first traces of Carnaval emerged from official attempts to eradicate it. The best and most detailed descriptions of the festivities come from a time when it had become a rarity and was on the way to extinction.[8] Despite the scarcity of historical sources, I will attempt a superficial reconstruction of Mexico City's Carnaval at the turn of the seventeenth century. My portrait is based upon an interpretation of the prohibitions to which it was subject as well as some subsequent accounts.

During the three days preceding Ash Wednesday, the city was gripped by an atmosphere of joy and liberty. There were dances, paseos, and balls in all parts of the city. People threw eggshells and aniseeds at one another and everybody was tipsy. Many disguised themselves with masks and roved the city making fun of individuals and of the authorities; and, taking advantage of their anonymity, they committed many excesses. Some even dressed as clerics. According to a 1731 viceregal *bando* (order), men frequently put on women's clothing and vice versa, although the former was probably more common. In 1722, the archbishop ordered the reading of an edict that aimed to "prevent the dishonest womanly transformations."[9] Young Indians dressed up as old men in colorful costumes to do the dance of the *huehuenches* (old men). On Mardi Gras (the Tuesday before Ash Wednesday), the Indians participated in the so-called ceremony of the hanged. In this parody of the judicial system, one of them was "hanged" from a tree. The ritual seems to have been a local version of the death of Carnaval, a ceremony that was common in many towns of Spain.[10]

According to María Sten, the Indians of the barrios and nearby villages certainly participated in the masquerades that took place within the *traza*. The archbishop's ban of 1722 dealt with the subject of the disguises used during Carnaval but also made reference to the devil. During the colonial period, the association of the Indians' idolatrous practices and the demonic was a common theme.[11] Apart from this connection, there were certain segments of Carnaval—the *huehuenches* and the ceremony of the "hanging," for example—in which only Indians took part. After the 1731 ban, these ceremonies continued to be performed in the same way as they had been previously in the heart of Mexico City, but only in the Indian villages of the Valley of Mexico. Finally, at the beginning of the nineteenth century, the Indians of Tlaltelolco received permission to organize festivities during Shrovetide. They were reminded, however, that they were not allowed to take their celebrations into the *traza* of the city, which seems to indicate that they had done so at one time. All of these facts point to the conclusion that Carnaval was once a festival exclusive to, or at least dominated by, the city's Indians and surrounding communities.

Many scholars of carnivals that occur in diverse regions of the world emphasize that this festival is primarily one of social inversion. For a couple of days, the forbidden is permitted, and social and sexual roles become interchangeable. For a brief moment, the oppressed impose their rules. At the same time, carnivals define the limits of social order. Although mockery, liberty, and pleasure rule in these days, not all acts are sanctioned. The carnival reveals and confirms those social principles that are sacrosanct. The same inversion of the social order has its principles and limits. During carnivals, men dress as women and the poor as the rich, but the opposite is indeed a rare occurrence.[12]

In fact, the possibilities of social inversion in highly stratified societies are actually a part of the very same social order. The hierarchies are never absolute and as such can be moved from one plane to another without modifications. Social ordering in traditional societies is, above all, an asymmetrical distribution of obligations and rights. The inequality that underlies this distribution is obvious in the whole but not in the individual parts of the system. The component elements of the traditional social hierarchy should not be visualized as steps on a lineal scale. Rather, they are interconnecting bodies in a multidimensional space. Each level has another corresponding surface that represents its partial inversion. Indeed, the system is legitimized as a whole by the existence of these multiple levels in which the general order is contradicted.[13]

This construct can be made clearer with some examples derived from the social life of colonial Mexico. For example, many of the descriptions of Indians constantly contrasted their virtues with their defects. Their lack of reasoning was contrasted with their ability as craftsmen.[14] The legal dispositions for the protection of Indians were derived from and were logical within this conception. At no time was the subordinated position of the Indian to the Spaniard questioned; only in some aspects their rights increased and their obligations decreased. For example, the Indians did not pay the *alcabala* sales tax, nor the tithe on nonindigenous agricultural products. In the same way, they were not subject to the same law as the Spaniards. The system was in fact legitimized by these differences among social categories; inferiority on one level was justified by superiority on another; the exploitation of Indians was compensated for by the particular attention that the monarch paid to them; and the misery of the poor in life would be offset by their reward in Heaven after death.

These variations in the social order according to perception of levels was clear in public ceremonies. The social position that the authorities and various groups held within colonial society was reflected in their actual location during ceremonies, and this place varied according to the reason for the celebration. Obviously, the precedence of civil over religious officials was not the same for a political occasion as for a religious festivity. Even though, in most processions, Indians usually occupied places of little or no importance, in some they were central to the whole event. In 1756, in the festivity to confirm the oath to the Virgin of Guadalupe as patroness of New Spain, the governors and authorities of the Indian communities of San Juan Tenochtitlán and Santiago Tlaltelolco played principal roles. In his "Diario de sucesos notables" (Journal of notable events), José Manuel de Castro Santa-Anna explained their prominent position at this event: "This function seemed very appropriate for them in consideration of the fact that it was to the fortunate Indian Juan Diego that the divine Lady appeared."[15]

Because every ceremony was different, the order of precedence for groups and individuals had to be established for each separate function. Each festivity had a particular series of conditions that regulated that order. This continual process allowed officials, corporate bodies, and distinguished persons to try to improve their position at the expense of others. The jockeying for position, of course, led to impassioned fights that could even result in physical violence. In 1697, for example, on Holy Thursday, the Franciscans and the Trinitarians disagreed over precedence; their words escalated into blows with fists and maces. They even used the crosses they carried as weapons, and many were wounded as a result.[16]

In traditional societies, carnivals are really a tangible representation of ideology and are part of a complex system that portrayed social order according to place. In these moments of celebration, some figures are placed in an inverted position that they do not normally occupy all year long. This inversion generally occurs in a period of great liberty and relaxation of social norms. The use of masks to disguise the social identity of the participants accentuates the "individuality" of human beings in society. Therefore, they are not defined so much by their psychological and moral characteristics as by their ranking within the social hierarchy of the world of work, family lineage, and the network of interchange of reciprocal or unequal favors.[17] Carnivals do not so much question the social order in its entirety as they remind society that the level of daily life is not the only one that exists, but is rather one of many. Carnivals also remind people that all hierarchies are ephemeral before the ethical and religious equality of humans. Thus, carnivals try to reestablish the customary equilibrium among the various levels of social life, in particular, between the obligations and the rights of the popular classes. This balance is constantly threatened by the growth of the elite's power. Carnivals become a mechanism to defend the people's traditional rights; they limit the social domination of the powerful.[18]

The descriptions of the Shrovetide festivities in Mexico City show many elements of social inversion. The Indians, briefly, occupied the *traza* of the city—the exclusive preserve and place of residence of the Spaniards. Laypersons had fun dressing as clerics in order to mock them. Sexual roles became interchangeable and the young danced disguised as elders.

Civil and religious authorities began to combat this grandiose festival of inversion in Mexico City at the end of the seventeenth century. The struggle achieved some momentum at the beginning of the eighteenth century. Apparently, the first skirmishes were provoked by the church. In 1679, on the Sunday of Shrovetide, the Holy Office ordered the reading of an edict that forbade the practice of seculars putting on clerical garb on these days.[19] On the same day three years later, Don José Lesamis, the confessor of the archbishop, roamed the streets of the city with an image of the Virgin and prayed the rosary. No doubt, his intention was the same as that of the monk Antonio Margil de Jesús who, in 1709, on the occasion of the San Luis Potosí Carnaval, went into the streets to preach and to disabuse the crowd of the vain passions that they sought there.[20] In 1700, the Inquisition repeated its prohibition against laypersons dressing as religious for amusement.[21] In 1722, the archbishop of Mexico City issued an edict that banned "the feminine transformations that in this Shrovetide suggest the presence of the Devil in such costumes." The viceroy backed the archbishop and ordered the publication of a *bando* that also prohibited the practice of going out with masks and of people covering their faces for the dances that occurred during this period. According to the *Gaceta de México,* thanks to these and other provisions taken that year, "The participants did not dare commit the least excess or mischief in public so that the attendance at the celebrations in church was much greater in the three days of Shrovetide."[22]

The campaign against Carnaval took on a stronger character and became more resolute under the government of Viceroy Juan de Acuña. While he ruled New Spain, from late 1722 to early 1734, Viceroy Acuña took over the crusade personally and increased the efforts to end the excesses that this festival seemed to engender. Many scholars believe that the viceregal government did not have the authority to do away with such popular traditions and that the *bandos* that were constantly reiterated, as well as the measures adopted, had only an ephemeral effect at best. It does seem that as to Mexico City's Carnaval, the viceroy stopped it in its tracks and it never recovered. On December 20, 1731, a *bando* was published in the city that prohibited cross-dressing and wearing masks and threatened a penalty of two hundred lashes and two years of presidio for Spanish transgressors who could not prove their blue blood, six years of presidio for nobles, and two hundred lashes and six years of work in an *obraje* for those of dark color.[23] This decree was not only a mortal blow for Carnaval, but it also stopped the popular masquerades that, only a short time before, the same viceregal authorities had encouraged.

In fact, the 1731 *bando* was only one of a series of many measures that the viceroys proclaimed against Carnaval over the years. Already, in 1728, the *Gaceta de México* noted the good order that had prevailed in the capital in the days preceding Shrovetide: "On [February] 8 and the following two days of Shrovetide (which in this city have been the occasion for taunting masks used for public dances by the residents), there were no incidents contrary to honesty and self-control; due to the prudent and discreet precautions of His Excellency, who has, during the years of his government, not permitted things that are contrary to modesty in these days."[24]

In 1821, an official receiver of the Ayuntamiento still considered that Viceroy Acuña had put an end to the masks and disorders of Carnaval. He dislodged all festivities from the center of the city by encouraging alternative entertainments that extended from the Sunday of Shrovetide until Easter—in particular, the paseo of Ixtacalco.[25] From this moment forward, the efforts of the following viceroys during the period of Carnaval were limited to the maintenance of a certain vigilance to prevent the resurgence of excesses within the city, the suppression of minor disorders, and the imposition of order in the the city's environs. This last duty was the most difficult.

Accounts of Carnaval in the decades following the government of Viceroy Acuña only comment on the tranquillity of Shrovetide in Mexico City. In 1783, the *Gaceta de México* published the following description: "On [February] 16 and the two following days of Shrovetide, numerous crowds attended the celebration in all the churches where it was held. During this period (in accordance with the strict decree published on the 12th and other just measures that were taken), neither concealing masks, costumes that disguise, alluring music, provocative dances, distracting games, nor many of the other prejudicial distractions which were so common in these days, were seen or heard."[26]

In 1757, José Manuel de Castro Santa-Anna wrote in his "Diario de sucesos notables": "On the afternoons of 20, 21, and 22 of the said month [February], throngs of people of all classes assembled on the delightful Avenue of the Alameda on the occasion of Shrovetide. But no scandalous behavior resulted in this area or other streets due to the vigilance of the grenadiers and cavalry who were on guard around the city." His description of these days was very similar for the next year as well.[27] In 1774, a royal order confirmed the 1731 prohibition against the use of masks in New Spain.[28]

Even then, the enlightened governments tried to do away with the disorders that still existed, even though these were minor compared with those that were common at the beginning of the century. The customs that persisted were the throwing of aniseeds and hollow eggs filled with various substances (*cascarones*), which took place mostly in halls or on the paseos.[29] In 1787, the Audiencia—which was governing as a result of the untimely death of Viceroy Bernardo de Gálvez—prohibited the throwing of "large aniseeds, covered almonds . . . barley, split peas, other seeds, and small stones" in the coliseum during Carnaval and only permitted people "to amuse themselves throwing small aniseeds, which are called *grajea* or *mostacilla*, and this practice, with moderation."[30] By 1797, the authorities had banned not only the "use of *cascarones*, aniseeds, and other projectiles commonly thrown during Shrovetide," but also "the great disorders" that resulted from these practices. That year the Ayuntamiento decided to make these prohibitions even more effective. They ordered confectioners to abstain from the sale of such sweets and instructed the judges of the plaza to ensure that *cascarones* were not present in the markets during the period of festivities.[31]

In 1780, at the request of the viceroyalty's general advisor, the king of Spain sent an order that mandated the end of the Carnaval festivities that the Indians traditionally organized in the center of the city. Upon being pushed out of this part of the city, however, the Indians simply transferred these activities to the interior of their villages, where the scrutiny of Spanish authorities was not quite so thorough. This order included a ban on the ceremony of the hanged and the dance of the *huehuenches*, which "the Indians of the villages of Ixtacalco, Mexicalcingo, Ixtapalapa, and others in the immediate surroundings still practice these days." The dances reminded the Spaniards of the Indians' "ancient pagan ways" that were "in opposition to religion, to Catholic dogmas, and offensive to the cult." The officials believed that "the irregular, indecent, and dishonest ceremonies" encouraged "many pernicious beliefs and apart from this and other many abuses, foment, extend, and propagate the incorrigible vice of drunkenness, because they start and end with this other custom of the said Indians."[32] Unlike the previous ban, these prohibitions do not seem to have had any effect. At the beginning of the twentieth century, the ceremony of the hanged continued to take place in the Plaza de Romita.[33]

In 1802, the Indians of the *parcialidad* of Santiago Tlaltelolco were given a license to "go out and shout" during the three days of Shrovetide. The permission did carry the conditions that they should not enter the city, nor allow men to dress as women or the opposite, nor engage in drunkenness, and, finally, that they were to make themselves scarce at the times of worship. The authorization should not come as a surprise. The officials had nothing against the organization of festivities by Indians during Carnaval so long as there was no disorder and they avoided ceremonies that had vague associations with paganism, as well as rites of social inversion—that is to say, when the festivities were stripped of all that was the very essence of Carnaval.[34]

After Independence, even though many of the dispositions taken by the viceregal government were forgotten, the Carnaval of Mexico City never recovered its former glory. Its resurgence in the middle of the nineteenth century was but a pale imitation, a denaturalized bourgeois invention that was only a prelude to its total disappearance. At that time, its celebration was reduced to elegant masked balls attended by high society, which took place at private homes or in theaters such as the Principal or the Iturbide. Certainly, groups of boys followed the elegant masked revelers in the street and threw *cascarones* of bran or honey and stinky water in the paseos of the city. But this only occurred in the period immediately before the initiation of the balls. Carnaval had been domesticated and privatized; it had become the almost-exclusive patrimony of upper classes.[35]

In the eighteenth century, Carnaval was weakened as a defense mechanism of the traditional social equilibrium and ceased to be a rite in which society put aside its customary rules in order to revitalize its foundations. The efforts of repression launched against it, as well as the efficiency of that campaign, especially within the urban core, were signs that the balance between the various social groups had altered to the benefit of the powerful and the state. The disappearance of rites of social inversion during this period represented a paralysis of the system of estates. It was a dangerous oversimplification that sought to fix the hierarchy on one level, to make it an immutable order, and to deprive it of its relative flexibility. Without a doubt, this new hardened attitude of the viceregal authorities toward the fleeting liberties enjoyed by Indians and *castas* during Shrovetide were related at least in part to the rebellion of 1692. A more important factor in this change was the advance of a modernizing tendency to uniformity that was beginning to erase all of the unpleasant social ambiguities of the past. When the common people fought for their present interests by harkening back to an idyllic past, their arguments were discounted by the necessity to complete reforms for the sake of progress. In this manner, a new society emerged in which change was not only the inevitable if unconscious result of men's actions but also their fundamental goal.

The most efficient measure to fight the excesses of Shrovetide was mitigation of the austerity of Lent. Therefore the officials accepted some varied distractions for the city residents during this holy period. From the 1740s on, they apparently allowed tightrope walkers to perform in the streets. By the end of the century, taking advantage of the absence of theater in the Coliseum from Ash Wednesday to Easter, acrobats of various types took over this venue to show off their talents. In the Valley of Mexico, villages had an ancient tradition of representing the passion of Jesus Christ. Many enlightened thinkers opposed these portrayals because they were not received with the proper respect. Despite this criticism, however, and after much hesitation and internal discord, the church continued to permit them as long as "human malice did not abuse them." Relatives, neighbors, and friends were invited as the audience for small religious plays that were mounted in private homes. The diversion was accompanied by conversation, snacks, and glasses of *chicha* (corn liquor). Of course, these meetings were not always so peaceful. On many occasions, they turned into lively revelry, with dancing and intoxicating drinks. During the Wars of Independence, public *colloquia* were even presented in the Coliseum and the Plaza de Gallos. The principal attraction of these particular gatherings was not so much the plays but some rather lewd dances.[36]

The paseos that took place on the banks of the *acequia real* (royal water canal) and of the canal that linked Mexico City with Chalco were the most characteristic diversion of Lent. These paseos were already very popular by the end of the seventeenth century, but in the following century they were improved and promoted by enlightened governments. The paseos began on the Sunday of

Shrovetide and ended on Easter Sunday, so that no difference was marked between the period of Carnaval and that of Lent. The activities followed a route from the neighborhood of Jamaica to that of Ixtacalco and along the Viga and Santa Anita. Food stands and crowded *pulquerías* appeared suddenly in the immediate area, and a multitude of *trajineras* (small boats that transported goods and people) with musicians on board, came and went among the *chinampas*, with visitors as passengers.[37]

Even though this lively distraction could provide an efficient remedy against the festivities of Carnaval, it was important to ensure that the excesses that had been eradicated during Shrovetide were not simply resurrected during Lent. This reasoning guided the decree of April 1748, which ordered that "during the period of the paseo of Jamaica, the justices of the city must attend it every night to watch and guard that no disorders occur and to make sure that at nine o'clock, everyone leaves the said paseo and the area of the canal without any exceptions."[38]

The royal decree of 1780 that banned the performance of the *huehuenches* and the ceremony of the hanged, also ordered that, around this paseo, the pulque stands should be controlled very closely and taverns that served brandy and ordinary and Castilian wines should be closed, because the mixture of these drinks with pulque gave rise to "superfluous excesses and public as well as private sins."[39]

In 1794, the Sunday of Shrovetide was a disaster because someone ordered the opening of the locks of San Lázaro and the canal began to empty. As a result, the canoes had to navigate in muddy waters.[40] In 1797, the keeper of the locks at La Viga supplied an account of the disorders that had occurred there on Sunday, March 19. He took the opportunity to denounce the fact that "many *trajineras* travel along this way and many of the rowers call out in loud voices to those on the paseo, offering a place in their boat for a half [real] with the attraction of music because they have some instruments on board, and so they take on many plebeians of different *calidades* [ranks], sexes, and conditions; this combination leads to singing and dissolute words, from which many offenses to God arise and much public scandal." In order to avoid these disorders, the lockkeeper proposed that the owners of the canoes and those who operated them "should be seriously warned that they should abstain from the excesses that they wanted to introduce by regularly chartering their canoes." Guided by his suggestion, the authorities cited the owners of the *trajineras* to make them aware of the new disposition, which prohibited the rental of the *trajineras* by the seat to individuals who did not know each other. Despite this ban, the practice was still common at least until 1809.[41]

The prohibition on the frequent rental of *trajineras* is quite revealing of the mentality of the colonial Mexican authorities. For them, disorder came from the mixture of groups, the breakdown of barriers among persons of "distinct ranks, sexes, and conditions." This fusion was really quite relative; all those who traveled in canoes were "plebeian individuals," that is to say, mestizos and other *castas* consorted with the Indian rowers in the canoes. But this negation of the differences among the estates was considered highly prejudicial to the social order.

None of the measures destroyed the liveliness that characterized these outings, and even though, in 1821, a syndic of the Ayuntamiento affirmed that these excursions had disappeared over the years, they reappeared after Independence with the same vitality.[42] In 1840, during Lent, Fanny Calderón de la Barca portrayed the scene at the Paseo de la Viga: "Two long lines of carriages are to be seen going and returning as far as the eye can reach, and hundreds of gay plebeians are assembled on the sidewalks with flowers and fruit and *dulces* [sweets] for sale, and innumerable equestrians in picturesque dresses, and with spirited horses, fill up the interval between the carriages, and the canoes are covering the canal, the Indians singing and dancing lazily as the boats steal along." She added that if a visitor to Mexico ignored "the number of *léperos* busy in exercise of their vocation," the notion that "it was the most flourishing, the most contented, and the most peaceful place in the world" would not seem farfetched.[43] After a long struggle, the viceregal authorities had managed to defeat Don Carnal (Mr. Appetite) and his licenses, but inevitably, they had also provoked the irreversible decadence of Doña Cuaresma (Mrs. Lent) and her contriteness.

## Not Too Hot Nor Too Cold . . . Just Right

Carnaval was not the only popular festivity of religious origin that provoked the wrath of the civil and religious authorities. In reality, in the eighteenth century, all the religious manifestations of the common people were perceived with great reservations. It is sometimes believed that the Enlightenment was an antireligious intellectual movement. In reality, the Enlightenment, more than fighting to end the faith, imposed new religious standards. This scenario was not only present in the Western world, but very much so in Spain and its empire. There, the thinkers imbued in modern ideas proposed the reform of the church and its cult to make faith and reason completely compatible. For this purpose, it was vital to end the abuses of clerics and the superstitions of the ignorant who defiled authentic piety. The church was sympathetic to these proposals; they imposed stricter rules for the lives of religious personnel and reinforced the fight against the false beliefs of the faithful, which led them to mistake interesting frauds for real miracles.[44]

In New Spain, the first victims of this enlightened policy were evidently the common people. They saw miracles and divine intervention all around them. They believed equally in the affirmations of Catholic priests and those of witches and healers. They attended the religious rites more for their sumptuousness and festive character than because of a rational understanding of their internal meaning. The common people's conception that religious festivities were joyful celebrations that interrupted the monotony of daily life, that allowed them to escape the habitual norms of conduct, and that liberated repressed desires had to be curbed.

The goal was not to do away with popular religious festivities, but more to make them fall into line with the more spiritual devotion that, according to the new ideas, should be dominant. The internal religious sentiment was supposed to guide and limit external manifestations of worship; all activities that did not coincide with the tone of solemnity, reserve, and seriousness required of such occasions had to disappear. The religious festivals, once purified of their disorders, abuses, and superstitions—all of which represented the common people—could finally take place in strict adherence to the norms of the church and of public order.[45]

The church's attacks on these festivities had begun much earlier. After the first missionaries had fostered popular manifestations within religious ceremonies, the hierarchy of the church considered that this participation represented an infiltration of idolatrous practices into the ceremonies and as such denounced them. Since the sixteenth century, the clergy in general had proposed to put an end to the enormous consumption of alcoholic beverages that took place during these festivals, all to no avail.[46] In fact, it was the upsurge of the church's opposition to the popular forms of religious participation as well as the viceregal government's constant intervention in this area that were novel in the eighteenth century. Also, lurking behind the enlightened project to separate superstition from authentic faith lay the bourgeoisie's goal of differentiating their beliefs and values from those of the common people in order to create a new vision of their own world.[47]

In Mexico City, there were many religious festivities that, according to the enlightened thinkers, were in urgent need of reform in order to curb the disorders and abuses that characterized them. In 1784, the members of the Royal Audiencia who composed the "Informe sobre pulquerías y tabernas" (Report on pulque shops and taverns) recommended placing religious festivities under the jurisdiction of the *juez mayor* (senior judge) of the *cuartel* where they took place. With the assistance of the army and the court of the Acordada, this official would try to prevent drunkenness and other excesses. Vigilance was deemed necessary over the festivities of San Antonio Abad, San Sebastián, Nuestra Señora de la Candelaria, San Juan de Dios, the birth of Saint John the Baptist in the neighborhood named for him, San Hipólito, the Ascension of Our Lady, San Lucas, the commemoration of the Day of the Dead in the Royal Hospital and that of the Immaculate Conception in the neighborhood of Salto del Agua, as well as that of Nuestra Señora de Guadalupe in the Villa (her sanctuary), and that of the Santos Inocentes in the Church of San Hipólito.[48]

The next year, Hipólito de Villarroel wrote, in *Enfermedades políticas que padece la capital de esta Nueva España . . .* (Political illnesses that afflict the capital of New Spain . . .), a critique of the abuses that were committed during the celebration of religious events in Mexico City, and he cited some incidents. For instance, in the religious procession to celebrate the Ascension of Our Lady in the parish of Santa María, some drunken Indians, without guidance from any priests, carried out the image of the Virgin amid colossal disorder and stopped in front of balconies to show it to the residents. On another occasion, on a Friday in Lent, the Indian water carriers put crosses with candles in the streets and then later, in the afternoon, took the crosses to the *pulquerías* where they proceeded to get drunk. On the day and the evening of November 2, the Day of the Dead, people placed offerings in the Portal of the Mercaderes (merchants), large crowds congregated, and, consequently, there was much pinching and grabbing among those assembled. Also on that date, people gave each other figures of monks, clerics, and other persons made of *masa* (the ground corn used to make tortillas) and candy. During Holy Week, individuals set up stands along the routes of the procession to sell food. Finally, for the procession of Corpus Christi, the Indians built indecent arbors.[49]

Quite clearly, the festivities denounced as disorderly in these documents were either those that took place in the poor neighborhoods of the city, or at which their adherents were exclusively Indian, or finally, because of their important religious significance, were those that attracted the entire population of the city. In order to put an end to all conduct that did not reflect modesty and seriousness in these festivities, the authorities began to regulate their planning. It became necessary to seek the authorization of the church and a license from the Ayuntamiento to organize processions or dances or to install lighting. Before granting permission, the town council required assurances that all festivities would take place with the necessary "decorum and tranquillity." No fireworks—either rockets or *castillos* (a form of fireworks)—were allowed. In the case of Corpus Christi, no food stalls were permitted in the vicinity of the procession's route. For the dances, men could not mix with women. The consumption of alcoholic beverages was strictly prohibited. The festival had to end early—before the evening prayers—and could not extend for days on end, because this practice meant that artisans and public employees would not work.[50]

Although clearly all these dispositions could not be enforced with the efficiency that the officials would have desired—popular resistance was too vigorous to permit it—the measures were not abandoned. At least three religious festivities were radically reformed—temporarily or permanently—in accordance with the will of the enlightened viceregal authorities. The festival of the Virgin of the Angels was the first of the three affected by the reforms. Her church was located in the indigenous barrios of Santiago Tlaltelolco and San Miguel Nonoalco. According to the devotees of this Virgin, in 1580, during a period of floods in the city, her image appeared miraculously on a cloth. People went to her temple to seek her assistance, principally for protection from natural disasters (floods, tremors, and the like). In his book *Paisajes y leyendas* (Landscapes and legends), Ignacio Altamirano defined this Virgin as "the Madonna of the poor." On August 2, a multitude of Indians crowded the temple for very lighthearted festivities. But the ecclesiastical hierarchy began to worry about the organization of such ceremonies. The free flow of pulque on this occasion only served to confirm suspicions that this celebration had little to do with faith and much more to do with dissipation, licentiousness, superstition, and idolatry. In 1745, Archbishop Don Juan Antonio Vizarrón y Eguirreta ordered the image covered and the church closed for seven months. After this period, the intensity of the cult of the Virgin of the Angels fell off dramatically, and the church was abandoned until 1776 when, because of a strong tremor, the barrio residents remembered their former protectress. Thanks to the perseverance of a tailor who collected alms and donations, the sanctuary was rebuilt.[51]

If the disorder formally associated with this festivity reappeared, it does not seem to have lasted many years. Undoubtedly, in the last decades of the colonial period, the Indians of the *parcialidad* of Santiago Tlaltelolco were obliged to maintain the same propriety for the festival of the Virgin of the Angels as they did in the ceremony for their patron saint. The feast of the Apostle James (Santiago) was also famous for its wildness and drunkenness, but in 1778, thanks to the provisions taken by the government, these disorders ceased for both festivities. By 1784, according to the authors of the "Informe sobre pulquerías y tabernas," the celebration took place in perfect order: "There could be no larger crowd than that which assembled for the last day [of the festivity] of Santiago nor could anyone say that the least excess was noted. That enormous plaza was filled with stands of fruit and other foodstuffs distanced from the transit of the procession. Strict vigilance efficiently ensured that there were no drinks of any kind, liquors, nor pulque, and as a result not a drunk was spotted, nor was there the least difficulty."[52] At the beginning of the nineteenth century, the modest church of the Virgin of the Angels was torn down to make room for a large and sumptuous temple in a sober neoclassical style. The new building clearly reflected the religious conception that the officials wished to implant in New Spain.[53]

The second of this series of transformed festivals was the one celebrated on November 2 in the cemetery of the Royal Indian Hospital. Men, women, and children paid a nocturnal visit to this and other graveyards where festivities and intoxication took place. These events reflected the complex relationship between life and death, which remained an integral part of the beliefs of Indians, *castas*, and poor mestizos. But this festivity, which blurred the line between the living and the dead, necessarily scandalized and even horrified the enlightened elites. These intellectuals were increasingly devoid of any rites and beliefs that helped them confront the reality of death. They sought to separate it strictly from life, to exile it from society, and to forget its existence.[54]

It should come as no surprise that on October 1, 1766, the criminal court of the Royal Audiencia prohibited attendance at the cemeteries and reminded all that it was against the law to sell alcoholic beverages after nine in the evening. It is harder to ascertain to what degree this *bando* was respected. Most likely, the Day of the Dead festivities continued to take place in the usual way in the areas surrounding the city, but were altered within the city limits.[55]

It is certain, however, that at the graveyard of the Royal Indian Hospital, much more drastic measures than the previous ones were implemented with great success for several years. The hospital was an institution exclusively for New Spain's Indians. The Indians who lived in Mexico City or its barrios and neighboring towns used its services in case of illness. In the frequent epidemics of the eighteenth century, the hospital lodged large numbers of patients. In 1770, it admitted 4,529 individuals, of whom 448 died. In 1776, 3,227 passed through its doors, of whom 426 died. The mortality was higher in 1779; of the 4,198 patients, 950 passed away. Those who drew their last breath in the hospital were usually interred in its burial ground so that few Indian families in the Valley of Mexico did not have a relative or friend who was buried in this place.[56]

Despite the significance of this cemetery for the native population, the administrator of the hospital, a petty official, ordered in 1773 that they could no longer enter it, alleging: "So many people of low category entered the hospital by the main door to visit the said graveyard that they caused inconveniences and disorder in the house." The measure, which totally ignored the beliefs and sentiments of the indigenous population of the Valley of Mexico, was a violent blow for them, especially in a decade, as we have seen, of very high mortality in the hospital. Because of the simple decision of an administrator, thousands of families were separated from their deceased because their contact with them on November 2 was cut off. The Indians showed their profound displeasure by ceasing to give alms to the chaplain in charge of praying for the souls of those buried in the cemetery. The chaplain, as a result, was forced to resign.

In 1777, his successor, the *bachiller* Don José María de Neve y Romero, petitioned the viceroy for permission to open the door that joined the graveyard to Victoria Street on the Day of the Dead. The main door of the hospital would remain closed so that the staff would not be inconvenienced by the Indians' comings and goings. The *bachiller* hoped that this measure would stimulate the Indians to give some alms, at least on this day. In 1779, the viceroy denied the request because the judge of the hospitals was totally opposed to the measure, citing his reason: "Of course, some donations resulted from the masses and prayers for the dead in the cemetery of the Royal Indian Hospital on the day commemorating the dead, but the people converted Victoria Street and the surrounding area into a paseo with lunches, drunkenness, and indecencies even in the very burial ground." The judge added that if "they want masses and prayers for the dead said for the blessed souls of these Indians, the public church of the hospital is open." So, according to him, there was no reason for the Indians to stop providing alms.

The judge's last statement was extremely revealing of the abstract spirituality within the religious concepts of the enlightened thinkers of the period. The common people, in contrast, understood religion in a totally distinct manner. The *bachiller* was aware of the difference in thinking and noted that "the Indians, who are so literal that if the prayers for the dead are not given precisely when they visit and over the very graves of the dead, will not offer any donations."[57] This example is a good illustration of the opposition prevalent in the eighteenth century between popular beliefs, which were deemed superstitions by the enlightened thinkers, and the rational faith that, in contrast, they hoped to promote.

Corpus Christi was the third festival that bore the brunt of the enlightened thinkers' policies. All social groups within Mexico City and its immediate surroundings participated in the procession for the festival of Corpus Christi: the guilds, lay sodalities, religious orders, secular clergy, the Inquisition, the parishes, the ecclesiastical *cabildo*, the archbishop, the viceroy, the Audiencia, the Ayuntamiento, the university, and royal officials—all took part. The indigenous population carpeted the streets with flowers and pungent herbs and built many arches formed with twigs, flowers, and multicolored birds.

The procession began with a lively group who danced, played games, and wore masks; it was composed of Indians, mulattoes, and mestizos. Various grotesque figures were interspersed in the procession, such as the crippled *cojuelo* (devil), the giants, and above all, the *tarasca*, an enormous dragon that symbolized sin defeated by grace, which was a major attraction.[58] This particular group within the procession came to the viceregal authorities' attention because their ebullience began to contrast with the solemnity of the rest of the procession.

In 1744, the Ayuntamiento broke with previous custom and did not contract groups to perform four dances for the procession on Corpus Christi's eighth day. In past years, the dancers had arrived for their performances inebriated, their faces covered, and they had proceeded to commit various acts of disrespect.[59] Later, in 1790, Viceroy Revillagigedo the second took up the campaign to end these disorders with renewed energy. He disallowed coaches so that the procession would not be slowed down, no seats were set up along the route, the cavalry did not take part, nor the coach of honor that traditionally followed the Host. The viceroy also prohibited the presence of badly dressed individuals in the procession as well as Indians who wanted to join in with images and drums. Finally, the lively group that had led off the procession was canceled and disappeared forever from the event as it occurred in Mexico City.[60] The task of purification that the viceroy undertook was not limited to this festival. Ten days after Corpus Christi took place without the *tarasca* and the giants, the procession of the Virgin of Remedios went forward in an atmosphere of perfect order. José Gómez wrote on this subject in his strange journal: "Never before had a more serious nor more cultivated function been seen."[61]

In 1792, the custom of taking chain gangs of prisoners out to beg on Holy Thursday and Good Friday was stopped.[62] The next year, officials suppressed the traditional visit that the local populace paid to the inmates of the insane asylum of the Hospital of San Hipólito on the day of the Holy Innocents, because the visit was detrimental to the patients. The corresponding day of visitation for the patients of the Hospital of San Juan de Dios, traditionally March 8, was also discontinued.[63] Not even the procession of Holy Week escaped the zeal of this reform-minded viceroy. In 1794, José Gómez wrote in his journal: "On April 17 and 18, no armed men, nor penitents, nor the cart of death, nor any of those who ridicule the august ceremonies of our religion took part in the processions of Holy Week."[64]

Religious festivities, in particular Corpus Christi, were occasions that fostered the unity of all of the faithful and the communion of all the distinct sectors of society. The measures undertaken by the viceregal governments of the eighteenth century, however, profoundly altered this aspect of religious festivities. Some members of the congregation began to be isolated from the rest. The dead, the poorly clothed, the prisoners, and the insane ceased to take part in the religious celebrations that had traditionally made room for them. A new system of social exclusion created newly marginalized groups of people, and its effects were felt in all areas, but especially in the religious sector. Of course, the colonial Mexican authorities had succeeded in moderating the religious festivities and had turned the traditional saying—"There is no procession without a *tarasca"*—on its head.

## *Colloquia, Posadas,* **and** *Jamaicas*

If the enlightened reformers and the church had been able to translate their wishes into reality, they would have eradicated not only Carnaval but also all of the disorders associated with religious festivities. These changes would have deprived the common people of all the pleasures that liberated them from their problems and the suffering of daily life. In the second half of the eighteenth century, the exploitation of the working classes increased—the rarely mentioned other side of the coin of the mining boom and surge of wealth among the upper classes. At the same time, the government prohibited the common people from getting drunk, setting off rockets, mingling with the opposite sex in religious dances, and finally, from enjoying themselves on feast days. It was not enough that they had to work more every day, to live one on top another in the city's *vecindades* (tenements) and *arrabales* (marginal neighborhoods), to suffer increased racial discrimination, but they even had to endure all this abuse cold sober and take part in religious processions with a serious and even severe manner.

Fortunately, the power of the state was not sufficient to do away with all the little pleasures of the common people. Apart from this weakness, the resistance and stubbornness of the poor must have indeed been formidable. In any case, because of the threats, the festival retreated into the interior space of the houses and *vecindades* where the common people gave it asylum.

Given that during Shrovetide and Lent they could no longer amuse themselves freely in public spaces, the Indians, *castas,* and mestizos began to organize private *colloquia* for their family, friends, and neighbors. These festivities became common both in this period and at Christmas. The pretext of such gatherings was always to present a *colloquium*—a little play on the theme of the religious event being commemorated on that day. In theory, these parties were motivated by noble and pure intentions. One of the defenders of this practice described its advantages in the following manner: "At the same time as these diversions serve to keep the public honestly entertained and to separate them from other pernicious occupations that arise from sloth, they also contribute to remembrance of the lofty mysteries that are embraced in the redemption of humankind, because their subject matter provides a beautiful link with the principal parts of this creed."[65]

The *colloquia* first took place behind closed doors, but then were moved into the open air within the patios of the *vecindades*. Friends and families acted in the representations and then afterward, in the entrance, they served a snack, which included "baked goods, sweets, and lime water, *horchata* and *chicha* [some popular beverages]." Clearly, people who attended often drank alcoholic beverages as well. Musicians were in attendance, and the most joyful and lively dances that could be imagined followed.[66]

The *colloquia* celebrated in the days before Christmas became more and more elaborate over the course of the eighteenth century. They evolved from the sixteenth-century tradition among the indigenous population of lighting fires, singing, playing drums and bells, and settting up sumptuous Nativity scenes. It was from these customs that the famous *posadas* (type of reenactment of Christmas and party) developed.[67] During the *posadas*, the faithful carried images of the Virgin and Saint Joseph from door to door. After a couple of orations, the people went inside, and a lavish supper was served, while the boys of the village went out to ask for half-*reales*, sweets, and *bizcochos* in the stores and taverns.[68] By the end of the eighteenth century, these customs had become extremely popular and provoked the indignation of the period's moralists. In 1796, the *bachiller* Don José Mariano de Paredes denounced "these types of novena or *septenario* named *posadas* . . . in which music such as *sones* and profane songs are introduced to provoke sensuality and are just as popular in the theaters and dances of all classes of people."[69]

Despite the fact that the *colloquia* took place mostly inside houses, they did not totally escape the scrutiny and control of the authorities. The Ayuntamiento controlled the licenses needed to organize a *colloquium*. They granted permission on the condition that there would not be "more mixture of the sexes than needed for the performance"—because by this time, in decent gatherings, the women were grouped together in a separate space, apart from the men—and that no intoxicating drinks would be consumed, and, finally, that the entertainment would end at eleven o'clock at night. The gathering had to be exclusively for family and friends and the hosts could not charge "any stipend," although it was at times acceptable for the guests to chip in with a small sum at the door to cover costs. Before the event, the text of the *colloquium* had to be submitted to the officials for revision and censorship. This condition was, of course, to prevent the presentation of propositions that were contrary to faith and good customs. In some cases, in order to ensure that all these dispositions were obeyed and that good order prevailed, the *alcalde del cuartel* attended.[70]

But the vigilance of officials over these *colloquia* was not sufficient. In 1808, after the removal of Viceroy José de Iturrigaray, the archbishop petitioned the new viceroy to outlaw these festivities outright. Viceroy Pedro Garibay agreed to this request immediately and ordered the publication of a *bando* that prohibited this type of festivity. The authorities maintained the ban until 1814.[71]

The popularity of the *colloquia* gave rise after 1814 to the organization of professional paid events that took place during Shrovetide and Lent and that were open to the public. In these gatherings, religious plays alternated with other more frivolous entertainments. The *colloquia* that were put on in 1821 in the Plaza de Gallos and the Veas Alley, however, were so indecent and scandalous—and because of the gaiety that reigned—that the authorities began to frown upon them again.[72] The repression of festivities that took place in the street, however, simply meant their emergence in other spaces. After all, the people had to have fun somewhere.

In the eighteenth century, the *jamaicas* (parties to aid a charity) appeared for much the same reasons as the *colloquia* and *posadas*. These events were simply parties in which the principal entertainments were "scandalous" and "sacrilegious" dances such as: "La llorona" (The weeping woman), "El rubí" (The ruby), "El pan de manteca" (Shortening bread) or "El pan de jarabe" (Syrup bread), "Las lanchas" (The boats), "El zape" (The brush-off), "La tirana" (The tyrant), "La poblanita" (The little woman from Puebla), "Los temascales" (The sweat baths), "La vals" (The waltz), "El toro viejo" (The old bull) and "El toro nuevo" (The new bull), "El jarabe gatuno" (The cat *jarabe*), "El sacamandú," "La cosecha" (The harvest), "El animal" (The animal), "El chuchumbé," "La maturranga," "La bolera del miserere" (The song of the Miserere, or Psalm 50), "El pan de jarabe ilustrado" (The enlightened syrup bread), "Los panaderos" (The bakers), "Las bendiciones" (The blessings), "Los mandamientos" (The commandments), "Las confesiones" (The confessions), and "El pan pirulo" (The meager bread).[73]

The authorities always distrusted these parties, in particular, because it was so difficult to keep a watchful eye on such private diversions. On top of this, the *jamaicas*, unlike the *colloquia* and *posadas*, did not hide their festive goals behind a facade of piety. For this reason, while the *colloquia* were tolerated with bad grace—except for the years from 1808 to 1814—as soon as the *jamaicas* appeared, clerics attacked them from the pulpit, and the Audiencia prohibited them in a *bando* of 1761 that was reissued in 1780.[74]

According to the bishop of Oaxaca, the Devil himself was the author of the dances. According to this prelate, some "not only led people to sin but [were] also sinful in and of themselves . . . because of the lasciviousness of the lyrics, the gestures and movements of the hips, the nudity of the bodies, the mutual touching of men and women, because they take place in suspicious lower-class houses, in the countryside, and in hidden places at night, and at times when the judges cannot keep an eye on them."[75]

The enlightened thinkers also denounced these dances as shameless and immoral. In the *Viajero universal*, for instance, a passage claims: "The dances of the ordinary people are quite lubricious; their songs are analogous to the hardly decent accompaning movements."[76] The writer José Joaquín Fernández de Lizardi was much more explicit and extreme in his critique. In his famous novel, *El Periquillo Sarniento*, he wrote an extensive description of the sins which, in the eyes of decent folk, were committed in the *jamaicas*. He wrote: "Those who organize these dances . . . are pimps and shady characters of a thousand indecencies. . . . Normally, the young men who dance or, as they say, the *útiles*, are good-sized knaves; they go to dances with only two things in mind: having a good time and mockery. These jokes are nothing more than their seductions or informality. If they can, they deflower the virgin and deceive the wife, and all this is done without love but rather as a vice or simply a way to pass the time." Lizardi continued to criticize these young men. He stated, "Even when they meet with obstacles, that is to say when all the young women at a dance are judicious, honest, and modest and know how to ward off these attempts at their virtue and keep their honor intact, . . . even in these unlikely cases, these young men reach their goal. . . . They continue to skip and jump with tranquillity, content with what they call *caldo* [groping]. This *caldo* . . . beware husbands and fathers who are honorable, and wish to preserve your family name! This *caldo* consists in the gropings of your daughters and wives, the thousands of liberties taken that become hidden and furtive kisses." But Lizardi did not reprimand men only, he also reprimanded women who attended these events. He continued, "What is worse is that for many women, these gropings and grabbings, accompanied by laughter and conversations, only represent a venial sin for their soul. But these venial sins soften and prepare the soul for mortal sins, and the gropings and *caldos* of which we talk, inflame some young women and send them on the road to their own dishonor as well as that of their fathers and husbands. No scruple is too exaggerated in order to avoid these excesses."[77]

Unlike the *jamaicas*, the *saraos* were elegant and exclusive *tertulias*, accompanied by a dance—or more accurately, they were the *jamaicas* of the rich. Although a few sleep-deprived moralists criticized these events, the civil and ecclesiastical authorities never opposed them—probably because they attended regularly themselves. Obviously, the jet set did not judge their own diversions according to the same criteria they used for those of the poor.

In the second half of the eighteenth century, individuals denounced many of the popular *sones* and dances to the Inquisition. Some songs and dances came to the Holy Office's attention, because they alluded to or represented the sexual act. For example, in the "Baile de los panaderos" (Dance of the bakers), a woman came out singing:

> She really is a baker
> who doesn't indulge herself.
> Take off your underpants
> because I want to party.
> And the man answered:
> He is really a baker
> who doesn't indulge himself.
> Lift your skirts higher
> because I want to party.[78]

According to a denunciation of "El toro viejo," this song was deemed to be "crude, scandalous, profane because of the way in which persons of both sexes execute the movements without any respect for the Holy Laws. They cannot control their passions, they use their movements, actions and the most suggestive signals of the carnal act even to the point of putting their arms around each other."[79]

People reported other dances to the Inquisition because of their attacks on priests or because they denied certain dogmas of the Catholic religion. One verse from "El chuchumbé" ran:

> A Mercederian monk
> is standing on the corner
> Lifting his habit,
> showing the *chuchumbé*.
> Whether you're good
> whether you're bad
> I have to blow your *chuchumbé*.[80]

In another example, "El pan de jarabe ilustrado" included this verse:

> Now Hell is finished,
> and the devils have died;
> Now, my honey,
> we won't be condemned.[81]

The Holy Office did not pay all that much attention to these accusations and simply published more edicts that banned this type of dance. Nevertheless, these dances became more and more popular and rapidly spread from place to place. The *chuchumbé*, for example, which seems to have been imported to New Spain from Cuba, made its first appearance in Veracruz in 1766, and by 1771, people danced it in Acapulco.[82] Fondness for this profane music even invaded churches. In 1746, the *cabildo* of the cathedral contracted Ignacio Jerusalem y Stella, music master of the Coliseum, who popularized the new Italian style in Mexico City. Despite his dissolute life, in 1750, Ignacio Jerusalem was promoted from violinist and teacher of boys to the master of the chapel, a position that he held until his death in 1769. Until this time, he had not been the center of any particular scandal. In the last decades of the eighteenth century, however, someone played indecent *sones*, such as "El chuchumbé" and "El pan de manteca," on the organ during religious services. These acts provoked the indignation of some—but not all—of the faithful and the priests.[83]

The *jamaicas* were so successful that they were held in the most unexpected locations. In 1782, several laypersons partied in the Convent of Santa Isabel. There were a fandango and some *seguidillas*, during which some nuns danced to "El pan de jarabe." In 1811, people participated in a *jamaica* in the Royal Indian Hospital, much to the indignation of the judge charged with oversight of the institution.[84]

The *jamaicas'* rapid diffusion as well as the "lascivious and lubricious" quality of much of the *sones* that were danced to at these events might seem to indicate that eighteenth-century New Spain was becoming sexually liberated. Although few scholars have studied this aspect of social life, the scant bits of information available seem to prove the opposite. First of all, New Spain was never a fertile field for the imposition of the type of sexual morality that the church professed. Both the indigenous culture, which held very distinct concepts of sexuality, as well as the constant arrival of higher numbers of men than women from Spain, made that task of priests very onerous. In Guadalajara, for example, in the seventeenth century, the rate of illegitimate births was more than 50 percent of all births. Nevertheless, the situation seems to have been changing in the eighteenth century. In this period, race mixture decreased while mixed marriages increased. This strange phenomenon can be explained only by the improved organization of the church, which permitted it to exert increased pressure on unmarried couples to regularize their status.[85] Also, officials seem to have made the punishment for the crime of procuring harsher by the end of the eighteenth century.[86] Finally, they transformed the *recogimientos* for women in this period.

At their inception, *recogimientos* were entered voluntarily by single women who wished to isolate themselves from the world or wanted to lead a truly Christian life. These institutions were also where prostitutes were jailed whether they wished to reform or not. Women accused—usually by irate wives—of being in adulterous relationships and wives who were waiting for the approval of a separation or ecclesiastical divorce from their husbands were also imprisoned there. In the *recogimiento* of Belén, for example, which existed from 1686 to the mid-eighteenth century, innocent maidens lived alongside *solteras* (nonvirgin single women) and prostitutes.

In contrast, the *recogimiento* of Santa María Magdalena, which functioned from the end of the seventeenth century until Independence, began with fallen women, and ended its institutional life as a prison for women. The transition came in 1783, when the institution was reformed, new disciplinary measures were imposed, and a new practice that obliged the prisoners to work was inaugurated. Some of the crimes that were punished with time in the *recogimiento* were: adultery, debauchery, prostitution on public byways, illicit unions, and other such sexual offenses. The sentences were harsh: An old Indian woman caught selling *tepache* (an alcoholic drink) was condemned to four years of imprisonment. Luckily for her, her advanced age led to an immediate commutation and her liberation. María Dolores Peña, a Spanish woman accused of adultery, was jailed for four years; her lover was sent to the presidio of San Juan de Ulúa for eight years. Juana Rodríguez, a Spanish woman, was given a sentence of six years for having a sexual relationship with two men; and Gregoria Piedra, also a Spanish woman, spent eight years in jail for the crime of dissoluteness and being an influence of perversion on those around her.

At the turn of the eighteenth century, houses of correction for women made an appearance and were tolerated and even protected by the neighborhood alcaldes although they were not strictly legal. These houses were usually located in cheap restaurants or *atolerías* (where *atole*, a corn drink, was sold). Poor women were jailed there for a few days, usually because of unpaid debts or for having illicit relations with married men. The women were forced to work for about fifteen hours a day. Over the course of the eighteenth century, "bad" women, adulterers, and debauched individuals were no longer considered sinners who could be redeemed and brought to eternal salvation by embracing a Christian life, but began to be seen as simple delinquents or criminals who should be punished.[87]

The reality of these punishments must make any sexual liberation that seemed to emanate from the *jamaicas* rather insubstantial. In addition, the dances and *sones* were scandalous only in the eyes of the enlightened thinkers, the moralists, and the easily frightened. After all, what happened at these gatherings? Some people sang some rather daring *sones*, some couples took the opportunity to caress each other with more or less discretion. In all, it was not the end of the world. In fact, the person who denounced the dance of "El toro viejo," which I cited previously, thought that the epitome of daring was reached when the dancing couple intertwined their arms. It seems far-fetched that the common people of the city and countryside only began, in the latter half of the eighteenth century, to allow their young folk to have some minimal sexual experience—such as the "furtive palpations" of the dances—before marriage or illicit unions. Also, the European peasantry of the sixteenth through eighteenth centuries—who did not have a reputation for lasciviousness—allowed their young, men and women, a much greater latitude in sexual experience than can be discerned in the accusations regarding the colonial Mexican *jamaicas*.[88]

The real novelty of the *jamaicas*, along with the *colloquia* and the *posadas*, was that it marked the start of the privatization of popular diversions. Ironically, the result of the repressive measures instituted by the civil and ecclesiastical officials against the religious festivities that had formed the diversions of the people was that these entertainments retreated into less public spaces where vigilance and control could not be so effective or strict. More than one person must have thought that since the Ayuntamiento, the viceroy, and the church had made it so difficult to go and dance for the Virgin, it was better to stay in the neighborhood and dance with that dark beauty who lived nearby.

# Pulques, *Tepaches*, and *Chinguiritos*

On December 31, 1771, Inspector General José de Gálvez reported to newly installed Viceroy Bucareli on the state of the Royal Treasury: "Nor are there sufficient judges in the criminal and the ordinary courts to verify the innumerable abuses of the *pulquerías*, which are the real center and originating point of all the crimes and public sins that overwhelm this numerous population."[89] Some historians concur with the inspector general and make a connection between the breakdown of customs in the eighteenth century and the consumption of alcohol. They take for granted that the level of alcoholism increased over the course of the century.[90]

The whole idea that New Spain in general and Mexico City in particular underwent a period of profound moral decay in the eighteenth century must be reconsidered. It is vital to examine the situation of intoxicating drinks in Mexico City at the end of the colonial period. Pulque, especially, is worthy of attention because it was the beverage with the highest level of consumption among the common people.

Was there really an increase in its consumption in the latter half of the eighteenth century? Was there also a concurrent rise in the drinking of the so-called prohibited drinks? Did *pulquerías* change into important centers of sociability, from which a popular culture in opposition to that of the elite and the enlightened governors emerged? How did the policy of the officials change in regard to the *pulquerías* and in what way?

Officialdom's preoccupation with the excessive consumption of pulque and other alcoholic drinks did not begin in the eighteenth century; it emerged shortly after the completion of the conquest of New Spain. Pulque and its regulation have a long history, of which the eighteenth century is but one part. Both must be placed in the context of this longer history in order to answer the questions posed above.

**I.** The pulque consumed in Mexico City was produced in haciendas located to the east, north, and west of the city. Muleteers transported it to the *pulquerías*, open-air stands located in little plazas only a few yards away from the walls of nearby houses.[91] Open on three sides, the *pulquerías* were protected from the rain by a roof of shingles. Barrels and basins of pulque, covered with big planks of wood, sat under these precarious constructions. Clients drank their pulque from gourds and earthenware pots. Apart from the pure, white pulque, other customers bought pulque *curado*—mixed with other substances such as lime, meat, orange or apple peel, or melon. Pulque had to be sold very quickly because it went bad after only three or four days.

At the beginning, women managed *pulquerías* exclusively. The stands opened early because they were obliged to close at sunset. At first, they were not permitted to serve any drinks before one in the afternoon on days of festivals—which were the days of greatest demand—but this rule was constantly violated.[92]

Pulque was very inexpensive. The price of three *cuartillos*, about 1.5 liters of the fine pulque, or five *cuartillos*, or 2.5 liters of the ordinary was a half real. There are some indications that the price rose toward the end of the eighteenth century because of rising taxation. In 1806, although the authorized price was for three *cuartillos* of the fine or four of the ordinary, many vendors gave only one and half *cuartillos* of the medium for this price.[93]

In 1724, the rules obliged *pulquerías* to have a name written on a sign located on their principal facade. Many of their names referred to the location, the owner, or to places in Spain or New Spain. However, many other names were more picturesque, such as "Sancho Panza," "Maravilla," "Juanico the Monster," and "Tumba Burros."[94]

Pulque dates back to the pre-Hispanic period. According to some historians, it was not consumed on a daily basis but rather was associated with certain religious ceremonies.[95] Whether pulque was a solely ritual drink then or not, after the Conquest, it became common among the entire indigenous population of New Spain. Mestizos, *castas*, and poor Spaniards also developed a taste for this alcoholic drink, as it was by far the cheapest available.

All the poor residents of the city frequented the *pulquerías*. "Persons of honor and decency" who were aficionados of the white liquid (most probably a minuscule group) could not patronize the *pulquerías* without the risk of dishonor, because the area around the few *pulquerías* was constituted as the exclusive space of the common people.[96] In these locations, large crowds of men and women congregated to drink, especially on days of compulsory attendance at mass and for the barrio-level religious festivals. Despite numerous prohibitions, vendors sold not only the white, pure pulque but also pulque mixed with herbs and roots and even peyote, which gave the drink a much greater kick. In another common violation of the rules, merchants set up food stands—sometimes even cheap restaurants—close to the *pulquerías* and sent food over to the drinkers. Musicians, with harps and guitars, played in the vicinity, and thus impromptu dances broke out in the middle of public streets. Sometimes, after the vast quantity of pulque consumed, tempers flared and fights erupted, which at times led to violent bloodshed. According to the authorities, the immoderate consumption of pulque and the other prohibited drinks led to such sexual transgressions as adultery and incest.[97]

To the viceregal officials, the *pulquerías* were dangerous not only because they seemed to be permanent centers of vice, disorder, crimes, and sins, but also simply because of the large numbers of the common people who congregated there. Among the authorities, they provoked a fear that the flames of subversive action could be kindled in their midst. At the same time, however, pulque was one of the principal sources of revenue for the Royal Treasury and an important moneymaker for the various estate owners. The government could not therefore contemplate any measures that would end or even diminish its consumption. It could only try to limit some of the many disorderly incidents that occurred in the *pulquerías*. Even so, in the second half of the eighteenth century, the preoccupation with increasing the revenues derived from pulque for the Royal Treasury canceled out the desire to combat the disorders. Thus, for a better understanding of these contradictory poles of official wishes, it is necessary to examine the importance of pulque within the Royal Treasury and the changes it underwent over the course of the colonial period.

**II.** Shortly after the conquest of the Aztecs, the Spanish noticed with alarm the indigenous practice of mixing pulque with various herbs and roots, causing an effect unknown to the Iberians. The conquerors began to take measures against the consumption of such drinks as early as 1529.[98] Although scholars have stated at times that the Crown disallowed not only mixed pulque but the white, pure variety in the sixteenth and early seventeenth centuries, in fact, unadulterated pulque was not only tolerated but also produced, transported, sold, and consumed freely. In addition, in 1608, Viceroy Velasco issued some dispositions that specified that all matters related to pulque should be managed by the Indians. In 1648, a commission of judges of pulque under the authority of the *corregidor* was created in Mexico City. By the 1650s, 212 *pulquerías* existed in the capital.[99]

In the 1650s, Viceroy Duke of Albuquerque gave Mexico City's Ayuntamiento the right to collect taxes on the pulque brought into the city. The Crown only discovered the existence of this duty and the amount collected—which rose to 40,000 pesos a year—a few years later in 1663. According to the report sent to Spain, the revenue from this scheme of taxation could easily reach 140,000 or 150,000 pesos annually.[100] The discovery of this unsuspected and promising source of revenue for the Royal Treasury made the Crown reconsider and repeal its traditional opposition to pulque. Many new virtues for this drink were discovered. The new position is evident in this affirmation that "the beverages [being] so common and well known for being healthy and medicinal such as this one, there does not seem to be any reason to ban it, and even with a light color such as when people abuse it, even so, this does not cause anything more than an increase in quantity but not the quality of the drink." The author added that if such a reason could be invoked, wine from Castile would also have to be outlawed.

In any case, the Crown solicited information from the viceroy as to whether pulque "caused the Indians more drunkenness than wine, if, from this drink, they engaged in public sins and other insults to the service of God" before coming to a decision on the matter of the new tax. In addition, the competition with the sales of wine from Andalusia and its benefits were another area of concern.[101]

On July 14, 1664, the *corregidor* of Mexico City, Don Francisco Sáinz Izquierdo, ordered that all the pulque in the city be thrown out. Despite this antagonistic act, the information that reached the king's ears must have been favorable, because, in 1665, the order came that all taxes collected on pulque would be remitted to Spain. In December 1668, the monopoly on this new branch of the Royal Treasury was publicly sold at auction.[102]

The straightforward authorization of pulque and the imposition of a tax on the drink brought angry protests, especially from the clergy. Around 1668, the viceroy wrote to the queen regent: "The uproar began to resonate and some of your subjects of noted virtue came to ask for a remedy for the grave insults and sins that resulted from the abuse of this drink, and although you charged the *corregidor* with the necessary warnings to amend these serious disturbances, the excesses did not cease nor the perplexity of these people, zealous in the service of God, who went on to publish proclamations from the pulpit."[103] Doctor Pedraza, a clergyman, even affirmed that he had seen the devil in a *pulquería*.[104]

In 1671, the bishop of Puebla wrote to the queen to explain that the new tax had very critical effects on the indigenous population. "Deserting their houses," these poor souls "went out into the streets to seek a remedy causing great extremes of sentiment."[105] Before such a deluge of protests, the queen had second thoughts about her decision's justness. She authorized the viceroy to close the *pulquerías* if the disorders continued and to decrease the tax that the Indians paid if he believed this measure to be expedient. The viceroy did not close the pulque stands, but he did lower the tax paid by the indigenous population.[106]

The Spanish Crown's indecision could not last very long. In 1693, as a result of a rebellion the previous year, the viceroy banned the sale and consumption of pulque in Mexico City. The king energetically condemned this measure and lifted the general prohibition, leaving only a restriction on yellow pulque, which was fortified with slaked lime, and on any other mixed pulque. In the royal order, the king asserted that the connection between the rebellion and the ingestion of pulque was tenuous, because this beverage was "very beneficial to the temperament and character of these Indians." Even the Protomedicato (the medical guild) had qualified it as "of intrinsic goodness without intervening mixtures or any additions." Its absolute interdiction could force the indigenous population to "use other substances that might result in a greater evil," without even considering "the devastation that the lack of earnings would cause to many Indian villages that grew magueys." Above all, "the loss that the Royal Treasury" would suffer "of the duty applied to such an important end as the maintenance of the armada of Barlovento" was a most salient argument to allow the pulque trade to continue.[107]

The viceroy, who was probably still trembling from the fright the rebellion gave him, did not obey the monarch's order, alleging that pulque was not imbibed in its pure form "nor could it be preserved without additions." It was, therefore, necessary to maintain the ban. Thus, the king had to reiterate his authorization of white pulque in a royal order of June 3, 1697. To clarify the question of whether pulque could be conserved without additives, he asked for the opinions of the Protomedicato. This body, after a few brief experiments, concluded that white pulque lasted in good condition for four days in winter and three in summer. Therefore the sale and consumption of pulque were once again permitted.[108]

The fact that the interests of finance prevailed over moral considerations was made even clearer in 1723. A Mercedarian monk tried to publish a tract in opposition to pulque. Viceroy Juan de Acuña forbade its publication and ordered the confiscation of the manuscript. The king approved the viceroy's measure the following year.[109] Because of the constant violations of the regulations and the frequent disorders in the *pulquerías*, in 1747, the Crown ordered Viceroy Revillagigedo the first to take various measures to end these abuses. At the end of this royal provision, the sovereign, without apparent fear of contradiction, also asked that the pulque industry be developed and expanded, although clearly "without any prejudice of the public cause."[110]

The king's concern for the branch of the Royal Treasury that oversaw taxes on pulque is easily understood. Upon its creation in 1668, the officials believed that taxes on pulque would easily produce between 140,000 and 150,000 pesos annually in the capital alone. After nearly a century, these optimistic numbers had not been reached. The stagnation in revenues from pulque was caused in part by the general growth of taxation on the beverage. Since the inception of taxation on pulque, each load cost twelve reales upon entering the city. But the practice of auctioning off contracts for the collection of pulque taxes to individuals was also to blame for the decline in revenues derived from pulque. Both these practices proved to be unfavorable to the royal finances. Since 1734 the value of the pulque monopoly had not increased; in fact, it had slightly decreased (see Table 1).

**Table 1: Contractors for the Pulque Monopoly, Mexico City (1668–1763)**

| Years | Contractors | Annual income (in pesos) |
|---|---|---|
| 1668 | Directly administered by León Dalza | 83,445[a] |
| 1669–1671 | Alonso de Flores de la Sierra y Valdés | 66,000 |
| 1671–1673 | Roque Alonso de Valverde[b] | 66,000[c] |
| 1674–1676 | Alonso de Narváez | 73,000 |
| 1677–1679 | Alonso de Narváez | 86,000 |
| 1680–1683 | Roque Alonso de Valverde | 95,000 |
| 1683–1688 | Juan Domingo de la Rea[d] | 95,000 |
| 1689–1692 | Juan Domingo de la Rea | 97,000 |
| | (Prohibition of pulque following the rebellion) | |
| 1698–1705 | Juan Domingo de la Rea and Juan Clavería | 70,000 |
| 1707–1709 | Juan Domingo de la Rea and Juan Clavería | 75,000[e] |
| 1709–1716 | Juan Antonio de Viar and Juan Clavería[f] | 100,000 |
| 1716–1725 | Juan Gutiérrez Rubín de Celis | 90,000 |
| 1725–1734 | Juan Esteban de Iturbide | 121,000 |
| 1734–1735 | Juan Esteban de Iturbide[g] | 130,000 |
| 1735–1743 | Sebastián de Ariburu Arechaga | 130,000 |
| 1743–1752 | Manuel Rodríguez Pedroso[h] | 128,500 |
| 1752–1757 | Jacinto Martínez de Aguirre[i] | 128,500 |
| 1757–1763 | Juan Manuel de Astiz[j] | 128,500 |

[a]This administration only lasted from September to December and collected 27,815 pesos. The annual income was calculated by taking the monthly average earnings and multiplying this figure by twelve.

ᵇAlonso Flores de la Sierra ceded him the monopoly.

ᶜAccording to José Jesús Hernández Palomo, *El aguardiente de caña en México (1724–1810)* (Seville, 1979), pp. 48 and 54–55, Alonso de Narváez obtained the monopolies of Mexico City and Puebla jointly for 92,000 pesos yearly from 1674 to 1676 and for 105,000 yearly from 1677 to 1679. Previously, the Puebla monopoly had been auctioned for 17,000 annually and in 1680, it was auctioned for 20,500 pesos. In order to calculate the amount corresponding to the Mexico City monopoly, I assigned a value of 19,000 pesos annually for the Puebla monopoly.

ᵈJuan Domingo de la Rea took over the monopoly upon the death of his father-in-law.

ᵉThe term auctioned of 1680 was for nine years. The monopolists agreed to pay 70,000 pesos for the first seven years and 75,000 for the remaining two years.

ᶠJuan Antonio de Viar took over after Juan Domingo de la Rea died in 1709.

ᵍJuan Esteban de Iturbide died in 1735. Fabián de Fonseca and Carlos de Urrutia, *Historia general de la Real Hacienda* (Mexico City, 1978) vol. III, p. 360, affirm that the moment of his death, the value of the monopoly was 147,000 pesos.

ʰFonseca and Urrutia, vol. III, p. 361 say that the monopolist was Sebastián de Ariburu Arechaga.

ⁱJosé Manuel de Castro Santa-Anna, "Diario de sucesos notables escrito por . . ." In *Documentos para la historia de México* (Mexico City, 1854), vol. VI, p. 158, affirms that Jacinto Martínez de Aguirre died on July 27, 1757.

ʲJuan Esteban de Iturbide died in 1735. Fonseca and Urrutia, vol. III, p. 360, affirm that at the moment of his death, the value of the monopoly was 147,000 pesos.

*Sources*: José Jesús Hernández Palomo, *El aguardiente de caña en México (1724–1810)* (Seville, 1979), pp. 44–45, 53–57, 60, 82, 123–124, 277, 412, 453, 456, 460, 465, 466, and 469. I have compared these figures with those which Fabián de Fonseca and Carlos de Urrutia, *Historia general de la Real Hacienda* (Mexico City, 1978), provide and in general, there are no major divergence. The numbers furnished by Manuel Payno, *Memorias sobre el maguey mexicano y sus diversos productos,* (Mexico City, 1864), pp. 93–94, and José María Marroqui, *La ciudad de México* (Mexico City, 1900–1903), vol. I., pp. 199–200, are quite different and are not at all reliable. José Manuel de Castro Santa-Anna, "Diario de sucesos notables escrito por . . ." In *Documentos para la historia de México* (Mexico City, 1854), vol. VI, p. 158, provides information on the monopoly for the years from 1752 to 1757.

For this reason, in 1761, the Crown decided to give in to the prevailing norms and allow pulque taxes to be administered directly by the Royal Treasury. From February 1763, the revenues from pulque flourished. Under the new system, revenues doubled, compared to the period when individuals under contract collected these taxes. This surge in revenues occurred despite the fact that the territory of the monopoly had included an area of five leagues around the city and the jurisdiction of Texcoco, while the new arrangement covered only Mexico City.[111] On the other hand, the growth in revenue happened when the tax on pulque was raised by nearly 60 percent. Officially, the tax went from twelve reales a *carga* (load) to one real per *arroba*. Because a *carga* was the equivalent of twelve *arrobas*, in effect the taxload was not raised. But, in the pulque industry of this period, a *carga* had eighteen *arrobas*.[112] Also, for some strange reason, the tax collected at the city entrance was one real and two-thirds *grano* (see Table 2).[113]

**Table 2: Taxation of Pulque Entering Mexico City (1668–1810)**

| | |
|---|---|
| From 1668 to 1762: | 12 reales per *carga*.[a] |
| From 1763 to 1766: | 1 real, 2/3 *grano* per *arroba* or 12.66 *granos* per *arroba*. |
| From 1767 to 1776: | 1 real, 1 *grano*, 1/6 *grano* per *arroba* or 13.16 *granos* per *arroba*. |
| In 1777: | 1 real, 4 *granos* per *arroba* or 16 *granos* per *arroba*. |
| From 1778 to 1779: | 1 real, 5 *granos* per *arroba* or 17 *granos* per *arroba*. |
| From 1780 to 1783: | 1 real, 11 *granos* per *arroba* or 23 *granos* per *arroba*. |
| From 1784 to 1810: | 2 reales, 1 *grano* per *arroba* or 25 *granos* per *arroba*. |

[a]Generally, a *carga* was equivalent to 12 *arrobas*, but in the eighteenth century, a *carga* of pulque was composed of 18 *arrobas*.
*Source*: "Informe sobre pulquerías y tabernas del año de 1784," *Boletín del AGN* 8:2 (1947):230–232 and 8:3 (1947):378; Fabián de Fonseca and Carlos de Urrutia, *Historia general de la Real Hacienda* (Mexico City, 1978) vol. 3, p. 423.

Encouraged by the increased income derived from its direct administration of taxation in Mexico City, the Royal Treasury started to take over control of all the other monopolies of pulque in New Spain.[114] The king then charged his officials with the promotion of the sale of this beverage, with the proviso, of course, that it should be "without prejudice of the precautions against rebellions."[115] In 1767, officials raised the pulque tax very slightly to one *tomin*, one *grano* and one-sixth of a *grano* per *arroba*.[116] From 1772, the income derived from pulque rose rapidly (see Tables 3 and 4). Until then, the Crown had considered the growth of the income derived from pulque taxation and the conservation of order and public morals in New Spain difficult to reconcile. Seemingly, only an expansion of the vigilance over and control of *pulquerías* could prevent the escalation of consumption that, in turn, would lead to disorder, sin, and crime. The Crown was determined that moral considerations would not stand in the way of the growth of income and so it had to reinforce and improve the mechanisms of repression that regulated the *pulquerías*. Until then, such controls had not had much effect. Despite the regulation and increased policing, disorders still erupted daily.

In 1771, Inspector General Gálvez proposed a measure that, according to him, would increase the treasury income derived from pulque while at the same time reducing the consumption of the drink and thus contributing to the public order. Gálvez believed that the reason for the excessive imbibing of pulque was its low price: "Because the half-real is the coin of least value, and for it, a

**Table 3: Pulque Taxation in New Spain (1765–1821)**

| Year | Income (in thousands of pesos) | Year | Income (in thousands of pesos) |
|------|------|------|------|
| 1765 | 378 | 1793 | 851 |
| 1766 | 352 | 1794 | 801 |
| 1767 | 479 | 1795 | 756 |
| 1768 | 341 | 1796 | 827 |
| 1769 | 367 | 1797 | 850 |
| 1770 | 361 | 1798 | 833 |
| 1771 | 349 | 1799 | 815 |
| 1772 | 376 | 1800 | 835 |
| 1773 | 424 | 1801 | 817 |
| 1774 | 433 | 1802 | 753 |
| 1775 | 469 | 1803 | 731 |
| 1776 | 488 | 1804 | 709 |
| 1777 | 523 | 1805 | 678 |
| 1778 | 734 | 1806 | 678 |
| 1779 | 835 | 1807 | 712 |
| 1780 | 862 | 1808 | 681 |
| 1781 | 958 | 1809 | 659 |
| 1782 | 996 | 1810 | 562 |
| 1783 | 1,016 | 1811 | 485 |
| 1784 | 1,047 | 1812 | 250 |
| 1785 | 946 | 1813 | 261 |
| 1786 | 713 | 1814 | 312 |
| 1787 | 715 | 1815 | 333 |
| 1788 | 878 | 1816 | 316 |
| 1789 | 834 | 1817 | 355 |
| 1790 | 879 | 1818 | 377 |
| 1791 | 849 | 1819 | 326 |
| 1792 | 870 | 1820 | 334 |
|      |     | 1821 | 267 |

*Source*: Manuel Payno, *Memorias sobre el maguey mexicano y sus diversos productos* (Mexico City, 1864), pp. 93–94. Fabián de Fonseca and Carlos de Urrutia, *Historia general de la Real Hacienda* (Mexico City, 1978), vol. 3, pp. 423–424, also provide a series on the income produced within the pulque sector of the Treasury of New Spain from 1765 to 1790. The figures are slightly lower than those presented by Payno. A systematic comparison between the figures for Mexico City provided by Fonseca and Urrutia, vol. 3, p. 423, and José Jesús Hernández Palomo, *El aguardiente de caña en México (1724–1810)* (Seville, 1979), pp. 369–370, makes those which Payno cites seem more likely. Hernández Palomo, pp. 369-370, found information for the years 1702 to 1810 in the Archivo General de Indias. Nevertheless, his own figures for Mexico City make these seem farcical. In 1786 and 1787, the income collected for all of New Spain is less than that collected in Mexico City. It is obvious that some of the reports from the rest of New Spain are missing in the Spanish archive.

customer is given up to five *cuartillos* of pulque, no one has to do without." He proposed to increase the tax sharply so as to also raise the price of pulque and thus wean the public from its habit of

**Table 4: Pulque Taxation in Mexico City (1763–1820)**

| Year | Income (in thousands of pesos) | Year | Income (in thousands of pesos) |
|------|--------------------------------|------|--------------------------------|
| 1763 | 247 | 1792 | 511 |
| 1764 | 269 | 1793 | —— |
| 1765 | 257 | 1794 | 452 |
| 1766 | 245 | 1795 | 426 |
| 1767 | 250 | 1796 | 459 |
| 1768 | 246 | 1797 | 471 |
| 1769 | 252 | 1798 | 443 |
| 1770 | 237 | 1799 | 431 |
| 1771 | 232 | 1800 | 451 |
| 1772 | 233 | 1801 | 437 |
| 1773 | 283 | 1802 | —— |
| 1774 | 304 | 1803 | —— |
| 1775 | 339 | 1804 | —— |
| 1776 | 366 | 1805 | —— |
| 1777 | 457 | 1806 | 284 |
| 1778 | 511 | 1807 | 298 |
| 1779 | 529 | 1808 | 285 |
| 1780 | 531 | 1809 | 276 |
| 1781 | 624 | 1810 | 283 |
| 1782 | 647 | 1811 | 263 |
| 1783 | 636 | 1812 | 98 |
| 1784 | 654 | 1813 | 119 |
| 1785 | 585 | 1814 | 179 |
| 1786 | 418 | 1815 | 202 |
| 1787 | 415 | 1816 | 140 |
| 1788 | 511 | 1817 | 177 |
| 1789 | 486 | 1818 | 167 |
| 1790 | 485 | 1819 | 172 |
| 1791 | 491 | 1820 | 138 |

*Sources*: Fabián de Fonseca and Carlos de Urrutia, *Historia general de la Real Hacienda* (Mexico City, 1978), p. 423 and José Jesús Hernández Palomo, *El aguardiente de caña en México (1724–1810)* (Seville, 1979), pp. 369–370 and 428. Various scholars have elaborated series of figures for the amount of pulque which entered Mexico City. Fonseca and Urrutia's series goes from February 1763 to June 1791. Hernández Palomo found data in the Archivo General de Indias which allowed him to construct a series from 1702 to 1801. The numbers presented in these two series are identical except for the period from 1767 to 1776. In that interval, Hernández Palomo's numbers are slightly lower than those of the other authors. The difference between the two is exactly a half grano per arroba. As such, the difference must be explained by the absence in the Archivo General de Indias of information regarding the tax recently imposed for the clothing of the military. This tax was in place from 1767 to 1776. For this reason, I chose to follow the figures of Fonseca and Urrutia for this interval. After 1791, I used those offered by Hernández Palomo because they are the only ones available. For the period from 1806 to 1820, I used those that Hernández Palomo found in the Archivo General de la Nación because, once again, they are the only ones available.

excessive consumption. Despite this measure, the inspector general also recommended that the "Royal Treasury should hire an adequate number of officials and employees who would monitor the *pulquerías* and squelch the excessive number of *tepacherías*."[117]

Local authorities put the advice of the inspector general into practice. Despite the fact that the level of taxation on pulque was already quite high—it represented approximately a quarter of the final price—in 1777, the tax was increased to one real, four *granos*; in 1778, it was further elevated to one real, five *granos*; in 1780, it went to one real, eleven *granos*; and in 1784, it reached two reales, one *grano* (see Tables 1 and 2). In the space of twenty years, the tax on pulque rose more than 100 percent. For this reason, in 1784, the taxes collected on pulque when it entered the city were slightly higher than the price paid to the producer.[118]

At first, the income derived from the sale of pulque increased very rapidly (see Tables 3 and 4). The general improvement of the fiscal structure of New Spain certainly played a part in this growth also. From 1784—the year of the last tax hike—the rise in income from this sector stagnated, and the amount of taxes collected each year began to decrease considerably. At first glance, it seems obvious that the plunge in revenues was linked to excessive taxation that affected the price and thus caused a decline in the demand for pulque. In fact, a similar phenomenon took place in many other areas of colonial Mexican production. The exorbitant tax burden began to drown the colonial economy.[119]

Apparently the policy inspired by Gálvez was successful. The Royal Treasury's coffers swelled while, at the same time, the consumption of pulque diminished. After 1786, however, the decline in drinking habits began to affect the royal income negatively. The collection of taxes descended to levels below those attained since 1778 (see Table 4). Undoubtedly, Alexander de Humboldt, who traveled in New Spain from 1803 to 1804, based his observations upon this set of circumstances. He asserted: "The desire of increasing the revenues of the Crown occasioned latterly a heavy tax on the fabrication of pulque, equally vexatious and inconsiderate. It is time to change the system in this respect, otherwise this cultivation, one of the most ancient and lucrative, will decline, notwithstanding the decided predilection of the people for the fermented juice of the maguey."[120] The economic growth that characterized the eighteenth century was coming to an end all over New Spain.

**III.** Not only did the Crown obtain succulent profits from the sale and consumption of pulque but the large-scale producers also made their fortunes in this trade. These large-scale producers were practically all *hacendados* (members of the landed class) who were involved in all stages of the business; they planted magueys, processed the juice, and organized the transport and sale of the pulque. In the eighteenth century, the production of the white liquor became a lucrative enterprise that attracted capital investment.

Interestingly enough, many of the powerful figures who invested in this business already had or were granted titles of nobility. The Count of Jala, the Marchioness of Herrera, the Count of Tepa, the Count of Medina y Torres, the Marquis of Castañiza, the Count of Bassoco, the Marquis of Bibanco, the Viscount of Bolaños, and the Count of Regla were just some of the notables involved in the pulque trade.[121] After all, if the Old World aristocracy owned large and reputable vineyards, why should the nobility of New Spain not acquire pulque estates?

Many of these pulque aristocrats had plebeian origins and had made their fortunes in commerce or mining during the eighteenth century. It was only after they had amassed their wealth that they purchased titles of nobility and bought their pulque estates. In this way, the Count of Jala, the Marquis of Castañiza, and the Count of Bassoco became rich through commerce and then bought their titles, respectively, in 1749, 1772, and 1811. In contrast, the Count of Regla and the Marquis of Bibanco, as well as the Viscount of Bolaños, made their fortunes in mining and acquired their titles in 1768 and 1791 respectively.[122]

The practice of investing capital derived from mines or trade into large estates was a common pattern in New Spain. Apparently, the supposed economic security of landholding as well as the inherent social prestige associated with land seems to explain the phenomenon. In reality, the haciendas were often burdened with mortgages and drowning under taxes that gobbled up the wealth of two or three generations of these families.[123] Possibly, the pulque estates were simply an exception to this pattern; instead of being the bane of such fortunes, they were a boon to them.

In any case, these estates had created complex production structures that responded to the sharp oscillations of the market in agricultural products and still managed to reap huge financial rewards. Rarely were the pulque estates characterized by maguey monoculture, but rather, other plants such as corn, beans, barley, fava beans, and peas were sown between the rows of cacti. Livestock of many types was also usually raised on these estates. The harvests from these activities were often used on the estates but some were sold.

In this manner, the owners of these estates protected themselves from the fluctuations of the market; they sold when conditions were favorable and consumed their harvests when there was no market.[124]

Even the market for pulque fluctuated. Although the estates were close to the largest center of consumption—Mexico City—this market rose and fell sharply. Moreover, pulque had to be sold expeditiously or spoil. It was for this reason that the large estates always tried to control the stands where pulque was sold in order to ensure the proper functioning of their enterprise. All pulque aristocrats noted above also owned one or more *pulquerías* in Mexico City.

In 1782, the Count of Jala rented his three *pulquerías* (the Pacheco, Bello, and Las Maravillas). The tenants pledged to buy all the pulque produced on the lands of the estates of the Count of Jala at the price of twenty-one reales for a *carga* in the period from October to June. In the months of July, August, and September, however, when pulque production diminished, and hence the demand and price rose, the Count was obliged to sell only 210 *cargas* a week, with the remaining pulque sold to the highest bidder. In this way, the Count of Jala guaranteed the sale of all his production without losing the opportunity to speculate during the months of scarcity.[125] This need to control the sale of pulque provides an explanation for a bitter lawsuit that took place in the 1780s among some of the competing pulque aristocrats.

Toward 1781, the consumption of pulque began to decline in Mexico City, and for that, it was vital to guarantee the markets for the produce of their estates. Don Antonio Bassoco, the Count of Jala, and the Marquis of Catañiza obtained licenses to open new *pulquerías*. The Count of Tepa, who at this time was a counsellor and member of the Council of Indies but also the owner of several *pulquerías*, was alarmed at the sudden increase in competition. He argued that these licenses violated the rules and asked the king to destroy these new stands. The other pulque estate owners defended their rights in a lawsuit against the Count of Tepa, which lasted until 1794. The new *pulquerías* remained open in the interim. The eventual verdict against the Count of Tepa was probably due, not to the impeccable logic of the plaintiffs, but rather to the fact that they were not only the owners of large pulque estates but also rich and influential merchants. The Count of Tepa's original charge that these new *pulquerías* broke the law was clear, but the power of money nullified the ordinances designed to promote public order.[126]

**IV.** In fact, the economic interests of both the Crown and the *hacendados* depended upon a deeply rooted appetite of the common people for pulque. Thus, regulations concerning this beverage were designed not so much to end its consumption, nor even to diminish it, but rather to control as much as possible the disorders it caused. Two bureaucrats in the Royal Treasury, Fonseca and Urrutia, defined the objectives of the Crown's policy in this way: "Despite its medicinal qualities as a product of the region, [pulque] has, as the result of its abuse, become the origin of an infinite number of crimes and illnesses, to such a degree that the religious zeal of our august monarchs, not able to extinguish it, has led to sound ordinances to suffocate them." They reiterated the contradiction in royal policy caused by the profits derived from pulque coupled with a concern for the social consequences of abuse of the alcoholic beverage. They stated: "In effect, an effort has been made to reconcile the removal of these excesses by means of these regulations, for the benefit of the Indians, and the advantage of the Royal Treasury. Public magistrates will continue to promote the vigilance, exactitude, and care of all the ministers charged with the growth of the royal patrimony."[127]

From the outset, the monarchs dispatched many orders whose goal was to prevent the disorders caused by drunkenness. The first recorded laws of 1529, 1545, and 1607 had as their main objective the prohibition of intoxicating beverages such as *tepache, vingui, cuarapo*, yellow pulque, and pulque that was mixed with roots, herbs, or other ingredients. Apparently, these drinks produced real frenzies in those who imbibed them.[128] Although the white, unadulterated pulque was not explicitly permitted, it was tolerated, and no restrictions or regulations hampered its sale or consumption.

It was only in 1608 that Viceroy Velasco put into effect some ordinances that, with the objective of doing away with the mixed pulque, explicitly allowed the consumption of pure, white pulque. These ordinances permitted one elderly Indian woman from every hundred Indians to sell pulque. They also limited the number of pulque vendors to one hundred and fifty persons in the city. The price was fixed at half a real for two *cuartillos*. Spaniards, mestizos, and *castas* were not allowed to produce or sell pulque. In 1629, Viceroy Cerralvo ordered the population to obey these ordinances. The viceroy also reiterated the rules in 1653.[129] At the beginning of the 1650s, Viceroy Count of Alva de Liste limited the number of *pulquerías* operating in Mexico City to fifty.[130]

In the 1660s, the enactment of a tax on pulque as it entered the city as well as the creation of the Pulque Branch of the Royal Treasury stimulated the composition in rapid succession of new ordinances on intoxicating drinks in 1671. These ordinances, which served as a model during the colonial period for all subsequent regulations on pulque, were composed of eight sections. The first section was a reminder of the prohibition of all mixed-pulque drinks; the second asked the church to strengthen the campaign against these drinks by threatening both producers and their clients with divine retribution; the third clarified that only the sale of pure, white pulque was permitted.

These first three sections of the ordinances of 1671 only repeated the previous dispositions. Innovations began in the fourth section. In this section, it was ordered that "the pulque stands must be separate from the walls and houses and must not have more than the roof and one solid wall to protect from the sun and the air, leaving all other three sides open so that the activities inside can be observed and noted from outside." The fifth section ordered that "there should be no contact between men and women who drink in the doorways, nor where they sit down to eat, nor should too many people congregate there, nor should they stay around after they have drunk, nor should there be harps, guitars, or other musical instruments, dances, or musicians." The sixth section indicated that the pulque stands should close at sunset.

In fact, these three sections formed the core of the new regulations. They were evidently not designed to do away with the excessive consumption of pulque but rather to destroy one of the meeting places of the common people. Any success depended upon the ease of oversight of the *pulquerías*, which would prevent the sale and consumption of drinks in stands that were supposed to be closed. The scheduled hours imposed on the *pulquerías* coincided with the workday and so, at least in theory, artisans and other workers were prevented from congregating there. In this way, the officials hoped to prevent the *pulquerías* from becoming, or most probably from continuing to serve as, an important meeting place for the plebeians. Because the lower classes met in the *pulquerías*, viceregal authorities worried that seditious ideas could be spread there and also that the convergence of plebeians would reinforce and strengthen their attachment to a lifestyle abhorent to the enlightened elite. The viceregal government tried to extirpate a privileged space of sociability that served Mexico City's common people exclusively. In its judgment, these spaces could easily become centers of subversion.

The sections that followed did not really add much to the first six. The seventh forbade the practice of sales on credit. The eighth specified the penalties for those who were caught in the streets in a state of drunkenness.[131]

The pulque contractor, Alonso Flores de la Sierra, objected to these ordinances and the Audiencia supported him. As a result, the viceroy was forced to make some concessions and so he authorized the sale of food in less popular *pulquerías*. But he also ordered the implementation of the royal order of 1669, which limited the number of *pulquerías* in Mexico City to twenty-four. Faced with a proliferation of prohibitions, Alonso Flores de la Sierra ceded the monopoly to Roque Alfonso de Valverde. Luckily for the latter, in 1672, the queen authorized an increase in the number of *pulquerías* to thirty-six; twenty-four were for men and twelve were for women.[132]

The viceregal government's fear that the *pulquerías* would become centers of sedition became a reality in 1692. According to Sigüenza y Góngora, the passions stimulated by drink ignited in the *pulquerías*, where the Indians and *castas* began to take courage in their cups until they rebelled on June 8, 1692.[133] Once the rebellion was quashed, the viceroy ordered the closure of all *pulquerías* and forbade drinking pulque within city limits. As noted earlier, the king did not share the viceroy's belief that the cause of the riot was pulque and the *pulquerías*, nor was he willing to forgo the income derived from this industry. Eventually, he overturned the measures taken by the viceroy, who reluctantly—and stalling as much as he dared—implemented the king's order. Thus, the viceroy once more authorized the consumption and sale of white pulque in 1697.[134]

Despite the proliferation of all kinds of regulations in the eighteenth century, there was little scope for improvement on the 1671 ordinances concerning alcoholic beverages. These dispositions continued to form the foundation for any subsequent rules. Although a great number of *bandos* and ordinances on pulque were published in the eighteenth century, most of these were simply repetitions of the previous regulations with a few additions. For instance, in 1724, the mixture of the *coapatle* stick with pulque was forbidden, despite the fact that, apparently, it was totally benign.[135] In 1748, a *bando* threatened strict penalties for anyone who was found to be drunk in a public place.[136] In 1752, all *pulquerías* that were located near churches were ordered removed.[137] During the term of office of Viceroy Revillagigedo the second, officials took several measures to try to improve standards of hygiene near pulque stands and to impose a more modest norm of conduct. In 1790, *pulquería* owners became responsible for the cleanliness of the streets around their businesses, and after 1794, they were obliged to have a "common space."[138] Thus, the object of the eighteenth-century governments was not so much to improve upon the ordinances of 1671—which had already outlined all forms of conduct that should be repressed in the interests of public order—but rather to make them more effective because the dispositions were constantly being violated. For this reason, in 1724, in order to facilitate the scrutiny of the *pulquerías*, it was ordered that "there should be a decent but eye-catching notice with an inscription of their name or title by which they are known on the principal facades of their shacks (as corresponds) to the good order of the police."[139]

In 1752, officials ended the segregation of men and women in *pulquerías*. It became a nuisance to try to separate the husband from the wife, the father from the daughter, the brother from the sister, because this practice could give rise to "their hiding and congregating in order not to suffer this division or separation (even those who did not share these ties) buying or sending someone to buy pulque so that they could drink it (together)."[140] Of course, the danger of the common people drinking pulque in hidden corners away from the gaze of public authorities outweighed the dangers of mingling with the opposite sex.

In 1793, a cartographer completed a map of Mexico City with the location of *pulquerías* clearly and precisely indicated as an aid to the vigilance of the officials.[141] Finally, that same year, officials closed the little *casillas* outside the city limits where pulque was sold. This measure was the result in part of pressures from the *pulquería* owners who disliked the competition, but it was also due to the difficulty of supervising these places properly.[142]

During the eighteenth century, officials also tried to bring the people who frequented *pulquerías* under greater control. To accomplish this task, the power of judges and alcaldes was reinforced and, at the same time, the corruption and arbitrary actions of these officials were curtailed. The power of the state rarely intruded into the *pulquerías* in the seventeenth and early-eighteenth centuries because of the custom of allowing the contractor/monopolist to name a private judge from among the ministers of the Royal Audiencia to take over the exclusive jurisdiction of all affairs related to the sale of pulque.[143] The practice of naming such a judge was an effort to counter the constant extortion that secondary officials had exerted on the owners of *pulquerías*, but the solution was not satisfactory. The contractor/monopolist just chose one of his friends or an easily influenced minister so that he could violate the ordinances with impunity whenever it suited his interests.

In 1697, the jurisdiction of all judges was reestablished over the sale and consumption of pulque. Around 1723, however, an applicant for the monopoly of pulque, Juan Bautista Marichalar, offered to pay a higher tariff than usual if he were given certain privileges. One of these, evidently, was to be able to name a private judge. Because, as usual, the Crown was short of money, it chose to give the monopoly to the highest bidder with the right to grant a private judge.[144] Finally, in 1748, the king did away with this custom, which interfered so much with his powers of scrutiny and repression in the world of the *pulquería*. He named Viceroy Revillagigedo the first and his successors as private judges of the monopoly of pulque. In 1752, the viceroy authorized the *alcaldes del crimen*, the *corregidor*, and the *alcaldes ordinarios* to inspect the *pulquerías* and put an end to the disorders that took place there. He specified that the jurisdiction of these officials remained subsumed under his own authority.[145] As noted above, in 1763 the monopoly of pulque came under the direct authority of the Audiencia, thus improving the control of the state over all affairs related to this beverage.

In reality, all of these legal modifications did not alter the basic problem, which was the corruption and arbitrary power of the judges and officials in charge of supervising the *pulquerías*. Already the ordinances of 1671 required that "the secondary ministers, *alguaciles* [mayores], and watchmen should not cause disturbances, nor gather unpleasant gossip."[146] In the same vein, these secondary justices were threatened in 1752 with being sent to a presidio in Africa for four years if they did not make sure that the ordinances concerning *pulquerías* were obeyed.[147] At the same time, the justices' powers were expanded. They were allowed to proceed in a summary fashion against those who violated the ordinances, and the accused had no possibility of appealing their decisions.[148] Despite these extraordinary powers, in 1771, Inspector General José de Gálvez estimated that there were not enough judges to combat the disorders that the excessive consumption of pulque caused.[149]

Partly in response to these two problems—the corruption of secondary officials and the lack of sufficient judges—the government divided Mexico City into eight *cuarteles mayores* in 1782. Each one was subdivided, and thirty-two alcaldes del barrio were put in charge of these *cuarteles*. The viceregal government hoped that this measure would finally put an end to the disruption caused by the *pulquerías*. Paradoxically, the costs incurred by this reform were covered by the taxes collected from pulque.[150] The expectations wrapped up in the creation of these *cuarteles* and their respective alcaldes were soon dashed because none of these positions was salaried; only persons of dubious morality applied for the posts, with the intention of using their powers to enrich themselves.

The author of "Discurso sobre la policía de México" (Discourse on the police of Mexico City) affirmed that, despite the fact that he himself had proposed the division of the city into *cuarteles*, after ten years, it was a resounding failure. He stated: "It is fitting to call attention to the fact that there were a few who occupied the post who were notorious *pulqueros* and who manipulated different posts for their own benefit and in these capacities openly allowed the most scandalous excesses, trampling upon or causing unjust accusations against their neighboring *pulquerías* so that, while consumption would drop in this tavern, it would rise in theirs, where because of the violence and the effect of the powerful stimulus of complete liberty many injustices were committed." He continued his critique with: "It is vain to consider or reflect whether the pulque is fresh or corrupted, whether it is pure or mixed with pernicious ingredients; whether the stand begins and stops serving at the times prescribed by the ordinances or whether they obey even one rule of those that have been established; because they [the *pulqueros*] are those in charge of enforcing the regulations in general, no one should doubt that, having the control of justice in their own district, they will be so indulgent to their own interests, and as strict and rigorous against those nearby who might prejudice them."[151] If the disruptions caused by the *pulquerías* were hard to combat, the deep-seated corruption of those entrusted with the enforcement of regulations made the disorder an intractable problem.

**V.** The Crown implemented several types of repressive measures to end the disorders in the *pulquerías* that turned out to be very inefficient. In contrast, those of an economic nature proposed by Inspector General José de Gálvez, were much more successful. I stated earlier, rather cavalierly, that the increase in the tax on pulque led to a rise in its price and, consequently, a decrease in its consumption, but to what extent is this affirmation correct? What sources support this position? Fortunately, the record of the quantity of pulque that entered Mexico City and was taxed for the periods from 1763 to 1801 and 1806 to 1810 has been preserved. Of course, these figures do not include all pulque drunk in Mexico City because they cannot include what was smuggled in by circumventing the Royal Treasury's vigilance and taxation. But the quantity of bootleg pulque probably did not vary much between 1763 and 1810. The figures from the gateposts of Mexico City are sufficient to allow us to form a more or less precise idea of the fluctuations in pulque consumption in the capital at the end of the colonial period.

Table 5 shows that, from 1764 to 1772, pulque consumption fell, but it began to rise again very rapidly from 1772 to reach its apex

Table 5: Volume of Pulque Brought into Mexico City (1763–1810)

| Year | Thousands of arrobas | Year | Thousands of arrobas |
|---|---|---|---|
| 1763 | 1,880 | 1787 | 1,592 |
| 1764 | 2,048 | 1788 | 1,964 |
| 1765 | 1,948 | 1789 | 1,865 |
| 1766 | 1,856 | 1790 | 1,861 |
| 1767 | 1,837 | 1791 | 1,887 |
| 1768 | 1,796 | 1792 | 1,962 |
| 1769 | 1,840 | 1793 | 1,805 |
| 1770 | 1,724 | 1794 | 1,735 |
| 1771 | 1,686 | 1795 | 1,634 |
| 1772 | 1,702 | 1796 | 1,761 |
| 1773 | 2,060 | 1797 | 1,810 |
| 1774 | 2,214 | 1798 | 1,702 |
| 1775 | 2,417 | 1799 | 1,657 |
| 1776 | 2,667 | 1800 | 1,735 |
| 1777 | 2,745 | 1801 | 1,679 |
| 1778 | 2,892 | 1802 | —— |
| 1779 | 2,985 | 1803 | —— |
| 1780 | 2,595 | 1804 | —— |
| 1781 | 2,603 | 1805 | —— |
| 1782 | 2,698 | 1806 | 1,092 |
| 1783 | 2,654 | 1807 | 1,145 |
| 1784 | 2,512 | 1808 | 1,095 |
| 1785 | 2,248 | 1809 | 1,061 |
| 1786 | 1,603 | 1810 | 1,088 |

*Source*: José Jesús Hernández Palomo, *El aguardiente de caña en México (1724–1810)* (Seville, 1979), p. 428, obtained this information from the Archivo General de Indias. The series goes from 1763 to 1801. This series is identical to the one provided by Fabián de Fonseca and Carlos de Urrutia, *Historia general de la Real Hacienda* (Mexico City, 1978), vol. 3, p. 423 for the years 1763 to 1790. Hernández Palomo obtained the data for the years from 1806 to 1810 in the Archivo General de la Nación.

in 1779. After this high point, it returned to its previous levels within the space of ten years. This trend seems to confirm the hypothesis advanced that excessive taxes made the consumption of pulque decrease at the end of the colonial period. The last period of decline coincided with the most radical tax increase on the beverage (in 1780, the tax went from seventeen *granos* per *arroba* to twenty-three *granos* per *arroba*).

Let us not jump to conclusions. The oscillations in pulque consumption also followed the fluctuations of the prices of agrarian goods. It seems logical to assume that the prices of basic goods would have had a direct effect upon the consumption of alcoholic beverages. If these foodstuffs rose in price, the common people had less money to spend on pulque and its consumption diminished.

In fact, if we compare the variations in the price of corn in Mexico City (see Table 6) with the ups and downs in the consumption of pulque, it is clear that they go in different directions.

**Table 6: Price of Corn in Mexico City (1763–1810)**

| Year | Price (*reales per* fanega) | Year | Price (*reales per* fanega) |
|------|------|------|------|
| 1763 | 9.62 | 1787 | 27.61 |
| 1764 | 9.81 | 1788 | ——— |
| 1765 | 8.66 | 1789 | ——— |
| 1766 | 8.79 | 1790 | 19.55 |
| 1767 | 9.95 | 1791 | 15.08 |
| 1768 | 10.90 | 1792 | 10 |
| 1769 | 10.39 | 1793 | ——— |
| 1770 | 12.4 | 1794 | ——— |
| 1771 | 12.60 | 1795 | 20.66 |
| 1772 | 19.86 | 1796 | 13.46 |
| 1773 | 17.47 | 1797 | 16.87 |
| 1774 | 15.42 | 1798 | 21.83 |
| 1775 | 12.42 | 1799 | 19.61 |
| 1776 | 15.30 | 1800 | 19.95 |
| 1777 | 9.95 | 1801 | 18.08 |
| 1778 | 9.05 | 1802 | 26.50 |
| 1779 | 11.15 | 1803 | 19.25 |
| 1780 | 14.38 | 1804 | 14.58 |
| 1781 | 20.10 | 1805 | 18.10 |
| 1782 | 20 | 1806 | 20.50 |
| 1783 | ——— | 1807 | 19 |
| 1784 | 11.06 | 1808 | 24 |
| 1785 | 23.33 | 1809 | 25.75 |
| 1786 | 40.67 | 1810 | 34.50 |

*Source*: Enrique Florescano, *Precios del maíz y crisis agrícolas en México (1708–1810)* (Mexico City, 1969), pp. 115–117.

Table 7 makes this comparison; it includes the inverse of the price of corn, that is, the number of *fanegas* (bushels) that could be purchased with 100 reales. The rise in the price of corn was translated /9. into a decrease in pulque consumption. The inverse also appears: a lowering of the price of corn provoked an expansion of pulque consumption.

**Table 7: Purchasing Power of 100 Reales in *Fanegas* of Corn, Mexico City (1763–1810)**

| Year | Number of fanegas *of corn* | Year | Number of fanegas *of corn* |
|------|------|------|------|
| 1763 | 10.4 | 1787 | 3.6 |
| 1764 | 10.4 | 1788 | — |
| 1765 | 11.5 | 1789 | — |
| 1766 | 11.4 | 1790 | 5.1 |
| 1767 | 10.1 | 1791 | 6.6 |
| 1768 | 9.2 | 1792 | 10 |
| 1769 | 9.6 | 1793 | — |
| 1770 | 8 | 1794 | — |
| 1771 | 7.9 | 1795 | 4.8 |
| 1772 | 5 | 1796 | 7.4 |
| 1773 | 5.7 | 1797 | 5.9 |
| 1774 | 6.5 | 1798 | 4.6 |
| 1775 | 8.1 | 1799 | 5.1 |
| 1776 | 6.5 | 1800 | 5 |
| 1777 | 10.1 | 1801 | 5.5 |
| 1778 | 11 | 1802 | 3.8 |
| 1779 | 9 | 1803 | 5.2 |
| 1780 | 7 | 1804 | 6.9 |
| 1781 | 5 | 1805 | 5.5 |
| 1782 | 5 | 1806 | 4.9 |
| 1783 | — | 1807 | 5.3 |
| 1784 | 9 | 1808 | 4.2 |
| 1785 | 4.3 | 1809 | 3.9 |
| 1786 | 2.5 | 1810 | 2.9 |

*Source*: Enrique Florescano, *Precios del maíz y crisis agrícolas en México (1708–1810)* (Mexico City, 1969), pp. 115–117.

Clearly, the decrease in pulque consumption was primarily related to the trend toward increases in the price of corn in the last decades of the colonial period, which caused a general impoverishment of Mexico City's common people in a period in which their wages remained static. If changes in the economic situation of the common people was the primary variable in the fluctuations in pulque consumption, there are still some discrepancies between the two phenomena—principally for the period from 1763 to 1771—that must then be explained in a different manner.

During that period, despite the fact that corn prices were low, pulque consumption remained at a low level as well. It is possible that, around 1770, pulque became even more popular and that afterward, the taste for this drink was simply maintained at this level for the rest of the colonial period, with the customers' ability to pay as the only other variable. Another possibility is that in the first ten years that the Royal Treasury took over the direct management of pulque, its system of tax collection improved to such a degree that the evasion of taxes of the producers and vendors decreased, and that by 1772, the tax collectors had reached a level of efficiency that would be difficult to surpass. So, in this reading, the amount of taxed pulque grew, although not the level of consumption. Finally, in the period from 1772 to 1810, total pulque consumption in Mexico City followed the same patterns as the price of corn; that is to say, there was a relationship between the cost of corn and the consumption of pulque, but this relationship was not so close between the price of corn and the per capita consumption.

New Spain's population expanded in general and, despite famines and epidemics, which made this demographic expansion irregular and subject to stops and starts, the capital's population grew markedly in the eighteenth century.[152] Even though the great famine of 1785–1786 claimed many lives, it is clear that, after it ended, Mexico City's population began to expand again at a rapid pace. Humboldt calculated, rather conservatively, that the population of New Spain increased at the rate of 20 percent in the years between 1793 and 1803.[153] This pattern of growth no doubt continued until 1810, and Mexico City was no exception to this trend. Because this demographic growth did not lead to an increase in pulque consumption in the city, evidently the per capita consumption went down in this period. The most likely explanation is that the excessive taxation on pulque was at the root of this decline.

In short, with the available information, it is impossible to state definitively—as many have done—that pulque consumption increased in the second half of the eighteenth century. On the contrary, clearly the per capita consumption decreased, especially from 1785 to 1810—a period that is commonly considered the apotheosis of the Enlightenment and thus consequently also of "the breakdown of customs." Undoubtedly, some readers will interject that, although the consumption of pulque declined in this period, it always remained at high levels. This belief is also a deeply seated myth. From Humboldt until today, it has been said and repeated that pulque consumption per inhabitant of Mexico City was outrageous but, according to my calculation, it was no more than half a liter a day.[154] This quantity may, at first, seem rather high but in the perspective of daily wine consumption in Paris in the same period, where a half-liter of wine daily was normal and, taking into account the higher level of alcohol in wine, it does not seem so outrageous.[155] Although it is true that the figures for Mexico City do not take into account smuggled pulque, the same is true for the calculations regarding wine-drinking habits in Paris, which fail to include either contraband wine or other drinks.

At the end of the nineteenth and the beginning of the twentieth century, pulque consumption in Mexico City was much higher than at the end of the colonial period. This increase occurred, despite the fact that, in the national period, the taste for many other alcoholic beverages had become common. In 1896 and in 1916, each resident of the capital drank, on average, 0.9 litres of pulque daily.[156]

**VI.** Scholars have stated that banned drinks became more common in the last half of the eighteenth century in New Spain. This change would explain why, despite the reduction in pulque consumption and its low level for the times, the drunkenness of Mexico City's residents seems to have increased. Yet this reasoning also seems rather dubious.

As previously stated, the problem of prohibited drinks did not emerge in eighteenth-century New Spain; their pernicious effects had been described as early as 1529: "And intoxicated (from a pulque and roots mixture, the Indians) perform their ceremonies and the sacrifices that they did before and as they are frenzied, they attack each other, and kill each other; and many carnal and evil sins result from this drunkenness, from which Our Lord is not well served."[157] From this date, the Crown tried all possible remedies to end the practice of drinking these substances, but all to no avail. The testimony of this policy's failure is evident in the repeated dispositions of 1545, 1635, 1650, 1657, 1671, 1724, 1736, 1742, 1748, 1755, and 1771.[158]

What differed in the eighteenth century was that the type of prohibited drinks began to change gradually, away from the more traditional ones, such as the combination of pulque and fruit, roots, or herbs, such as *tepache* (pulque with dark honey), *guarapo* (pulque, sugar from cane or corn, with dark honey in a warm container to accelerate fermentation), *charangua* (leftover pulque, syrup, chile colorado, and toasted corn husks, all slowly warmed), *chilode* (pulque, *ancho* chile, an herb called *epazote*, garlic, and salt), and *sangre de conejo* or rabbit blood (pulque and the juice of red prickly pears). These combinations lost favor as more modern distillations such as *mezcal* and cane brandy or *chinguirito* replaced them in the public's taste. Cane brandy had made an incursion into the drinks scene by 1631 when it was mentioned in a prohibition. The term *chinguirito* only came into use around 1714.[159]

It is most unlikely that the substitution of one type of beverage for another could account for an increase in public drunkenness, and in fact, the substitution was incomplete—*tepache*, for instance, continued to be all the rage among the common people. To the contrary, if pulque had been combined with hallucinogenic substances such as peyote, the switch from these drinks to the more modern ones marks an advance of the Western and bourgeois morality to the detriment of the indigenous customs.[160] New Spain's enlightened elites perceived this substitution of one type of drink for another as an act of civilization and constantly promoted it.

Over the course of the eighteenth century, many eminent persons in the colony asked the king to lift the ban on cane brandy, arguing that it was much less noxious than pulque, but they made no such arguments for the other prohibited drinks. In 1758, the Protomedicato also deemed cane brandy less prejudicial to health than Spanish brandy derived from grapes.[161] In 1765, and later in 1767, as minister of the Council of the Indies, José de Gálvez argued for *chinguirito*'s authorization. In 1766 and in 1768, Mexico City's and Puebla's bishops, through the viceroy, proposed to the king that he approve the production of *chinguirito*. They reasoned that it would put an end to pulque consumption. In 1788, Don Silvestre Díaz de la Vega, the accountant general of the tobacco monopoly, wrote an essay on *chinguirito*, "Discurso sobre la decadencia de la agricultura en el reino de la Nueva España, medios de reestablecerse con sólo la habitación, uso y arreglo de un ramo que se propone con ventajas considerables al Estado y al real erario" (Discourse on the decadence of agriculture in the kingdom of New Spain, methods to reestablish it with solely the occupation, use, and repair of a sector that promises considerable advantages for the state and Royal Treasury). The product in question was, of course, cane brandy. In 1790, the bishop of Durango asked the viceroy to lift the prohibition against the production and consumption of *chinguirito*.[162]

The Crown did not give in to these appeals immediately. The king refused, not because he believed that *chinguirito* was particularly harmful or that it had led to great crimes and sinful behavior as it had been described several times in the royal orders of the period. Rather, the Crown hesitated because of a conviction that this authorization would lead to a decrease in pulque consumption and, consequently, a reduction in the revenues generated from this commerce. That the trade in wine and brandy from Spanish vineyards in the New Spain market would suffer was another concern.[163] From 1750 to 1780, the Crown, responding to these same worries, continued its efforts to uproot the practice of distilling cane brandy in New Spain, all without any tangible results.[164]

It was only in 1796, in a royal order of March 19, that the king finally legalized cane brandy and created a branch of the Royal Treasury to manage it. The king was finally convinced that, rather than interfering with the pulque revenues—which had been decreasing annually—they would be added to and thus these receipts would increase.[165] Officials also expected that the taxes on cane brandy would swell the royal coffers but the reality did not match their hopes. The lifting of the ban on cane brandy had come at an inauspicious moment. The colony's residents were facing an agricultural crisis and, although the consumers of cane brandy were not part of the poorest class and thus not so vulnerable to the ups and downs of corn prices as the pulque drinkers, the consumption of cane brandy also started to decrease rapidly (see Table 8).

**Table 8: Income from the Cane Brandy Department, New Spain (1797–1821)**

| Year | Income (thousands of pesos) | Year | Income (thousands of pesos) |
|------|------|------|------|
| 1797 | 200 | 1809 | 184 |
| 1798 | 233 | 1810 | 192 |
| 1799 | 215 | 1811 | 151 |
| 1800 | 206 | 1812 | 66 |
| 1801 | 221 | 1813 | 61 |
| 1802 | 172 | 1814 | 48 |
| 1803 | 163 | 1815 | 53 |
| 1804 | 157 | 1816 | 96 |
| 1805 | 150 | 1817 | 102 |
| 1806 | 153 | 1818 | 93 |
| 1807 | 180 | 1819 | 88 |
| 1808 | 172 | 1820 | 82 |
|      |     | 1821 | 48 |

*Source*: José Jesús Hernández Palomo, *El aguardiente de caña en México (1724–1810)* (Seville, 1979), pp. 134–136.

**VII.** If pulque consumption did not really increase in such a dramatic fashion in late eighteenth-century Mexico City and this level of drinking was no higher than that of wine in many European cities, and if the consumption of prohibited drinks did not rise in this period, why did so many travelers describe a capital city infested with drunks? Humboldt, for example, wrote: "In New Spain drunkenness is most common among the Indians who inhabit the Valley of Mexico and the environs of Puebla and Tlascala (*sic*), wherever the maguey or agave are cultivated on a great scale." In Mexico City, he continued, the police "send around tumbrils, to collect the drunkards to be found stretched out in the streets. These Indians, who are treated like dead bodies, are carried to the principal guard-house." Then he states: "In the morning an iron ring is put around their ankles (*sic*) and they are made to clear the streets for three days. On letting them go on the fourth day, several of them are sure to return in the course of the same week."[166] Perhaps this impression of a level of intoxication that was much more generalized in New Spain than in other nations can be explained by the fact that the consumption of alcohol there was less well integrated into daily life than in other places.

In eighteenth-century Paris, for example, it was normal for a man of the common people to drink two or more liters of wine daily. But he did so in small cabarets in which all the customers knew each other. There, in a warm and lively atmosphere, he met with friends, neighbors, relatives, and workmates, and over the course of several hours, in the course of conversations, he calmly drank several—even many—glasses of wine, usually along with various dishes that were prepared on site or brought in from a nearby restaurant. In these cabarets it was not uncommon to see entire families—husbands, wives, and children—eating and drinking.[167]

In contrast, drinking alcoholic beverages in general and pulque in particular differed radically in eighteenth-century Mexico City. It was a much more compulsive act. The common people did not seem to have any other goal than to get drunk as quickly as possible. It would be a great leap to suggest that this pattern of behavior was linked to historic and psychologial motives on the part of the residents of New Spain and Mexico City in particular. It is clear, however, that during the seventeenth and eighteenth centuries, the regulations imposed by Spanish officials on *pulquerías* implanted this compulsive manner of drinking. These regulations prohibited *pulquerías* in enclosed locales to have any sort of distractions there, such as musicians or dances, to have food stands nearby, or to have any seats. Thus, patrons were forced to remain standing in the expectation that they would not remain very long. The predictable result was that customers drank their pulque as quickly as possible.

Paradoxically, the Crown's attempt to prevent the transformation of *pulquerías* into centers of popular sociability meant that pulque consumption was not an act that was integrated into daily life. It became more of a compulsive unwinding in response to the reality of daily misery and constant humiliations and thus led to multiple and regular disorders. The authorities treated the *pulquerías* as if they were zones of tolerance.

This same policy to exclude the *pulquerías* from the social life of the common people and maintain a stringent scrutiny over them also implied a strict limitation of their numbers. The big change caused by this policy occurred at the midpoint of the seventeenth century, along with the other alterations, when Viceroy Count Alva de Liste reduced the number from 212 to only 50 *pulquerías*. There were 36 in the central core of the city and 14 in the surrounding area. From then on, the number of *pulquerías* was not allowed to increase until 1812. At several times, this total dipped even lower. In 1664, only 24 authorized stands existed. In 1671, this number grew slightly to 36. Nevertheless, the colonial officials continued to grant licenses, so that by 1784 there were 45 pulque stands. But in the city plan ordered by Viceroy Revillagigedo the second in 1793, only 35 *pulquerías* were still functioning in the entire city (see Table 9).

Clearly, in the plazas and outskirts of the city, some Indians sold pulque *tlachique*, which they produced themselves, but this trade operated with very small quantities. Also, in 1793, the authorities shut down the *casillas* that sold pulque in the vicinity of the city boundaries. In 1800, a *bando* that prohibited the sale of pulque outside an official *pulquería* was published.[168] From 1650, the number of *pulquerías* decreased, despite the fact that the urban population had grown considerably. At the end of the eighteenth century, there was only 1 *pulquería* per 3,857 residents in the capital.[169] The contrast with previous periods or with European cities illuminates the difficulties faced by the *pulquerías* of Mexico City.

In 1608, Viceroy Luis de Velasco gave permission for 1 elderly Indian woman per 100 residents to sell pulque. Before 1650, there were 212 *pulquerías* in the city despite the small population. In a city such as eighteenth-century Paris, there was a tavern for every 200 residents.[170] The scarcity of *pulquerías*, combined with the regulations that disallowed lengthy stays, explains why, rather than restful centers of sociability, they were veritable drinking troughs for intoxication. In contrast, in 1784, persons of a higher social stratum had 194 taverns at their disposal (158 in the central core and 36 in the vicinity). They were located in cozy annexes where patrons could sip their drinks in peace.[171] Faced with *pulquerías* always overflowing with people and constantly scrutinized by the authorities, many of the common people took refuge in the clandestine *tepacherías*.

**Table 9: Number of *Pulquerías* in Mexico City (1650–1864)**

| Year | Number of pulquerías | Added details |
|---|---|---|
| before 1650 | 212[a] | |
| about 1652 | 50[b] | 36 downtown, 14 outskirts[c] |
| 1664 | 24[a,b] | |
| 1669 | 24[d] | |
| 1672 | 36 | 24 for men, 12 for women[a,e] |
| 1698 | 36[f] | |
| about 1722 | 50 | 36 downtown, 14 outskirts[g] |
| before 1753 | 46[h] | |
| 1753 | 36[h] | |
| 1784 | 45 | 18 downtown, 27 outskirts[i] |
| 1793 | 35[j] | |
| 1812 | — | *Pulquerías* mushroomed as a result of the promulgation of the Constitution of Cádiz[k] |
| 1825 | 80[k,l] | |
| 1831 | 250[m] | |
| 1864 | 513[l] | |

[a]AGN, Reales Cédulas, vol. 15, exp. 179.

[b]José María Marroqui, *La ciudad de México* (Mexico City, 1900–1903), vol. 1, pp. 190–191.

[c]Ibid., vol. 1, pp. 207–208.

[d]AGN, Reales Cédulas, vol. 10, exp. 113, and José Jesús Hernández Palomo, *El aguardiente de caña en México (1724–1810)* (Seville, 1979), p. 62.

[e]Fabián de Fonseca and Carlos de Urrutia, *Historia general de la Real Hacienda* (Mexico City, 1978), vol. 3, pp. 344–346, and Hernández Palomo, p. 62.

[f]Ibid., p. 82.

[g]Marroqui, vol. 1, p. 200.

[h]Fonseca and Urrutia, vol. 3, pp. 375–383.

[i]*Informe sobre las pulquerías . . .*, no. 2, pp. 203–206.

[j]Plano de la ciudad de México de 1793, AHA.

[k]Ibid., tomo 1, pp. 209–211.

[l]Manuel Payno, *Memorias sobre el maguey mexicano y sus diversos productos* (Mexico City, 1864) pp. 80–91.

[m]Juan Felipe Leal and Mario Huacuja Rountree, *Economía y sistema de hacienda en México. La hacienda pulquera en el cambio. Siglos XVIII, XIX, y XX* (Mexico City, 1982), p. 104.

The segregation of pulque from the flow of daily life was aggravated in 1748 when the viceregal authorities forbade the sale of this beverage in *almuercerías*. They alleged that the pulque sold in these locales was smuggled in from the *casillas* and thus had not been taxed.[172] The *almuercerías* were small restaurants that served food only in the morning "and in no way [served] dinners, snacks, or suppers," because they only opened in the morning and at noon. They were located in annexes or outbuildings and, generally, poor women who were supporting large families ran these businesses. For a half *real*, they offered a dish, a piece of bread, and a *cuartillo* of pulque. The *almuercerías* were extremely popular because of "the customary practice in this capital of eating an *almuerzo* [midday snack], not only among the common people but also among the merchants, office workers, and other classes," and because their work was "quite far away from their places of residence, they could not go home to eat it [the *almuerzo*]."[173]

After 1784, the owners of the *almuercerías* fought to recover their lost right to sell a small quantity of pulque with meals. They intensified their lobbying after 1793, when the pulque *casillas* outside city limits were closed. This action removed the pretext with which the prohibition on serving pulque at the *almuercerías* had been implemented. Despite this change, in 1800, the ban still had not been not lifted. Around 1806, licenses to sell pulque were once more available to the *almuercerías*, but only to those that had been open for more than five years. Also, the officials used any old excuse to refuse or revoke these permissions if the establishment was called a *fonda* (tavern) instead of an *almuercería*, if meals and snacks were sold.[174] Clearly, the officials could not fathom that pulque might have any other purpose than that of a cheap means to get drunk.

**VIII.** As previously stated, the place of alcoholic beverages in colonial Mexican society underwent profound changes in the period of the Enlightenment. Average consumption of pulque per inhabitant decreased in the twenty-five years preceding the Wars of Independence. The old drinks derived from the indigenous past, which were considered diabolical by the Spanish authorities, were being displaced by others more to the liking of enlightened thinkers. Finally, the marginalization of alcohol in daily social intercourse became even more accentuated.

Faced with this array of facts, it is hard to continue to maintain that this period was marked by a laxness about drinking customs. On the contrary, the strict control of pulque consumption from the middle of the seventeenth century must be recognized. This management became even tighter in certain of its aspects in the eighteenth century.

The author of the "Discurso sobre la policía de México," unlike so many of his contemporaries, saw clearly the significance of the transformations in mores that were occurring around him. In his discussion of *pulquerías* and *vinaterías*, he pointed out that it was in the latter type of institution that disorder prevailed, even though persons of a higher social standing tended to frequent the *vinaterías*. He stated: "The people seen in the *pulquerías* are all from the lowest of the plebeians or the most impoverished artisans. It is almost possible to advance the proposition that among these people there are no scandals, because unquestionably they [scandals] are, in all the world, not absolute, but relative to the person who sees an action or hears an immoderate expression that he has experienced or heard since birth, [then] the continuation of this custom will not cause any novel effect against virtue nor foster or suggest depravity in morality." He continued to point out that "those who frequent or live near the pulque stands are of this coarse riffraff and character, and consequently their customs are not debased by the presence of drunks or the immoderation of those who surround them."[175]

According to this author, Mexico City's plebeians had always been depraved and degenerate: "From their birth they have no edification, their parents give them the example of their debased practices, which they inherit from example and tradition."[176] Finally, the author affirms that the evil did not arise from the consumption of alcohol, which in itself was not pernicious. "Most wise authors, very skillful merchants, and most adept manufacturers" of all times have been "great drunkards." It was not the ingestion of intoxicating drinks, but rather the lack of "any nurture" of the common people that led to the continuous public disorders.[177] This text clearly shows that the problem facing the eighteenth-century officials was not to put an end to the further degeneration of the common people's lifestyle because this was a constant. Rather, they needed to uproot traditions that were beginning to be considered most pernicious.

The enlightened thinkers suggested that the state should take over the education of the common people's children. In this way, they would be able to inculcate the moral values of the nascent bourgeois society in them and thus break the chains of tradition. Lizardi did not hesitate on this matter; according to him, the education of the lower classes' children could not be entrusted to their parents. The latter were "irrational brutes" who "would imbue them [their children] with their errors and worries, and with their perverse example would form in them devilish hearts."[178] The state's plans to eradicate the people's traditional culture and impose upon them the upper classes' values, attitudes, and conduct were hidden behind the false problem of the degeneration of customs.

**IX.** The Wars of Independence accentuated the viceregal government's contradictory policy toward pulque. One year after the outbreak of the Hidalgo revolt, Spanish officials began to worry that the *pulquerías* and *vinaterías* would become centers for the transmission of insurgent ideas and hatcheries of plots against the goverment, just as in the revolt of 1692. In order to resolve this dilemma, they intensified all the measures taken during the colonial period. If the dispositions against music, dancing, meals, or even seats had been successful in keeping people from lingering in the *pulquerías* for one and a half centuries, Viceroy Venegas pushed the logic further in a police regulation of September 27, 1811. He ordered that, while alcoholic beverages could be purchased in *pulquerías* and *vinaterías*, they could not be consumed on the premises.[179]

The common people reacted to this measure in the same way that they had to previous ones. Because this ban was radical, however, the population's reaction was also drastic. Clandestine *pulquerías*, *tepacherías*, and *vinaterías* mushroomed at an alarming rate.

The city's police superintendent then tried to convince the viceroy that this measure was not sensible because it would not put an end to drunkenness; drinkers, instead "of getting drunk in public places where no plots could be hatched without all knowing and seeing it, . . . will do so in secret hiding places of an annex or other such place far from the population centers and the observation of ministers of justice." The only solution, according to the superintendent, lay in the education of the people. This recommendation ignored the fact that Viceroy Venegas's ruling aimed to do away with subversion, not intoxication.[180] In any case, clearly, if the officials bore down too harshly on the disorders of the street, the people would simply retreat to closed shops, which were clandestine, and thus avoid all scrutiny. Although it would only work over the long term, the only solution to this dilemma was to wean the common people away from their "bad habits" by education.

Suddenly, in 1812, a number of *tabernas*, *vinaterías*, and *tepacherías* opened in the barrios surrounding the city. This growth was a response to a number of factors. On the one hand, the

Reglamento of 1811 distanced people from the *pulquerías*, but pulque began to be in short supply in the city.[181] Thus, it became even more common to mix it with other liquids that had an even higher alcoholic content. Finally, the Constitution of Cádiz had guaranteed complete freedom of commerce, which made the control of vendors of alcoholic beverages difficult to justify.[182]

That year, too, the residents of the barrios of Santa Cruz and La Palma denounced the clandestine *tepacherías* and *vinaterías* that operated there under the guise of being cafeterias. Among these taverns, some had irreverent names such as "Infiernito" (Little Hell) or "El paso de Lucifer" (The passage of Lucifer). Others commemorated the great victories of the insurgents, such as the battles of Cuautla and Zitácuaro. Those who complained about these establishments charged: "They [these establishments] take goods of value and of no value, stolen and not stolen; day after day there are fandangos without respite whether it is a holy day or a workday, there is gambling, very insolent dances, and songs of the same nature: and this happens in the public's sight because, even if the ministers of justice pass by, they fear no one. Also, many deserters and prostitutes hide in there."[183]

The viceroy feared that such places could become the sites of hatching plots against the government and he asked to be informed as to the danger that these taverns represented. The police superintendent answered that, even though, in these places, "many disorders are committed, they are not aimed at public security, nor do the conversations there promote anything seditious. Thus, Your Excellency should entrust the *corregidor* to zealously repress the cited disturbances, because this is really his duty and within his jurisdiction."[184] The superintendent's reply was in the same vein as his opposition to the Reglamiento set out in 1811. He considered that the problem posed by the *pulquerías* was solely moral and had nothing to do with political subversion.

By 1820, the situation had worsened, according to a bureaucrat of the Ayuntamiento who reported: "Suddenly the city is full of *casillas* that sell pulque and *tepache*, of which the latter is notoriously harmful to public health because of the noxious liquids that are its ingredients. In some of these said *casillas*, there are partitions or screens that hide the patrons; at their tables they gamble, men and women sit on the same bench, there is so much scandal, from which many quarrels are provoked with such grievous results, because most of the public, who are *léperos* and plebeians, are armed with knives and razors."[185]

By July 1821, the government had no control whatsoever over the *pulquerías* and taverns. Insurgent troops were threatening the city. The officials were so embroiled in juridical problems caused by the restitution of the Constitution of Cádiz that they had lost their legitimacy among the city's residents and could not make *pulquería* owners obey their orders. When a *regidor* in charge of street cleaning discovered some *pulquerías* serving drinks on holy days and tried to stop them, all he got for his pains was insults. In despair, he consulted the syndics of the Ayuntamiento to see if the control of *pulquerías* fell under his jurisdiction within the new constitution. The syndics replied in a long disquisition, written in a pedantic and edifying tone, that concluded that the *regidor* should have imposed his authority and imprisoned the infractors on the spot.[186] This reply reflected the blindness of the Ayuntamiento to the disappearance of the petty bureaucrats' legitimacy and power.

A few days later, probably because of this incident, the Ayuntamiento published a *bando*, which began thus: "Because the vice of drunkenness has spread to such an extent as to lead to extreme dissolution, as everyone painfully notes the excessive number of *vinaterías* and *pulquerías*, inside which men and women leer at each other at all hours, [where] without any concern for modesty or shame they prostitute themselves at the merchants' urging, and cause many disturbances among them, evils of which the consequences cannot be calculated, the putrid festivities never end."[187] The measures adopted were none other than those always invoked; what else could they do? The *pulquerías* were to close at the first ringing of the curfew; they could not open on holy days; they had to be on the street and not in shops; and for the *n*th time, the rules disallowed *tepache* and threatened drunks with jail. As usual, the *bando* was totally ineffective. It was only the last gasp of authority of the colonial polity regarding pulque and alcoholic beverages.

After Independence, the situation changed rapidly. In 1825, the number of *pulquerías* that were allowed in the city increased to 80. By 1831, there were 250, and in 1864, there were 513 authorized (see Table 9). By this late date, there was a *pulquería* for every 410 residents. This ratio was much more reasonable than the one that had existed at the turn of the eighteenth century, when there was only 1 *pulquería* for 3,857 residents.[188]

In 1854, the authorities also ordered that the *pulquerías* move from the city center to the outlying areas.[189] The Mexican government accepted the disturbances occasioned by the presence of *pulquerías* so long as they were excluded from the public space used by the elites and were only to be found outside city limits. This compromise, however, meant that they did not have the same measure of control over these establishments, which reverted to their role as places to congregate for the lower classes. The golden age of the *pulquerías* had begun.

## Acrobats, Puppeteers, and "Scientific" Charlatans

In eighteenth-century Mexico City, and particularly away from the city center and in the barrios, the streets were bustling and lively. Much to the delight of the people, entertainment was never lacking in these spaces. Acrobats, puppets, exotic animals, *fuegos ilíricos*, women and children with deformities, machines that made men invisible, and other such marvels were all on display.

These diversions did not seem harmful to the authorities; they were, after all, among the most benign types of entertainment that one could imagine. And, after all, the common people needed to amuse themselves in their moments of leisure. The officials hoped that these peaceful diversions would lure the artisans and other workers away from the vices in which they so often indulged, such as gambling and drinking.

Despite this reasoning, these street entertainments were banned during part of the eighteenth century. The prohibition did not stem from the disorder that they might cause, but, rather, because the Coliseum saw them as competition for its audience. The measure seems to have been instituted around 1750, and in 1760 it was still in effect.[190] In the following decades, however, the government realized that if it controlled the life of the streets and the amusements of the common people too harshly, they would simply organize parties in their homes. Those festivities would be much more difficult to police and control with any efficacy. They opted to allow the street entertainments once more.

The change in the viceregal government's position was so complete that, in March 1821, a syndic of the Ayuntamiento defended the right of street performers to work during the entire period of Lent. He stated: "In such a populous city as this capital where there is no other public entertainment but that which occurs on the sides of streets, . . . the residents must make available all the diversion possible in order to avoid even worse evils and insults to God."[191] Despite this new policy, the viceregal government still tried to maintain an adequate control over street shows. After all, the common people, with their notorious ingenuity, were capable of transforming the most innocent pastime into a biting social satire. The acrobats, most of all, often lapsed into this kind of subversive game, and their performances were usually something more than feats of physical agility. Many of the acrobats were Spaniards, who, by all appearances had not "made it" in America. They lived a life of bare subsistence, which was probably not such a big change from their previous existence in their homeland. The acrobats seem to have traveled not only from barrio to barrio but also from city to city. At times, their wives and children toured with them.

These traveling showmen of the people would brighten the patios and the streets with an atmosphere of exuberant festivity, much needed in a city more and more in need of such jollity. In defiance of the law, many roamed the streets playing big and small drums as well as violins and bass guitars to attract the residents and passersby. Men dressed as women; this inversion allowed them to play the buffoon by committing "ridiculous mistakes" and "abuses."[192]

In reality, these marginal performers, these denizens of social isolation, these public fools, concentrated in themselves all the latent capacity for inversion and social satire that the people could not show openly in the street. They formed a type of small, traveling, semiprivate carnival. Their physical skills were only one facet of a complex system of social inversions. They seemed to defy the laws of gravity with their feats of acrobacy; up and down, right and left were blurred as they flew through the air. In the system of inversions, their acrobatic superiority placed them in the role of simple folk, poor souls, fools, and the insane on a spiritual level. It was in this sense that the common people identified with them.

The enlightened thinkers believed—as expressed with devastating clarity by Lizardi—that the common people were "a monster with many heads, with little or no understanding," who "did not have any critical faculties; rather they argue based on the superficial appearances and, because their contentions are not in line with reason, most of the time they are discordant and are constructed in the same ignorance as that of the insane."[193] The common people accepted the role of the ignorant peasant in the same way that the lower classes generally in most traditional societies accept the dominant values. But, in Mexico, they subverted their role; they transformed the character of the ignorant peasant into a form of resistance and adapted it to their needs.

This logic meant that blindness became prophetic of life after death, and of destiny. Was it only the poor and humble who could see through banal external aspects? By the same token, they were the only ones who knew that the emperor wore no clothes and that he was mortal like them. Were they really unable to argue according to the rules of logic? For this reason, only they understood and experienced all that which was not encompassed by these rules. As such, death—which terrorized the upper classes—was their constant companion. Did Nature remain unvanquished by the plans of science? The common people compromised in this regard. Furthermore, were not the people, like children, the simple, and the insane, closer to God?[194]

The acrobat held a mirror to the people. His quips were like poisonous darts pointed at the abuses of the rich and powerful; his disjointed mumblings were the truths that, although denied by the powerful, were known to all. The acrobat restored the common people's capacity for social inversion, he shed light on the day-to-day realities of the people, and as such, this capacity gave the street entertainers a measure of dignity.

It is not entirely surprising that one day, along with a crowd from the neighborhood, the residents of a *vecindad* housing particularly poor and miserable individuals in Arsinas Street, decided to crown an acrobat as king. This act followed the observation of the acrobat that the social order was similar to a mortal leap. The preparations for the coronation reflected the usual pomp and elegance; residents hung banners from the entrance; in the patio, they suspended curtains and streamers; and they installed a construction to accommodate a large quantity of fireworks—an *árbol de fuego* (tree of fire).

Unfortunately, the ceremony was canceled. One of the neighbors informed the Ayuntamiento of the plans; the officials intervened to prevent this contestation of the structures of power. With prudent leniency, the acrobat was not punished nor was he prevented from continuing his performances in the area so long as he avoided "any hint of a scandal."[195] In any case, this type of incident provides an explanation for the extreme caution exercised by the authorities when they granted licenses for such diversions.

The conditions that the officials imposed on the entertainers when they gave permission for shows were: that no forbidden beverages be served; that the performers should not attract their public by playing musical instruments, especially those associated with the military; that they should not "whistle" to the public or engage in "other types of subversion"; that they should appear in decent clothes appropriate to their gender; that their program should end before evening prayers; and finally, that they should not transfer the entertainment to another house without warning the Ayuntamiento.[196] When the authorities discovered "abuses," they canceled licenses. They did so, not to forbid such entertainments indefinitely, but only to force the street entertainers to petition for the permissions once more, and thus allow the officials some leverage to stop the disorders.[197]

Because of their immense popularity, the street entertainers extended their range of activities beyond the public byways and the patios of tenements. The ban on street entertainment that the Coliseum instigated lasted for years, but its purpose was not only to do away with some annoying competitors but also to monopolize a diversion that attracted such a large public. When ticket sales slumped at the Coliseum, its adminstrators organized acrobatic functions, with tightrope walkers and tumblers, in order to fill the hall.[198] Even after these types of diversions were authorized in public places, the Coliseum continued to present them, particularly during Lent when no theatrical productions were mounted. Such events were also staged in the Plaza de Toros.[199]

Over time, these forms of entertainment included a greater variety of performers and became more and more flashy. In 1792, the Coliseum organized a show with acrobats, tightrope walkers—with and without balancing poles, on jumping ropes, or on loose wires— and balance artists. Then, in 1802, a show of equestrian exercises engaged the public.[200]

Obviously, the originally simple street shows were changing and needed a new space in which to continue their evolution. Because the Coliseum had for so long fought to keep these plebeian performers out of their midst, it was not the ideal place. In 1822, a series of spectacles was presented in the Plaza de Toros. It was the most grandiose of this type of entertainment, far surpassing previous efforts in the same genre. The program was as follows:

Friday, February 7: Acrobats and a *jamaica*, with artificial lighting, until 7:00 P.M.

Sunday, March 2: Acrobats and four young bulls in celebration of the glorious and unforgettable Cry of Iguala.

Monday, March 3: Acrobats and *fuegos ilíricos*, with intermittent lighting.

Sunday, March 9: Acrobats and a representation of the coronation of our august monarchs.

Monday, March 10: Acrobats and four bulls.

Sunday, March 16: Acrobats and a corrida of rings.

Monday, March 17: Acrobats and four brave bulls.

Wednesday, March 19: Acrobats and four hydrogen balloons.

*Note*: The companies of acrobats who perform on these days will be among the three best that are in the city upon that date and will perform in three corners of the plaza so that the public will be totally pleased with the show.[201]

The performers who put on these shows could not develop a regular following if they were allowed to work only once a year during Lent and then, for the rest of the year, had to wander from place to place begging for a location. But these types of events could not be presented continuously in one set locale because their attraction was in their exoticism. With repetition, the spectators became blasé and lost interest. The nature of these entertainments made it difficult for performers to change their acts constantly and maintain the continued interest of the audience. In order to succeed, these shows had to continue the custom established by the acrobats who began the practice of staying in one place for a couple of weeks and then changing locations. They adopted a gypsylike lifestyle, which evolved into the beginnings of the circus in Mexico.

Despite their seeming innocuousness, puppet shows presented more challenges to the authorities than acrobats. At first glance, what could be less offensive than little mannequins manipulated either by women or Indians? When hidden away inside stores, however, far from the intrusive gaze of judges and alcaldes de barrio, the puppeteers pushed the genre to its limit. Puppet shows were generally presented in the homes of retired actors. At night, at the conclusion of the shows in the Coliseum, many of the performers from this theater went to the houses of their old friends to assist in the manipulation of the puppets. In this friendly atmosphere, the actors presented biting satires to lower-class audiences, in which men and women mixed without barriers. The puppeteers often continued into the wee hours of the morning, and the shows culminated in disorder and drunkenness.[202]

A 1749 decree banned puppet theaters "to avoid the notable excesses, scandals, quarrels, and public sins that are committed in these puppet playhouses because of their nighttime functions."[203] Despite a softening of this ban and the permission to renew performances with licenses from the Ayuntamiento, the hostility toward these shows never disappeared. Not only were they subjected to the same vigilance as the acrobats but also to the same strategic withdrawal of licenses; and, as we have already seen, the Coliseum forbade its actors to attend these places.[204]

The officials imposed enlightened reforms on the puppet shows in much the same manner as on its sister art—the theater. By the end of the colonial period, certain individuals tried to implement a professionalization of the art form and attempted to transform it into a purely educational kind of entertainment. In 1814, Don Ignacio Miranda petitioned for a license to start a theater school which, according to him, would be the first of its kind in New Spain, but would have as an annex a puppet theater. Don Ignacio Miranda assured the licensing authorities that he would not allow "the indecencies, the indolence, and the disorder" that prevailed in so many other puppet theaters and that made this diversion into "a useless spectacle, both disagreeable and pernicious." Instead, his institution would promote the "Enlightenment" as well as "agreeable and honest entertainment." The building would be provided with "separate entrances and the proper division of seating [so that] the public could enjoy the show without having to mix with others, without the stigma of contact with other classes, [but rather] as an honest rational diversion."

At this time, officials were trying to implement just such policies in the Coliseum and so they gave him the license. They argued that the plan "is most suitable because it proposes to provide an honest form of recreation and, at the same time, to train actors in the practice and good discipline needed for work in the theater, all goals that are desired by such an enlightened government as the one required and always present in this metropolis."[205] Although, as previously mentioned, this school had a very short existence, the project does show that even street entertainments, such as puppets, could not entirely escape the reforming zeal of the enlightened officials.

The puppet theaters were not, in fact, the only diversions to suffer the impact of the ideas of the Enlightenment. Much to the delight of the authorities, strange little shows that reflected the ideas of the reformers began to appear in the streets. These new entertainments were all characterized by a mission to inform the popular classes of strange and curious novelties that, until then, had been largely unknown to the majority of city residents. As such, the shows fulfilled an educational role by showing the realities of daily life or by revealing exotica, anomalies, or the advances of "science." In 1817, a retired second lieutenant of the dragoons wandered the streets charging one real per person to see a baby leopard. At the time, such an experience must have seemed totally singular.[206]

The very educational *fuegos ilíricos* were another such commonly organized experience. These were lighted perspectives that represented "buildings of antiquity, from fables, and some of the most important edifices of this capital" and that were constructed "according to the rules of optics."[207] Certainly, given the public's passion for images, these spectacles must have attracted large crowds ftom among the passersby.

The exhibition of deformed human beings was another street diversion. In 1810, for the price of one real, people could observe an Indian woman who was only one *vara* (about a yard) tall with arms only a quarter of a *vara* long, and entirely double-jointed. Despite these "deformities," she could "sew, thread a needle, and fix a handkerchief"; she also danced and, more to the point in this age of Enlightenment, she was "becoming civilized with all due decorum."[208] No doubt, many of the enlightened thinkers would have agreed with the account from the *Diario de México*, which ended: "God permit that this should happen with all the other Indians and plebeians in New Spain."

The enlightened thinkers' "scientific" curiosity was awakened by just about anything. The study of abnormalities, for example, was thought to provide a bridge to the understanding of the secrets of Nature. In 1811, when an illiterate woman from Oaxaca, María Gertrúdiz Pérez, asked for a license to display her twenty-year-old son "who because of Nature's defects had never grown beyond the height of about three-quarters of a *vara*, although with perfectly formed limbs," the notary, in a tone of reverence calculated to pique the interest of the authorities, added that this permission would not only assist the woman but also "would become quite a phenomenon." Corregidor del Mazo wrote to Viceroy Venegas to lend support to María Gertrúdiz's petition, explaining that "according to the observations of experts, the presentation of this phenomenon can contribute to the objectives of physics as well as the other sciences and natural disciplines." Faced with such a convincing argument, the viceroy granted the license. In the document, the *corregidor*, imbued by an unquenchable thirst for knowledge, but indelicate in a manner not so foreign from our own discipline, added as one of the conditions to the permission that "if [the youth] died while in this capital city, the proper authorities must receive prompt notification so that, for the betterment of humanity, his cadaver can be inspected to add to the knowledge of anatomy."[209]

Within the group of people of moderate levels of culture, the Enlightenment inspired a strange mixture of the spirit of scientific inquiry with the credulity that was also found among those who considered themselves enlightened thinkers. The impact of information that shattered old systems of belief, long part of the collection of certainties of everyday life, was that any type of tomfoolery that cloaked itself in the mantle of science was easily accepted at face value.[210] In his youth, Jean-Jacques Rousseau tried to earn his keep by selling jars with false bottoms to unsuspecting villagers who believed that these transformed water into wine.[211]

The public in Mexico City was never completely safe from pseudoscientific charlatans. Both Alzate and Díaz de Gamarra denounced them vehemently. In his essay "Errores del entendimiento humano" (Errors of human understanding), the latter wrote: "There are others [who are impostors] who are even more harmful to society. These are those who coax their victims to spend large amounts of money to discover the secret of the philosopher's stone, to build some kind of new machine with admirable springs, and there, like a parrot, they perorate from memory on the center of gravity, the forces of friction, strength, and resistance, concluding their speech with promises of the great usefulness and many advantages of their newly invented machine."[212]

Nevertheless, some of these confidence tricksters were extremely ingenious and their mechanical skills were so developed that rather than being described as charlatans, they should be characterized as inventors. The makers of "the invisible man machine" should be categorized in this latter group. The following description documents the presence of such curious artifacts on the city streets around 1805. The invisible man machine was "a square frame measuring about one and a half *varas* in height. There is a little box hanging from two thick wires in the center, which measures three-quarters of a *vara* in length and one in width. In the middle of the upper part, there is a small wooden cup, from which a thin metal wire emerges and is connected to the roof with three glass bulbs, two in the center of the sides and one in the lower part; also there are two mouthpieces, one on each side, through which people talk and are answered in a most categorical manner." The author of this description believed that the quality of the answers that "are even clearer than those of the first-known invisible man machine, which is today in the San Felipe de Jesús Street," made this version of the machine superior. He also stated that "this one is improved in that it emits pleasant smells in its surroundings; and, upon request, it will play music, which was verified the other day when it played a minuet, boleros, and other songs of the country, all quite perfectly and in a tone that could not be improved."[213]

In contrast, other scientific shows proved to be even more fraudulent, such as that of "Señor Falconi, eminent physicist, engineer, and mathematician," who, in 1786, presented himself in the Coliseum. His show was nothing more than a series of crude magic tricks. The next day, members of the public denounced the "scientist" by posting a lampoon of the show on the doors of the Coliseum before the first show of the day.[214] Others were much more skilled in their presentations. Around the time of Mexican Independence, one illusionist was so skillful that Lizardi had to use the forum of newspapers to counter the rumor that the magician had a pact with the Devil by explaining the natural laws on which his tricks were based.[215] At the same time that acrobats were sowing the seeds of the modern circus, and professionalization became more common in the puppet theater, the "scientists" burst upon the stage. It was in this way that street theater took a turn toward modernity.

## Enlightened Paseos

Unlike most other street diversions that were attacked and reformed during the century of Enlightenment, the paseos were promoted and improved. In fact, at the end of the colonial period, Mexico City's principal paseos had either been built by the viceregal government or remodeled and enhanced by it.

The first paseo that the capital's population enjoyed was the Alameda. It was built in 1572 on one of the first extensions of the lagoon that the Spaniards had drained. For a long time, the Alameda was the only paseo near the city; it was the object of several reforms during the eighteenth century. In 1771, Viceroy de Croix ordered that the area be extended into the space once occupied by the small squares of Santa Isabel and San Diego, and the Alameda was thus radically transformed in its appearance. Viceroy Bucareli also ordered the paseo's remodeling. The two avenues that cross it diagonally were then created, and five fountains were installed in a symmetrical pattern. Finally, it was enclosed with a continuous bench along the wall. In addition, regimental musicians played there on holidays.[216]

The paseo in the woods of Chapultepec was also older; it was located at a distance from the city so that residents went there only when they could spend the day. This place, which had been the playground of the Mexican leaders, was transformed into a paseo for Spaniards at the beginning of the sixteenth century. A small palace for the enjoyment and relaxation of the viceroys was built at the bottom of the hill, near a large spring. By 1783, the woods and the palace were in ill repair. Viceroy Matías de Gálvez petitioned for funds from Spain to recondition them in order that the ceremonial handing over of the staff of authority from one viceroy to his successor could be held there. The king, however, did not give his permission for such repairs.

In 1785, Viceroy Gálvez ordered the contruction of a palace at the top of the mountain to be used as a resting place for the viceroys. The work continued even after his death in 1786. In 1787, however, the Crown suspended the construction because of a rumor that the recently deceased viceroy had hoped to lead New Spain to independence and planned to use the palace as a fortress in the ensuing fight against the Spaniards. Viceroy Revillagigedo the second envisioned the completion of the palace as an archive for the kingdom, but this plan did not come to fruition either. It was only during the reign of Viceroy Iturrigaray that the builders took up the project again, but the Wars of Independence interrupted their labors once more.[217]

In 1785, Viceroy Bucareli ordered the creation of a paseo that carried his name. Later, adjacent to that one, the Paseo Nuevo was inaugurated in 1778.[218] Apart from these paseos, there were others such as La Viga, which I mentioned earlier. This most popular paseo ran along the banks of the *acequia real* (royal water canal) and the canal that joined the city to the town of Chalco. Viceroy Pedro Cebrián y Agustín, who governed from 1742 to 1746, was particularly fond of this paseo and sponsored several improvements to it. Viceroy Revillagigedo the second also enhanced it.[219]

All these paseos were extremely popular. According to the authors of the "Informe sobre pulquerías y tabernas," in 1784, the Alameda attracted between five and six thousand persons on holidays.[220] The elite and even the viceroy attended these paseos regularly. The moralists of the Enlightenment believed this activity to be the fount of many virtues. First of all, it was healthy but, more important, it distracted people from other and sinful diversions.[221]

These laudable activities were not, however, without some problems. Members of the upper classes complained of the unwholesome odors emanating from food stands and of the close proximity of people of the lowest social orders. These individuals were practically nude, dirty, and flea-bitten, and they stayed there until the wee hours of the morning, involved in entertainments of dubious morality.[222] In order to counter these abuses, the authorities began to post guards and patrols along the paseos on days of rest. Also, Viceroy Revillagigedo the second ordered that, on holidays, eighteen grenadiers commanded by two corporals and one officer should be posted at the entrances of the Alameda from 4 P.M. to prevent access to "all this class of persons in shawls or blankets, beggars, barefoot, nude, or indecent."[223]

There was no shortage of reform proposals for the paseos among the enlightened class. The author of the "Discurso sobre la policía de México" dedicated several pages to his ideas. This text clearly illustrates the ideal that guided the design of these paseos. In a period when the Mexican elite worshiped the French, the models for such designs, not surprisingly, were the paseos of Paris and the gardens of Versailles. Consequently, geometrical forms dominated the paseos. Trees had to be placed in straight lines; the plants and shrubs had to form clear and simple figures. Exuberant vegetation was frowned upon; in fact, it was ruthlessly pruned so that it remained uniform and controlled. All the details were regulated, one might even say monitored, so that the impression for a spectator was of an ambiance of regularity and, above all, order.[224]

The ideals of enlightened despotism in the area of gardening reveal the preoccupation with neatness, which was the foundation of the conception of social order and even of policing, as it was envisaged in this period. Enlightened thinkers hoped to transform the entire society into a French-style garden in which each person would remain in his appointed place; individuals would not try to escape or flee the gaze of others. The fate of those who defied this order was pruning. Each person's position was to be determined by the enlightened despot, who came to these determinations guided by the rule of reason.[225] The education of lower-class children was an integral part of this project, because it is common sense that twisted trees cannot be straightened late in their life cycle. In contrast, "trees, especially their branches, when still young, can be guided as to their final shape."[226]

The coherence of the ideals of urban planning and gardening in these enlightened governments should not be too surprising. Houses, like trees, had to be of the same height and placed on a straight line. The city, like the paseos, had to be symmetrical, clean, and pleasant.[227] The viceregal governments dreamed of transforming the city into one large paseo, in which the elite could walk about showing off clothes and carriages without any worry about the importunate class of the homeless and other riffraff. In a city that had been reformed along these lines, in which social forces as well as Nature had been submitted to the will of the absolute monarch and the principles of reason, men—but enlightened men, of course —could dedicate themselves to the appropriate devotions to God without material considerations or worry over uprisings of the people.[228]

## Urban Reforms

The enlightened governments hoped to attain this ideal of urban planning through a multiplicity of projects undertaken during the second half of the eighteenth century. These ventures aimed to increase cleanliness and beautify and make the city rational. They were just one part of the struggle to recover control of the streets that took place in this period between the state and the elite on one side and the common people on the other. The authorities and the upper classes no longer accepted that the streets should be in effect dominated by the plebeians and their activities. Rather, they wanted to transform the streets into an attractive environment, decorated and regulated according to the laws of beauty, hygiene, safety, efficiency, and reason. The viceregal governments did not flinch from this task, which, given the standard filth, lack of hygiene, violence, and disorder that reigned in the streets, seemed a formidable one.

The first step in this campaign was to provide clear points of reference so that the city could be easily visited. They named the streets and assigned numbers to houses and rooms. As seen previously, in 1724, *pulquerías* were ordered to affix a visible sign with their names on their premises.[229] In the 1790s, the Ayuntamiento had the names of plazas and streets, clearly marked with blue and white tiles, placed on the street corners.[230] These measures were not for the benefit of residents, who knew their way around, but to make the government's task of administration and control of the population that much easier. Not too surprisingly, the state sponsored the elaboration of many city maps.

The civil and ecclesiastical jurisdictions were overhauled in this period. Parochial divisions in the capital had been based upon residential separation between the Spaniards and Indians.[231] In the sixteenth century, parishes were established in the *traza*, the central core of the city where only Spaniards were supposed to live, and *doctrinas*, an alternate form of parish, were created in the Indian-

dominated surroundings. These two supposedly separate popula-
tions mixed, and the *doctrinas* began to encompass parts of the *traza*,
while the parishes extended into the barrios outside the city center. The two distinct forms of jurisdiction thus were superimposed
over the same spaces. The situation became even more complicated
in the seventeenth century, when an indigenous-language parish
was created for Mixtecs and Zapotecs and another was established
for "extravagant and Chinese Indians," that is to say, migrants from
the Philippines. In 1768, after having secularized all the *doctrinas*,
Archbishop Lorenzana ordered José Antonio de Alzate to elaborate a new distribution of the parishes that would regularize them
so that the formerly overlapping jurisdictions would be eliminated.
Alzate proposed the creation of thirteen parishes of more or less
equal size, which would include Spanish, *casta*, mestizo, and Indian parishioners. The Crown approved the plan in 1771 and implemented it the next year.[232]

At the same time, the civil authorities reorganized their administrative and territorial units. In the first half of the eighteenth century, three new plans for the reformulation of divisions in Mexico
City were advanced but none was approved. In 1713, the idea of
creating nine *cuarteles* was put forward. The plan specified that of
these nine sections, six would be under the supervision of the
*alcaldes del crimen*, one would be overseen by the *corregidor*, and
two would be managed by the *alcaldes ordinarios*. In 1720, the proposal of dividing the city into six *cuarteles* was floated, and then, in
1750, the allocation was changed to seven *cuarteles*. Although this
last proposal included rules and dispositions to implement the new
division, in practice it would not have worked because the area
included in the *cuarteles* was simply too large for one alcalde to
patrol it adequately.

Despite these many failures, the officials continued to consider
the reorganization of urban space one of their central goals, because it was a fundamental part of the project to increase their social control of the capital's residents. In 1778, José de Gálvez dictated
an order to Viceroy Bucareli that mandated that the alcaldes should
live in their respective *cuarteles*, so that they could put an end to all
of the scandals that occurred in the *pulquerías*. Obviously seven
alcaldes could not begin to make a dent in a problem of this magnitude. In 1780, in response to this problem, Viceroy Mayorga, imi-
tating recent Spanish reforms, instituted a new category of
bureaucrats—the alcaldes del barrio. He commisioned the *oidor*
Baltasar Ladrón de Guevara to propose a new division of *cuarteles*

and barrios. In 1782, the officials created eight *cuarteles mayores* and subdivided each into four smaller jurisdictions. The five *alcaldes del crimen*, the *corregidor*, and the two *alcaldes ordinarios* were put in charge of the *cuarteles mayores*. The thirty-two alcaldes del barrio supervised the *cuarteles menores* under the supervision of their respective *alcaldes de cuartel*. The king confirmed this new division and its accompanying ordinances in 1786.[233] The city's transformations clearly reflect the authorities' desire to impose a new spatial division.

The city's previous organization was the result of history's processes. The parochial division, for example, simply reiterated the pre-Hispanic religious and territorial divisions and added on a new unit: the parish reserved for the Spaniards.[234] The past was given a concurrent reality with the present in many urban spaces, and thus created a complex and changeable system of references. Streets had several names simultaneously, their titles altered as the point of reference disappeared or was lost to memory. One precise place could belong to several distinct ecclesiastical divisions if the residents needed several types of religious attention. The city's traditional organization was based upon a conception of the city as heterogeneous, existing on several levels, each of which had its own system of reference. None of these systems hoped to encompass the whole city but only one aspect of each sector.

In contrast, the new concept of space that was imposed upon the city in the eighteenth century was abstract and totalitarian. It was based upon two of Descartes's clear mathematical hypotheses. The first premise was that two bodies would not occupy the same space at the same time, and the second affirmed that all points must be defined from the vantage of only one system of coordinates, which should be chosen arbitrarily. Also, in direct contradiction to the traditional vision, space was not a social creation but rather predated society. Humans and their activities did not define space; they simply existed within it. The interpretation of administrative divisions and the plurality of denominations were inimical to this modern conception and had to be eliminated. On the other hand, places that escaped categorization within this new system of reference could not be tolerated. All had to be inscribed within this system.

The reform of urban space was intimately linked to the new conception of the social order. Just as every space was defined unidimensionally, all human activity and all social groups had to occupy a precise place. The ordinances that governed the alcaldes de barrio included the obligation to imprison smugglers; banish Indians who resided inside the *traza* and oblige them to live in the villages and barrios on the outside; encourage schools and *amigas* (women who looked after and taught young children), and make sure that parents understood that it was their obligation to send their children to these establishments; look for homes for young orphans or, if they were older, seek apprenticeships in a workshop for them; send sick poor people to the hospitals and slackers to the presidio.[235] These ordinances provide a clear picture of the new system of restrictions and exclusions that was envisaged.

The manner in which these projects were implemented demonstrates that one of the principles of modernity—the narrow interrelation between knowledge and power—had made an appearance in New Spain. The task of formulating new civil and ecclesiastical divisions was delegated to persons who knew the city intimately: José Antonio de Alzate and Baltazar Ladrón de Guevara. Despite their scholarly backgrounds, both carefully studied the urban landscape and the distribution of population in the capital before rendering their plans. The *oidor* Ladrón de Guevara wrote: "Without depending upon the practical knowledge that was so useful to me, at the beginning I walked around the city many times. I passed through the center to reach the slums and the outlying districts; and keeping an eye on the maps that I found to be the most precisé, I meditated on the diversity of persons, and the enormous pleb of all *castas* who live both in the interior and the extreme edges of the city." According to this author, the plebeians lived in barrios, "some of which are composed of intricate alleyways, others are built between broken-down buildings between canals that made passage there almost impossible, many people live in adobe or cane-stalk huts arranged without any order on large tracts of land, separated one from the other by long distances." After his wanderings and examinations, he proceeded to divide the barrios physically and mapped out the *cuarteles*.[236]

Once this division was implemented, the ordinances specified that the alcaldes de barrio should undertake a census of all establishments (workshops, businesses, stalls, offices, inns, taverns, restaurants, and others) in their jurisdiction as well as a register of all the residents, house by house. A daily logbook of all deaths, travelers, and inhabitants who changed residences was also mandatory.[237] Even though all of these plans were not immediately fulfilled, in the term of Viceroy Revillagigedo the second, new plans of the city were drawn, and a census of the city's residents was concluded, as well as of those of the colony, at the same time as the massive urban reforms were completed.[238]

The dialectic between knowledge and power manifested itself again in 1811 when Viceroy Venegas decided to increase vigilance over and control of the population in order to prevent subversive outbreaks in the capital. He created the Junta de Policía y Seguridad Pública (Directorate of Police and Public Security). One of the first tasks of this new council was to assemble a general census of the city's population.[239]

The division of the city into *cuarteles* as well as the creation of the post of alcalde del barrio improved the authorities' scrutiny and their control over the residents, but at night, without adequate lighting, the streets returned to their previous state: lawless disorder. In 1762, the officials made their first attempt to provide the city with public lighting. That year the *corregidor* issued an order that the residents of houses should provide a glass lamp in every balcony and door, which were to remain lighted until eleven o'clock in the evening. Because the residents refused to pay from their own pockets for street lighting, the first effort failed. The Ayuntamiento tried to set a good example by placing lamps on its building and later, in 1783, 1785, and 1787, it reiterated the order of 1762 but without success. It was only in 1790, when Viceroy Revillagigedo the second ordered the installation of a thousand oil lamps—instead of the meager fifty that had been the custom—that the city finally could count on a stable and practical public system of lighting. These lamps were paid for and maintained by the Ayuntamiento. A corps of nightwatchmen, armed with sabers and charged with keeping good order during the night, patrolled the streets.[240] This new public lighting meant that the city never escaped the gaze of the powerful; it was permanently under scrutiny. Drunks and revelers, clandestine lovers and thieves could no longer escape into the night, and the streets were no longer their refuge.

Shortly after taking charge, Viceroy Revillagigedo the second embarked upon a project to transform the capital from top to bottom. His plans were based upon the information that was available for the city and the many schemes proposed by enlightened reformers over the years. His most central preoccupation was to improve the cleanliness of the city. Several canals where putrid water had accumulated were blocked, and others were widened so that the water flow was unconstrained. Generally, the canals were cleaned more frequently. In addition, officials ordered residents to sweep the streets twice a week and to wet them down daily. The officials created two cleaning services: one group collected garbage, and the other picked up excrement. The government built latrines in streets provided with drains, and all new tenements had to have "common places." Many of the city services improved substantially; the aqueducts were repaired, and a carriage rental service was established.

The viceroy's endeavors contributed considerably to the beautification of the city. Empty lots were fenced; streets were paved and provided with sidewalks and drains. Roads such as Guadalupe, San Cosme, La Piedad, and San Antonio Abad were repaired, and three new ones, Tlaxpana, Verónica, and another that linked La Piedad to La Viga, were built. More than two thousand trees were planted along boulevards, roads, and streets. The Plazas de Jesús, Paja, Arbol, and Vizcaínas were cleaned up. The boulevards of Bucareli, Alameda, and La Viga were improved.

The other major goal of Viceroy Revillagigedo the second's urban reforms was to do away with the disorder of the city streets. The first victims of his policy were the animals—no longer allowed to wander freely on the streets. Washing horses or mules in the streets was also prohibited. The nightwatchmen were given instructions to poison any dogs found out in public after midnight. But the officials also strove to redistribute economic activities more equitably in the city. The establishment of new bakeries or *tocinerías* (pork processors) in the city center was forbidden, and the ironworkers were banned from the central core. The usual food and drink stalls were limited to authorized markets. Public diversions, as we have seen, were also the subject of strict controls, but further, boys were no longer even allowed to play in the public streets, and bonfires for "illuminations," which were the custom on religious holidays, were curtailed. Acrobats and puppeteers had to obtain licenses from the Ayuntamiento in order to perform, and even the private *colloquia* had to receive official sanction. On top of all this, *beatas* (devout women who isolated themselves, but not in convents) had to display their ecclesiastical licenses before setting up in the streets.

The ragged and poorly dressed were the subject of several governmental decrees; they could no longer work in the tobacco factory. State workers could not show up for their jobs in a state of "undress" (that is to say, wearing only socks and wrapped in a big shawl). Indians were instructed to present themselves at public functions dressed in frock coats or in capes. They were also expected to be clean and well turned out. People who did not meet this standard were prevented from entering the Plaza de Gallos and the Alameda.

Vagabonds and the drunks who had always been a concern became the target of renewed and increased repression. People who dirtied the streets were no longer tolerated but punished and even jailed. The long-standing rules governing *pulquerías* were enforced with greater rigor, while drunks were condemned to forced labor in the streets. The campaign to rid the streets of vagabonds and vagrants by jailing was expanded.[241]

The Plaza Mayor was also totally transformed; the wall that had enclosed the cathedral's atrium was taken down. Before the government of Viceroy Revillagigedo the second, Francisco Sedano had described the viceregal palace as "an honorable tenement." He stated that "inside there were rooms for those who ran the food stalls in the plaza, storage space for the fruit and other foodstuffs, restaurants, and a winery called Botillería; billiards; a working bakery where pulque was sold openly and *chinguirito* was provided under the table; public card games in the guards' offices, where another game called el Parque was played; a game of *boliche* (a kind of bowling); mounds of garbage and manure piles."[242] Viceroy Revillagigedo the second banned all the stalls, exiled all those who caused disorder and abuses, and remodeled the building.

Taking advantage of the booths' removal from in front of the Flores portal in the Plaza Mayor for the celebration of the coronation of Charles IV, the viceroy forbade their reinstallation. A few years later, when the Plaza del Volador was declared the principal market for food supplies and the Mercado del Factor, or flea market, was created, all the stands located in the Plaza Mayor were obliged to relocate. The Parián was the only commercial establishment allowed in this area, and it was located in the Portales.[243]

Revillagigedo the second's successor, the Marquis of Branciforte, finished the task of remodeling the plaza. An equestrian statue of Charles IV completed the picture. At first it was a wood and stucco sculpture with an elliptical stone balustrade surrounding it. Later, Viceroy Iturrigaray inaugurated the famous bronze statue.

The extent of the changes in the city center can be appreciated by comparing a typical scene in the Plaza Mayor under Viceroy de Croix—overflowing with people, pulque, and wine stands—to an etching of the same place in 1797. By then, it was devoid of humans; the equestrian statue formed the focus, but the scene corresponds to the spatial rules of neoclassical style. Of course, this etching does adjust reality somewhat in order to fulfill the enlightened ideal. The monument to Charles IV appears to be located in the exact center of the plaza as if the Parián did not exist. In reality, the horse was to the east of the Parián. Also, it is quite probable that the absence of people and the tranquillity that are depicted were not quite the everyday reality that the engraver and others experienced there.

Nevertheless, by the beginning of the nineteenth century, there is no doubt that the city center appeared much more orderly and civilized than it had in previous years. Disorder had not been entirely banished from the city; instead, it had been moved to the outskirts. Viceregal governments continued their campaigns in these outlying regions in an attempt to subdue all unruliness.

In 1794, the architect Ignacio Castera, *maestro mayor* [official architect] of the city, gave shape to an ambitious urban project in two regulatory plans. He proposed to extend the uniform streets of the city core into the peripheral barrios and to build a major drainage canal enclosing the whole city—including the slums—in a square. On its inside corners, there would be large plazas where military exercises would be held. The project went ahead; but the first acts—tearing down houses in order to extend the streets of the center—caused such acrimonious protests from the residents that the plans had to be put on hold. Nevertheless, to the southwest of the city, a few streets had been opened.[244]

The viceregal authorities continued to favor such proposals at the start of the nineteenth century. In 1800, in the instructions that he left his successor, Viceroy Miguel José de Azanza wrote of the urban reforms that he had completed: "They could reach paramount perfection of which they have the potential if the reform of the barrios that I had planned was accomplished; this would make the whole city uniform, even its exits, streets, and paseos."[245]

On the eve of the Wars of Independence, Mexico City had changed. Its streets had names made visible to all, its houses were numbered. Detailed city plans homogenized the new divisions— civil and ecclesiastical. The neighborhoods were patrolled by the *alcaldes mayores* and alcaldes del barrio, scrutinized by enlightened reformers, and illuminated at night by lamps. The paved streets were clean and beautified. Economic activities were more evenly distributed in the city. Public diversions were subdued. The powers-that-be had the city well under control. The state and the elites had won the battle for the streets, at least within the *traza*.

In the long term, however, this process was not so irreversible as it appeared. The Wars of Independence, as well as the weakness of the governments that ruled immediately after the end of hostilities, allowed the common people to recover, at least temporarily, the freedom that they had lost. In any case, it would be foolhardy to equate the order that reigned in the city center at the end of the colonial period with the ideals of the Enlightenment. In reality, it was a much more despotic and arbitrary order that ruled the day. The creation of thirty-two *cuarteles* and their corresponding alcaldes del barrio, who took charge of policing the population, were among the most important elements of these reforms. But, almost immediately, these posts were filled by shady individuals who used their powers for personal enrichment. Only six years after the establishment of this system, the author of the "Discurso sobre la policía de México" declared that the alcaldes del barrio, instead of "restraining or guarding against abuses," had become "the open conduits for the propagation and commission of outrages and irregularities."[246]

The new commissioners of the barrios turned out to be as corrupt as their predecessors, and sometimes they even surpassed them. Because the new officials had more extensive powers, the consequences of their acts were more harmful. The reforms of the enlightened despots of the state were carried out by veritable criminals. The rules and regulations were of no use in ending the city's abuses and disorders, but they were an ideal route to the enrichment of the alcaldes del barrio, who used them as legal "tools" to extort money from the population. The exorbitant power of a corrupt police force that would strike terror in the hearts of Mexico City's residents was beginning to take form.

# 4

# The New Order, or Pelota

Mother, unto gold I yield me,
He and I are ardent lovers;
Pure affection now discovers
How his sunny rays shall shield me!
For a trifle more or less
All his power will confess. . . .
He makes cross and medal bright,
And he smashes laws of right. . . .
Noble are his proud ancestors
For his blood-veins are patrician;
Royalties make the position
Of his Orient investors;
So they find themselves preferred
To the duke or country herd,
the very powerful gentleman
Sir Money.

—Francisco de Quevedo

Of all the public diversions in eighteenth-century Mexico City, pelota occupied a privileged position. A forerunner of jai alai, pelota is played by throwing a hard ball against the far wall of a court. The game was the favorite pastime of Basque merchants who undoubtedly introduced it into New Spain. Study of this game allows us a glimpse of the almost unknown daily life of these merchants. It permits us to approach those most important personages who, until this point, have been relatively absent from the pages of this book.

Most of the merchants had emigrated from northern Spain in general and the Basque region specifically. Most frequently, they were young peasants following the example of relatives who had already made their fortunes in the Americas. The pattern was that upon their arrival, they worked as clerks or cashiers in the shops of their fellow Basques or of their relatives—usually their uncles. After a certain time, the relatives either made them partners or lent them the capital to start up their own businesses. Most often, this financial assistance came with a strengthening of the family ties: the nephew married his cousin, the daughter of the merchant. At the death of the uncle, the nephew / son-in-law inherited the business. This peculiar system of inheritance was based on tradition. Male heirs were usually left goods that were considered socially superior and prestigious, such as the landed estates that the father had acquired with the profits of commerce. The dowries of the daughters were the stores that had produced the wealth and so, upon the death of the patriarch, the commerce fell into the hands of the nephew through marriage to the daughter. This system explains the predominance of immigrants rather than Creoles in New Spain's commerce.[1] Lorenzo de Zavala wrote a caustic description of the Spanish merchants: "The majority of those who managed this country's commerce, with very few exceptions, were *polizones* (tramps): the name given to the poor youths who left the provinces of Spain to come to America. Their possessions consisted of their clothes: a pair of pants, a vest, and a jacket with two or three shirts." Their education and professional formation were minimal: "Many barely knew how to read and write, and they had no other knowledge of the world than that which they acquired on the trip over here; in their village they heard hardly anything more than their priests' sermons or their mothers' advice. They had no conception of the *peso fuerte* of America's value; many believed that there was no leader other than the king of Spain, no other religion but Christianity, no other language than Spanish." In New Spain, they joined a relative's establishment and led a drab existence: "They were assigned to the business of some relative in whose trade they were apprenticed. Early in the morning they got dressed to go to a daily mass. Then, they went home to take their chocolate for breakfast; they opened the shop and sat down to read a book of devotions after checking the accounts. They ate at nine and at midday they closed the shop to eat and rest for the siesta. At three, they said the rosary and after their devotions, they opened the shop again until seven in the evening, when they said the rosary again and sang praises to the Virgin." This uninspiring existence extended to their employees, who "followed the example of their masters and few left their employment. Conversations were limited to the prices of the goods in which there were few fluctuations, because all was regulated by the strict monopoly controlled by Cádiz and

Barcelona." Even so, their lives revolved around business and "did not include public roles, nor evenings at the theater, nor society, nor dances, nor any of those gatherings in which men distinguished themselves or where the two sexes tried to please each other by the refinement of their taste and thus softened their daily customs and perfected nature." The author commented upon the isolation inherent to this type of existence: "This type of education must have made men into creatures much different from those we know today. How could the ideas of reform be adopted by individuals who grew up in these customs and hardened, shall we say, into the routines of a semimonastic life?"[2]

This description of the daily life of the merchant community is only missing one detail: the game of pelota. The diversion was so popular among the wealthy merchants that if their employees showed any talent, the businessmen trained them in the secrets of the game and then made them compete, placing bets on their own men.[3] In fact, this game was ideally suited to the merchants. Because most of them had little education, they were not particularly interested in the diversions of the enlightened crowd such as the theater, so popular in this period. Pelota provided one of the few distractions from their daily worries. Apart from this, it supplied a forum to reaffirm their links with the place of their birth, and after a day of standing behind a counter, it provided simple exercise that meant that they could move a bit and shake off their indolence. For their employees, the game had another virtue. Given that they rarely married before the age of forty, they needed some vigorous exercise to let off steam and to withstand the frustrations of their celibacy.[4]

Yet, pelota did not affect only Basque merchants and their employees, but also other sectors of the population. The game spread quickly in New Spain and was extremely popular among the common people. In Mexico City, besides the courts at San Camilo (about which I will provide more details later), there were others at the Alameda although they were not always in use. There were also courts in the cities of Puebla, Oaxaca, and Zacatecas. In addition, the game was played in the slums as well as in public squares in Mexico City. In fact, many of the professional players got their start in the streets.[5]

The Basque merchants were not at all pleased at the populace's adoption of their sport. Then common people began to frequent the San Camilo courts, where the merchants went to play and to place bets after work. After the people's discovery of pelota, the courts were always full. The public mocked the merchants, who did not inspire any sympathy. Those businessmen then began to meditate on ways to stop the riffraff from coming into the San Camilo courts. They did not want to share their game with plebeians nor did they wish to endure their impertinences. They needed a means to exclude the plebeians from the game of pelota.[6]

Pelota was also significant in other ways. With an extremely long history, by the eighteenth century the game was forward looking. Its modernity was undisputed; it was the only sports diversion of the period. As we know now, such amusements were destined to become excessively important, as is seen with the examples of soccer, football, tennis, and many other sports. Moreover, the game was easily converted into a defense of free enterprise. In a justification of their pastime, the merchants stated: "In this game, only physical agility that is visible to all wins; no one joins the game without knowledge of his competitor's advantage."[7]

According to these same merchants, the sport fostered two qualities in its adherents that were considered essential for the new spirit of the nascent bourgeoisie: moderation and health. Pelota was not only useful to society, but it also helped to banish vices and harmful diversions. It was, in fact, a "virtue that corresponds to that of *Eutropelia* (the virtue that moderates the excess of diversions)."[8]

Finally, pelota did not distract the merchants from their primordial preoccupation in life: the accumulation of wealth. The high bets that were common at the courts only made the games all the more exciting. This diversion combined health, moderation, free enterprise, and the desire for wealth. It represented the emerging modernity with dignity and foreshadowed the new order of bourgeois society.

## Life Struggles with Death in Pelota

No information remains about the first games of pelota in New Spain, when or where they were played. The monks of San Camilo had a court for their own use by the middle of the eighteenth century, but undoubtedly this was not the first nor the only one that existed. It must have been in the best condition, and, for this reason, in 1758, pelota fans asked the monks to open it to the public. The monastic order relented and rented it to a widow for 650 pesos a year. In return, she was allowed to charge a fee per game and for the balls. At this time, access to the stands was still free.[9]

The sport functioned in this manner for years but, according to the merchants, the common people who came to the games caused serious disorders. The merchants began to seek ways to prevent the attendance of this troublesome rabble. In 1787, with the support of the commissioner general of the order of San Camilo, the merchants petitioned the Archbishop Viceroy Núñez de Haro y Peralta to allow them to develop a series of regulations that would end the disorders that the common people caused during play.[10]

The merchants provided rules, which were confirmed in a royal decree of March 14, 1788. In the first instance, the rules prohibited "the entry of dissolute persons and of the lowest plebeians who spoiled the occasion and caused irreparable damage." Only "respectable folk" were allowed to attend the games. This disposition was not extraordinary in the social context of the times; it was the way in which the merchants decided to put the ruling into practice that was innovative. With their practical spirit, the merchants did not believe that the measure would be easy to apply. New Spain's rulebooks were full of just such dispositions, which had had no effect whatsoever. In order to make the rule effective, the merchants added a second point. From this moment forward, they would charge half a real to enter the stands. Doing so, they made entry impossible for the poor.[11] The solution, however, opened a hornets' nest, given that arguments over the use of the ticket money continued for a long time. At first, the merchants decided to name an administrator. The widow was given a lifetime pension and retired. The income from ticket sales would be destined for the new San Andrés Hospital. The king approved of such a pious decision.[12]

By 1800, the court was in disrepair and the monastery of San Camilo, as the owner, undertook its restoration. As a result, games were suspended for six months. The Order of San Camilo had spent considerable sums on these works at a time when its financial situation was not particularly healthy, and the monastery as well as the chapel were also deteriorating. At the grand reopening, in order to recover the costs of the repairs, the order increased the annual rent from 650 pesos to 1,000 pesos a year. Despite the increased rent, the order's financial problems were far from resolved. That same year, they asked the viceroy to allow them to keep the profits from ticket sales, which had been given over to the San Andrés Hospital as charity.[13]

To support their petition to the viceroy, the members of the Order of San Camilo underlined the fundamental importance of their services to the community. They rescued the spirits of Mexico City's dying residents: "Since the year 1756, when this institute was established in the capital, the priests have been serving the public with constant fervor, effort, and generosity for which they are so well known; they are continually helping the dying at all hours of day and night without even accepting a mug of hot chocolate in the houses, even when they spend the whole night at the bedside of an invalid." The priests of San Camilo, they continued, "cannot do more because of the situation [the poverty of the monastery] that makes it impossible to find the funds for their subsistence, and without those they request, all of Mexico will lament the absence of the services of ministers who with piousness provide to the residents *services that are really important* in the struggle with death, at the time when even those who most loved the invalid in life often abandon him because they do not want to witness the pain of this state."[14]

The monks were not exaggerating their merits. New attitudes regarding death among New Spain's elite in the eighteenth century made the services of the priests vital. Death was no longer a personage who, for better or worse, coexisted side by side with the population. Members of the elite opted to forget its existence in order to push into the background the terror that it inspired and the unavoidable encounter at the end of their days. Cemeteries were pushed out of the city limits; funerals began to be more austere, less showy; the inscriptions and epitaphs on gravestones were shortened to the bare minimum; and above all, the dying were abandoned.[15]

In those circumstances, because of their terror, family members and friends did not have the strength to help the ailing one in his last moments; they had to depend on the services of others. They turned to specialists who helped the dying spiritually. These were members of the Order of San Camilo, who were known as the priests of death.

Their petition to receive the ticket revenues from the pelota game provoked an angry response from the previous beneficiary, the San Andrés Hospital.[16] This institution's members wrote to the viceroy to assert that their services were much more important than those of the monastery of San Camilo. They stated that, although the monks of San Camilo "believe themselves in need and worthy of greater kindness from the public, as in effect they are because of their piousness and the value of their institution, . . . the rules of justice do not permit our silence when they ask for measures or expedients for their subsistence by trying to take from another what they have acquired with perfect legitimacy." They were indignant that the deprived would be an object *"as laudable and pious* as the General Hospital, which *not only saves the poor moribunds with spiritual aid,* which are the object of their ministry, *but also with corporeal assistance* for their recovery and food, *thus saving the lives* of many unfortunates, who otherwise would die as a result of their poverty and misery."[17]

The terms that the San Andrés Hospital laid out in its response to the Order of San Camilo placed government officials in a quandary typical of the period of the Enlightenment. Who deserved the revenues from the pelota game? Did those who helped the dying meet their Maker appropriately have more merit than those who saved the ailing from death? Did a happy death, one in which repentance and faith opened the doors of the "true" life in Paradise to the soul, have a higher value than this earthly life, so common and savage?

In fact, during the century of Enlightenment, the elite had already made their choice. Although they could not make such an admission openly, they had decided for life. They preferred worldly goods over the eternal life. The struggle between the Order of San Camilo and the San Andrés Hospital was extremely embarassing for the colonial officials—both civil and ecclesiastical—because they found it impossible to express this preference. How could they tell the monks of death that the enlightened society did not want to be reminded of death and that they valued the doctors who remedied the ailments of the body over those who saved the soul? To do so, they would have had to admit this fact to themselves as well.

Their solution was bureaucratic delay. Despite numerous letters asking for a final decision, many years passed without an answer to the order's petition. Finally, in August 1805, the archbishop discovered a solution that allowed an end to this matter without implicating the church in the fundamental question that lurked in the background. In a letter to the viceroy, the prelate noted that if the hospital received the ticket revenues as a result of a royal decree, only another decree could change the situation.[18]

This breakthrough was coincidental to the arrival of a royal decree from Charles IV that resolved a conflict between the Basque merchants and the San Andrés Hospital. The merchants won this round; they had requested a permanent judge for the game. The salary of the official would be paid out of the charity money

destined for the hospital. With great audacity, the viceroy interpreted this order as an endorsement of the hospital as the recipient
of the ticket revenues. Without taking any responsibility, the viceroy rejected the Order of San Camilo's petition.[19]

Actually, the monks of death were fighting against the tide. Not
only had the Enlightenment fostered a choice of life over the happy
death, but even the very monks whose purpose was the latter shared
the mentality of New Spain's elite. They also considered good health
and a long life to be virtues. In fact, it was for this reason that they
built the pelota court. In 1787, the commissioner general of the order had written: "Through the uninterrupted passage of centuries,
from the Greeks, the Romans, and more civilized and cultured nations, the spheroid or game of pelota has been deemed one of the
most honest and useful exercises as it provides for relaxation, *health*,
and recreation."[20]

In 1818, the commissioner general expressed this idea once
again but with greater clarity: The game of pelota "is much more
beneficial for one's health, because in it the corporeal forces are
exercised."[21] Pelota was really the only diversion that meshed with
the new cult of health that enlightened thinkers adopted; it counterbalanced their terror of death.[22] Whenever the Basque merchants
had to list the virtues of the sport, they never forgot to mention the
benefit to health. They based this affirmation on scientific authority: "Without question, the game of pelota is one of the most honest, useful, and innocent of diversions in which one can engage. Its
origins in time immemorial, its almost universal practice, and the
unanimous opinions of scientists all favor it. This diversion, which
pits friends against each other, amuses the elderly and adults, and
excites the young in a healthy manner."[23]

Its adherents also credited pelota with fostering another virtue
that the bourgeoisie associated with health and physical vigor:
moderation. The merchants wrote: "All the moralists agree that a
game, played in the proper moderation, is a virtue of *eutropelia*;
and if this opinion extends without discrimination to all games, all
the more reason to apply it to the game of pelota." They continued:
"Other games develop ambition more than entertainment, and
when they do not harm health, they do nothing to improve it, as
occurs, when combined with vice, they lead to the practice of remaining seated and keeping at it day and night. Only this occupation provides a corporeal exercise that is beneficial to health and a
medicinal agitation that does not allow the player to extend the
hours of play beyond what his physique allows and, in any case,

playing always comes to an end with the night. In short, no game provides better circumstances for its honesty, the little risk to one's fortune or family."[24]

The last part of this defense of pelota was a bald-faced lie. The sport was no doubt healthy but it was certainly neither innocent nor honest. Sizeable bets were placed on the outcome of games and, at times, some gamblers arranged their bets before the games so that they could wager large amounts of money. This fact was confirmed by an adviser to the viceroy in 1801: "In effect, according to the information I have acquired and what I have observed personally, I understand the need to reserve this game for decent and up-standing persons only as was resolved by His Majesty. Although it should be an honest diversion, it is riddled with vice, probably because of the class of persons who attend, maybe because of the ne'er-do-wells who laze around there without any other purpose in life; or perhaps because of the large quantities of money that are wagered."[25] For most participants the bets were, in fact, the major interest, and actually the game itself was not much more than a smoke screen to fool the authorities and give the sport an air of respectability.

Bets, however, are rarely mentioned in the documents relating to problems arising from this sport. In contrast, the regulations elaborated in 1801 place great importance on the gambling factor. That year, an influential group of Basque merchants, alledging that "various abuses" had crept into the game, proposed a new set of rules that included the hiring of a permanent judge to be paid from ticket revenues. Naturally, the San Andrés Hospital opposed this measure because its revenues were threatened. It argued that the disorders in the game of pelota were exaggerated.[26] This riposte forced the merchants reluctantly to specify the types of abuse to which they referred: "If none other, it would be a great boon to prevent the freedom and impetuousness of some sons and employees of principal families who bet in excessive amounts; this would be a very worthy goal."[27]

In fact, the principal difference between this new set of rules and the previous ones was the inclusion of several points—28 to 36—which specified in great detail the way in which bets were to be placed.[28] In the game of pelota, as in the century of the Enlightenment, in the struggle between a happy death and earthly life, the winner was not life—as might be concluded at first glance—nor were the players the victors, but rather the gambler, the powerful gentleman Sir Money.

## The Controversy of Disorder

The documents on the game of pelota reveal that both the merchants and the monks of the Order of San Camilo shared a constant obsession: to prohibit the entry of the common people into their court and stands at any price. They always blamed the "plebeians" for all the disorders that occurred there. In the Regulations of 1787, for example, the group of merchants, fans of the game, stated the following:

> 1. That this assembly agrees that to put an end to the disorders that have plagued this place for several years, there is no remedy that is more convenient than to root out the cause, that is to say, to strictly prohibit the entry of any depraved person of the riffraff who tarnish this diversion and cause irreparable problems; therefore, they believe it necessary and are now resolved that from this day forward, no persons who do not belong to the category of decent folk will be admitted into the game of pelota.[29]

In 1800, the same committee of merchants elaborated upon its reasons for the adoption of this rule: "There came a time when such a large group of this riffraff infiltrated the place, that their constant drunkenness, insolence, and provocations were a continual embarassment and put us at risk of perdition."[30] According to these men, the excesses of the common people were such that many respectable persons were forced to abandon their fondness for the game.

But were the affirmations of these merchants all true? Had the common people of Mexico City become a constant source of continually serious disorders? This question is at the center of this study. Did the customs of the common people really suffer such a decline in the eighteenth century? The documents on the game of pelota allow a clear answer to this question, although only as it relates to that sport.

This rare opportunity arises from the fact that with the diversion of pelota, unlike others, the campaign to restrict the common people ran into the obstacle of the economic interests of two institutions: first, the San Andrés Hospital and then later, the Order of San Camilo. As noted above, in 1801 the merchants came to the conclusion that the best way to end the disruptions caused by the plebeians was to hire a full-time judge. This measure, because it was to be funded out of the ticket revenues destined for the hospital, however, did not sit well with this institution. By 1817, during the Wars of Independence, the game of pelota was no longer so popular. Ticket sales no longer even covered the rent charged by the Order of San Camilo and the judge's salary. The monks proposed that the position of judge be eliminated so that the savings on his salary could restore the rent they received.[31] In both cases, the groups whose economic interests were prejudiced by the hiring of the judge alleged that there had never been any important disorders at the games. These arguments forced the merchants and then the judge to try to provide some evidence of these grave disorders. This confrontation, therefore, is very useful in resolving the question of the decline in the customs of the common people in the eighteenth century. Let us examine the arguments on both sides of this debate as it relates to the game of pelota.

In 1787, when the first regulations governing the game of pelota were drafted, no financial interests were at risk; but when the benefits of the ticket revenues had begun going to San Andrés Hospital, everyone agreed that very serious disorders were an everyday occurrence at the games. The Basque merchants who fostered the regulations were the first to identify the problems.[32] The merchants had the support of the commissioner general of the Order of San Camilo, who stated that: "As if the door to a theater designed only for respectable people was opened, even this worthy sport [pelota] does not stop the introduction of disorder by the riffraff. It would be interminable to list the insults that the most dignified men hear at every step from this dirty, idle, and slovenly group who are not distinguished in any way, nor worthy of any respect." He attributed the problem of disorder to the inherent unruliness of the plebeians: "Suffice it to say that it is common knowledge that as soon as they can speak, it is to insult, just like the hidden knife underneath the mantle, which barely covers the rebelliousness always at the back of their minds, because of the hate they feel for those not of their ilk, nor of their vile lineage."[33] Obviously, the cleric believed that the common people who attended the games were not only poorly behaved but actually criminals.

In 1800, the merchants stated that the regulations of 1787 had stopped the disorders but that over time, some abuses had crept back in. For this reason, they wished to reform the previous regulations and to name a permanent judge who would oversee the good order of the game.[34] In the absence of the archbishop, the cathedral chapter rose to the defense of the hospital. The chapter categorically denied the need for a judge, arguing that it was unnecessary because the game of pelota did not provoke disorders. To bolster their reasoning, they noted that a diversion that was much more likely to stimulate all sorts of excesses, such as the theater, did not enjoy the services of a special judge. They also reiterated the virtues—health, moderation, and such—that the merchants had listed as characteristics of the game. In defense of their position, the cathedral chapter declared: "It should be stated that in the case of theater, obviously a judge is needed because it takes place only at night, and misdemeanors can flourish in the shadows. But the diversion of pelota takes place in the light of the day, which serves as a deterrent to these misdeeds." They continued with, "In the former, all types of persons, from the riffraff who are naturally prone to such transgressions, are admitted, and in the latter, by order of His Majesty, this class of person is not admitted, rather only respectable individuals, known for their good manners." They also pointed out that "in the former, people of both sexes mix, which often puts innocence at risk, while in the latter, only men attend so that these situations simply do not arise." Finally they concluded, "The plays conspire to excite the most spirited and violent passions, while the game of pelota diverts, entertains, and even serves to moderate emotions by the moderating effect of exercise and activity. And, undoubtedly, it is for this reason that, although there are numerous authors who denounce the theater, not one criticizes the moderate exercise of pelota, and in contrast with the constant turmoil in the Coliseum, the game is problem-free." They reinforced their argument with the opinion of the "*mayordomo* [who was] not aware of such outrages, and said so when questioned by some of the judges; and because there were no problems, the picket of soldiers, stationed there by royal decree, was considered useless and removed."[35] These last affirmations—the unfamiliarity of the judges with any problems and the removal of the soldiers—were arguments that were hard to refute for those who wished to create the position of judge of the game of pelota.

One of the viceroy's advisers tried to mitigate the impact of this argument by stating that certain types of disorders were frequent. He cited the presence of loafers and the excessive gambling.[36] But were these problems of a sufficiently serious nature to warrant the creation of a position of judge especially for the game? In fact, the merchants were unable to come up with more serious problems to bolster their claims. Their response to the letter revealed their inability to counter this logic, and instead, to sway the viceroy, they resorted to declamations of good intentions and accused the cathedral chapter of sacrificing good order to their own economic interests. Despite this attempt at obfuscation, it was still clear that they could not provide examples of serious mayhem that the judge was supposed to repress. Believing it to be an unassailable argument, the *mayordomo* added that, "because he considered their ignorance to be an absurd argument that proved nothing, he asked some of the judges whether they knew of any disorders in the courts of San Camilo." The merchants then stated, "Since we do not want to suffer further, and we do not need any other proof of the lack of precision with which they have operated, it is clear that the *mayordomo* does not care whether there are excesses in the game of pelota so long as there is enough revenue to support the hospital. It is to be hoped that others who are not blessed with our temperate characters do not hear of this convenient blindness, so scandalous in persons imbued with the sacred soul and the ministries of the church."

The merchants continued, "The office of the magistrates and of justice should not be involved in all these vices and excesses. They do not punish but rather muddy the waters with external actions. Legislators cannot chastise all the avaricious, the haughty, the wrathful, those of ill will and other similar vices, as a wise statesman once said, because there would be no more citizens if every person dominated by some vice was condemned." They concluded that, "from this, we can assume that not all the excesses and disorders are reported to the judges and many go unpunished even though they are an open offense to morality. But, even taking this into account, that the judges are unaware of these vices that we have to regulate, it would still be a laudable goal to achieve good order by the establishment of a council and the naming of a judge."

The merchants argued further that "men do not suddenly reach the limits of perversity to commit crimes that disturb social order. The passions become stronger and more audacious if the acts are not challenged and stopped but, rather, repeated; they must be regulated with some small penalties, much in the same manner as a father uses in his family." They concluded, "This is not to say that these measures should be absent from the theater where youths who could profit from such discipline might be in attendance, but rather that we have provided this discipline for the good of our employees and all the people who attend the games for their enjoyment. Even if this would simply restrain some of the sons and employees from betting excessively, this would indeed be a worthy goal."[37]

Clearly, it was this last point that really preoccupied the merchants, who had suddenly developed moralistic tendencies. They believed that the naming of a judge was wholly justified if only to prevent their sons and employees from gambling excessively and to avoid the possible negative consequences for their businesses. Apart from this concern, however, they could not point to any other regular source of disorder, except perhaps when the common people jeered at the merchants and poor players. Even this excess ceased when "the plebs" were banned in 1787. In any case, the affirmations of the merchants were much tamer than those made by the commisioner general of the Order of San Camilo, when in 1787, he had referred to knives hidden under cloaks. The only vices mentioned were not really the responsibility of criminal justices, but rather offenses that could be repressed with warnings. Despite the weakness of their case, the authorities did finally give them the right to hire an exclusive judge for the game of pelota. Undoubtedly, the merchant's enormous economic and political power tipped the balance in the decision.

A similar discussion emerged in 1818, although on this occasion it was between the Order of San Camilo and the pelota judge. The Wars of Independence had caused a decline in interest in the game, which translated into a deterioration in revenues. The Order of San Camilo could no longer collect the full amount of rent for the use of their court and so they changed their tune. In 1787, they had stated that the game occasioned horrendous excesses but, in the new situation, they affirmed that never in the history of the game had there been any chronicle of notable disorders, which meant that the cost of the private judge was an unnecessary luxury. They argued that "the removal of the private judge does not imperil the game, the constant experience of half a century confirms this statement, as does logic and the evidence, because under normal circumstances, one or another player might commit a fraud in the bets or in the game." The merchants believed that peer pressure would resolve such situations. They argued that "the greatest penalty for them is to lose the good opinion of their peers, which is the equivalent of losing their profession, and falling into poverty, for which reason these frauds are extremely rare, and in addition, the person who is caught will be denied entry to the game if he acts this way even only once."[38]

Faced with these and other similar arguments that the San Andrés Hospital and the cathedral chapter had made previously, and the unblemished record of lack of public scandals, in January 1819, the viceroy allowed the monks to continue the game of pelota without the private judge. Prudently, he also ordered them to make use of the "assistance of a lieutenant and two soldiers as was the custom previously," if the circumstances warranted, and to advise "of the slightest disorder so that it can be remedied."[39]

Deprived of such an important source of income during a troublesome period, the judge appealed to the Audiencia to protest this decision. He tried to demonstrate the inherent dangers of the game of pelota, reverting to the time-honored argument that the mere presence of the common people was always the cause of disorders. He also referred to another more original contention, that an assembly of many people, in these difficult times for the colony, might easily veer into subversive activities. As usual, however, his allegations did not contain any concrete evidence of disorder except for those that were induced by the high-stakes gambling. The judge considered: "It should be useful to be reminded of the basis and experiences that caused the establishment of the commission of judge of the game of pelota, which today has been eliminated." He worried about the mixing of people there: "In effect, a multitude of people of all classes, but particularly plebeians, who have no manners, or shame, congregate in one place for a game that exalts greed and other harmful emotions, and these people, excited by the well-known ease that the game of pelota allows for frauds, deceptions, and tricks, were quite prone to disorders and *even* misdemeanors."

His experience as a judge made it "quite painful to see artifices between the players every day and spectators, with their excessive gambling, bankrupting fathers and sons and leading to quarrels and dangerous arguments." He concluded by arguing for the position: "There were the many circumstances . . . that . . . led Your Majesty to create the position of a judge who was charged with the prompt prevention of excesses among the players and whose experience and knowledge would help in the deterrence of such intemperance; it was impossible to control these abuses in another manner even by the counsel of respectable members; and the urgent need and public expediency that no large crowds be allowed to congregate without someone in charge who has proper authority." The judge affected incomprehension: "It is hard to fathom that these same considerations are not even stronger today in the midst of a rebellion that makes even the most innocent of assemblies suspicious and inspires fear and, consequently, resources have diminished while the demands have increased." He argued that "the players of the game of pelota are not immune from the effects of the terrible dissipation of customs among the residents of this kingdom and now they have the same chances to transgress and upset the order of the game." Finally, the judge concluded: "It is hard to see how circumstances have changed, that is to say, there are public dangers or private frauds to prevent or quickly thwart, because the causes of all these wrongs have increased."[40]

The viceroy's adviser cut through this sophisticated argument with a scathing and definitive reply that closed the door on the argument over disorder in the game of pelota: "According to the records of complaints, there have never been any murders, deaths, quarrels, *or scandals, or anything that requires the attention of a judge*, but rather only the worries of the same monks that the riffraff, indecent and disgusting plebeians, should not be allowed to enter; which has been achieved with the simple expedient of the care of the same clerics."[41] This answer shows that, despite the fact that no disorders of particular importance occurred in the game of pelota, the monks of San Camilo shared a conviction with the merchants and the viceregal authorities that excluding the common people from the game was paramount. The fundamental basis of the regulations of 1787 was not to do away with plebeian abuses, which did not amount to much, but simply to make sure that respectable people at their diversions did not have to rub shoulders with the riffraff.

## "We Reserve the Right of Admission"

At the end of the colonial period, there were a number of successful attempts to forbid plebeians from attending the game of pelota. These campaigns were not motivated by the disorders caused by the common people—although this was regularly alleged—because, as we have seen, no problems of any great magnitude really existed. This desire to segregate diversions actually sprang from a much more complex set of causes.

First, the Mexican elite, of which the monks were an integral part, was horrified by the people of "the pleb" who represented nothing less than an overwhelming majority of Mexico City's population. In 1787, the commissioner general of the order of San Camilo wrote: "The riffraff of this most populous city are the most filthy, most disgusting, most obscene, most impolite, most heedless, and most discourteous and shameless, so that they are beyond human imagination."[42]

Also, in eighteenth-century New Spain, the elite class believed that all social evils were rooted in the erosion of social barriers and in "the mixing of all types of persons."[43] Nothing was more harmful than a person of the lower classes who tried to pass as an equal of members of the upper classes, blending in with them in public places. Proper social order implied that different spaces be established for genteel persons and for those of the pleb. This concern is evident in a missive to the archbishop-viceroy: "The general adviser to the viceroyalty will only state to Your Illustrious Excellency that the said people [of the plebeian class] must be prevented on high holidays from presenting their diversions as equal to those of distinguished and high-ranking persons of this court; it is imperative to avoid the option in this most orderly Republic of ignoring class distinctions."[44]

In 1803, the monks of San Camilo again expressed their concern that elite men not mix with others of different classes. They pointed out: "The commissioner general noted the disorder occasioned in the game by the open admission policy, which allowed respectable persons to mingle with the lowest plebeians, and wishing to avoid the nefarious consequences of this fact, he tried to alter the conditions so that the many decent persons would feel more comfortable when they attended this honest diversion."[45]

Strangely, the idea that the common people should have their own diversions and particular spaces for them was also threatening, because the transformation of such spaces into breeding grounds of subversion seemed a short step away. It was for this reason that, in 1817, a judge of the pelota game contended that the worst possible scenario was that the game might become entirely the preserve of the common people: "The paucity of good players as well as the circumstances of the times have made the previous competitors withdraw (that is to say, respectable people) from this diversion . . . so that only two possible outcomes seemed likely, that it would be totally abandoned or that it would be attended only by the riffraff; either of these would be prejudicial for the public."[46]

Evidently, the only appropriate place for the common people, apart from churches and their homes, was their workplace. In the eyes of the Mexican elite—when outside these spaces—the common people were nothing but riffraff. The viceregal authorities vented this prejudice when they decreed that on workdays, no person of the lower classes should be seen at the game of pelota. Only respectable people, the rich, were accorded the right to enjoy a few hours of leisure every day. The viceroy's adviser expressed this sentiment in 1787: "On workdays when respectable persons gather for a sensible period of worthwhile relaxation from their tasks in the said game after having completed their work, the general adviser believed that there was no need to prevent the riffraff from mixing with the upper classes, because the artisans and workmen should be laboring without interruption and it would be sufficient only to see them at the pelota game to arrest them as vagabonds and bad examples for their peers."[47]

The merchants, the monks of the Order of San Camilo, and the viceregal authorities did not skimp on means to exclude the common people from the game. In the first place, all people deemed of lower class extraction were barred from entry. The criterion for differentiating between the two groups—upper and lower class—was simple. Clothes were the defining feature: "That the ticket salesman or the doorman should not allow any person who is not decent to enter for any reason and that those who enter must at least be dressed in military garb or with a cape, but none of those who walk around in skins or wrapped in counterpanes, sheets, or blankets or using these as capes, which, because only a few threads remain, are called raindrops."[48]

To make this prohibition even more effective, the officials decided to charge a half-real for admission. And, as if this were not enough, they also added a rule to the effect that "if, because of some negligence of the employee, one of those who is banned enters, one of the spectators can report this occurrence to the administrator so that the official or the sentinel might, without any scandal, effect the prompt expulsion of the said individual."[49] This text makes it clear that the Basque merchants had a small group of soldiers at their disposal to enforce the rules. These men were commissioned expressly to maintain order during pelota matches.[50]

The goal of all these regulations was to make the game and the courts an exclusive space for the colonial Mexican elite in general and for the Basque merchants in particular. When these merchants arrived at the San Camilo courts after a hard day working behind the counter at their shops, they found it intolerable to discover the courts occupied by slothful plebeians and vagrants. With the bald-faced arrogance that comes with wealth, the merchants included a condition in the Regulations of 1801 that would guarantee that when they arrived at the courts, they would be empty of riffraff:

> 21. That every workday, the court must be unoccupied at five o'clock in the afternoon so that the merchants and other respectable persons can play their games at this time when they are free from their occupations and for the benefit of their relaxation and

their taking some moderate exercise for the benefit of their health.[51]

On holidays, the merchants went to the courts as spectators and, most of all, as gamblers, and they expected the games and players to be top-notch. In order to ensure that this was the case, they instituted the following rules:

18. That because the hospital has suffered because of the stubborn lack of concern of some bumblers who monopolize the courts on holidays without reprieve in either the mornings or afternoons, in order that decent players can get access and attract more spectators, it is appropriate that all unskilled players, known as *molonguetes*, should be limited to the usual three sets and on holidays must desist at 10:30 in the morning and at 4:00 in the afternoon.

19. That first- and second-class players can play as many games as time allows; they will pay for the balls that they lose at a rate of two reales on holidays per game of three sets and one real on workdays as is current.

20. That the good players get preference over the bumblers at all hours and that they take turns among themselves, but if poor players are competing before the periods specified in Article 18, the game in progress must finish before any new game can be started.[52]

The rules even covered many small details that were included so that it would be clear that the game of *pelota* was a first-class diversion:

17. That the game attendants must be dressed with the decency appropriate to their class; to which effect, money from the contribution fund will be allocated in the necessary amounts for light clothing for them, which they must wear only while in service, as was disposed and foreseen by His Illustrious Excellency the Archbishop in a decree of the August 3, [17]87.[53]

The superintendent of the hospitals threatened to increase the restrictions that affected plebeian aficionados of pelota when, in order to raise the money for the San Andrés Hospital, he proposed a ban on street games and the imposition of an entrance fee for all courts in the city and not just the San Camilo court. He stated: "It seems appropriate to me that in the other pelota courts in the city, the entrance fee as well as the charges for players should be instituted for the benefit of the hospital because this subsidy belongs to it except for the new expenses, which are discounted as a result of the new regulation [1801]." He argued: "This undertaking would be possible if the game is prohibited from plazas and the outlying regions and with the proviso that people who are not, nor consider themselves to be, respectable should not be allowed to enter the court of San Camilo. And, as such, all those who want to play must perforce go to some of the other courts, whose better surfaces as well as gloves and balls will be incentive enough so that no violence will be necessary; and even though the price will be less, it will compensate for the new expenses."[54]

Evidently, the proposal was not realistic. Pelota had become so popular that it was impossible to prevent people from playing it in the streets. But, even so, this proposal was in harmony with the spirit of the times. Had not Carnaval been banished from the city center? Was it not the intention of the authorities to do away with the consumption of "prohibited" drinks? Were the street performers and puppeteers not under constant vigilance? Were "excesses" not prevented at religious festivals? Why not try to bar pelota from the streets if it was in the interests of the San Andrés Hospital?

Fortunately, the superintendent of hospitals' idea was not adopted. The Basque merchants opposed it unabashedly. At this time, the games in the San Camilo court were the only ones functioning in Mexico City. If street games were disallowed, it would be an open invitation to the entire plebeian population to come to San Camilo. Also, many players began in these street games, and if they were banned, the breeding grounds for new players would be eliminated. The merchants wrote: "As for the idea to prohibit any playing in the plazas or slums, in order to force all classes of people to play in the courts and thus contribute to the maintenance of the hospital, it is so absurd that it defeats itself and can only be rejected." They asked: "Who would provide courts in sufficient numbers for the many men who play in the plazas and slums free of charge if there is only the closed court of San Camilo (where the riffraff cannot enter), if the Alameda remains unrepaired?" Finally, they concluded: "If this measure was implemented, the consequences for the family, the state, and even the very San Andrés Hospital would be disastrous. Because new, skillful players would not be developed, there would be no attraction in the courts of San Camilo and thus, naturally, there would be no audience."[55]

The game of pelota demonstrates that the notion of hierarchy was still quite firmly in place among the colonial Mexican elites. The idea of equality among men, so dear to the Enlightenment in

France, does not seem even to have crossed the minds of the authorities, or the religious personnel, or even less the merchants who intervened in the regulation of this sport. Within this traditional mentality of hierarchy, one clearly modern trait must be noted. In 1787, when the Basque merchants and the monks of San Camilo decided to charge a half-real to enter the courts, they did so explicitly to prevent the admission of the poorer spectators, in essence, the plebeians. Yet, actually, the goal of this obligatory donation was not financial gain. The revenues were given to the San Andrés Hospital as charity. Also, by the end of the colonial period, many individuals were frequently exempted from this fee. Most certainly, those who enjoyed this privilege were respectable folk. In 1821, the assistant *regidor* wrote of the game of pelota that "the earnings are derived from the games, which are so much more profitable than *the miserable entrance fee of half a real* that it seems to me worthwhile to overlook the fee forever, as long as people feel welcome."[56]

By imposing a financial barrier to exclude the common people from the game, the merchants and the monks of San Camilo inaugurated a mechanism of social segregation that presaged the society to come. Economic differences became the most important social distinction. The backlash and the strictly hierarchical attitude coexisted in the most modern diversion of the century of Enlightenment. Within the efforts to impose the old principles of social segregation efficiently, the new order made its first appearance.

## Dissipated and Dominated

In his novel *El Periquillo Sarniento*, Lizardi compares the New Spain that he experienced with a mining town: "After . . . one or two mines have been discovered, it is said that the town is enjoying a bonanza, and this is precisely when things are at their worst. As soon as the veins are discovered, prices skyrocket; luxury is the rule of the day; strangers, often the most debased people, fill the town; they corrupt the original inhabitants; in short, the mining town becomes a scandalous den of criminals; in all parts, people gamble, get drunk, fight, wound each other, rob and kill, and commit all sorts of disorders."[57]

For a long time, historians believed that such moralist harangues were faithful descriptions of the social environment of the eighteenth century. In reality, they reflected the preoccupations of Lizardi and the other enlightened thinkers, who worried about the new disorders. Yet these new disorders were just old customs that the moralizing discourse and the struggle against "dissipation" targeted. This contradiction characterized New Spain's spirit during the last colonial century.

The Enlightenment proclaimed a life of moderation to be its ideal. As such, public diversions had to be guided by the corresponding virtue, or *eutropelia*. In 1815, Lizardi wrote: "Games, taken rationally, are not only not vices but rather represent a moral virtue named *eutropelia*." He defined *eutropelia* as "that moral circumspection that teaches us to rest when physically or spiritually tired, after a moderate diversion, which happily restores the natural restfulness of our spirit, makes us more happy and at peace with our work."[58]

The common people's pastimes were far from this ideal. Their noisy participation in the theater, their unfettered Carnaval, their sarcastic street entertainers and puppeteers, their stupendous drunks, and their cathartic parties scandalized and horrified New Spain's enlightened thinkers. Thus, the viceregal authorities decided to take on the task of ending these "disorders" and to put the people on the straight-and-narrow path of moderation and replace their diversions with those of *eutropelia*. For this reason, the bullfight was suppressed as a retrograde, barbaric, and bloodthirsty diversion. The conduct of the common people was strictly controlled in the theater; the shows themselves were professionalized and made to conform with the rules of bourgeois realism, while at the same time, they were transformed into a tool for political and moral propaganda. At the beginning of the eighteenth century, Carnaval—a bastion of popular culture—was exiled from the city center and then still fought vigorously. The officials were also outraged by the "disorders" and "excesses" that occurred during religious celebrations and so forced these festivities off the streets into private homes.

It was because of these policies that the *colloquia* and *jamaicas* began to be so common but these observances did not meet with the authorities' approval either. The *jamaicas* were forbidden, although undoubtedly without much success. Meanwhile, the *colloquium* became the subject of strict monitoring but with equally poor results. The population's increasing poverty as well as the exorbitant taxes on pulque fulfilled the desires of many of the moralists of the period—the consumption of this alcoholic beverage declined. At the same time, distilled beverages, which were more acceptable within the bourgeois morality of the day, partially replaced the "prohibited" ones; the mixtures of pulque and roots that had their origins in pre-Hispanic practices were condemned as diabolical. The street performers and puppeteers had to seek licenses to perform and, in order to keep their permissions, they had to moderate the tone of their acts and dialogues, especially because at this time, the "scientific" and "educational" diversions much in vogue began to compete for the same public. New Spain's elites had engaged in the reconquest of the streets, which once had been the common people's domain. For this reason, the viceregal authorities undertook their repair and renovation so that they would be transformed into appealing paseos. As for the game of pelota, the merchants had expelled the plebeians without any consideration whatever.

Was there not a breakdown of customs in the eighteenth century? In fact, there was, but only within New Spain's elite. This group imitated the French and started to follow bourgeois standards of conduct. Their morality was secularized and became more "natural." The exaltation of Christian contrition, which had been more theoretical than practical, was supplanted by praise for a moderate enjoyment of earthly pleasures. Outings in carriages, *tertulias,* and *saraos* became most fashionable in New Spain. Luxury and a pleasant lifestyle became the norm for the upper classes. But, at the same time that these elites afforded themselves less rigid rules of conduct, they became more intolerant in their attitude toward the common people. In previous periods, it was received wisdom that vices did not stain the good names of people of the lower classes as they did for those who were at the top of the social hierarchy and who, theoretically, had to preserve their honor and reputation. On the other hand, it was a common belief that humans were naturally sinners. Transgressions of the rules of religion and morality only confirmed this fact. Fortunately, the sacrament of confession, along with sincere repentance—often rather fleeting—could wash away the sins of the penitent.

In contrast, bourgeois morality considered people responsible for their own fate. Therefore, individuals, through their acts, did not simply confirm their natures but formed them. Violations of the moral order then took on a much more serious, objective character, and no subjective repentance could erase them. The guilty party had to pay and be punished. Finally, the fact that it was people of the lower classes who committed the crimes did not lessen their gravity. The bourgeoisie started to believe that they did not owe their wealth and their social position to divine grace or their parentage, but that they were the result of their daily efforts, their work, and their moderate behavior, which conformed to morality and decency. In contrast, the poor created their situations because they surrendered to vices that were contrary to middle-class virtues. The poor sought their own fate through their laziness, their immorality, and their lack of decency. The elite thus believed that to control the poor with a paternal severity would not be cruel, but rather a way to help them discard their dissipated customs and to place them on the straight-and-narrow path—in short, to educate them.[59]

This transformation is at the root of the eighteenth-century state's campaign, with the elites, the enlightened thinkers, and even, at times, the church, to crush firmly the diversions, the lifestyles, and the culture of the common people. In eighteenth-century New Spain, some people had dissipated lifestyles and others suffered from the domination of rigid authority, but the two characters were not of the same social group. The elites belonged to the first, and the common people to the second.

Clearly, the authorities' new attitudes were not exclusive to New Spain but were, indeed, common to all of the countries and colonies where the ideas of the Enlightenment spread and where the new bourgeoisie had made its decided appearance. In addition, this new enlightened intolerance did not emerge from forces internal to New Spain but from European realities. The people who formulated these policies regarding popular diversions and those who were in charge of implementing them were by and large Spanish bureaucrats. They were not acquainted with Mexican society and rarely stayed long enough to become familiar with it. They came with preconceived ideas and tried to find ways to impose these notions. One of these ideas was that the urban lower classes lacked propriety and that when they were composed of Indians, mestizos, and mulattoes, such a debasement was much more likely. To put an end to these disorders, they turned to policies that had been effective in Spain and only reinforced their provisions due to the greater defects within the colonial population. The Creole enlightened thinkers had a much more simplistic vision of society, but they shared the ideal of modernity with the Europeans. They frequently assisted by offering their greater knowledge of the local conditions and hoped to bring to light the moralizing reforms and get reality in line with the new standards. The measures that were to govern public diversions in New Spain were directly inspired by those that were applied or at least attempted in Spain. A few examples illustrate this connection.

Generally, Spanish thinkers opposed the bullfights. Jovellanos y Ramírez criticized this festivity because it had lost its noble quality and had become a plebeian entertainment in which the bullfighter risked his life for a meager sum of money. Also, it had become a barbarous and bloodthirsty diversion.[60] The Count of Campomanes objected to the bullfights because, according to him, they were a drain on the economy.[61] Finally, as we have already discussed, the Bourbons, who had never been fans of the *corridas*, outlawed them in 1785 and reiterated the measure in 1805.[62]

In contrast, modern men of culture favored the theater. Juan Pablo Forner defended this art form decisively as long as it "served to teach and improve, while amusing."[63] Jovellanos acclaimed the theater as the first among spectacles, the most rational and the most beneficial.[64] The ministers of Charles III also resolutely supported the theater. A royal decree of 1767 repealed all prohibitions against plays and enjoined local authorities to reopen theaters that had been closed.[65] Nevertheless, all the defenders of the dramatic arts agreed that the stage was in a deplorable state. The public, particularly those members of it seated in the balconies, were disruptive and caused disorder. The shows were of a very inferior quality and, on top of all this, they were immoral. In his report on the reform of the theater and public diversions, Jovellanos proposed in 1790 that one or two distinguished citizens—preferably members of a dramatic academy—be named in each theater who would direct and make sure that the spectators were orderly. It seemed to him that acting schools were also needed to end the vices and defects of the actors; and clearly, doing away with the dances that were presented on stage and which were, according to him, nothing other than "a miserable imitation of the riffraff's free and indecent dances" was necessary.[66] In Madrid, the enlightened thinkers denounced the *sainetes* and *tonadillas*.[67]

In general, the taste of the majority of the public had nothing in common with that of the enlightened thinkers. While the former embraced the works of Spain's Golden Age, especially those plays of love and magic—such as *El mágico de Salerno*—the latter criticized these plays and proposed their replacement with works in the neoclassical style.[68] According to the standards for drama emitted from Valladolid, if plays were to fulfill their objective of educating while entertaining, they had to teach proper religion, be moral, inculcate appropriate attitudes; the language had to be seemly, the characters had to be tasteful, and the scenery had to be realistic.[69] This verisimilitude was the idea of the enlightened thinkers, and they believed that the rule of the three unities was the best means to achieve this goal. Nicolás Fernández, as early as 1762, wrote plays that respected the unities of space, time, and action.[70] Verisimilitude and realism, which encompassed so much, had clear and precise limits. "The object of the [theatrical] fable," wrote Forner, "is to represent not all that is possible but rather that which can be represented without great repugnance."[71] The theater, according to Jovellanos, should present "good and magnanimous princes, humane and uncorruptible magistrates, virtuous citizens, faithful and devoted friends."[72]

All this was far from embodying verisimilitude. Jovellanos, in fact, believed that the Royal Academy of Language should be responsible for the censorship of theater, which meant that it should be based upon stylistic considerations.[73] Nevertheless, he also believed that the theater should fulfill a political function by presenting dramas that displayed a reverence for the Supreme Being and the Catholic religion, in which all loved the king, the law, and the authorities in general.[74] He was not the only intellectual who thought it appropriate to use drama as a political tool to maintain the established order. In a 1797 letter to Manuel de Godoy, Leandro de Moratín wrote that good theater should "instruct the common people in what by necessity they must know, that they must be obedient, modest, humane, and virtuous, that they must avoid concerns and errors that harm good customs and Christian morals, without which neither the laws nor the authority will be respected." Furthermore, according to this author, "[Theater] must prepare and direct the public opinion as appropriate, so they do not use nor abuse the very ordinances that the government has implemented in order to advance the happiness of all."[75]

Of course, all these laudable goals were not easy to put into practice, as they were in opposition to many economic interests. In a practical and almost visionary spirit, Jovellanos conceived of making the theatrical reforms compatible with the economic survival of the performance halls. First, these establishments would no longer contribute to charity. Second, as the performances improved, more people of a respectable class would attend, and thus the price of tickets could be increased. Of course, the common people would beat a retreat from the theater but, after all—stated Jovellanos—this diversion was a drain on their pocketbooks and not really necessary. Later, who knew when, shows that were educational and cheap would be provided for this class of persons.[76] A few years later, in 1800, the Council of Direction and Theater Reform put these ideas into practice in Madrid. The officials did away with all the shows that were popular among the lower classes and raised the prices.[77]

Unlike their efforts for the theater, the enlightened monarchs diligently fought Carnaval. In fact, the first prohibitions against carnavalesque jests appeared in the last years of the sixteenth century. Royal authorities repeated these injunctions throughout the seventeenth and eighteenth centuries. In Madrid alone, such bans were published in 1586, 1599, 1606, 1607, 1608, 1612, 1613, 1624, 1644, 1646, 1651, and 1673. Between 1721 and 1773, forty of these prohibitions were proclaimed. Their appearance continued sporadically until 1816.[78] The very abundance of these decrees designed to combat the Shrovetide festivities is testimony to their ineffectiveness. Still, from the eighteenth to the nineteenth century, Carnaval lost ground in the city. The common people's cathartic festivities were gradually replaced by sumptuous balls and luxurious displays of horsemanship, masquerades, and carriage displays organized by the aristocracy and the bourgeoisie and supported by the enlightened thinkers.[79] Jovellanos, for example, argued for the practice during the days of Carnaval of organizing sensible and tasteful *saraos* in the theaters and other closed settings and that the use of masks be permitted only in these places.[80]

Priests, governors, and the Spanish enlightened thinkers also rejected popular participation in religious festivities. Various bishops tried to contain the disorders by obliging the religious celebrations to end early and by banning the practice of carrying altars, chapels, and pyramids with saints through the streets. In 1780, Charles III proscribed the dances and giants in the churches as well as in processions, but apparently without success.[81] When Campomanes became minister and then the governor of the Council of Castile, he persecuted the *cofradías*, who generally organized these festivities, and many were suspended. The Holy See, after the king's many requests, also reduced the number of holy days.[82]

The taverns were in the same boat. The officials did everything possible to make sure that they could not function as meeting places.[83] In their writings the enlightened thinkers harangued the artisans to take more pride in their work and not to lose their time and money in snacks and drunken sprees.[84]

Over the course of the eighteenth century, street performances multiplied in Spanish cities. At the beginning of the nineteenth century, other forms of entertainment, including the exhibition of animals and marvels as well as optical illusions, such as the perspective machine, *titilimundos* [peep shows], magic lanterns, and dioramas, were added to the more traditional diversions of acrobats and puppets.[85] By the middle of the eighteenth century, "scientific" charlatans began to give shows in the theaters with machines that answered questions in writing or manipulated puppets.[86] The enlightened thinkers tolerated these performances as a lesser evil than the money-wasting the common people tended toward in gambling, the taverns, and dances.[87] The authorities controlled these shows through the licenses granted by the theater judge and by obliging the puppeteers to present their scripts to the censors of the Inquisition.[88]

Charles III initiated an ambitious program of urban reforms in Madrid. The city was cleaned and the streets cobbled, lit at night, and beautified. The wearing of long capes and round hats was forbidden, because these garments could hid the identity of criminals. These measures—in particular, this last one—as well as a shortage of food and growing political and social unrest led to the famous mutiny of Esquilache in 1766. The common people of Madrid took to the streets and destroyed seven thousand streetlights that had only recently been installed. The king escaped to Aranjuez, lifted the ban on capes and hats, lowered the price of food, and exiled his unpopular minister, Don Leopoldo de Gregorio, Marquis of Esquilache.[89] The mutiny, however, did not derail the plans for urban reform. On the contrary, the Count of Aranda's government hurried the program's implementation to prevent any further disturbances. In 1768, he divided the city into small *cuarteles* under the supervision of alcaldes del barrio who, in turn, were subordinated to the *alcaldes del cuartel*. Later that year, this form of division was applied to other cities.[90] Also, shortly after the mutiny ended, the authorities expelled the unemployed, vagabonds, and persons of dubious lifestyle from Madrid.[91] The Spanish enlightened thinkers generally favored the policies of enlightened despotism as they applied to vagabonds and beggars being shut away in hospices or workhouses.[92]

To sum up this brief overview of the attitudes of the enlightened politicians and thinkers in Spain, suffice it to say that the game of pelota was quite popular among their ranks. Campomanes and Jovellanos both considered it a virtuous and healthful activity. The latter wrote that "the public games of pelota are inherently of great usefulness, because in addition to providing an honest form of recreation for those who play and the spectators, they substantially improve the agility and strength of those who practice the sport and, for that, improve the physical education of the young."[93]

All this information confirms that the policy regarding public diversions in New Spain was a direct copy, point by point, of the statutes that were applied in Spain, despite the vast differences in the two societies. As a result, the outcry against the common people's moral decay and their customs, as well as the measures taken to curb this trend, were not local responses to the appearance of new attitudes and behavior of Mexico City's plebeians, nor did it reflect the reality of New Spain. Rather, the outcry and reactions echoed European concerns provoked by a new intolerance on the part of governments and the enlightened thinkers toward the common people's diversions and plebeian culture in general. The texts that document the excesses of the scandalous plebeians do not really tell us anything about the life of the common people. Such facts were of no interest to the enlightened thinkers and the governments they represented, but they are a testament to the new bourgeois mind-set that began to spread to New Spain.

Nevertheless, the similarities between one set of policies and the other should not be confused with a unidirectional flow of influences from Spain to New Spain. Nor should it be believed that the enlightened reforms were always applied first in the metropolis and then, afterward, in the colonies. The Spanish empire, especially at the level of the elites, was one economic, political, and intellectual unit in which the parts were interdependent, although not equal in status. It was possible, although exceedingly rare, for Creole intellectuals to influence Spanish society.

Father José Mariano Beristáin, the author of the *Biblioteca hispanoamericana septentrional*, represents one of these exceptions. He was a native of Puebla, where he studied rhetoric, philosophy, and theology. He traveled to Spain as the secretary of the bishop of Puebla, Don Francisco Fabián y Fuero, when the latter was named bishop of Valencia in 1773. Several years later, he quarreled with the bishop and so moved on to Valladolid where he gave classes at the university. There, he engaged in an active intellectual life. At the begining of 1787, he started *El Diario Pinciano*, the first newspaper of Valladolid, which continued regular publication until the middle of the next year. He wrote theater reviews of the plays presented in Valladolid and, through this medium, he was able to spread the aesthetic and moral values of the Enlightenment. He fought the popularity of dramas about magic and love affairs and promoted those reflecting neoclassical values. Shortly after the failure of the newspaper, Beristáin returned to New Spain to promote the ideals of the Enlightenment in his native country.[94]

Sometimes the reforms that were dreamed up in Spain were first implemented in New Spain, in that, at times, the opposition and the groups that resisted these changes were not so strong in the colony as in the mother country. Carnaval, for example, was brought under control in Mexico City before it was in Madrid. This contrasting situation might have been due to the longer tradition of Carnaval in Spain and the population's more deep-seated attachment to its traditions. The viceregal colonial governments backed the theater firmly as early as 1753, and the church gave this distraction at least some lukewarm support. In contrast, in Spain, these traditional enemies of the theater remained steadfast throughout the entire eighteenth century. Until 1767, when Charles III eliminated them, many prohibitions against plays remained on the books. Even as late as 1780, theater musicians in Madrid had to ask the Council of Castile for exemption from legal proceedings of infamy. The church continued to denounce the theater in sermons and did not allow actors to be buried with church rites. When natural disasters struck, the clerics managed to convince the faithful that these events were a divine punishment for the licentious lives led by the actors, and as a result, they were able to have plays banned in many cities. In 1746, after a destructive storm in Valencia, the theater was torn down at the bishop's insistence. When an earthquake shook Granada in 1778, theater performances were suspended. In 1800, on the island of León, the owner of a theater himself asked for permission to tear down his building in the midst of an epidemic. Also, after Aranda (minister to Charles III) was ousted, those who campaigned against the theater renewed their efforts, and even Charles III decreed that only large cities could have theaters.[95]

At times, the differences between New Spain and Spain were so marked that spiritual trends that caught on strongly in one place had no success in the other. This was so for *costumbrismo* (a literary genre emphasizing customs and manners). Some European enlightened thinkers promoted an idealized image of peasants; they envisioned simple, austere, and thrifty workers at their diversions. This impression appears in some guise in many paintings of the period, of which the most famous are Goya's drawings.[96] Jovellanos defended the people's dances: "There are many villages where the people, protected from the infection of vices, do not have any other form of recreation but these joyful gatherings and the innocent games and dances that provide for their delight."[97]

In New Spain, however, the peasants were by and large Indians, and the Spanish and Creole elites were not disposed to see any good qualities in them. Who would adopt their dances, which were still suspected of idolatrous overtones? There are only a few colonial Mexican paintings in which *costumbrismo* can be detected. One of them is a screen that depicts popular scenes along the canal of La Viga—one of the paseos that the viceregal government favored—and the paintings show the different castes of which this society was composed. The portrayal does not evoke any sympathy for the common people, but reflects a desire to catalogue the racial mixtures in order to pigeonhole men and women of the pleb. It was an attempt to reinforce the moribund hierarchical system based on race.[98]

It seems absurd to imagine—as some historians have—that certain groups within the elite were attracted to the common people's diversions and sought to participate in them.[99] We believe this book has shown that the viceregal government and the colonial Mexican elite fought against these popular diversions and tried to reform others according to bourgeois values. They tried to create separate public spaces for respectable people that could not be infiltrated by the common people. Finally, they tried to put an end to the worldly mingling of the different social classes.

The Bourbon reforms' influence as well as the ideals of the Enlightenment caused New Spain to become immersed in a serious contradiction. At the same time as the economic transformations opened new channels of social mobility—both upward and downward—the portrayal of the ethnic/racial hierarchies within society no longer had much foundation. From this situation came a reaction, which was to try to revive the social differences portrayed in this idealized view of society and to increase the obstacles to social mobility. The Spaniards deprived the Creoles of many of the high positions that they had acquired previously.[100] In 1779, the government published the Royal Pragmatic (decree), which aimed to curtail marriages between unequals. Its goal was to end the union of men or women of superior racial ranking with those of inferior—or dark—racial backgrounds.[101] Mestizos were accused of trying to "whiten" themselves by providing false information about the Spanish ancestors in their background. For this reason, the officials began to consider and treat them the same as Indians.

With strong racist overtones, a *colloquium* of 1790 ridiculed a "whitened" Indian by having him say:

I's not no dark Indian
but kinda Spanized.
On the side of my granmaw
I's noble, no doubt at all.
On the side of my paw
it don't matter
'cause he was a good guy,
but then they hanged him.
On the side of my maw
it is clear
since although she was dark, dark
her eye was white, white;[102]
and contemplate my person, go'sir,
am I good or am I bad?
Also you have to know
I am a bit cultured
and I know how to sing a requiem
or secular singing.
I can study the praises
without any tomfoolery.[103]


The act of declaring a mestizo an Indian had economic advantages for the Crown, because the latter paid tribute and the former did not. This denial of racial mixture was also part of a campaign to increase tribute revenues. Around 1770, in León, Commissioner Monteverde declared that only three ethnic categories existed: the Spanish, the Indian, and the mulatto. Of course, the mulattoes paid tribute.[104]

Hipólito de Villarroel proposed a method to cleanse the city of rogues; he suggested that all the idlers be dispatched to their communities of origin and then a wall be built around the city, leaving the barrios excluded.[105] Clearly, this was not a realistic proposal, but it does give an insight into the extreme of racial and social prejudices to which the elites could ascribe. Of course, Villarroel was among a group whose intolerance was most exacerbated.

These ideas were not absent from the works of other well-known and respected thinkers who have—perhaps unjustly—been categorized as liberals. In his novel *El Periquillo Sarniento*, Lizardi formulated the fate of his characters according to their racial identity. Mestizos or mulattoes died or ended in disgrace, while Creoles such as Trapiento or even Periquillo, despite their immoral conduct, inherited a *mayorazgo* and lived happily ever after. The novel reinforced the Creoles' elitist beliefs and showed them the dangers of rubbing shoulders with people of the lower classes. Finally, it urged them to preserve their moral values.[106] In another novel, La Quijotita y su prima, Lizardi wrote that, in matters of dress, "the lady should not be like the plebeian, nor the mistress like her servant, nor anyone in clothes that are not fitting, because otherwise all would be disorder and a frightening confusion."[107] Of course, there were also many people who opposed the notion of difference based upon racial criteria—in particular, Abad y Queipo—but they were in the minority, and certainly people in the upper ranks of society did not deign to pay attention to them until it was too late.[108]

Concurrently with the economic transformations, in the eighteenth century new systems of social ordering and exclusion were being blindly adopted in New Spain without any consideration of their profound inconsistencies. During the period of the Bourbon reforms, Mexico City experienced neither the phenomenon of slumming nor a generalized deterioration of customs. Rather, a head-on collision between two phenomena occurred, both of which obeyed different logic: On the one hand, there was the dissemination of the ideas of the Enlightenment and the changes within the value system of the elites. This dismantling of the system of social hierarchies was accompanied by the paradoxical and useless endeavor to try to revitalize this very system. These events occurred during a period of incredible growth and strengthening of the state. All these trends are well documented and originated outside New Spain.

On the other hand, the popular culture formed an underground current that developed silently out of many sources. This culture came from the daily resistance to exploitation and survival strategies within situations of extreme poverty. It also originated from the effort to find small pleasures within a miserable and oppressive life; these diversions were gleaned from elements of upper-class culture but transformed to serve other goals. Finally, indigenous traditions contributed; they were renewed through the constant migration of Indians from the countryside to the city. All these elements gave rise to a reality that is, even today, almost totally unknown. But in order to delve into this undercurrent, it was first necessary to destroy the myth of the deterioration of customs, which suggested that urban popular culture of the eighteenth century was a passive imitation and a result of the changes initiated by the dominant classes of colonial Mexican society.

## The Power of Money

The hardening of the caste system limited the social mobility of Creoles and wealthy mestizos. The upsurge in the despotic power of the Spanish Crown as well as the agricultural crises, which were increasingly severe and caused famine and misery, added to the weakening of Spanish domination over its colonies. Napoleon's invasion of Spain exacerbated this weakness, and then the internal conflicts between absolutists and liberals gave rise to insurgency, and later, Independence in Mexico.

One of the first acts of the independent government was to outlaw the categorization of residents by their racial origins. In this way, the officials hoped to put an end to the odious practice of socio-racial discrimination that was the norm during the entire colonial period. Thus, Mexicans became equal before the law.[109]

Within the area of public diversions, the effect of the new social order was, at first glance, rather surprising. With the end of the legal system of castes, the tendency toward avoiding the mixing of various social categories in the diversions within public spaces did not disappear; rather, this trend became even stronger than in the colonial period. Shortly after Independence, new theaters were instituted that quickly specialized in order to please different social groups. "Cultivated" theaters were the favorites of the elites, while "light" theaters were aimed at the common people.[110] Merchants discovered that public diversions could be very profitable, and they began to produce shows and entertainments of diverse content and quality according to the social class of the target audience. As popular diversions began to be simply "products," they lost the subversive quality that they had enjoyed previously. On the other hand, the age-old dream of the colonial Mexican elites and the viceregal governments of expelling the Indians as well as the plebeians from the city center, for which they undertook so many campaigns, became a reality around 1844. Then the city center became the preserve of the upper classes as the poor and needy vacated it.[111]

The separation of diversions and public spaces was accomplished without decrees or rules. It occurred silently, without visible coercion, and in a "natural" manner. Quite simply, once market forces were unshackled and promoted by the state, they proved to be a much more efficient mechanism of social differentiation and exclusion than decrees and prohibitions.[112] In reality, by the end of the colonial period, money had begun to show its power. No law or any reinforcement of police or any state control had been enough to reduce pulque consumption, but the general increase in the cost of living and the rise in the price of pulque caused by higher taxes achieved this goal. Merchants were able to put an end to the common people's presence at pelota games simply by charging a half-real for a seat in the stands.

In the new post-Independence social order, all men were equal. Individuals could not be exluded because of social or racial origins from attending a diversion or from being in a public place. There were those who could pay the entry fee and those who could not. For the latter group, there were always cheap shows that they could afford and that no one from the wealthy upper classes would wish to attend. The differentiation of diversions and public spaces that was initiated in the eighteenth century, therefore, was accomplished "without violence" and "spontaneously."

One of the goals of colonial society had been reinforcement of the social barriers among different groups but, in practice, this ideal was never approached with much efficiency. During the colonial period—although more so at the beginning than at the end—the hierarchical ordering in religious processions and festivities as well as the regulated contact among racial groups in public spaces was rarely enforced. The great gap between the law that organized individuals according to social criteria and the economic factors that were more often pragmatically applied made the Spanish Crown's segregationist policies impossible to implement.

In contrast, although modern society proclaims the integration of all groups into social life as its goal, financial inequalities ensure an efficient discrimination within public spaces. Modern societies have a discourse of inclusion but practice a policy of exclusion.[113] The institutions of exclusion, for example, all proclaim the reintegration of "deviants" into social life as their principal purpose. Asylums are supposed to cure the insane, and penitentiaries propose to reeducate prisoners into model citizens. Surely it was not a simple coincidence that in the eighteenth century, among other public works, the Crown commissioned the Mexican Consulado—the guild of merchants—to build an insane asylum and a prison.[114] This group, more than any other, presaged the coming society.

Over the course of the eighteenth century, two ideological positions diverged over the notion of the proper strategy to eliminate the disorders that the common people occasioned when they attended the same public diversions as the elite. The enlightened thinkers proposed the education of the plebeians in the theater as a remedy and the inculcation of the new bourgeois values. In contrast, the merchants adopted a simpler and more efficient solution for the game of pelota, for example, which was to exclude the riffraff through economic sanctions.

Despite the legacy of Enlightenment ideas, in post-Independence Mexico, the new social order postponed the common people's education until more propitious times and allowed free rein to the power that money conveyed to discriminate and exclude. The consequence of these decisions was that Mexican society began to resemble the social ideal that the Spanish merchants had proclaimed during the colonial period. These businessmen, who were expelled from Mexico in 1828, were not able to witness the fulfillment of their dreams. Ironically, it was only when Sir Money's most faithful allies left the country that the period of his most despotic and absolutist reign of power began.

## "A Well-Ordered Republic"

The ideal derived from enlightened despotism of a society in which social classes would not mingle in public spaces and diversions is not a dead letter in today's Mexico. It is not a dream buried beneath two centuries of history. On the contrary, it is not only alive, it seems close to realization. The "distinction of classes," which was so clear in the eighteenth century, is currently respected with a surprising spontaneity.

In performances for the elite in which an entrance fee is required, such as those at Bellas Artes, high-class theaters, art film houses, and upper-end night life, it would be very surprising to encounter even one individual from the common people. But it would be a mistake to think that this separation is due only to the high price of the tickets to these diversions. Even in public places, the spatial differentiation of social classes is completely established. In Chapultepec Park, for example, on Sundays, the lower classes gravitate toward the area around the castle and the old lake, while the middle classes prefer to celebrate their children's birthdays near the highway and in the newer parts of the park. For a day out in the country, the common people chose a destination like Contreras, which can be reached by bus, while the elite, who own cars, prefer the Ajusco. In Acapulco, the poorer tourists swim on the beaches near the city center, such as Hornitos and others, while the "snobs" prefer to take the sun at Condesa and those privileged condominium owners go to the beaches near the naval base.

This separation seems "natural" and "obvious" to everyone. There are no rules that regulate it, nor do any officials make sure that it is obeyed, nor is there any need to do so. In many cases, the division is not even caused by any kind of economic pressure. Quite simply, this "class distinction," which is necessary for any "well-ordered republic," this horror of the mingling of different social classes, has been interiorized by the entire population.

A simple test will confirm that this is, indeed, a reality. When masons stop to eat, they often have to purchase food in the high-class neighborhoods where they work. They always go in groups of four or five to the supermarket as a kind of psychological protection against the hostile environment. They never take a cart, although they are customers. Rarely do they get out of the supermarket without having suffered some insult, through words or gestures, from the cashiers. Such examples from daily life could easily be multiplied many times over. But the proof is in the pudding.

The ideal of enlightened despotism, which is a reality almost in its entirety today, was impossible to achieve in the eighteenth century because the methods used by the officials to reach their goal were totally inadequate. Rules and the patrols of judges could not do away with the long traditions of daily contact among the various social groups in the same public spaces. Also, the elites and the colonial governments were always fighting against the current. Instead of allowing the economic forces to create class distinctions, they tried to mitigate this influence and obstinately tried to impose a hierarchical division that had little to do with the economic reality of the day. Once market forces were liberated from legal and social trammels in post-Independence Mexico, the process of differentiation of social spaces accelerated considerably and prepared the ground for a future internalization of the horror of "social mingling."

It is often said that modern society has a tendency to reduce the distinctions between individuals and to erase differences. The reality seems quite the opposite. Human diversity is not reduced to a single social type but rather to a large number of these types, rigidly graded along one unique social scale. Cultural values become common to the society in general but are distributed in an unequal manner. These phenomena, along with the unstoppable growth of the state, bring contemporary societies closer every day to the hierarchical bureaucratic totalitarianism that Max Weber predicted in his darkest moments of despair.[115] Perhaps the enlightened despotism of the eighteenth century and the union of power with knowledge to strengthen and modernize the state while maintaining a rigid hierarchy was just a failed and premature trial run for the totalitarian society that awaits us in the future.

# Notes

## Introduction

1. José Miranda, *Humboldt y México* (Mexico City, 1962), 17–22.
2. José Miranda first advanced this thesis in *Sátira anónima del siglo XVIII* (Mexico City, 1953), 15–17. Since then, several other historians have expressed it with more or less important variations. See Pablo González Casanova, *La literatura perseguida en la crisis de la Colonia* (Mexico City, 1958), 145; Luis González y González, "El Siglo de las Luces," in *Historia mínima de México* (Mexico City, 1977), 76–77, and "El linaje de la cultura mexicana," *Vuelta* 72 (1982): 17–18; and María del Carmen Velázquez, "El siglo XVIII," in *Historia documental de México* (Mexico City, 1974), 333–334, and "El despertar ilustrado," *Historia de México* (Mexico City, 1978), vol. 7, 1454–1457.
3. Miranda, *Humboldt y México*, 57.
4. This expression comes from Jean-Pierre Berthe (personal communication).
5. Some recent studies that have characterized the eighteenth century in this way are Enrique Florescano, *Precios del maíz y crisis agrícolas en México (1708–1810)* (Mexico City, 1969); Enrique Florescano and Isabel Gil Sánchez, "La época de las reformas borbónicas," in *Historia general de México* (Mexico City, 1977), vol. 2; Claude Morin, *Michoacán en la Nueva España del siglo XVIII. Crecimiento y desigualdad en una economía colonial* (Mexico City, 1979), and his "Sentido y alcance del siglo XVIII en América Latina: el caso del centro-oeste mexicano," in *Ensayos sobre el desarrollo económico de México y América Latina (1500–1975)*, ed. Enrique Florescano (Mexico City, 1979).
6. For the Valenciana, see David A. Brading, *Miners and Merchants in Bourbon Mexico, 1763–1810* (Cambridge, Eng., 1971), 136. For the tobacco factory, see Florescano and Gil Sánchez, "La época de las reformas borbónicas," 219.
7. Florescano and Gil Sánchez, "La época de las reformas borbónicas," 220.
8. On the movements of protest, see Cuauhtémoc Velasco A., "Los trabajadores mineros de la Nueva España," in *La clase obrera en la historia de México*, vol. 1: *De la colonia al imperio* (Mexico City, 1981), 292–299. On the movements in the tobacco factory, see José Gómez, "Diario curioso de México . . .," in *Documentos para la historia de México* (no place, 1854), vol. 7, 401; and Florescano and Gil Sánchez, "La época de las reformas borbónicas," 220.
9. Edward Shorter, *The Making of the Modern Family* (London, 1976), 255–268.

10. Brading, *Miners and Merchants*, 33–92; Florescano and Gil Sánchez, "La época de las reformas borbónicas," 203–231.

11. Irving Leonard, "The 1790 Theater Season of the Mexico City Coliseo," *Hispanic Review* 19 (1951):107.

12. Cited in Enrique de Olavarría y Ferrari, *Reseña histórica del teatro en México* (Mexico City, 1961), vol. 1, 156–157.

13. "Informe sobre pulquerías y tabernas del año de 1784," *Boletín del AGN* 28:2 (1947):201–202.

## Chapter 1

1. AGN, Reales Cédulas, vol. 1, exp. 103.

2. Jonathan Israel, *Race, Class, and Politics in Colonial Mexico, 1610–1670* (Oxford, 1980), 135–189.

3. AGN, Reales Cédulas, vol. 1, exp. 103.

4. Ibid., exp. 215.

5. Ibid., vol. 2, exp. 102.

6. Ibid., vol. 15, exp. 130.

7. Ibid., vol. 17, exps. 11, 12.

8. Ibid., vol. 2, exp. 102.

9. Gregorio Marañón, *Don Juan* (Buenos Aires, 1944), 11–13.

10. Ibid., 58–59.

11. AGN, Reales Cédulas, vol. 19, exp. 1.

12. Julio Jiménez Rueda, "Documentos para la historia del teatro en la Nueva España," *Boletín del AGN* 15:1(1944):115–116, 121–129.

13. Israel, *Race, Class, and Politics*, 125–126, 146–147.

14. José María Marroqui, *La ciudad de México* (Mexico City, 1900–1903), vol. 1, 191.

15. Fabián de Fonseca and Carlos de Urrutia, *Historia general de la Real Hacienda* (Mexico City, 1978), vol. 3, 344–346.

16. AGN, Reales Cédulas, vol. 22, exps. 59, 62; vol. 23, exps. 6, 92. For a complete history of the official attitudes regarding cockfights, see María Justina Sarabia Viejo, *El juego de gallos en Nueva España* (Seville, 1972), 13–27.

17. Cited in Vicente Riva Palacio, *México a través de los siglos. Historia del virreinato* (U.S., no date), vol. 4, 267–268.

18. AGN, Reales Cédulas, vol. 15, exp. 130.

19. Cited in Riva Palacio, *México a través*, vol. 4, 271–272.

20. AGN, Reales Cédulas, vol. 7, exp. 4; vol. 5, exp. 181; vol. 8, exp. 13.

21. Ibid., vol. 17, exp. 81. See also vol. 19, exp. 59, and vol. 20, exp. 43.

22. One of these orders was given in 1671: ibid., vol. 12, exp. 23; another was given in 1676: vol. 15, exp. 44.

23. Ibid., vol. 12, exp. 23.

24. Carlos de Sigüenza y Góngora, "Alboroto y motín de México, del 8 de junio de 1692," *Relaciones históricas* (Mexico City, 1972), 152; for the description of the riot and its causes, see pp. 95–174. See also Rosa Feijó, "El tumulto de 1692," *Historia Mexicana* (April–June 1965): 656–679.

25. Israel, *Race, Class, and Politics*, 58–59.

26. Edmundo O'Gorman, ed., "Sobre los inconvenientes de vivir los indios en el centro de la ciudad," *Boletín del AGN* 9:1(January–March 1938), and his "Reflexiones sobre la distribución urbana colonial de la ciudad de México," *Seis estudios históricos de tema mexicano* (Jalapa, Veracruz, 1960), 33–44.

27. O'Gorman, "Sobre los inconvenientes," 7.

28. Sigüenza y Góngora, "Alboroto y motín," 145.

29. This chapter and those following that touch upon the subject of bullfights owe a lot to Benjamín Flores Hernández, "Con la fiesta nacional, por el Siglo de las Luces. Un acercamiento a lo que fueron y significaron las corridas de toros en la Nueva España en el siglo XVIII" (thesis, Universidad Nacional Autónoma de México, 1976). Despite this fact, our assessments of the festival are opposed. Flores Hernández is an enthusiastic defender of the bullfights as a symbol of "national unity." Roberto Moreno y de los Arcos also made some extremely useful suggestions about this matter.

30. Flores Hernández, "Con la fiesta nacional," 12–14.

31. Ibid., 12–14.

32. Nicolás Rangel, *Historia del toreo en México* (Mexico City, 1980), 60.

33. M. G. Jovellanos y Ramírez,"Memoria para el arreglo de la policía de los espectáculas y diversiones públicas y sobre su origen en España," in *Obrás escogidas* (Madrid, 1955), vol. 1, 113.

34. Cited in ibid., 138–149.

35. Cited in Rangel, *Historia del toreo*, 7.

36. Cited in ibid.

37. Cited in ibid.

38. Cited in ibid., 305–306.

39. Ibid., 5–6, 25, 28, 193; Flores Hernández, "Con la fiesta nacional," 68, 138–140.

40. Rangel, *Historia del toreo*, 25–26, 96.

41. Ibid., 26; Flores Hernández, "Con la fiesta nacional," 66.

42. Cited in Rangel, *Historia del toreo*, 306–307.

43. Flores Hernández, "Con la fiesta nacional," 66.

44. AHA, vol. 855, exp. 18.

45. Ibid., exp. 25.

46. Ibid., exps. 3, 4, 7, 8, 11, 12, 13, 14, 15, 17, 19, 27, 29, 31, 34, 36, 39, 40, 47, 48, and 50.

47. Ibid., exp. 18.

48. Ibid., exp. 22.

49. Rangel, *Historia del toreo*, 100.

50. Hipólito de Villarroel, *Enfermedades políticas que padece la capital de esta Nueva España en casi todos los cuerpos de que se compone y remedios que se la deben aplicar para su curación si se quiere que sea útil al rey y al público* (Mexico City, 1937), 210.

51. Flores Hernández, "Con la fiesta nacional," 50.

52. Ibid., 26–27.

53. Ibid., 29, 45.

54. Ibid., 43–44; Rangel, *Historia del toreo*, 55–56, 105.

55. For more information on the frequently flouted prohibition of bullfights in the Plaza del Volador outside official celebrations, see Rangel,

*Historia del toreo,* 193. Flores Hernández, in "Con la fiesta nacional," 137, 158–160, comments upon the locations of bullfights.

56. Rangel, *Historia del toreo,* 261, 263–264; Flores Hernández, "Con la fiesta nacional," 112–115.

57. For more information on the diversions added to the bullfights, see Rangel, *Historia del toreo,* 138, 146–147, 163, 191–192, 185, 186 and 234–235.

58. Ibid., 146, 198–90, 269–271.

59. Ibid., 192.

60. Ibid., 241–266. Already in 1785, Villarroel, *Enfermedades,* 205–212, had proposed several reforms for the bullfights, of which one was to build a permanent stadium.

61. On this plaza, see Rangel, *Historia del toreo,* 362–363; Flores Hernández,"Con la fiesta nacional," 55–88, and his "Sobre las plazas de toros en la Nueva España del siglo XVIII," *Estudios de Historia Novohispana* 7 (1981):155, 158.

62. José Joaquín Fernández de Lizardi, *Obras* (Mexico City, 1970), vol. 4, 30–31. Also Villarroel, *Enfermedades,* 306, criticized the bullfights harshly and asserted that God disapproved of them.

63. Rangel, *Historia del toreo,* 194–197.

64. Jovellanos y Ramírez, "Memoria para el arreglo," 116–117. Part of the criticism of Campomanes is cited in Jean Sarrailh, *La España ilustrada de la segunda mitad del siglo XVII* (Mexico City, 1974), 74. On the general attitude of the enlightened thinkers, see Antonio Domínguez Ortiz, *Sociedad y Estado en el siglo XVIII español* (Barcelona, 1976), 486.

65. Flores Hernández, "Con la fiesta nacional," 26, 262–263.

66. Rangel, *Historia del toreo,* 179–191.

67. Ibid., 143–150, 161,177. See also Flores Hernández, "Con la fiesta nacional," 43–44.

68. Flores Hernández, "Con la fiesta nacional," 54.

69. Rangel, *Historia del toreo,* 191.

70. Flores Hernández, "Con la fiesta nacional," 262–263.

71. Rangel, *Historia del toreo,* 301–310.

72. Cited in Flores Hernández, "Con la fiesta nacional," 262–263.

73. Ibid., 268.

74. *Translators' note: Cañas* was derived from an Arab game. The players were dressed in armor and mounted on horseback to throw fragile sticks of about two meters in length at each other.

75. Cited in Hildburg Schilling, *Teatro profano en la Nueva España: fines del siglo XVI a mediados del XVIII* (Mexico City, 1958), 167–171; Rangel, *Historia del toreo,* 81.

76. Rangel, *Historia del toreo,* 93.

77. Cited in Flores Hernández, "Con la fiesta nacional," 260–261.

78. Cited in Rangel, *Historia del toreo,* 346.

79. Timothy E. Anna, *The Fall of Royal Government in Mexico City* (Lincoln, NE, 1978), 100–108.

80. Ibid., 129.

81. The first text appears in integral form in Rangel, *Historia del toreo,* 353–359.The second is in Fernández de Lizardi, *Obras,* 27–29.

82. Anna, *Fall of Royal Government,* 129–130.

83. AHA, vol. 855, exp. 56.

84. As defined by Max Weber, *Economía y sociedad* (Mexico City, 1979), vol. 1, 25–31.

85. On the loss of legitimacy of the Spanish in Mexico City, see Anna, *Fall of Royal Government*, 191–209.

86. Rangel, *Historia del toreo*, 351–352.

87. Ibid., 361–371; Flores Hernández, "Con la fiesta nacional," 56–58.

88. Flores Hernández, "Sobre la plazas de toros," 155–158, and "Con la fiesta nacional," 181.

## Chapter 2

1. On the importance of ideas regarding magic in eighteenth-century Mexico and its relative substitution by modern ideas among the elite during the last decades of the colonial period, see Luis González y González, "El siglo mágico," *Historia Mexicana* 2:5 (July–September 1952):66–86. On the concepts of the magic world and the rational world, see Max Weber, *Historia económica general* (Mexico City, 1979), 295–309. On the affirmation of this earthly world as true and not a simple apparition on the part of the eighteenth-century bourgeoisie, see the fascinating book by Bernard Groethuysen, *Origines de l'esprit bourgeois en France. L'Eglise et la bourgeoisie* (Paris, 1972).

2. Jean Duvignaud, *Sociología del teatro* (Mexico City, 1966), 17, 80–81, 92–95.

3. Ibid., 115.

4. An abundant bibliography on the theater of evangelization exists. Among the first works that examined this theme are: Robert Ricard, *The Spiritual Conquest of Mexico: An Essay on the Apostolate and the Evangelizing Methods of the Mendicant Orders in New Spain, 1523–1572*, trans. Lesley Byrd Simpson (Berkeley, CA, 1966), 194–206; and José J. Rojas Garcidueñas, *El teatro en la Nueva España en el siglo XVI* (Mexico City, 1935).

5. This is Bishop Palafox's expression. Hildburg Schilling, *Teatro profano en la Nueva España: fines del siglo XVI a mediados del XVIII* (Mexico City, 1958), 167–171.

6. María Sten, *Vida y muerte del teatro nahúatl. El olimpo sin Prometeo* (Mexico City, 1974).

7. Ibid., 110.

8. Rojas Garcidueñas, *El teatro en la Nueva España*, 110–111.

9. Ibid. On the scarcity of actors in the eighteenth century, see Julio Jiménez Rueda, "Documentos para la historia del teatro en la Nueva España," *Boletín del AGN* 15:1 (1944):116–120.

10. Schilling, *Teatro profano*, 11–45; and Irving A. Leonard, *Baroque Times in Old Mexico; Seventeenth-Century Persons, Places, and Practices* (Ann Arbor, MI, 1959), 105.

11. 11–20.

12. Armando de María y Campos, *Los payasos; poetas del pueblo, el circo en México. Crónica* (Mexico City, 1939), 15.

13. This information comes from a 1770 document in which the administrator of the Royal Indian Hospital provides a summary of the history of the institution. ABMNAH, Ramo Hospital Real de Naturales, vol. 74, exp. 1. On the history of theaters of the said hospital, see Schilling,

*Teatro profano*, 11–45; Manuel Mañón, *Historia del teatro principal de México* (Mexico City, 1932), 15–16; and Jesús Romero Flores, *México, historia de una gran ciudad*, ed. B. Costa-Amic (Mexico City, 1978), 342–349.

14. For example, from 1756 forward it was rented to individuals. Mañón, *Historia del teatro*, 17; ABMNAH, Ramo Hospital Real de Naturales, vol. 97, exp. 5; vol. 100, exp. 18. In 1786, the viceroy ordered the creation of a subscribers' society composed of distinguished citizens who took charge of the theater. Silvestre Díaz de la Vega, *Discurso sobre los dramas* (Mexico City, 1786), 14–16. But in less than three years, this society folded. Harvey L. Johnson, "Disputa suscitada en la ciudad de México, entre los alcaldes del crimen y los ordinarios, por el auto del año de 1819 que mandó a las actrices no vestir traje de hombre en las funciones del Coliseo," *Revista Iberoamericana* 10:19 (November 1945):134. In 1789, the New Coliseo was rented to Don Manuel Lozano, the sublieutenant of the Provincial Militias of Toluca. Mañón, *Historia del teatro*, 34–35. In 1792, the hospital administered its theater directly. ABMNAH, Ramo Hospital Real de Naturales, vol. 100, exp. 18; vol. 104, exp. 16.

15. On the function of the Royal Indian Hospital, see Carmen Venegas Ramírez, *Régimen hospitalario para indios en la Nueva España* (Mexico City, 1973), 41–65.

16. On the expenses for maintenance of the theater, see ABMNAH, Ramo Hospital Real de Naturales, vol. 84, exp. 11; vol. 97, exp. 5; vol. 104, exp. 12. There were epidemics and famines in 1707, 1710–1711, 1714, 1727–1728, 1731, 1734, 1736–1739, 1749–1750, 1760–1762, 1768, 1772–1773, 1778–1780, 1785–1786, 1789–1790, 1790–1793, 1798, 1800–1802, 1803, and 1812–1813. Enrique Florescano and Isabel Gil Sánchez, "La época de las reformas borbónicas," *Historia general de México* (Mexico City, 1977), vol. 1, 252–255.

17. Schilling, *Teatro profano*, 11–45; AHA, vol. 796, exp. 3.

18. On the conflictive relations between the church and the theater in Europe, see Duvignaud, *Sociología del teatro*, 67; and Eugène André Despois, *Le théâtre français sous Louis XIV* (Paris, 1886), 246–283; in Spain, Antonio de Domínguez Ortiz, *Sociedad y Estado en el siglo XVIII español* (Barcelona, 1976), 483–486; and Gonzalo Anes, *El antiguo régimen: Los Borbones* (Madrid, 1981), 135–136. On the Inquisition as censor of the theater, see Sten, *Vida y muerte*, 85–86. Bishop Palafox y Mendoza was the principal adversary of the theater in New Spain. Schilling, *Teatro profano*, 167–171.

19. On the ups and downs of the theater in Spain, see Enrique de Olavarría y Ferrari, *Reseña histórica del teatro en México (1538–1911)* (Mexico City, 1961), vol. 1, 17–18. On the support of the viceroys in New Spain, see Rojas Garcidueñas, *El teatro en la Nueva España*, 102–106, 110–111; Jiménez Rueda, "Documentos para la historia," 116–120; Leonard, *Baroque Times*, 159; and Rodolfo Usigli, *México en el teatro* (Mexico City, 1933–1934), xxxviii.

20. Olavarría y Ferrari, *Reseña histórica*, vol. 1, 20–21; and Lauro E. Rossell, *Iglesias y conventos coloniales de México; historia de cada uno de los que existen en la ciudad de México* (Mexico City, 1961), 331–332.

21. Alzate's text is cited in José Antonio de Alzate y Ramírez, "Periódicas," *Obras* (Mexico City, 1980), vol. 1, 52–58, 64, 128–130. The quotes are taken from the latter pages. I based my interpretation on Roberto Moreno y de los Arcos' introduction to *Obras*, vol. 1, xii–xiii.

22. On the Enlightenment, see Ernst Cassirer, *La filosofía de la Ilustración* (Mexico City, 1981), 9–53; Hans Barth, *Verdad e ideología* (Mexico City, 1951), 9–61. For a critical analysis of the Enlightenment, see Eduardo Subirats, *La ilustración insuficiente* (Madrid, 1981). On the Enlightenment in Spain, see Jean Sarrailh, *La España ilustrada de la segunda mitad del siglo XVI a mediados del XVIII* (Mexico City, 1974); Rafael Segovia Canosa, *Tres salvaciones del siglo XVIII español* (Jalapa, Veracruz, 1960); and Gaspar Gómez de la Serna, *Los viajeros de la Ilustración* (Madrid, 1979).

23. Max Weber, *El Político y el científico* (Mexico City, 1981), 70–72.

24. Cited in J. Sarrailh, *La España ilustrada*, 233.

25. Cited in ibid., 170.

26. On enlightened despotism and its impetus for the inquiries in New Spain, see José Miranda, *Las ideas y las instituciones mexicanas. Primera parte, 1521–1820* (Mexico City, 1978), 143–149, and "La ilustración y el fomento de la ciencia en México durante el siglo XVIII," in *Vida colonial y albores de la independencia* (Mexico City, 1972), 199–212.

27. Cited in Sarrailh, *La España ilustrada*, 190.

28. Cited in ibid., 192.

29. Cited in Miranda, *Las ideas y las instituciones*, 159.

30. Cited in Sarrailh, *La España ilustrada*, 252–253.

31. Cited in Miranda, *Las ideas y las instituciones*, 168.

32. Daniel Roche, *Le peuple de Paris. Essai sur la culture populaire au XVIIIᵉ siècle* (Paris, 1981), 204–237.

33. Antonio Magaña Esquivel, *Los teatros en la ciudad de México* (Mexico City, 1974), 22.

34. Cited in Olavarría y Ferrari, *Reseña histórica*, vol. 1, 80.

35. Cited in ibid., 183.

36. Gaspar Melchor de Jovellanos y Ramírez, "Memoria para el arreglo de la policía de los espectáculos y diversiones públicas, y sobre su origen en España," in *Obras escogidas* (Madrid, 1955), vol. 2, 25–27.

37. Cited in Duvignaud, *Sociología del teatro*, 312.

38. Cited in Armando de María y Campos, *Andanzas y picardías de Eusebio Vela: autor y comediante mexicano del siglo XVIII* (Mexico City, 1944), 209.

39. See, in particular, Marquis de Sade, *Justine ou les malheurs de la vertu, suivie de l'Histoire de Juliette, sa soeur*, various editions.

40. Alzate y Ramírez, *Obras*, vol. 1, 56.

41. Cited in Mañón, *Historia del teatro principal*, 56–57.

42. Considerandos del Reglamento de Teatro de 1786.

43. Ibid.

44. Irving A. Leonard, "La temporada teatral de 1792 en el Nuevo Coliseo de México," *Nueva Revista de Filología Hispánica* 5 (1951): 395.

45. For a reconstruction of the atmosphere of the Coliseo, see the works of Díaz de la Vega, *Discurso sobre los dramas*, 7–16; José Gómez, "Diario curioso de México . . .," in *Documentos para la historia de México* (No place, 1854), vol. 7, 93–94, 98, 102–108; *El Viajero Universal o noticia del mundo antiguo y nuevo* (Madrid, 1799), vol. 26, 277–285; José Joaquín Fernández de Lizardi, "Periódicos. Alacena de frioleras; Cajoncitos de la alacena; Las sombras de Heráclito y Demócrito; El conductor eléctrico," in *Obras* (Mexico City, 1970), vol. 4, 56–59; and various journalists of the period. The journalist who wrote in 1806 was cited in Olavarría y Ferrari,

*Reseña histórica*, vol. 1, 158, and the other two who wrote in 1821 were cited in Mañón, *Historia del teatro principal*, 52–59. The building is described in ibid., 16. I also used documents in ABMNAH, Ramo Hospital Real de Naturales, vol. 74, exps. 1, 20; vol. 84, exps. 11, 25, 64. Other documents of interest are reproduced in de María y Campos, *Andanzas*, 86–112, and *Guía de representaciones teatrales en la Nueva España, siglos XVI al XVIII* (Mexico City, 1959), 192–193. Apart from the Theater Regulations of 1786, I consulted many *bandos*, decrees, and official dispositions, in particular those of 1786 and 1790, cited in Mañón, *Historia del teatro*, 33, 35–36; and those of 1787, cited in Olavarría y Ferrari, *Reseña histórica*, vol. 1, 50; and those of 1811 and 1819 in AHA, vol. 797, exp. 29.

46. ABMNAH, Ramo Hospital Real de Naturales, vol. 106, exp. 25.

47. Cited in Leonard, "La temporada teatral," 107. On the Café Tacuba, see Artemio de Valle-Arizpe, *Calle vieja y calle nueva* (Mexico City, 1949), 322.

48. ABMNAH, Ramo Hospital Real de Naturales, vol. 104, exp. 7.

49. Cited in María y Campos, *Andanzas*, 86–112.

50. Alzate y Ramírez, *Obras*, vol. 1, 55.

51. Díaz de la Vega, *Discurso sobre los dramas*, i–iv, 14–16.

52. Reglamento de Teatro de 1786. In his discussion of the plays, Díaz de la Vega, *Discurso sobre los dramas*, 10–11, also mentions the royal decrees of 1703, 1741, 1764, and 1767 and the magistrates' decrees of New Spain from 1746, 1770, 1775, and 1783.

53. Jiménez Rueda, "Documentos para la historia del teatro," 138–140.

54. Reglamento de Teatro de 1786, point 5.

55. Ibid., point 21.

56. Ibid., point 18.

57. Ibid., point 15.

58. On the addenda of 1786, see Mañón, *Historia del teatro principal*, 33. I have not been able to locate the royal decree of 1792 nor the regulations of 1794 or 1813, but they are mentioned in AHA, vol. 796, exp. 3; vol. 797, exp. 29.

59. The regulations and other projects after 1821 are documented in AHA, vol. 796, exp. 3.

60. Cited in Schilling, *Teatro profano*, 99–100.

61. ABMNAH, Ramo Hospital Real de Naturales, vol. 28, exp. 18; vol. 101, exp. 11.

62. Gómez, "Diario curioso," 92.

63. Mañón, *Historia del teatro principal*, 34–35.

64. Ibid., 38.

65. Jiménez Rueda, "Documentos para la historia," 131–133, 135–137.

66. Cited in Olavarría y Ferrari, *Reseña histórica*, vol. 1, 146. In this document, the administrator states that the actress was imprisoned for "some homicide that it is said that she committed." Josefina Muriel also studied the case of the actress, but she does not mention any homicide; rather, she states that the actress was jailed for the scandalous life that she led. See her *Los recogimientos de mujeres. Respuesta a una problemática social novohispana* (Mexico City, 1974).

67. Cited in Mañón, *Historia del teatro principal*, 41–42.

68. Reglamento de Teatro de 1786, point 15.

69. Cited in Olavarría y Ferrari, *Reseña histórica*, vol. 1, 72–76.

70. ABMNAH, Ramo Hospital Real de Naturales, vol. 104, exp. 16.

71. AHA, vol. 797, exp. 21.

72. On the salaries of actors, see Olavarría y Ferrari, *Reseña histórica*, vol. 1, 37–46, and Luis González Obregón, *La vida de México en 1810* (Mexico City, 1979), 103–104. In calculating these wages, the high cost of costumes for which the actors were responsible must be taken into consideration. On the debts of the actors, see ABHNAH, Ramo Hospital Real de Naturales, vol. 101, exp. 11; vol. 107 bis, exp. 5, and María y Campos, *Andanzas*, 124–129.

73. Sten, *Vida y muerte*, 140; and María y Campos, *Andanzas*, 214–215.

74. Mañón, *Historia del teatro principal*, 33–34; Olavarría y Ferrari, *Reseña histórica*, vol. 1, 53–54; and AHA, vol. 797, exps. 20, 23.

75. AHA, vol. 797, exp. 21.

76. ABMNAH, Ramo Hospital Real de Naturales, vol. 100, exp. 6.

77. Cited in Olavarría y Ferrari, *Reseña histórica*, vol. 1, 142.

78. ABMNAH, Ramo Hospital Real de Naturales, vol. 101, exp. 11.

79. Ibid., vol. 103, exp. 8.

80. Cited in Olavarría y Ferrari, *Reseña histórica*, vol. 1, 144. On this labor conflict, see also Mañón, *Historia del teatro principal*, 39–40.

81. Ricard, *Spiritual Conquest*, 201.

82. Jiménez Rueda, "Documentos para la historia," 116–120, 137–138.

83. María y Campos, *Andanzas*, 68–69; Olavarría y Ferrari, *Reseña histórica*, vol. 1, 20–21.

84. Schilling, *Teatro profano*, 91; Muriel, *Los recogimientos de mujeres*, 69–70.

85. ABMNAH, Ramo Hospital Real de Naturales, vol. 107, exp. 2.

86. Díaz de la Vega, *Discurso sobre los dramas*, 15.

87. María y Campos, *Andanzas*, 124–129.

88. I hope Weber will forgive my version of his theories, *Economía y sociedad* (Mexico City, 1979), vol. 1, 21–23, 43–53, and vol. 2, 1074.

89. ABMNAH, Ramo Hospital Real de Naturales, vol. 101, exp. 11; and María y Campos, *Andanzas*, 192–193.

90. Muriel, *Los recogimientos de mujeres*, 66–69.

91. ABMNAH, Ramo Hospital Real de Naturales, vol. 100, exp. 6.

92. Ibid., vol. 107bis, fol. 126–127.

93. Mañón, *Historia del teatro principal*, 19–21.

94. Duvignaud, *Sociología del teatro*, 131–155.

95. Ibid., 260.

96. Alzate y Ramírez, "Periódicos," 129.

97. Cited in Olavarría y Ferrari, *Reseña histórica*, vol. 1, 81. This same idea, although in a more developed form, is found in Díaz de la Vega, *Discurso sobre los dramas*, 34.

98. For the titles of the plays, *tonadillas*, *seguidillas*, and *sainetes* that were presented in the Coliseo, see Olavarría y Ferrari, *Reseña histórica*, vol. 1, 28–29, 62–63, 158.

99. On these spectacles, see ABMNAH, Ramo Hospital Real de Naturales, vol. 28, exp. 22; vol. 107bis, exp. 5; María y Campos, *Los payasos*, 18–23; Olavarría y Ferrari, *Reseña histórica*, 63–66; and Mañón, *Historia del teatro principal*, 17–18.

100. Mañón, *Historia del teatro principal*, 17–18. It is interesting to note that in 1806, in Madrid, bullfights were also part of a spectacle of *sainetes*.

René Andioc, *Teatro y sociedad en el Madrid del siglo XVIII* (Valencia, 1976), 33.

101. ABMNAH, Ramo Hospital Real de Naturales, vol. 28, exp. 22.

102. Díaz de la Vega, *Discurso sobre los dramas*, 7. In 1790, the administrator of the Coliseo repeated these criticisms. Olavarría y Ferrari, *Reseña histórica*, vol. 1, 78.

103. Cited in Olavarría y Ferrari, *Reseña histórica*, vol. 1, 156–157.

104. Cited in ibid., 158.

105. Theater Regulations of 1786, point 5.

106. ABMNAH, Ramo Hospital Real de Naturales, vol. 103, exp. 53; and Olavarría y Ferrari, *Reseña histórica*, vol. 1, 149–150.

107. Olavarría y Ferrari, *Reseña histórica*, vol. 1, 154–156.

108. ABMNAH, Ramo Hospital Real de Naturales, vol. 106, exp. 64.

109. Cited in María y Campos, *Andanzas*, 134–135.

110. ABMNAH, Ramo Hospital Real de Naturales, vol. 106, exp. 81.

111. Ibid., vol. 107bis, exp. 10.

112. Mañón, *Historia del teatro principal*, 33–34, and Olavarría y Ferrari, *Reseña histórica*, vol. 1, 53–54.

113. Díaz de la Vega, *Discurso sobre los dramas*, 1–7.

114. These criteria to distinguish tragedy from comedy were presented by the author of a letter on the theater published in 1768 in the *Diario Literario de México*: Alzate y Ramírez, "Periódicos," xxx, also by Díaz de la Vega, *Discurso sobre los dramas*, 1–4.

115. ABMNAH, Ramo Hospital Real de Naturales, vol. 106, exp 64; vol. 107bis, exp. 5; and Olavarría y Ferrari, *Reseña histórica*, vol. 1, 150.

116. Cited in Mañón, *Historia del teatro principal*, 41.

117. On this characterization of the bourgeois vision of the world, see Groethuysen, *Origines de l'esprit*.

118. Paul Blanchart, *Histoire de la mise en scène* (Paris, 1948), 10.

119. Cited in Emilio Orozco Díaz, *El teatro y la teatrilidad del barroco: ensayo de introducción al tema* (Barcelona, 1969), 62.

120. Alzate y Ramírez, "Periódicos," 57.

121. Duvignaud, *Sociología del teatro*, 266.

122. Cited in Schilling, *Teatro profano*, 47–64.

123. Cited in ibid., 47–64.

124. Ricard, *Spiritual Conquest*, 203.

125. José Juan Arrom, *Historia del teatro hispanoamericano (época colonial)* (Mexico City, 1967), 32.

126. Cited in ibid., 100.

127. Duvignaud, *Sociología del teatro*, 236.

128. Cited in Olavarría y Ferrari, *Reseña histórica*, vol. 1, 150.

129. Reglamento de Teatro de 1786, point 21. On this conception of the spectator, see Duvignaud, *Sociología del teatro*, 222.

130. Orozco Díaz, *El teatro y la teatrilidad del barroco*, 39–53.

131. Reglamento de Teatro de 1786, points 7, 8, 10, 11, 12, 15, and 18.

132. Cited in Mañón, *Historia del teatro principal*, 41.

133. Cited in Olavarría y Ferrari, *Reseña histórica*, vol. 1, 182.

134. Alzate y Ramírez, *Obras I*, 57.

135. Cited in Luis Reyes de la Maza, *El teatro en México durante la Independencia, 1810–1839* (Mexico City, 1969), 63.

136. Reglamento de Teatro de 1786, point 6.

137. Cited in Mañón, *Historia del teatro principal*, 41.

138. Cited in María y Campos, *Andanzas*, 203–204. On the rule of the three unities and verisimilitude, see Blanchart, *Histoire de la mise en scène*, 53; and Duvignaud, *Sociología del teatro*, 260.

139. Cited in Olavarría y Ferrari, *Reseña histórica*, vol. 1, 78.

140. Usigli, *México en el teatro*, 29; Jiménez Rueda, "Documentos para la historia," 111–112; and Leonard, *Baroque Times*, 104.

141. Jiménez Rueda,"Documentos para la historia," 115–116.

142. Ibid., 121–129.

143. Leonard, *Baroque Times*, 111–116.

144. Julio Jiménez Rueda, *Herejias y supersticiones en la Nueva España* (Mexico City, 1946), 238–239.

145. Reglamento de Teatro de 1786, points 1 and 2.

146. Father Rincón's criteria for and censorship of these works are published in Olavarría y Ferrari, *Reseña histórica*, vol. 1, 77–81.

147. The narration of the reactions this drama provoked can be found in Olavarría y Ferrari, *Reseña histórica*, vol. 1, 83–87.

148. Cited in Usigli, *México en el teatro*, 68.

149. Ibid., 72; ABMNAH, Ramo Hospital Real de Naturales, vol. 107bis, exp. 5.

150. ABMNAH, Ramo Hospital Real de Naturales, vol. 107bis, exp. 5. Father Beristáin y Souza published theatrical critiques in Valladolid, Spain, in the *Diario Pinciano*, which he created. It was from this platform that he condemned the same plays that he authorized in Mexico. Celso Almuiña Fernández, *Teatro y cultura en el Valladolid de la Ilustración. Los medios de difusión en la segunda mitad del siglo XVIII* (Valladolid, 1979), 83–89, 141–181.

151. Anna, *Fall of Royal Government*, 103–129.

152. ABMNAH, Ramo Hospital Real de Naturales, vol. 107 bis, exp. 5.

153. *El Viajero Universal*, vol. 26, 257–297.

154. Duvignaud, *Sociología del teatro*, 11–12, 80–89.

155. *Translators' note*: For a more complete discussion of the festival of Corpus Christi, see Linda Curcio-Nagy, "Giants and Gypsies: Corpus Christi in Colonial Mexico City," in *Rituals of Rule, Rituals of Resistance: Public Celebrations and Popular Culture in Mexico*, ed. William Beezley, Cheryl English Martin, and William E. French (Wilmington, DE, 1994), 1–26.

156. For descriptions of the festival see *El Viajero Universal*, vol. 26, 292, in Mariano Cuevas, *Historia de la iglesia en México* (Mexico City, 1946–1947), vol. 3, 511–516; and in Manuel Carrera Stampa, *Los gremios mexicanos: La organización gremial en Nueva España (1521–1861)* (Mexico City, 1954), 102–104. A more detailed portrait of this festival as it was by the mid-nineteenth century can be found in Antonio García Cubas, *El libro de mis recuerdos* (Mexico City, 1978), 470–486.

157. On this ceremony, see *El Viajero Universal*, vol. 26, 293–296; and González Obregón, *La vida de México*, 61–68.

158. On this festival, see *El Viajero Universal*, vol. 26, 296–297; and Romero Flores, *México, historia de una gran ciudad*, 117–118.

159. María y Campos, *Los payasos*, 18–23.

160. On the topic of these performances in 1810, see González Obregón, *La vida de México*, 104–105.

161. Ibid., 105–106.

162. Mañón, *Historia del teatro principal*, 50; and Anna, *Fall of Royal Government*, 86.

163. Anna, *Fall of Royal Government*, p. 129.

164. Mañón, *Historia del teatro principal*, 50–51; Olavarría y Ferrari, *Reseña histórica*, vol. 1, 167; and Reyes de la Maza, *El teatro en México*, 11–12.

165. Mañón, *Historia del teatro principal*, 51.

166. Ibid., 54.

167. Ibid.

168. Cited in Olavarría y Ferrari, *Reseña histórica*, vol. 1, 252.

169. Cited in ibid., 156–157.

170. On the addenda of 1786, see Mañón, *Historia del teatro principal*, 33. On those added in 1792 and 1794, I have found references to these only in AHA, vol. 797, exp. 29. On the disorders, see María y Campos, *Guía de representaciones teatrales en Nueva España*, 192–193.

171. Olavarría y Ferrari, *Reseña histórica*, vol. 1, 158, 183; María y Campos, *Andanzas*, 214–215; and ABMNAH, Ramo Hospital Real de Naturales, vol. 107bis, exp. 5.

172. ABMNAH, Ramo Hospital Real de Naturales, vol 107, exp. 7; vol. 107bis, exp. 5.

173. AHA, vol. 797, exp. 25.

174. Olavarría y Ferrari, *Reseña histórica*, vol. 1, 175–176.

175. Ibid.; and Harvey L. Johnson, "Disputa suscitada en la ciudad de México," 150.

176. ABMNAH, Ramo Hospital Real de Naturales, vol. 107bis, exp. 5.

177. All these critiques are cited in Olavarría y Ferrari, *Reseña histórica*, vol. 1, 181–183, 200–202.

178. ABMNAH, Ramo Hospital Real de Naturales, vol. 107bis, exp. 5.

179. Cited in Jiménez Rueda, "Documentos para la historia," 138–140.

180. ABMNAH, Ramo Hospital Real de Naturales, vol. 102, exp. 8.

181. AHA, vol. 797, exps. 33, 34, and 35. In 1821, there were other disorders at another public *colloquium*. Ibid., exp. 31.

182. Olavarría y Ferrari, *Resseña histórica*, vol. 1, 187; and García Cubas, *El libro de mis recuerdos*, 353–354.

183. Susan R. Bryan, "The commercialization of the theater in Mexico and the rise of the 'teatro frívolo,' " (unpublished manuscript, 1984), 3.

184. Magaña Esquivel, *Los teatros en la ciudad*, 67–68; García Cubas, *El libro de mis recuerdos*, 347–348.

185. On the failure of the intellectuals to create a spiritual nourishment to the taste of the people and on the production of this popular drama by the elite of the industry, see Leon Tolstoi, "¿Qué hacer?" In *Los anarquistas. La teoría* (Madrid, 1975), 274–278.

186. Cited in Mañón, *Historia del teatro principal*, 60–63.

187. AHA, vol. 796, exp. 3.

# Chapter 3

1. The numbers that I cite are by no means exact but should give the reader a general picture of the size and composition of Mexico City at the turn of the eighteenth century. For the statistics of total population, and racial breakdown, see Alexander de Humboldt, *Political Essay on the King-*

*dom of New Spain*, trans. John Black (London, 1811), Book 2, 209–210, who gives the total population as 137,000, with 2,500 whites or Europeans, 65,000 Creoles, 33,000 Indians, 26,500 mestizos, and 10,000 mulattoes. He places the military population at about 5,000 to 6,000. The author of the "Discurso sobre la policía de México . . .," in *Antología de textos sobre la ciudad de México en el periodo de la Ilustración, 1788–1792*, ed. Sonia Lombardo de Ruiz (Mexico City, 1982), 99, notes that undoubtedly the plebeian sector of the population comprised four-fifths of the total. Jorge González Angulo Aguirre, *Artesanado y ciudad a finales del siglo XVIII* (Mexico City, 1983), 11, states that in 1794 the population of Mexico City was 120,000 residents, of whom 40,000 had some occupation, 5,211 labored in workshops, to which must be added 1,520 owners of these workshops, which gives a total of 6,731 artisans. On top of this, 7,500 individuals worked in the Royal workshops and 5,000 worked in their own homes. Flora Salazar, "Los sirvientes domésticos," in *Ciudad de México. Ensayo de construcción de una historia*, ed. Alejandra Moreno Toscano (Mexico City, 1978), 42, calculates that, in 1822, of the 150,000 residents in Mexico City, 20,000 lacked any housing or the means to earn their living. I have reduced this figure since at the end of the eighteenth century the population of Mexico City was smaller, and without doubt the number of beggars was augmented as a result of the Wars of Independence.

2. For the description of the life of the streets in Mexico City, see "Discurso sobre la policía"; Hipólito de Villarroel, *Enfermedades políticas que padece la capital de esta Nueva España* (Mexico City, 1937); and the works of contemporary historians Luis González Obregón, *México viejo. Noticias históricas, tradiciones, leyendas y costumbres* (Mexico City, 1976), and his *La vida en México en 1910* (Mexico City, 1979); Jesús Romero Flores, *México, historia de una gran ciudad*, ed. B. Costa-Amic (Mexico City, 1978); Sonia Lombardo de Ruiz, "Ideas y proyectos urbanísticos de la ciudad de México, 1788–1850," in *Ciudad de México. Ensayo de construcción de una historia*, ed. Alejandra Moreno Toscano (Mexico City, 1978).

3. "Discurso sobre la policía," 67.

4. AHA, vol. 797, exp. 33.

5. González Angulo Aguirre, *Artesanado y ciudad*, 73.

6. "Discurso sobre la policía," 52.

7. By 1840, the situation remained the same. Frances Calderón de la Barca, *Life in Mexico* (New York, 1970), 105, provides a description of the conditions: "And though a few ladies in black gowns and mantillas do occasionally venture forth on foot very early to shop or to attend mass, the streets are so ill kept, the pavements so narrow, the crowd so great, and the multitude of *léperos* in rags and blankets so annoying, that all these inconveniences, added to the heat of the sun in the middle of the day, form a perfect excuse for their nonappearance in the streets of Mexico."

8. I have used a variety of types of sources: (1) Chronicles of notable events and gazettes of the period: Antonio de Robles, *Diario de sucesos notables* (Mexico City, 1946), vol. 1, 258–259; vol. 2, 12; vol. 3, 92; José Manuel de Castro Santa-Anna, "Diario de sucesos notables escrito por . . .," in *Documentos para la historia de México* (Mexico City, 1854), vol. 6, 103, 227–228; José Gómez, "Diario curioso de Mexico," in *Documentos para la historia de México* (Mexico City, 1854), vol. 7, 291; *Gacetas de México* (Mexico City, 1949), vol. 1, 14, 77, 136, 370; vol. 3, 88. (2) Diverse prohibitions: Eusebio Ventura Beleña, *Recopilación sumaria de todos los autos acordados de la real*

*audiencia y sala del crimen de esta Nueva España y providencias de su superior gobierno* (Mexico City, 1981), vol. 1, 3rd pagination, 225–226; AGN, Ramo Civil, vol. 796, exp. 13. (3) Documents relating to the concession of licenses by the Ayuntamiento of Mexico City: AHA, vol. 797, exp. 21 and 33. The descriptions of Carnaval, which appeared after the end of the colonial period, were those of "La Romita," Lauro E. Rosell, *Iglesias y conventos coloniales de México; historia de cada uno de las que existen en la ciudad de México* (Mexico City, 1961), 132–143, and that of Ixcateopa, in the State of Mexico, Higinio Vázquez Santa Ana and J. Ignacio Dávila Garibi, *El carnaval* (Mexico City, 1931), 29–33.

9. On the 1731 *bando*, see *Gacetas de México*, vol. 1, 370; Ventura Beleña, *Recopilación sumaria*, vol. 1, 3rd pagination, 225–226. On the archbishop's edict, see *Gacetas de México*, vol. 1, 14.

10. The only information I could find on the ceremony of "hanging" in the eighteenth century is its prohibition in a Royal Decree of 1780 (AGN, Civil, vol. 194, exp. 3). Unfortunately, this document does not provide any information about the actual form of the ceremony, only that it took place at Shrovetide among the Indians of Ixtacalco, Mexicalcingo, Ixtapalapa, and some other nearby villages. This same decree asserts that the ritual was a holdover from the Indians' pagan ways. Some historians also believe that its origin is pre-Hispanic. (Roberto Moreno y de los Arcos argued this position at my thesis defense, when I presented an earlier version of this book.) The question is not easily resolved. Subsequent descriptions of the ceremony closely resemble the death of Carnaval (or Zampanar, Peirote, Meco, Antruido, Judas, Pero-Palo) in the small towns of Spain, which also takes place on the Shrovetide Tuesday. Julio Caro Baroja, *El carnaval, (análisis histórico-cultural)* (Madrid, 1984), 113, 115–116, 120, 122, and 124–125. On the other hand, some aspect of the Mexican version—for example, the dances of the *huehuenches*—are clearly of pre-Hispanic origin, although the costumes have undoubtedly been influenced by Spanish ones, at least as to the disguises. At mid-nineteenth century, according to Antonio García Cubas, *El libro de mis recuerdos* (Mexico City, 1978), 407, the *huehuenches* were "people of the lower classes, or Indians, whose only pleasure consisted in aimlessly roaming the streets of God, disguised with threadbare and greasy costumes, *generally of moors.*"

11. María Sten, *Vida y muerte del teatro náhuatl. El olimpo sin Prometeo* (Mexico City, 1974), 137.

12. Caro Baroja, in *El carnaval*, provides an excellent study on Carnaval and its social significance. See also Roberto da Matta, "Le dilemme brésilien. Individu, individualisme et personne dans les sociétés semi-traditionnelles," *Esprit* 7 (1983):32–35.

13. Louis Dumont, "La valeur chez les modernes et chez les autres," *Esprit* 7 (1983): 14–21.

14. See, for example, the description of Gemelli Careri, *Le Mexique à la fin du siècle XVIIᵉ vu par un voyageur italien* (Paris, 1968), 124.

15. Castro Santa-Anna, "Diario de sucesos notables," 56–61.

16. Careri, *Le Mexique à la fin*, 133. On the conflicts over the positions in processions, see Andrés Lira and Luis Muro, "El siglo de la integración," in *Historia general de México* (Mexico City, 1977), vol. 2, 160–161.

17. Matta, "Le dilemme brésilien," 33–36.

18. This dual aspect of Carnaval (defense of traditional rights of the common people and the consolidation of the social order) are demonstrated

in the following examples. In 1637, in the Carnaval of Madrid, participants criticized the policy of the Count Duke in increasing taxes and selling public offices with ridicule and satire. It has also been asserted that the famous Carnaval of Venice was nothing other than a safety valve for society to escape the excessive pressures of the state in the face of inequality. Finally, Caro Baroja has convincingly shown that the inversions of authority, which are celebrated in Carnaval and other similar festivals, actually strengthen the established authority. All these examples are found in Caro Baroja, *El carnaval*, 92–93, 156, 338–339. Carnaval was indeed nothing more than a section of a much larger phenomenon. Edward P. Thompson, "Eighteenth-Century English Society: Class Struggle without Class?" *Social History* 3:2 (May 1978):150–165, shows that the English revolts of the eighteenth century all had the goal of defending the interest of the common people by invoking a traditional order—even if fictitious—which the participants hoped to restore.

19. Robles, *Diario de sucesos*, vol. 1, 258–259.

20. Ibid., vol. 2, 12; Vázquez Santa Ana and Dávila Garibi, *El carnaval*, 20.

21. Ibid., vol. 3, 92.

22. *Gacetas de México*, vol. 1, 14.

23. Ventura Beleña, *Recopilación sumaria*, vol. 1, 3rd pagination, 225–226. See also *Gacetas de México*, vol. 1, 370. The note of the *gaceta* is reproduced in Sten, *Vida y muerte*, 136.

24. *Gacetas de México*, vol. 1, 77.

25. AHA, vol. 797, exp. 33.

26. *Gacetas de México*, vol. 3, 88.

27. Castro Santa-Anna, "Diario de sucesos," vol. 6, 103, 227–228.

28. Ventura Beleña, *Recopilación sumaria*, vol. 1, 3rd pagination, 226.

29. Gómez, "Diario curioso," 291.

30. Cited in Enrique de Olavarría y Ferrari, *Reseña histórica del teatro en México, 1538–1911* (Mexico City, 1961), vol. 1, 50.

31. AHA, vol. 796, exp. 13. See also "Compendio de providencias de policía," 22.

32. AGN, Civil, vol. 194, exp. 3.

33. Rossell, *Iglesias y conventos coloniales*, 132–134.

34. AHA, vol. 797, exp. 21.

35. Descriptions of Carnaval at mid-nineteenth century can be found in Guillermo Prieto, *Memorias de mi tiempo* (Mexico City, 1948), vol. 1, 188–190; García Cubas, *El libro de mis recuerdos*, 373, 404–409. See also Luis Reyes de la Maza, *El teatro en México durante la Independencia, 1810–1839* (Mexico City, 1969), 30; and Manuel Mañón, *Historia del teatro principal en México* (Mexico City, 1932), 81. On the takeover of Carnaval by the middle classes in Europe, see Caro Baroja, *El carnaval*, 157.

36. On the authorization of acrobats during Lent, from the time of the viceroy Marquis of Casa Fuerte, see AHA, vol. 797, exp. 33. On the functions of acrobats in the Coliseum, see Armando de Maria y Campos, *Los payasos; poetas; del pueblo, el circo en México* (Mexico City, 1939), 18–22. On the discussion of the morality of representations of the Passion, see Julio Jiménez Rueda, *Herejías y supersticiones en la Nueva España* (Mexico City, 1946), 23–24; Pablo González Casanova, *La literatura perseguida en la crisis de la Colonia* (Mexico City, 1958), 46–52; and especially, Armando de Maria y Campos, *Guía de representaciones teatrales en la Nueva España, siglos*

*XVI al XVIII* (Mexico City, 1959), 171–181. After Independence, the attacks of enlightened thinkers on these representations continued; see Olavarría y Ferrari, *Reseña histórica*, vol. 1, 202–203, and Reyes de la Maza, *El teatro durante la Independencia*, 30. I devote the next chapter to private *colloquia*. Some of the licenses for the Lenten period are found in AHA, vol. 797 exp. 32, and vol. 796, exp. 10. I have already dealt with the public *colloquia* in Chapter 2 at "The Denouement of the Theater." The source for this section is AHA, vol. 797, exp. 31, 33, 34, and 35; ABMNAH, Ramo Hospital Real de Naturales, vol. 107 bis, exp. 5; vol. 102, exp. 8; and Julio Jiménez Rueda, "Documentos para la historia del teatro en Nueva España," *Boletín del AGN* 15:1 (1949):138–140.

37. On the subject of these paseos, see Carreri, *Le Mexique à la fin*, 136, 162, 163–164, 165, 171, and 174; Castro Santa-Anna, "Diario de sucesos notables," vol. 6, 122–123, 237, 249; AHA, vol. 796, exp. 141; vol. 797, exp. 33; AGN, Civil, vol. 194, exp. 3; Olavarría y Ferrari, *Reseña histórica*, vol. 1, 157–158; and González Obregón, *La vida de México*, 96. See also the oil-painted folding screen that represents the canal of the Viga, and which is reproduced in Miguel Salas Anzures, "La ciudad de México," *Artes de México* 1:49–50 (January 1964):no pagination.

38. Ventura Beleña, *Recopilación sumaria*, vol. 1, 3rd pagination (no pagination).

39. AGN, Civil, vol. 194, exp. 3.

40. José Antonio Alzate y Ramírez, "Textos sobre la ciudad de México," in *Antología de textos sobre la ciudad de México en el periodo de la Ilustración, 1788–1792*, ed. Sonia Lombardo de Ruiz (Mexico City, 1982), 351.

41. AHA, vol. 796, exp. 14.

42. The opinion of the syndic is found in AHA, vol. 797. Descriptions of these outings in the nineteenth century can be found in Manuel Payno, *Los bandidos de Río Frío* (Mexico City, 1983), 380–381; García Cubas, *El libro de mis recuerdos*, 414–421; and Rossell, *Iglesias y conventos coloniales*, 153–154.

43. Calderón de la Barca, *Life in Mexico*, 112.

44. On the Enlightenment and religion in general, see Ernst Cassirer, *La filosofía de la Ilustración* (Mexico City, 1981), 156–221. For Spain, in particular, see Jean Sarrailh, *La España ilustrada*, 612–707; and Rafael Segovia Canosa, *Tres salvaciones del siglo XVIII español* (Jalapa, 1960), 17–55. For New Spain, see Pablo González Casanova, *El misoneísmo y la modernidad cristiana en el siglo XVII* (Mexico City, 1948), 167–226.

45. The author of the "Informe sobre pulquerías y tabernas del año de 1784," *Boletín del AGN* 18:2 (1947):196, proposes to ban the sale of food and drink during the processions, not only because fasting was required during this period but also because the vendors made a great commotion, "causing scandal by actions that are so foreign and distant from the *interior sentiments* that in this holy time every good Catholic should have and demonstrate with *exterior signs*."

46. On the encouragement of an indigenous participation in religious ceremonies, see Robert Ricard, *The Spiritual Conquest of Mexico; An Essay on the Apostolate and the Evangelizing Methods of the Mendicant Orders in New Spain*, trans. Lesley Byrd Simpson (Berkeley, CA, 1966), 176–193. See also Charles Gibson, *The Aztecs Under Spanish Rule; A History of the Indians of the Valley of Mexico, 1519–1810* (Stanford, CA, 1964), 99–135; and Sten,

*Vida y muerte,* 69–84. Gibson, *Aztecs Under Spanish Rule,* 135; Hidburg Schilling, *Teatro profano en la Nueva España: fines del siglo XVI a mediados del XVIII* (Mexico City, 1958), 166; Rodolfo Usigli, *México en el teatro* (Mexico City, 1932), 29; and Sten, *Vida y muerte,* 85–86, provide some of the church's critiques of these religious manifestations.

47. Bernard Groeythuysen, *Origines de l'esprit bourgeois en France. L'Eglise et la bourgeoisie* (Paris, 1977), 20–36.

48. "Informe sobre pulquerías y tabernas," 3:376–377.

49. Villarroel, *Enfermedades,* 184–191.

50. AHA, vol. 796, exp. 5, 6, 8, 10; also vol. 1066, exp. 3. See also Castro Santa-Anna, "Diario de sucesos notables," 115–116; and Gómez, "Diario curioso," 42.

51. González Obregón, *México viejo,* 173–180; Rosell, *Iglesias y conventos coloniales,* 71–75.

52. "Informe sobre pulquerías y tabernas," no. 2:199–200.

53. Rosell, *Iglesias y conventos coloniales,* 75.

54. On the concept of death held by eighteenth-century elites, see Philippe Ariès, *L'homme devant la mort* (Paris, 1977), 293–399. On this conception in New Spain, see Juan Pedro Viqueira Albán, "El sentimiento de la muerte en el México ilustrado del siglo XVIII a través de dos textos de la época," *Relaciones* 5 (1981):45–54.

55. Ventura Beleña, *Recopilación sumaria,* vol. 1, 3rd pagination, 54.

56. The source of the numbers of patients and deaths at the hospital for the 1770s were taken from Carmen Venegas Ramírez, *Régimen hospitalario para indios en la Nueva España* (Mexico City, 1973), 44–45.

57. The documents on the closure of the Royal Hospital's graveyard are located in ABMNAH, Hospital Real de Naturales, vol. 81, exp. 8; vol. 61, exp. 6.

58. Descriptions of the feast of Corpus Christi can be found in Mariano Cuevas, *Historia de la Iglesia en México,* vol. 3, 511–516; Manuel Carrera Stampa, *Los gremios mexicanos: la organización gremial en Nueva España, 1521–1861* (Mexico City, 1954), 102–104; and in *El viajero universal o noticia del mundo antiguo y nuevo. Obra recopilada de los mejores viajeros* (Madrid, 1799), vol. 26, 292.

59. Schilling, *Teatro profano,* 148.

60. Gómez, "Diario curioso," vol. 7, 341; "Compendio de providencias de policía en México del segundo conde de Revillagigedo," ed. Ignácio González-Polo, in *Suplemento al Boletín del Instituto de Investigaciones Bibliográficas* (Mexico City, no date), 32; and García Cubas, *El libro de mis recuerdos,* 470.

61. Gómez, "Diario curioso," 342.

62. "Compendio de providencias de policía," 32.

63. Ibid., 57; Gómez, "Diario curioso," 399.

64. Gómez, "Diario curioso," 405.

65. AHA, vol. 796, exp. 10.

66. Ibid.; and vol. 797, exp. 19; and González Casanova, *La literatura perseguida,* 57–60.

67. Sten, *Vida y muerte,* 70; Luis González Obregón, *Vetusteces* (Mexico City, 1917), 146–147.

68. González Obregón, *Vetusteces,* 135–143.

69. Cited in Julio Jiménez Rueda, *Historia de la cultura en México: el virreinato* (Mexico City, 1950), 257.

70. AHA, vol. 796, exps. 10 and 21.

71. Ibid., vol. 797, exps. 19 and 21; González Obregón, *Vetusteces,* 137–138.

72. Ibid., vol. 797, exps. 31, 33, and 34.

73. On the topic of these dances, see González Casanova, *La literatura perseguida,* 65–77; María del Carmen Velázquez, "El siglo XVIII," in *Historia documental de México* (Mexico City, 1974), 417–418; and José Antonio Robles-Cahero, "La memoria del cuerpo y la transmisión cultural: las danzas populares en el siglo XVIII," in *La memoria y el olvido. Segundo simposio de historia de las mentalidades* (Mexico City, 1985), 167.

74. Ventura Beleñas, *Recopilación sumaria,* vol. 1, 3rd pagination, 60.

75. Cited in Velázquez, "El siglo XVIII," 416–418.

76. *El viajero universal,* vol. 26, 378.

77. José Joaquín Fernández de Lizardi, *El Periquillo Sarniento* (Mexico City, 1965), 99–100.

78. Cited in González Casanova, *La literatura perseguida,* 74.

79. This text is found in ibid., 69, but the author did not provide the final section, thus giving the impression that the dance was actually more audacious than the last words indicate. The paragraph in its complete form is found in Robles-Cahero, "La memoria del cuerpo," 174.

80. Cited in Robles-Cahero, "La memoria del cuerpo," 169.

81. Cited in González Casanova, *La literatura perseguida,* 75.

82. On the importation of the *chuchumbé* into New Spain, see Robles-Cahero, "La memoria del cuerpo," 168; on its diffusion to Acapulco, see González Casanova, *La literatura perseguida,* 67.

83. On Ignacio Jerusalem and the increase of profane music, see Jesús Estrada, *Música y músicos del virreinato* (Mexico City, 1973), 123–127. "*El chuchumbé*" was played on Christmas Day in 1792 in the convent of San Francisco in Jalapa, apparently at the request of the monks. González Casanova, *La literatura perseguida,* 68 and Robles-Cahero, "La memoria del cuerpo," 175. "El pan de manteca" was played in 1796 in a convent of cloistered nuns in Mexico City. Velázquez, "El siglo XVIII," 413–415.

84. On the dance in the Convent of Santa Isabel, see Robles-Cahero, "La memoria del cuerpo," 175. On the *jamaica* in the hospital, see ABMNAH, Ramo Hospital Real de Naturales, vol. 104, exp. 39.

85. For information on the illegitimate births in Guadalajara, see Thomas Calvo, "Familia y registro parroquial: el caso tapatío en el siglo XVII," *Relaciones* 10 (Spring 1982):58–61. On the decrease of race mixture and the increase in mixed marriages, and the accompanying explanation, see Magnus Mörner, *Race Mixture in the History of Latin America* (Boston, 1967), 66–67.

86. Gómez, "Diario curioso," 9–10, 32–33, 88, 120.

87. On the *recogimientos* in general, see Josefina Muriel, *Los recogimientos.* On the *recogimiento* of Belen, see, in particular, pp. 81–102; on Santa María Magdalena, see pp. 100–139. For the sentencing practices, see pp. 123–128. Muriel believes that the rise in numbers of prisoners in the second half of the eighteenth century was due to a moral decay in customs at the time. In contrast, I believe that this increase was linked to a new intolerance and the severity of the authorities under the influence of enlightened ideas. This second line of reasoning seems more coherent with the institutional changes in the *recogimientos* clearly laid out by Josefina Muriel, *Los recogimientos de mujeres: respuesta a una problemática social*

*Novohispana* (Mexico City, 1974), 217–218. On the houses of correction for women, see ibid., 146–148.

88. Among European peasantries of the same period, young people were allowed to flirt and sexually caress each other during their engagement. One of these customs in the Germanic region was the *Kiltgang*, which permitted a young woman to sleep in the same bed as her suitor so long as sexual intercourse did not occur. On these customs, see Jean-Louis Flandrin, *Le sexe et l'Occident. Evolution des attitudes et des comportements* (Paris, 1981), 285–291; Jacques Solé, *L'amour en l'Occident à l'époque moderne* (Paris, 1976), 30–38; Edward Shorter, *The Making of the Modern Family* (London, 1976), 102–108, who affirms that during the *Kiltgang*, the couple lay very chastely next to each other simply chatting. His affirmation seems hard to believe.

89. Cited in Fabián de Fonseca and Carlos de Urrutia, *Historia general de la Real Hacienda* (Mexico City, 1978), vol. 3, 403–407.

90. See for example, Velázquez, "El siglo XVIII," 333; Juan Felipe Leal and Marío Huacuja Rountree, *Economía y sistema de hacienda en México. La hacienda pulquera en el cambio. Siglos XVIII, XIX, XX* (Mexico City, 1982), 83, state that the consumption of pulque increased in Mexico City in the eighteenth century, but they do not relate this trend to the breakdown of customs.

91. On the cultivation of maguey, the plant from which pulque is derived, its elaboration and transport, see "Respuesta que dio el guardia mayor a las 35 preguntas que le hace el Superintendente," Museo Naval de Madrid, Ms. 569, doc. 2, fol. 50–63. I wish to thank T. Rojas for telling me about this manuscript and for giving me a copy of this document. See also Humboldt, *Political Essay*, vol. 2, 520–521; Leal and Huacuja, *Economía y sistema*, 79–84; José Jesús Hernández Palomo, *El aguardiente de caña en México (1724–1810)* (Seville, 1974), 1–30. Jesús Ruvalcaba Mercado, *El maguey manso. Historia y presente de Epazoyucan, Hidalgo* (Mexico City, 1983), 41–96, provides one of the most complete studies of maguey and its production.

92. The most useful sources on the topic of pulque and *pulquerías* in the eighteenth century are: Fonseca and Urrutia, *Historia general de la Real Hacienda*, vol. 3, 338–428; José María Marroqui, *La ciudad de México* (Mexico City, 1900–1903), vol. 1, 189–211; and Hernández Palomo, *El aguardiente de caña*. On mixed pulques (pulques *curados*), see Fonseca and Urrutia, *Historia general de la Real Hacienda*, vol. 3, 353–357; and Hernández Palomo, *El aguardiente de caña*, 30.

93. "Informe sobre pulquerías y tabernas," no. 2, 223–224; Fonseca and Urrutia, *Historia general de la Real Hacienda*, vol. 3, 403–407; and Hernández Palomo, *El aguardiente de caña*, 316–317. On the prices in 1806, see AHA, vol. 3719, exp. 25.

94. Ibid., exp. 7, and "Informe sobre pulquerías y tabernas," no. 2, 205.

95. See, for example, Gibson, *Aztecs Under Spanish Rule*, 150.

96. AHA, vol. 3719, exp. 41.

97. On these violations of the rules, see AHA, vol. 3719, exp. 8 and 37; "Informe sobre pulquerías y tabernas," no. 2, 202–229; Fonseca and Urrutia, *Historia general de la Real Hacienda*, vol. 3, 361–366; Marroqui, *La ciudad de México*, vol. 1, 208; Virginia Guedea, "México en 1812: control político y bebidas prohibidas," in *Estudios de historia moderna y*

*contemporánea de México* (Mexico City, 1980), vol. 8, 59; and Hernández Palomo, *El aguardiente de caña*, 75–76. On the use of pulque with peyote, sometimes for magical-religious ends, see AGN, Ramó Civil, vol. 59, exp. 7; and also Irving A. Leonard, *Baroque Times in Old Mexico* (Ann Arbor, MI, 1959), 159–160.

98. Fonseca and Urrutia, *Historia general de la Real Hacienda*, vol. 3, 346.

99. On the supposed prohibition of pulque, see ibid., 339. Hernández Palomo, *El aguardiente de caña*, 31–37, shows that pulque was tolerated. On the number of *pulquerías* in 1650, see AGN, Reales Cédulas, vol. 15, exp. 179.

100. AGN, Reales Cédulas, vol. 7, exp. 131; Fonseca and Urrutia, *Historia general de la Real Hacienda*, vol. 3, 340–346; "Informe sobre pulquerías y tabernas," no. 2, 230; and Hernández Palomo, *El aguardiente de caña*, 37–47. The figure of 40,000 pesos a year was taken from AGN, Reales Cédulas, vol. 7, exp. 131. Hernández Palomo, *El aguardiente de caña*, 40–41, using another document, states that the revenue was only 5,000 pesos annually.

101. AGN, Reales Cédulas, vol. 7, exp. 131.

102. Marroqui, *La ciudad de México*, vol. 1, 190–191; Fonseca and Urrutia, *Historia general de la Real Hacienda*, vol. 3, 340–341; Hernández Palomo, *El aguardiente de caña*, 45–47; and Gregorio Martín de Guijo, *Diario 1648–1664* (Mexico City, 1952), vol. 3, 222.

103. AGN, Reales Cédulas, vol. 10, exp. 113.

104. Cited in Marroqui, *La ciudad de México*, vol. 1, 196–197.

105. AGN, Reales Cédulas, vol. 12, exp. 17.

106. AGN, Reales Cédulas, vol. 10, exp. 113; vol. 11, exp. 106; and vol. 12, exp. 17.

107. Cited in Fonseca and Urrutia, *Historia general de la Real Hacienda*, vol. 3, 354.

108. Ibid., 353–359; Hernández Palomo, *El aguardiente de caña*, 67–84.

109. Ibid., 360.

110. Ibid., 363.

111. Hernández Palomo, *El aguardiente de caña*, 119–125. According to Hernández Palomo, 130–131, Texcoco and the five leagues around the city (Coyoacán, Mexicalzinco, Tacuba, Guadalupe, and Xochimilco) were given as a monopoly for a year and 230 days for 49,382 pesos. This was the equivalent of an income of 30,000 a year.

112. Ibid., 208; "Informe sobre pulquerías y tabernas," no. 2, 230–231. According to Fonseca and Urrutia, *Historia general de la Real Hacienda*, vol. 3, 370, in 1752, a *carga* was defined as composed of twelve *arrobas* for fiscal reasons. Since this order was probably never carried out, the authorities decided in 1763 to specify the tax by *arroba*, not *carga*.

113. "Informe sobre pulquerías y tabernas," no. 2, 230–231. Neither Hernández Palomo, in *El aguardiente de caña*, nor Fonseca and Urrutia, in *Historia general de la Real Hacienda*, mentions the two-thirds of a *grano*, but Graph 2 of the income derived from pulque and the taxes collected, which is provided in the work of these authors (vol. 3, 423), clearly shows that the actual amount charged by the officials was one real and two thirds of a *grano*.

114. Hernández Palomo, *El aguardiente de caña*, 135–141.

115. Cited in Fonseca and Urrutia, *Historia general de la Real Hacienda*, vol. 3, 392.

116. Ibid., 416–417, 423. The "Informe sobre pulquerías y tabernas," no. 2, 231, states that officials began to collect this tax in 1764, but this is probably a typographical error in the text; it should read 1774. In any case, the date seems to be wrong. Hernández Palomo, *El aguardiente de caña*, 220, affirms that there was no increase; rather, one real per *arroba* was deducted to pay for the clothing of the military. Indeed, the information he presents (p. 369), from the Archivo General de Indias on the receipts for 1767 and 1776 and for the pulque brought into the city (p. 428), indicate that this increase was not implemented. The most plausible explanation is that the amount collected for the clothing of the military was kept in a separate account and so does not appear in the documentation of the Archivo General de Indias.

117. Cited in Fonseca and Urrutia, *Historia general de la Real Hacienda*, vol. 3, 405–406. On Gálvez's policy regarding pulque, see "Informe sobre las pulquerías y tabernas," no. 3, 378–379; and Hernández Palomo, *El aguardiente de caña*, 209, 315–316.

118. "Informe sobre pulquerías y tabernas," no. 3, 392.

119. See Claude Morin, "Sentido y alcance del siglo XVIII en América Latina: el caso del centro-oeste mexicano," in *Ensayos sobre el desarrollo económico de México y América Latina (1500–1975)*, ed. Enrique Florescano (Mexico City, 1979), 162–163.

120. Humboldt, *Political Essay*, vol. 2, 527.

121. AHA, vol. 3719, exps. 4, 6, and 38; Fonseca and Urrutia, *Historia general de la Real Hacienda*, vol. 3, 410–412; Romero Flores, *México, historia de una gran ciudad*, 446; and David Brading, *Miners and Merchants in Bourbon Mexico, 1763-1810* (Cambridge, Eng., 1971), 105, 216.

122. Brading, *Miners and Merchants*, 148, 234.

123. Ibid., 283–297.

124. See the case of the Hacienda de Jala in Leal and Huacuja Rountree, *Economía y sistema*, 38–45.

125. AHA, vol. 3719, exp. 4.

126. Fonseca and Urrutia, *Historia general de la Real Hacienda*, vol. 3, 411–412; and Marroqui, *La ciudad de México*, vol. 1, 206–207.

127. Fonseca and Urrutia, *Historia general de la Real Hacienda*, vol. 3, 339.

128. Ibid., 339, 346.

129. Hernández Palomo, *El aguardiente de caña*, 33–36; the unabridged ordinances appear on pp. 433–435. On the order of Viceroy the Duke of Albuquerque, see Guijo, *Diario 1648–1664*, vol. 1, 229–230.

130. Marroqui, *La ciudad de México*, vol. 1, 191.

131. These ordinances are published in Fonseca and Urrutia, *Historia general de la Real Hacienda*, vol. 3, 345–348.

132. Hernández Palomo, *El aguardiente de caña*, 58–62.

133. Carlos de Sigüenza y Góngora, "Alboroto y motín de México, del 8 de junio de 1692," *Relaciones Históricas* (Mexico City, 1972), 138, 144–145, 154.

134. AHA, vol. 3719, exp. 2; Fonseca and Urrutia, *Historia general de la Real Hacienda*, vol. 3, 353–357.

135. Fonseca and Urrutia, *Historia general de la Real Hacienda*, vol. 3, 360; Marroqui, *La ciudad de México*, vol. 1, 202; "Informe sobre pulquerías y tabernas," 219; Hernández Palomo, *El aguardiente de caña*, 12, 28–30.

136. Fonseca and Urrutia, *Historia general de la Real Hacienda*, vol. 3, 361–366.

137. Ibid., 369.

138. ABMNAH, Ramo Hospital Real de Naturales, vol. 84, exp. 9; AHA, vol. 3719, exp. 8.

139. AHA, vol. 3719, exp. 7.

140. Fonseca and Urrutia, *Historia general de la Real Hacienda*, vol. 3, 368.

141. This map is displayed in AHA.

142. Marroqui, *La ciudad de México*, vol. 1, 207–209.

143. This practice began with the first monopoly in 1669. In 1671, the viceroy tried to reestablish the authority of the subordinate ministers over matters related to pulque. But the opposition of the contractor/monopolist in tandem with the Royal Audiencia made the viceroy back down. In 1674, the position of private judge was abolished, but was then reinstated in 1685. Hernández Palomo, *El aguardiente de caña*, 58–60, 64–67, 81, 104–106, 122.

144. Hernández Palomo, *El aguardiente de caña*, 81, 104; Marroqui, *La ciudad de México*, vol. 1, 199–200.

145. Fonseca and Urrutia, *Historia general de la Real Hacienda*, vol. 3, 361, 371.

146. Ibid., 348.

147. Ibid., 372.

148. Ibid., 371.

149. Ibid., 405–406.

150. Eduardo Báez Macías, ed., "Ordenanza de la división de la nobilísima cudad [*sic*] de México en cuarteles, creación de los alcaldes de ellos, y reglas de su gobierno: dada y mandada observar por el excelentísimo señor don Martín de Mayorga, virrey, gobernador y capitán general de esta Nueva España," *Boletín del AGN* 10:1–2 (1969):103.

151. "Discurso sobre la policía," 69–72.

152. See Enrique Florescano and Gil Sánchez, "La época de las reformas borbónicas,"in *Historia general de México* (Mexico City, 1977), vol. 2, 251–255; Sherburne F. Cook and Woodrow Borah, *Essays in Population History: Mexico and the Caribbean* (Berkeley, CA, 1971), vol. 1, 300–375; Claude Morin, *Michoacán en la Nueva España del siglo XVIII. Crecimiento y desigualdad en una economía colonial* (Mexico City, 1979), 39–91; and Humboldt, *Political Essay*, Book 2, 81–83.

153. Humboldt, *Political Essay*, 37.

154. On this idea of very high pulque consumption, see Humboldt, *Political Essay*, Book 2, 98; and Gibson, *Aztecs Under Spanish Rule*, 409, who also repeats this statement in his conclusion. Figures provided in Hernández Palomo, *El aguardiente de caña*, 428, indicate that the average annual consumption in Mexico City for the period 1763 to 1810 was 39,545 *arrobas*. According to Humboldt, *Political Essay*, Book 2, 98, the population of Mexico City in 1793—a date at more or less the midpoint of our period—was 135,000 residents. This would mean that the annual consumption per inhabitant was 14,376 *arrobas*. Hernández Palomo, *El aguardiente de caña*, 320–321, provides the official equivalencies for units of measure

used in pulque: 1 *carga* equals 18 *arrobas*, or 450 *cuartillos*. Since 1 *cuartillo* was the equivalent of half a liter, then 1 *arroba* of pulque was the same as 12.5 liters. So, the annual pulque consumption per inhabitant was 179.7 liters; and daily, a little less than half a liter. Gibson, *Aztecs Under Spanish Rule*, 396, estimates the annual consumption at about 75 gallons, which would be the equivalent of 0.77 liters daily, a quantity that seems a long way off from the excesses that he imputes. He does not explain the manner in which he obtained this figure, so it is not possible to critique it.

155. On wine consumption in Paris, see Daniel Roche, *Le peuple de Paris. Essai sur la culture populaire au XVIIᵉ siècle* (Paris, 1981), 269.

156. Leal and Huacuaja Rountree, *Economía y sistema*, 103.

157. Cited in Fonseca and Urrutia, *Historia general de la Real Hacienda*, vol. 3, 346.

158. Ibid., 344–346, 363–366, 403; Vicente Riva Palacio, *México a través de los siglos: Historia del virreinato* (United States, n.d.), vols. 3 and 5, vol. 4, 220; Marroqui, *La ciudad de México*, vol. 1, 190–191; and Hernández Palomo, *El aguardiente de caña*, 438–439, 446.

159. The recipes for these fermented beverages are taken from "Explicación del modo de beneficiar cada una de las diversas bebidas que se usan en el reino de la Nueva España," Museo Naval de Madrid, Ms. 335, doc. 6, fols. 28–34v. This document, which undoubtedly dates from 1791, is published in Iris Higbie Wilson, ed., "Pineda's Report on the Beverages of New Spain," *Arizona and the West* 5 (1963):79–90. The book also contains many other recipes, including other distillations. (I thank Teresa Rojas for providing me with a copy of the original document and its English version.) On *chinguirito*, see Hernández Palomo, *El aguardiente de caña*, 7, 45–61.

160. On the mixture of pulque and peyote, see AGN, Civil, vol. 59, exp. 7; and Leonard, *Baroque Times*, 101–102.

161. "*Chinguirito*," in *Enciclopedia de México* (Mexico City, 1978), vol. 3, 782.

162. Fonseca and Urrutia, *Historia general de la Real Hacienda*, vol. 3, 402–403; Marroqui, *La ciudad de México*, vol. 1, 203–204; and Hernández Palomo, *El aguardiente de caña*, 65–84, 91–104.

163. Fonseca and Urrutia, *Historia general de la Real Hacienda*, vol. 4, 373.

164. Hernández Palomo, *El aguardiente de caña*, 25–26, 86–88.

165. Ibid., 91–104; Gómez, "Diario curioso," 452, 461.

166. Humboldt, *Political Essay*, Book 2, 149–150.

167. Roche, *Le peuple de Paris*, 256–273.

168. Marroqui, *La ciudad de México*, vol. 1, 207–208. The author confuses the *casillas*, which were closed in 1793, with the *pulquerías* outside the city limits. In fact, these were quite distinct businesses. The *casillas* were located beyond the city entrances and, as such, the pulque sold there was not taxed. This distinction is clear in AHA, vol. 3719, exp. 17.

169. According to Humboldt, *Political Essay*, Book 2, 98, the population of Mexico City was then 135,000.

170. Viceroy Luis de Velasco's ordinances on pulque are reproduced in Hernández Palomo, *El aguardiente de caña*, 433–436. On the number of *pulquerías* before 1650, see AGN, Reales Cédulas, vol. 15, exp. 179. Roche, *Le peuple de Paris*, 258, provides the number of taverns in Paris. It would have been interesting to compare the number of *pulquerías* in Mexico City

with the equivalent number of taverns in Spanish cities, but unfortunately, this last statistic was unavailable.

171. "Informe sobre pulquerías y tabernas," no. 2, 227.

172. AHA, vol. 3719, exp. 17.

173. For a description of the food stands, see AHA, vol. 3719, exps. 17, 40, 41, and 42.

174. AHA, vol. 3719, exps. 17, 19, 25, 40, 41, and 42.

175. "Discurso sobre la policía de México," 60.

176. Ibid., 63.

177. Ibid., 61–63.

178. Fernández de Lizardi, *El Periquillo Sarniento*, 104.

179. Guedea, "México en 1812," 45–47.

180. Ibid., 48.

181. Ibid., 51–52. Hernández Palomo, *El aguardiente de caña*, 224–225, states that the cause for this apparent scarcity of pulque in the city was that the insurgent troops knew that the tax levied on pulque financed the Royalist troops. The rebels therefore took every opportunity to cut the roads that served to transport pulque to the capital city.

182. Marroqui, *La ciudad de México*, vol. 1, 209.

183. Cited in Guedea, "México en 1812," 59.

184. Ibid., 63.

185. AHA, vol. 3719, exp. 50.

186. Ibid., exp. 52.

187. Ibid.

188. Leal and Huacuja, *Economía y sistema*, 105. In 1864, the city population was 210,000.

189. Payno, *Los bandidos*, 86–94, and Prieto, *Memorias de mi tiempo*, vol. 1, 48–50, 81–82, describe the atmosphere in the nineteenth-century *pulquerías*.

190. ABMNAH, Ramo Hospital Real de Naturales, vol. 106, exp. 81.

191. AHA, vol. 797, exp. 33.

192. Ibid., vol. 796, exps. 9, 10, 11, and 15.

193. Fernández de Lizardi, *El Periquillo Sarniento*, 399.

194. Caro Baroja, *El carnaval*, 313–314; Bartolomé Bennassar, *Un siècle d'or espagnol* (Paris, 1982), 39.

195. AHA, vol. 796, exp. 9. Acrobats seem to have flocked to Arsinas Street to entertain. They continued to do so in the first half of the nineteenth century. Artisans were in the habit of bringing their children to this street to see the performances. Payno, *Los bandidos*, 87.

196. AHA, vol. 796, exps. 9, 10, 11; vol. 797, exp. 21.

197. This strategy was used in 1797, ibid., exp. 11, and in 1813, ibid., exp. 22.

198. ABMNAH, Ramo Hospital Real de Naturales, vol. 106, exp. 81.

199. AHA, vol. 797, exp. 23, 38; María y Campos, *Los payasos*, 18–23.

200. María y Campos, *Los payasos*.

201. AHA, vol 797, exp. 21.

202. Ibid., exp. 20, exp. 21; ABMNAH, Ramo Hospital Real de Naturales, vol. 107bis, exp. 5; Olavarría y Ferrari, *Reseña histórica*, vol. 1, 53–54; Mañón, *Historia del teatro principal*, 33–34.

203. Ventura Beleñas, *Recopilación sumaria*, vol. 1, 3rd pagination, 129.

204. AHA, vol. 796, exp. 11; Mañón, *Historia del teatro principal*, 33–34; Olavarría y Ferrari, *Reseña histórica*, vol. 1, 53–54.

205. AHA, vol. 797, exp. 21.

206. Ibid., exp. 28.

207. Ibid., exp. 30. J. E. Varey, *Los títeres y otras diversiones populares de Madrid, 1758–1840. Estudio y documentos. Fuentes para la historia del teatro en España* (London, 1972), vol. 7, 41–42, states that these *fuegos ilíricos* seem to have been the same as those called "perspective machines" in Spain.

208. González Obregón, *La vida de México*, 98.

209. AHA, vol. 797, exp. 20.

210. Peter Gay, *The Enlightenment: An Interpretation*, Vol. 2: *The Science of Freedom* (New York, 1969), 27–45.

211. Jean-Jacques Rousseau, *Les Confessions* (Paris, 1964), 110–111.

212. Juan Benito Díaz de Gamarra, "Errores del entendimiento humano," in *Tratados* (Mexico City, 1947), 47. González Casanova, in *El misoneísmo*, 202, cites Alzate's criticism taken from the *Gacetas de literatura* on May 3, 1791.

213. AHA, vol. 797, exp 17.

214. María y Campos, *Los payasos*, 18–23; and Mañón, *Historia del teatro principal*, 33.

215. Olavarría y Ferrari, *Reseña histórica*, vol. 1, 196–197.

216. Romero Flores, *México, historia de una gran ciudad*, 387–389; Salvador Novo, *Los paseos de la ciudad de México* (Mexico City, 1980), 10–13; "Informe sobre pulquerías y tabernas," no. 2, 200–201.

217. Romero Flores, *México, historia de una gran ciudad*, 464–471; Novo, *Los paseos*, 54–58; and Humboldt, *Political Essay*, vol. 2, 102–103.

218. Romero Flores, *México, historia de una gran ciudad*, 390–391; Novo, *Los paseos*, 23–24; Gómez, "Diario curioso," 51.

219. "Discurso sobre la policía," 92–93; *El viajero universal*, vol. 28, 248; Romero Flores, *México, historia de una gran ciudad*, 391; Novo, *Los paseos*, 31–33.

220. "Informe sobre pulquerías y tabernas," no. 2, 200–201.

221. "Discurso sobre la policía," 75; AHA, vol. 797, exp. 33; Castro Santa-Anna, "Diario de sucesos," vol. 6, 148–151.

222. Villarroel, *Enfermedades*, 182–183; Castro Santa-Anna, "Diario de sucesos," vol. 6, 148–149.

223. Castro Santa-Anna, "Diario de sucesos," vol. 6, 148–149; "Compendio de providencias de policía," 31–64.

224. "Discurso sobre la policía," 75–87.

225. This analysis is based upon the descriptions of the gardens of La Granja in Spain in Benito Pérez Galdós, *Los apostólicos* (Madrid, 1917), 269.

226. "Discurso sobre la policía," 76.

227. Lombardo de Ruiz, "Ideas y proyectos," 171–172, discusses the coincidence between the proposals for urban design and gardening in the "Discurso sobre la policía," 36–41 for Urbanism and 75–87 for Paseos.

228. Olavarría y Ferrari, *Reseña histórica*, vol. 1, 157–158. This description of the Paseo de la Viga was already cited in the Introduction.

229. AHA, vol. 3719, exp. 7.

230. Marroqui, *La ciudad de México*, vol. 1, 7–8; "Compendio de providencias," 21.

231. O'Gorman, "Reflexiones," 19–22.

232. Roberto Romero y de los Arcos, 1982, 152–173.

233. Marroqui, *La ciudad de México*, vol. 1, 104–108; Eduardo Báez Macías, ed., "Ordenanzas para el establecimiento de alcaldes de barrio en la Nueva España. Ciudades de México y San Luis Potosí," *Boletín del AGN* 10:1–2 (1969):51–61, and his "Ordenanza de la división," 75–81, 102–105.

234. Roberto Moreno de los Arcos, "Los territorios parroquiales de la cuidad arzobispal, 1325–1981," in *Gaceta oficial del Arzobispado de México* 22 (September–October 1982): 152–173.

235. Báez Macías, "Ordenanza de división," 97–100, points 14, 19, 22, 23, 24, and 27.

236. Ibid., 80–81; Moreno de los Arcos, "Los territorios parroquiales," 152–173, comments on the work of Alzate.

237. Ibid., 98–99 (points 17, 18, and 20).

238. José Miranda, "La ilustración y el fomento de la ciencia en México durante el siglo XVIII," in *Vida colonial y albores de la independencia* (Mexico City, 1972), 206; "Compendio de providencias de policía," 30–31.

239. Anna, *Fall of Royal Government*, 80–83.

240. Ernesto Lemoine Villicaña, "El alumbrado público en la ciudad de México durante la segunda mitad del siglo XVIII," *Boletín del AGN* 4:4 (1963):783–818; Artemio de Valle-Arizpe, *Calle vieja y calle nueva* (Mexico City, 1949), 363–393; "Compendio de providencias de policía," 17–18.

241. "Compendio de providencias de policía," 15–59.

242. Cited in González Obregón, *México viejo*, x–xi.

243. Romero Flores, *México, historia de una gran ciudad*, 375–377; Marroqui, *La ciudad de México*, vol. 2, 401–402; Adriana López Monjardín, *Hacia la ciudad del capital: 1790–1870* (Mexico City, 1985), 75–76.

244. Lombardo de Ruiz, "Ideas y proyectos," 176–179.

245. Cited in Guedea, "México en 1812," 29–30.

246. "Discurso sobre la policía," 72. Viceroy Revillagigedo the second had planned to end the corruption of the alcaldes de barrio by changing the way they were named to their positions. Instead of the usual practice with the priest naming three residents who would choose the alcalde from among them, the viceroy ordered that the outgoing alcalde propose three names to the head judge who would then choose one as the next alcalde. "Compendio de providencias," 56. It is difficult to imagine that such a change would have made a dent in the prevailing corruption.

# Chapter 4

1. D. A. Brading, in *Miners and Merchants in Bourbon Mexico, 1763–1810* (Cambridge, 1971), 147–159, 238–297, writes about the merchants and this peculiar system of inheritance.

2. Cited in ibid., 154–155. This description is quite similar to that contained in a sonnet written in 1604 by Baltazar Dorantes de Carranza, which Jorge Alberto Manrique reproduces in "Del barroco a la ilustración," in *Historia general de México* (Mexico City, 1977), vol. 2, 360.

3. Most of the information on pelota is contained in the Archivo Histórico del Ayuntamiento, vol. 796, exp. 16. This section deals with the San Camilo game in the period from 1787 to 1821, but the papers are not organized or numbered systematically. Hence, it is not possible to provide accurate citations. For this reason, I provide general information about

the documents in question in order to facilitate the efforts of historians who decide to consult this documentation.

4. The merchants' lack of interest in the Enlightenment seems to have been general to the Western world. For Spain, see Antonio Domínguez Ortiz, *Sociedad y estado en el siglo XVIII español* (Barcelona, 1976), 490, 491. For France, see Emmanuel Le Roy Ladurie, "Lo cuantitativo en historia; la sexta sección de l'Ecole Pratique des Hautes Etudes," in *Perspectivas de la historiografía contemporánea*, ed. Ciro F. S. Cardoso and Héctor Pérez Brignoli (Mexico City, 1976), no. 280, 85, who summarizes the conclusions of Daniel Roche, *Livre et société dans la France du XVIIIᵉ siècle* (Paris, 1981). Brading, *Miners and Merchants*, 339, comments upon the age at marriage of merchants.

5. AHA, vol. 796, exp. 16, September 15, 1801, October 21, 1818, and July 31, 1801.

6. AHA, vol. 819, exp. 2, July 16, 1787.

7. Ibid.

8. Ibid. *Eutropelia* applied to games or occupations that were honest and moderate. See also AHA vol. 796, exp. 16, September 15, 1801.

9. AHA, vol. 796, exp. 16, March 9, 1819. Jesús Romero Flores, *México, historia de una gran ciudad*, ed. B. Costa-Amic (Mexico City, 1978), 391–392, states that the first court was located at the corner of Independencia and Revillagigedo Streets. It is clear that games were held there at the end of the eighteenth century, but its location—so distant from the city center— makes it an unlikely candidate for the first court. Also, Romero Flores clearly based this conclusion on José María Marroqui, *La ciudad de México* (Mexico City, 1900–1903), vol. 3, 182–185, but he totally misinterpreted the text, attributing events of the nineteenth century to the eighteenth century.

10. AHA, vol. 796, exp. 16, November 8, 1800; AHA, vol. 819, July 16, 1787.

11. The rule is found in AHA, vol. 796, exp. 16, July 16, 1787. Its confirmation is located in ibid., November 18, 1800.

12. Ibid., July 16, 1787.

13. Ibid., August 9, 1805, September 15, 1801, and January 17, 1803.

14. Ibid., January 17, 1803.

15. For more information on this phenomenon in New Spain, see Juan Pedro Viqueira Albán, "El sentimiento de la muerte en el México ilustrado del siglo XVIII a través de las textos de la época," *Relaciones* 5 (1981):45–54; for Europe, see Philippe Ariès, *L'homme devant la mort* (Paris, 1977), 293–299; and Norbert Elias, "La soledad del moribundo en nuestros días," *Vuelta* 69 (August 1982):17–24.

16. AHA, vol. 796, exp. 16, January 17, 1803, February 23, 1805, August 9, 1805, August 20, 1805, and September 19, 1805.

17. Ibid., August 9, 1805.

18. Ibid., August 20, 1805.

19. Ibid., September 19, 1805.

20. AHA, vol. 819, exp. 2.

21. AHA, vol. 796, exp. 16, October 21, 1818.

22. On the cult of health, see Juan Benito Díaz de Gamarra, "Errores del entendimiento humano," *Tratados* (Mexico City, 1947), 6–37, and the text published in *Mercurio Volante* by the Italian, Luis Carnaro, in nos. 11,

12, 13, and 14; see also José Ignacio Bartolache, *Mercurio Volante* (Mexico City, 1979), 109–152.

23. AHA, vol. 796, exp. 16, February 24, 1801.

24. AHA, vol. 819, exp. 2.

25. AHA, vol. 796, exp. 16, July 24, 1801.

26. AHA, vol. 797, exp. 16, November 8, 1900, February 24, 1801, March 30, 1801, April 4, 1801, June 2, 1801, and March 30, 1805.

27. AHA, vol. 796, exp. 16, September 15, 1801.

28. Compare this to the rules of 1787. AHA, vol. 796, exp. 16, July 16, 1801 and March 30, 1801.

29. Ibid., July 16, 1787.

30. Ibid., November 8, 1800.

31. Ibid., June 18, 1817, July 15, 1817, September 19, 1817, October 29, 1817, December 2, 1817, January 19, 1818, January 26, 1818, April 7, 1818, April 9, 1818, April 24, 1818, May 29, 1818, July 1, 1818, July 18, 1818, August 19, 1818, October 21, 1818, November 19, 1818, January 9, 1819, March 9, 1819, July 30, 1819, March 31, 1821, and December 6, 1821.

32. AHA, vol. 796, exp. 16, July 16, 1787.

33. Ibid., vol. 819, exp. 2.

34. Ibid., vol. 796, exp. 16, November 8, 1800.

35. Ibid., June 2, 1801.

36. Ibid., July 24, 1801.

37. Ibid., September 15, 1801.

38. Ibid., October 21, 1818.

39. Ibid., January 9, 1819.

40. Ibid., March 9, 1819.

41. Ibid., May 24, 1819.

42. Ibid., vol. 819, exp. 2.

43. Andrés Lira and Luis Muro, "El siglo de la integración," in *Historia general de México* (Mexico City, 1977), vol. 2, 180–181, comment on the beginnings of this type of concern.

44. AHA, vol. 819, exp. 2. The document dates from 1787.

45. Ibid., vol. 796, exp. 16, January 17, 1803.

46. Ibid., December 2, 1817.

47. Ibid., vol. 819, exp. 2.

48. Ibid.

49. Ibid., vol. 796, exp. 16, July 16, 1787.

50. On the deployment of the soldiers, see ibid., June 2, 1801.

51. Ibid., March 30, 1801.

52. Ibid.

53. Ibid.

54. Ibid., July 31, 1801.

55. Ibid., September 15, 1801.

56. Ibid., December 6, 1821.

57. José Joaquín Fernández de Lizardi, *El Periquillo Sarniento* (Mexico City, 1965), 309.

58. José Joaquín Fernández de Lizardi, *Obras* (Mexico City, 1970), vol. 4, 80–81.

59. See Bernard Groethuysen, *Les origines de l'esprit bourgeois en France. L'Eglise et la bourgeoisie* (Paris, 1977), 130–163, 280–295, for a discussion of the bourgeois conception of sin, wealth, and morality.

60. Gaspar Melchor de Jovellanos y Ramírez, "Memoria para el arreglo de la policía de los espectáculos y diversiones públicas, y sobre su origen en España," in *Obras escogidas* (Madrid, 1955), vol. 1, 113–117.

61. Cited in Jean Sarrailh, *La España ilustrada de la secunda mitad de siglo XVI a mediados del siglo XVIII* (Madrid, 1974), 74.

62. Domínguez Ortiz, *Sociedad y estado*, 486.

63. Rafael Segovia Canosa, *Tres salvaciones del siglo XVIII español* (Jalapa, 1960), 85; Domínguez Ortiz, *Sociedad y estado*, 485.

64. Jovellanos y Ramírez, "Memoria para el arreglo," vol. 2, 25–27.

65. Domínguez Ortiz, *Sociedad y estado*, 483–486.

66. Jovellanos y Ramírez, "Memoria para el arreglo," vol. 2, 36–38, 40–41, 41–45.

67. René Andioc, *Teatro y sociedad en el Madrid del siglo XVIII* (Valencia, 1976), 524.

68. Ibid., 32–37, 198–201; Celso Almuiña Fernández, *Teatro y cultura en el Valladolid de Ilustración* (Valladolid, 1979), 99–100, 135; Gonzalo Anes, *El antiguo régimen: Los Borbones* (Madrid, 1981), 473, all comment on the taste in theater of the common people of Spain. Jovellanos y Ramírez, "Memoria para el arreglo," vol. 1, 136, and Segovia Canosa, *Tres salvaciones*, 141–181, comment on the enlightened thinkers' critique of the plays of the Golden Age.

69. Almuiña Fernández, *Teatro y cultura*, 141–181.

70. Anes, *El antiguo régimen*, 474.

71. Cited in Andioc, *Teatro y sociedad*, 531.

72. Jovellanos y Ramírez, "Memoria para el arreglo," vol. 2, 28–30.

73. Ibid., 35.

74. Ibid., 28–30.

75. Cited in Andioc, *Teatro y sociedad*, 517–518.

76. Jovellanos y Ramírez, "Memoria para el arreglo," vol. 2, 45–49.

77. Andioc, *Teatro y sociedad*, 43–44.

78. Julio Caro Baroja, *El carnaval (análisis histórico-cultural)* (Madrid, 1984), 154–155.

79. Ibid., 157.

80. Jovellanos y Ramírez, "Memoria para el arreglo," vol. 2, 21–23.

81. Sarrailh, *La España ilustrada*, 73.

82. Domínguez Ortiz, *Sociedad y estado*, 378–380.

83. Ibid., 396.

84. Sarrailh, *La España ilustrada*, 73.

85. J. E. Varey, *Los títeres y otras diversiones populares de Madrid, 1758–1840. Estudio y documentos* (London, 1972), vol. 7, 41–44.

86. Ibid., 32, 41–44.

87. Almuiña Fernández, *Teatro y cultura*, 102.

88. Varey, *Los títeres*, 12–16, 33–35.

89. Pierre Vilar, "Coyunturas. Motín de Esquilache y crisis del antiguo régimen," in *Hidalgos, amotinados y guerrilleros. Pueblos y poderes en la historia de España* (Barcelona, 1982), 106–109; Domínguez Ortiz, *Sociedad y estado*, 308; Anes, *El antiguo régimen*, 371–372.

90. Eduardo Báez Macías, "Ordenanzas para el establecimiento de alcades de barrio en la Nueva España. Ciudades de México y San Luis Potosí," *Boletín del AGN* 10:1–2 (1970), 53–54; Vilar, "Coyunturas," 118; Anes, *El antiguo régimen*, 324.

91. Vilar, "Coyunturas," 118.

92. Sarrailh, *La España ilustrada*, 80–84, 528–537; Domínguez Ortiz, *Sociedad y estado*, 342–344.

93. Jovellanos y Ramírez, "Memoria para el arreglo," vol. 2, 24; Sarrailh, *La España ilustrada*, 75, provides information on Campomanes' opinions on pelota.

94. Almuiña Fernández, *Teatro y cultura*, 83–89.

95. On eighteenth-century theater in New Spain, see Chapter 2. For Spain, see Sarrailh, *La España ilustrada*, 595–597; Domínguez Ortiz, *Sociedad y estado*, 483–486; and Anes, *El antiguo régimen*, 135–136, 474.

96. Anes, *El antiguo régimen*, 473, 482, 484.

97. Jovellanos y Ramírez,"Memoria para el arreglo," vol. 1, 92–93, vol. 2, 7–15.

98. Gonzalo Aguirre Beltrán, *La población negra de México. Estudio etnohistórico* (Mexico City, 1972), 175–177.

99. José Miranda, *Humboldt y México* (Mexico City, 1962), 19, for example, states that "people of all classes mixed in the dances and popular diversions." It seems to me that the author was extrapolating too freely from the slumming, which was, according to José Ortega y Gasset, *Goya* (Madrid, 1963), 47–49, such an important trend in eighteenth–century Spain. On *majismo* (slumming) in Spain, see also Sarrailh, *La España ilustrada*, 87–89, 519; and Domínguez Ortiz, *Sociedad y estado*, 326–327.

100. Brading, *Miners and Merchants*, 37–44.

101. Magnus Mörner, *Race Mixture in the History of Latin America* (Boston, 1967), 65; José Gómez, "Diario Curioso de México," in *Documentos para la historia de México* (no place, 1854), vol. 7, 68; Domínguez Ortiz, *Sociedad y estado*, 328.

102. *Translator's note*: Here the *colloquium* refers to a person with cataracts, whose eyes became cloudy and white.

103. Cited in Enrique de Olavarría y Ferrari, *Reseña histórica del teatro en México, 1538–1911* (Mexico City, 1961), vol. 1, 91–92.

104. Claude Morín, *Michoacán en la Nueva España del siglo XVIII. Crecimiento y desigualdad en una economía colonial* (Mexico City, 1979), 78.

105. Hipólito de Villarroel, *Enfermedades políticas que padece la capital de esta Nueva España en casi todos los cuerpos de que se compone y remedios que se la deben aplicar para su curación si se quiere que sea útil al rey y al público* (Mexico City, 1937), 253–255.

106. Cecilia del Carmen Noriega Elio, "Fernández de Lizardi; un proyecto de sociedad. (Ideología y modelos de conducta)" (unpublished thesis, Universidad Nacional Autónoma de México, 1975), 156–179, 197–212, and 92, states that *"El Periquillo Sarniento* is the celebration of creolism for having resisted race mixture."

107. Cited in ibid., 176.

108. José Miranda, *Las ideas y las instituciones mexicanas. Primera parte, 1521–1820* (Mexico City, 1978), 170–174.

109. Andrés Lira, *Comunidades indígenas frente a la ciudad de México, Tenochtitlán y Tlaltelolco, sus pueblos y barrios, 1812–1919* (Mexico City, 1983), 63–64.

110. Susan E. Bryan, "The commercialization of the theater in Mexico and the rise of the 'teatro frívolo' " (unpublished manuscript, 1984), 3.

111. Alejandra Moreno Toscano and Jorge González Angulo, "Cambios en la estructura interna de la ciudad de México (1753–1882)," in *Asentamien-*

*tos urbanos y organización socioproductiva en la historia de América Latina*, ed. Hardoy and R. P. Schaedel (Buenos Aires, 1977), 177–188.

112. Karl Polanyi, *The Great Transformation* (Boston, 1944), 201–248, explains the appearance of the self-regulated market when it is left to its own devices and also comments upon its destructive effects.

113. Gladys Swain, "Une logique de l'inclusion: les infirmes du signe," *Esprit* 5 (May 1982):61–75, comments on the discourse of inclusion as a characteristic of modernity.

114. Brading, *Miners and Merchants*, 159. The insane asylum was actually a reconstruction of the San Hipólito Hospital, which was inaugurated in 1777.

115. Max Weber, *Economía y sociedad* (Mexico City, 1979), vol. 2, 1074.

# Glossary

Acordada: both a court and a police force founded in the eighteenth century. Originally, its purpose was to fight highwaymen.

alcaldes: officials within towns who held some bureaucratic and judicial functions. There were several variants. *Alcaldes mayores* were district governors. *Alcaldes del crimen* were responsible for justice. Alcaldes in charge of a particular area were called *alcaldes del cuarteles* or alcaldes del barrio.

*alguacil mayor*: the constable of an *alcalde mayor*.

Audiencia: the high court and also governing body, it was composed of a president and four judges (*oidores*).

Ayuntamiento: town council.

*bando*: a proclamation usually announcing regulations.

Bourbons: the dynasty that began to rule Spain, and consequently the colonies, in the eighteenth century. These rulers are associated with the changes of this period called "the Bourbon reforms."

*cabildo*: the elected council of a town.

*cascarón*: an empty eggshell filled with chalk, starch, confetti, or the like which Mexicans tossed at each other in celebration of Shrovetide.

*casillas*: places outside Mexico City where pulque was sold.

*castas:* racial categories that emerged from miscegenation.

*cazuela*: literally "a pot," but in this context a type of enclosure or balcony of a theater.

*chinampa*: raised field.

*chinguirito*: low-quality cane brandy.

*chuchumbé*: a dance known for its "obscene" movements and daring words, thought to have derived from African dances.

*colloquiums*: little plays based on a theme corresponding to the day's religious celebration.

Corpus Christi: the celebration of the rite of the Eucharist.

*corrales*: an early form of theater; usually uncovered patios where plays were presented.

*corregidor*: royal district governor.

*corrida*: bullfight.

*cuartel*: in this context, a city sector.

*donjuanismo*: a man's emulation of the literary character, Don Juan, by the seduction of women and other libertine conduct.

*fuegos ilíricos*: lighted perspectives that represented buildings from antiquity, from fables, and from the important cities of the world.

*horchata*: a drink made of water and ground nuts, usually almonds.

*huehuenches*: a dance and also the dancers who dress as old men.

*jamaicas*: parties to aid a charity.

*jarabe*: a dance characterized by intricate footwork.

*lépero*: a dirty, badly dressed person.

*luneta*: a section of theater seating.

maguey: a cactus used for the production of pulque.

mestizo: a person of mixed racial heritage, usually Indian and Spanish.

Monte de Piedad: an institution where people could pawn goods.

*mosquete*: a section of the theater.

*obraje*: a workshop, usually for textiles.

*oidores*: the judges of the Audiencia.

*parcialidades*: sections of Mexico City outside the *traza* and populated mostly by Indians.

paseo: a promenade, a place where members of the elite walked or rode in carriages in order to relax and be seen.

*pastoral*: a kind of play that re-created biblical stories.

pelota: a precursor of the game of jai alai, which originated with the Basques. It is played on a court against an end wall.

*petate*: a rush mat.

*Posada*: a festivity in the days before Christmas, when the participants re-create the trip of Joseph and Mary to Bethlehem by singing special songs outside the hosts' houses where they ask for room at the inn. After being ritually refused several times, finally all enter and enjoy food and drink.

pulque: an alcoholic beverage based on the fermented sap of the maguey cactus. It existed in Mexico before the Spanish Conquest.

*pulquerías*: places where pulque is sold.

Recogidas: an institution originally meant as shelter for respectable women whose husbands were absent, but by the eighteenth century, it had become a place where women were placed as punishment.

*regidor*: councilman, secondary officer of the *cabildo*.

*sainete*: short dramatic work, usually a farce.

*sarao*: an evening gathering with music and dancing.

*seguidilla*: a composition of seven verses used for popular songs, which became characteristic of Spanish song, and an accompanying dance.

*síndicos*: officials who take charge of the affairs of a corporate group.

*solares*: small plots of land within city limits.

*sones*: popular songs suitable for dancing.

*tarasca*: a dragon figure used in the procession on the day of Corpus Christi.

*tepache*: an alcoholic drink made from fermented fruit (usually pineapple), sugarcane, and brown sugar.

*tertulia*: a social gathering in which the participants meet regularly to discuss various topics, usually with some intellectual pretensions.

*tonadilla*: a short popular song.

*trajineras*: small boats that transported goods and people.

*traza*: the core of the city reserved, in theory, for Spanish residents.

*vecindades*: tenements.

*vinaterías*: places where wine was served and sold.

*visitador*: an inspector.

# Bibliography

## Sources

Most frequently, historical monographs are based upon a series of documents. This was not the case for this book. On the contrary, the selection of primary sources followed the exigencies of the historical problem that I proposed to resolve.

In the sections on bullfights and the theater, my work in the archives was minimal. The abundant literature on these topics and the extensive use and direct quotation of documents within these works made me believe that it would be more useful to concentrate on a critical analysis of this literature rather than a fruitless search for new material. However, I did find some previously undocumented material in the Ramos Toros and Diversiones Públicas of the Archivo Histórico del Ayuntamiento of Mexico City as well as in the Ramo of the Hospital Real de Naturales of the Archive of the National Museum of Anthropology and History.

On the other hand, for the section on street diversions and the game of pelota, I used the collections of the Archivo del Ayuntamiento of Mexico City intensively, since historical works on these topics were rare. I worked principally in the following series: Diversiones públicas, Gallos, billares y pelota, Festividades religiosas, and Pulquerías.

Finally, I filled in some gaps, particularly for the chapter on the seventeenth century. This information was gleaned from the Ramo of Reales Cédulas in the Archivo General de la Nación.

All the documents I used—either directly or taken from published sources—were for the most part regulations, *bandos*, decrees, official memoranda, and requests for licenses. Of course, these documents reflect the vision of the viceregal governments and only indirectly that of the common people who devised or attended these diversions. If my goal had been to study these diversions, these sources would not have been the appropriate instrument, but since I proposed to analyze the attitudes of the ruling classes toward the entertainments of the poor and the policies that they chose to follow, these documents were ideal. The reader might question this choice and pine for a study of the popular culture of Mexico City in the eighteenth century and not the story of its persecution. But it seems to me that this is the necessary first step before obtaining valid information on popular culture. The archives, of course, are the repositories of the memories of the ruling classes; and, to rescue some of the fragments of the distant past of those without power, these sources must be used critically.

This work has no other goal than to dispel an illusion, to end the simplistic reading of the past, and to forge a critical apparatus with which to examine, on a more solid basis, the thesis of the decline of customs and to allow an accurate study of popular culture in the eighteenth century.

## Published Works

Aguirre Beltrán, Gonzalo. *La población negra de México. Estudio etnohistórico,* Mexico City, 1972.

Almuiña Fernández, Celso. *Teatro y cultura en el Valladolid de la Ilustración. Los medios de difusión en la segunda mitad del siglo XVIII.* Valladolid, 1979.

Alzate y Ramírez, José Antonio de. "Periódicos," *Obras,* vol. 1. Mexico City, 1980.

———. "Textos sobre la ciudad de México." In *Antología de textos sobre la ciudad de México en el periodo de la Ilustración (1788–1792),* ed. Sonia Lombardo Ruiz. Mexico City, 1982, 159–370.

Andioc, René. *Teatro y sociedad en el Madrid del siglo XVIII.* Valencia, 1976.

Anes, Gonzalo. *El antiguo régimen: Los Borbones.* Madrid, 1981.

Anna, Timothy E. *The Fall of Royal Government in Mexico City.* Lincoln, NE, 1978.

Ariès, Philippe. *L'homme devant la mort.* Paris, 1977.

———. "Préface" to *Le mariage. Les hésitations de l'Occident,* by Marie-Odile Metral. Paris, 1977, 7–11.

Arrom, José Juan. *Historia del teatro hispanoamericano (época colonial).* Mexico City, 1967.

Báez Macías, Eduardo, ed. "Ordenanzas para el establecimiento de alcaldes de barrio en la Nueva España. Ciudades de México y San Luis Potosí." *Boletín del AGN* 10:1–2 (1969):51–74.

———, ed. "Ordenanza de la división de la nobilísima cuidad [*sic*] de México en cuarteles, creación de los alcaldes de ellos, y reglas de su gobierno: dada y mandada observar por el excelentísimo señor don Martín de Mayorga, virrey, gobernador y capitán general de esta Nueva España." *Boletín del AGN* 10:1–2 (January–June 1969):75–106.

Barth, Hans. *Verdad e ideología*. Mexico City, 1951.

Bartolache, José Ignacio. *Mercurio Volante*. Mexico City, 1979.

Benítez, Fernando. *Historia de la ciudad de México*. 9 vols. Mexico City, 1984.

Bennassar, Bartolomé. *Un siècle d'or espagnol*. Paris, 1982.

Blanchart, Paul. *Histoire de la mise en scène*. Paris, 1948.

Brading, D. A. *Miners and Merchants in Bourbon Mexico, 1763–1810*. Cambridge, Eng., 1971.

Bryan, Susan E. "The commercialization of the theater in Mexico and the rise of the 'teatro frívolo' '. Unpublished manuscript, 1984.

Calderón de la Barca, Frances. *Life in Mexico*. New York, 1970.

Calvo, Thomas. "Familia y registro parroquial: el caso tapatío en el siglo XVII." *Relaciones* 10 (Spring 1982):53–67.

Caro Baroja, Julio. *El carnaval (análisis histórico-cultural)*. Madrid, 1984.

Carrera Stampa, Manuel. *Los gremios mexicanos: La organización gremial en Nueva España (1521–1861)*. Mexico City, 1954.

Carreri, Gemelli. *Le Mexique à la fin du XVIIᵉ siècle vu par un voyageur italien*. Paris, 1968.

Cassirer, Ernst. *La filosofía de la Ilustración*. Mexico City, 1981.

Castro Santa-Anna, José Manuel de. "Diario de sucesos notables escrito por . . ." In *Documentos para la historia de México*. Vols. 4, 5, and 6. Mexico City, 1854.

"Compendio de providencias de policía de México del segundo conde de Revillagigedo." In *Suplemento al Boletín del Instituto de Investigaciones Bibliográficas*, trans. and ed. Ignacio González-Polo. Mexico City, 1983, 14–15.

Cook, Sherburne F., and Woodrow Borah. *Essays in Population History: Mexico and the Caribbean*. Berkeley and Los Angeles, 1971.

Cuevas, Mariano. *Historia de la iglesia en México*. 5 vols. Mexico City, 1946–1947.

Despois, Eugène André. *Le théâtre français sous Louis XIV*. Paris, 1886.

Díaz de Gamarra, Juan Benito. "Errores del entendimiento humano." In *Tratados*. Mexico City, 1947.

Díaz de la Vega, Silvestre. *Discurso sobre los dramas*. Mexico City, 1786.

"Discurso sobre la policía de México." In *Antología de textos sobre la ciudad de México en el periodo de la Ilustración (1788–1792)*, ed. Sonia Lombardo de Ruiz. Mexico City, 1982.

Domínguez Ortiz, Antonio. *Sociedad y estado en el siglo XVIII español*. Barcelona, 1976.

Duby, Georges. *Los tres órdenes o lo imaginario del feudalismo*. Barcelona, 1980.

Dumont, Louis. "La valeur chez les modernes et chez les autres." *Esprit* 7 (July 1983):3–29.

Duvignaud, Jean. *Sociología del teatro. Ensayo sobre las sombras colectivas.* Mexico City, 1966.

Elias, Norbert. "La soledad del moribundo en nuestros días." *Vuelta* 69 (August 1982):5–11, and 70 (September 1982):17–24.

*Enciclopedia de México.* Mexico City, 1978.

Estrada, Jesús. *Música y músicos del virreinato.* Mexico City, 1973.

"Explicación del modo de beneficiar cada una de las diversas bebidas que se usan en el reino de la Nueva España." Museo Naval de Madrid. Ms. 335, doc. 6, fols. 28–34v.

Febvre, Lucien. *Le problème de l'incroyance au 16ᵉ siècle, La religion de Rabelais.* Paris, 1968.

Feijó, Rosa. "El tumulto de 1692," *Historia Mexicana* (April–June 1965):656–679.

Fernández de Lizardi, José Joaquín. "Periódicos. Alacena de frioleras; Cajoncitos de la alacena; Las sombras de Heráclito y Demócrito; El conductor eléctrico." *Obras.* Vol. 4. Mexico City, 1970.

———. *El Periquillo Sarniento* (originally published 1816). Mexico City, 1965.

Flandrin, Jean Louis. *Le sexe et l'Occident. Evolution des attitudes et des comportements.* Paris, 1981.

Flores Hernández, Benjamín. "Con la fiesta nacional, por el Siglo de las Luces. Un acercamiento a lo que fueron y significaron las corridas de toros en la Nueva España en el siglo XVIII." Honors thesis, Universidad Nacional Autónoma de México, 1976.

———. "Sobre las plazas de toros en la Nueva España del siglo XVIII." *Estudios de Historia Novohispana* 7 (1981):99–160.

Florescano, Enrique. *Precios del maíz y crisis agrícolas en México (1708–1810).* Mexico City, 1969.

———, and Isabel Gil Sánchez. "La época de las reformas borbónicas." In *Historia general de México.* Vol. 2. Mexico City, 1977.

Fonseca, Fabián de, and Carlos de Urrutia. *Historia general de la Real Hacienda.* Mexico City, 1978.

*Gacetas de México.* 3 vols. Mexico City, 1949.

García Cubas, Antonio. *El libro de mis recuerdos.* Mexico City, 1978.

Gay, Peter, *The Enlightenment: An Interpretation.* Vol. 2: *The Science of Freedom.* New York, 1969.

Gibson, Charles. *The Aztecs under Spanish Rule; A History of the Indians of the Valley of Mexico, 1519–1810.* Stanford, CA, 1964.

Gómez, José. "Diario curioso de México . . ." In *Documentos para la historia de México.* Vol. 7. No place, 1854.

Gómez de la Serna, Gaspar. *Los viajeros de la Ilustración.* Madrid, 1974.

González Angulo Aguirre, Jorge. *Artesanado y ciudad a finales del siglo XVIII.* Mexico City, 1983.

González Casanova, Pablo. *La literatura perseguida en la crisis de la Colonia.* Mexico City, 1958.

———. *El misoneísmo y la modernidad cristiana en el siglo XVIII.* Mexico City, 1958.

González y González, Luis. "El linaje de la cultura mexicana." *Vuelta* 72 (November 1982):14–23.

———. "El Siglo de las Luces." In *Historia mínima de México.* Mexico City, 1977.

———. "El siglo mágico." *Historia Mexicana* 2:5 (July–September 1952):66–86.

González Marmolejo, Jorge René. "Curas solicitantes durante el siglo XVIII." In *Familia y sexualidad en Nueva España.* Mexico City, 1982.

González Obregón, Luis. *México viejo. Noticias históricas, tradiciones, leyendas y costumbres.* Mexico City, 1976.

———. *Vetusteces.* Mexico City, 1917.

———. *La vida de México en 1810.* Mexico City, 1979.

Groethuysen, Bernard. *Origines de l'esprit bourgeois en France. L'Eglise et la bourgeoisie.* France, 1972.

Guedea, Virginia. "México en 1812: control político y bebidas prohibidas." In *Estudios de historia moderna y contemporánea de México.* Mexico City, 1980.

Guijo, Gregorio Martín de. *Diario 1648–1664.* Vol. 3. Mexico City, 1952.

Hernández Palomo, José Jesús. *El aguardiente de caña en México (1724–1810).* Seville, 1974.

———. *La renta del pulque en Nueva España.* Seville, 1979.

Humboldt, Alexander de. *Political Essay on the Kingdom of New Spain,* trans. John Black. London, 1811.

"Informe sobre pulquerías y tabernas del año de 1784." *Boletín del AGN* 18:2 (1947):201–202.

Israel, Jonathan. *Race, Class, and Politics in Colonial Mexico, 1610–1670.* Oxford, 1980.

Jiménez Rueda, Julio. "Documentos para la historia del teatro en la Nueva España." *Boletín del AGN* 15:1 (1944):101–144.

———. *Herejías y supersticiones en la Nueva España.* Mexico City, 1946.

———. *Historia de la cultura en México: el virreinato.* Mexico City, 1950.

Johnson, Harvey L. "Disputa suscitada en la ciudad de México, entre los alcaldes del crimen y los ordinarios, por el auto del año de 1819 que mandó a las actrices no vestir trajes de hombre en las funciones del Coliseo." *Revista Iberoamericana* 10:19 (November 1945):131–168.

Jovellanos y Ramírez, Gaspar Melchor de. "Memoria para el arreglo de la policía de los espectáculos y diversiones públicas, y sobre su origen en España." In *Obras escogidas.* 2 vols. Madrid, 1955.

Lahisse, Jean. "La revolución silenciosa." *Diógenes* (1981):113–114.

Leal, Juan Felipe, and Marío Huacuja Rountree. *Economía y sistema de hacienda en México. La hacienda pulquera en el cambio. Siglos XVIII, XIX, XX.* Mexico City, 1982.

Lemoine Villicaña, Ernesto. "El alumbrado público en la ciudad de México durante la segunda mitad del siglo XVIII." *Boletín del AGN* 4:4 (1963):783–818.

León Cázares, María del Carmen. *La plaza mayor de la ciudad de México en la vida cotidiana de sus habitantes. Siglos XVI y XVII.* Mexico City, 1982.

Leonard, Irving A. *Baroque Times in Old Mexico: Seventeenth-Century Persons, Places, and Practices.* Ann Arbor, MI, 1959.

———. "La temporada teatral de 1792 en le Nuevo Coliseo de México." *Nueva Revista de Filología Hispánica* 5 (1951).

Le Roy Ladurie, Emmanuel. "Lo cuantitativo en historia; la sexta sección de l'Ecole Pratique des Hautes Etudes." In *Perspectivas de la historiografía contemporánea*, ed. Ciro F. S. Cardoso and Héctor Pérez Brignoli. Mexico City, 1976.

Lira, Andrés. *Comunidades indígenas frente a la ciudad de México, Tenochtitlán y Tlaltelolco, sus pueblos y barrios, 1812–1919.* Mexico City, 1983.

———, and Luis Muro. "El siglo de la integración." In *Historia general de México.* Mexico City, 1977.

Lombardo de Ruiz, Sonia. "Ideas y proyectos urbanísticos de la ciudad de México, 1788–1850." In *Ciudad de México. Ensayo de construcción de una historia*, ed. Alejandra Moreno Toscano. Mexico City, 1978.

López Monjardín, Adriana. *Hacia la ciudad del capital: 1790–1870.* Mexico City, 1985.

Magaña Esquivel, Antonio. *Los teatros en la ciudad de México.* Mexico City, 1974.

Mañón, Manuel. *Historia del teatro principal de México.* Mexico City, 1932.

Manrique, Jorge Alberto. "Del barroco a la ilustración." In *Historia general de México.* 2 vols. Mexico City, 1977.

Marañón, Gregorio. *Don Juan.* Buenos Aires, 1944.

María y Campos, Armando de. *Andanzas y picardías de Eusebio Vela: autor y comediante mexicano del siglo XVIII.* Mexico City, 1944.

———. *Guía de representaciones teatrales en la Nueva España; siglos XVI al XVIII.* Mexico City, 1959.

———. *Los payasos; poetas del pueblo, el circo en México. Crónica.* Mexico City, 1944.

Marroqui, José María. *La ciudad de México.* 3 vols. Mexico City, 1900–1903.

Matta, Roberto da. "Le dilemme brésilien. Individu, individualisme et personne dans les sociétés semi-traditionnelles." *Esprit* 7 (1983):30–47.

Maza, Francisco de la. *La ciudad de México en el siglo XVII.* Mexico City, 1985.

Miranda, José. *Humboldt y México.* Mexico City, 1962.

———. *Las ideas y las instituciones mexicanas. Primera parte, 1521–1820.* Mexico City, 1978.

————. "La ilustración y el fomento de la ciencia en México durante el siglo XVIII." In *Vida colonial y albores de la independencia.* Mexico City, 1972.

————, and Pablo González Casanova, eds. *Sátira anónima del siglo XVIII.* Mexico City, 1953.

Moreno de los Arcos, Roberto. "Introducción." *Obras.* José Antonio de Alzate y Ramírez. Vol. 1. Mexico City, 1980.

————. "Los territorios parroquiales de la ciudad arzobispal, 1325–1981." *Gaceta oficial del Arzobispado de México* 22 (September–October 1982):152–173.

Moreno Toscano, Alejandra. "Introducción. Un ensayo de historia urbana." In *Ciudad de México. Ensayo de construcción de una historia.* Mexico City, 1978.

————, and Jorge González Angulo. "Cambios en la estructura interna de la ciudad de México (1753–1882)." In *Asentamientos urbanos y organización socioproductiva en la historia de América Latina,* ed. Hardoy and R. P. Schaedel. Buenos Aires, 1977.

Morin, Claude. *Michoacán en la Nueva España del siglo XVIII. Crecimiento y desigualdad en una economía colonial.* Mexico City, 1979.

————. "Sentido y alcance del siglo XVIII en América Latina: el caso del centro-oeste mexicano." In *Ensayos sobre el desarrollo económico de México y América Latina (1500–1975),* ed. Enrique Florescano. Mexico City, 1979.

Mörner, Magnus. *Race Mixture in the History of Latin America.* Boston, 1967.

Muriel, Josefina. *Los recogimientos de mujeres. Respuesta a una problemática social novohispana.* Mexico City, 1974.

Noriega Elio, Cecilia del Carmen. "Fernández de Lizardi; un proyecto de sociedad. (Ideología y modelos de conducta)." Unpublished thesis, Universidad Nacional Autónoma de México, 1975.

Novo, Salvador. *Los paseos de la ciudad de México.* Mexico City, 1980.

O'Gorman, Edmundo. "Reflexiones sobre la distribución urbana colonial de la ciudad de México." In *Seis estudios históricos de tema mexicano.* Jalapa, Veracruz, 1960.

————, ed. "Sobre los inconvenientes de vivir los indios en el centro de la ciudad." *Boletín del AGN* 9:1 (January–March 1938).

Olavarría y Ferrari, Enrique de. *Reseña histórica del teatro en México.* 5 vols. Mexico City, 1961.

Orozco Díaz, Emilio. *El teatro y la teatralidad del barroco: ensayo de introducción al tema.* Barcelona, 1969.

Ortega y Gasset, José. *Goya.* Madrid, 1963.

Ortiz de Ayala, Simón Tadeo. *Resumen de la estadística del imperio mexicano, 1822.* Mexico City, 1968.

Payno, Manuel. *Los bandidos de Río Frío.* Mexico City, 1983.

Pérez Galdós, Benito. *Los apostólicos.* Madrid, 1917.

Polanyi, Karl. *The Great Transformation.* Boston, 1944.

Prieto, Guillermo. *Memorias de mis tiempo*. 2 vols. Mexico City, 1948.

Rangel, Nicolás. *Historia del toreo en México*. Mexico City, 1980.

Reyes de la Maza, Luis. *El teatro en México durante la Independencia, 1810–1839*. Mexico City, 1969.

Ricard, Robert. *La conquista espiritual de México*. Mexico City, 1947.

Riva Palacio, Vicente. *México a través de los siglos. Historia del virreinato*. Vols. 3 and 4. U.S., no date.

Robles, Antonio de. *Diario de sucesos notables*. 3 vols. Mexico City, 1946.

Robles-Cahero, José Antonio. "La memoria del cuerpo y la transmisión cultural: las danzas populares en el siglo XVIII." In *La memoria y el olvido. Segundo simposio de historia de las mentalidades*. Mexico City, 1985.

Roche, Daniel. *Le peuple de Paris. Essai sur la culture populaire au XVIII$^e$ siècle*. Paris, 1981.

Rojas Garcidueñas, José J. *El teatro en la Nueva España en el siglo XVI*. Mexico City, 1935.

Romero Flores, Jesús. *México, historia de una gran ciudad*, ed. B. Costa-Amic. Mexico City, 1978.

Rosell, Lauro E. *Iglesias y conventos coloniales de México; historia de cada uno de los que existen en la ciudad de México*. Mexico City, 1961.

Rousseau, Jean-Jacques. *Les Confessions*. Paris, 1964.

Ruvalcaba Mercado, Jesús. *El maguey manso. Historia y presente de Epazoyucan, Hgo*. Mexico City, 1983.

Sade, Marquis de. *Justine ou les malheurs de la vertu, suivie de l'Histoire de Juliette, sa soeur*. Various editions.

Salas Anzures, Miguel. "La ciudad de México." *Artes de México* 1:49–50 (January 1964): no pagination.

Salazar, Flora. "Los sirvientes domésticos." In *Ciudad de México: ensayo de construcción de una historia*, ed. Alejandra Moreno Toscano. Mexico City, 1981.

Sarabia Viejo, María Justina. *El juego de gallos en Nueva España*. Seville, 1972.

Sarrailh, Jean. *La España ilustrada de la segunda mitad del siglo XVI a mediados del XVIII*. Madrid, 1974.

Schilling, Hildburg. *Teatro profano en la Nueva España: fines del siglo XVI a mediados del XVIII*. Mexico City, 1958.

Segovia Canosa, Rafael. *Tres salvaciones del siglo XVIII español*. Jalapa, Veracruz, 1960.

Shorter, Edward. *The Making of the Modern Family*. London, 1976.

Sigüenza y Góngora, Carlos de. "Alboroto y motín de México, del 8 de junio de 1692." In *Relaciones históricas*. Mexico City, 1972.

"Sobre los inconvenientes de vivir los indios en el centro de la ciudad." *Boletín del AGN* 9 (January–March 1938).

Solé, Jacques. *L'amour en Occident à l'epoque moderne*. Paris, 1976.

Sten, María. *Vida y muerte del teatro nahúatl. El olimpo sin Prometeo*. Mexico City, 1974.

Subirats, Eduardo. *La ilustración insuficiente*. Madrid, 1981.

Swain, Gladys. "Une logique de l'inclusion: les infirmes du signe." *Esprit* 5 (May 1982):61–75.

Thompson, Edward P. "Eighteenth-Century English Society: Class Struggle without Class." *Social History* 3:2 (May 1978):150–165.

Tolstoi, Leon. "¿Qué hacer?" In *Los anarquistas. La teoría.* Madrid, 1975.

Usigli, Rodolfo. *México en el teatro.* Mexico City, 1932.

Valle-Arizpe, Artemio de. *Calle vieja y calle nueva.* Mexico City, 1949.

Varey, J. E. *Los títeres y otras diversiones populares de Madrid, 1758– 1840. Estudio y documentos. Fuentes para la historia del teatro en España.* Vol. 7. London, 1972.

Vázquez Santa-Ana, Higinio, and J. Ignacio Dávila Garibi. *El Carnaval.* Mexico City, 1931.

Velasco A., Cuauhtémoc. "Los trabajadores mineros de la Nueva España." In *La clase obrera en la historia de México.* Vol. 1: *De la colonia al imperio.* Mexico City, 1981.

Velázquez, María del Carmen. "El siglo XVIII." In *Historia documental de México.* Mexico City, 1974.

―――. "El despertar ilustrado." *Historia de México.* México City, 1978, vol. 7:1454–1457.

Venegas Ramírez, Carmen. *Régimen hospitalario para indios en la Nueva España.* Mexico City, 1973.

Ventura Beleña, Eusebio. *Recopilación sumaria de todos los autos acordados de la real audicencia y sala del crimen de esta Nueva España y providencias de su superior gobierno.* Mexico City, 1981.

*El viajero universal o noticia del mundo antiguo y nuevo. Obra recopilada de los mejores viageros.* Madrid, 1799. Vols. 26, 28.

Vilar, Pierre. "Coyunturas. Motín de Esquilache y crisis del antiguo régimen." In *Hidalgos, amotinados y guerrilleros. Pueblos y poderes en la historia de España.* Barcelona, 1982.

Villarroel, Hipólito de. *Enfermedades políticas que padece la capital de esta Nueva España en casi todos los cuerpos de que se compone y remedios que se la deben aplicar para su curación si se quiere que sea útil al rey y al público.* Mexico City, 1937.

Viqueira Albán, Juan Pedro. "El sentimiento de la muerte en el México ilustrado del siglo XVIII a través de dos textos de la época." *Relaciones* 5 (Winter 1981):45–54.

Weber, Max. *Economía y sociedad.* 2 vols. Mexico City, 1979.

―――. *Historia económica general.* Mexico City, 1979.

―――. *El político y el científico.* Mexico City, 1981.

Wilson, Iris Higbie, ed. "Pineda's Report on the Beverages of New Spain." *Arizona and the West* 5 (1963):79–90.

# Index

# Latin American Silhouettes
## Studies in History and Culture

*William H. Beezley and*
*Judith Ewell*
Editors

## Volumes Published

Silvia Marina Arrom and Servando Ortoll, eds., *Riots in the Cities: Popular Politics and the Urban Poor in Latin America, 1765–1910* (1996). Cloth ISBN 0-8420-2580-4  Paper ISBN 0-8420-2581-2

Roderic Ai Camp, ed., *Polling for Democracy: Public Opinion and Political Liberalization in Mexico* (1996). ISBN 0-8420-2583-9

Brian Loveman and Thomas M. Davies, Jr., eds., *The Politics of Antipolitics: The Military in Latin America*, 3d ed., revised and updated (1996). Cloth ISBN 0-8420-2609-6  Paper ISBN 0-8420-2611-8

Joseph S. Tulchin, Andrés Serbín, and Rafael Hernández, eds., *Cuba and the Caribbean: Regional Issues and Trends in the Post-Cold War Era* (1997). ISBN 0-8420-2652-5

Thomas W. Walker, ed., *Nicaragua without Illusions: Regime Transition and Structural Adjustment in the 1990s* (1997). Cloth ISBN 0-8420-2578-2  Paper ISBN 0-8420-2579-0

Dianne Walta Hart, *Undocumented in L.A.: An Immigrant's Story* (1997). Cloth ISBN 0-8420-2648-8  Paper ISBN 0-8420-2649-5

Jaime E. Rodríguez O. and Kathryn Vincent, eds., *Myths, Misdeeds, and Misunderstandings: The Roots of Conflict in U.S.-Mexican Relations* (1997). ISBN 0-8420-2662-2

Jaime E. Rodríguez O. and Kathryn Vincent, eds., *Common Border, Uncommon Paths: Race, Culture, and National Identity in U.S.-Mexican Relations* (1997). ISBN 0-8420-2673-8

William H. Beezley and Judith Ewell, eds., *The Human Tradition in Modern Latin America* (1997). Cloth ISBN 0-8420-2612-6  Paper ISBN 0-8420-2613-4

Donald F. Stevens, ed., *Based on a True Story: Latin American History at the Movies* (1997). Cloth ISBN 0-8420-2582-0  Paper ISBN 0-8420-2781-5

Jaime E. Rodríguez O., ed., *The Origins of Mexican National Politics, 1808–1847* (1997). Paper ISBN 0-8420-2723-8

Che Guevara, *Guerrilla Warfare*, with revised and updated introduction and case studies by Brian Loveman and Thomas M. Davies, Jr., 3d ed. (1997). Cloth ISBN 0-8420-2677-0  Paper ISBN 0-8420-2678-9

Adrian A. Bantjes, *As If Jesus Walked on Earth: Cardenismo, Sonora, and the Mexican Revolution* (1998). ISBN 0-8420-2653-3

Henry A. Dietz and Gil Shidlo, eds., *Urban Elections in Democratic Latin America* (1998). Cloth ISBN 0-8420-2627-4  Paper ISBN 0-8420-2628-2

A. Kim Clark, *The Redemptive Work: Railway and Nation in Ecuador, 1895–1930* (1998). ISBN 0-8420-2674-6

Joseph S. Tulchin, ed., with Allison M. Garland, *Argentina: The Challenges of Modernization* (1998). ISBN 0-8420-2721-1

Louis A. Pérez, Jr., ed., *Impressions of Cuba in the Nineteenth Century: The Travel Diary of Joseph J. Dimock* (1998). Cloth ISBN 0-8420-2657-6  Paper ISBN 0-8420-2658-4

June E. Hahner, ed., *Women through Women's Eyes: Latin American Women in Nineteenth-Century Travel Accounts* (1998). Cloth ISBN 0-8420-2633-9  Paper ISBN 0-8420-2634-7

James P. Brennan, ed., *Peronism and Argentina* (1998). ISBN 0-8420-2706-8

John Mason Hart, ed., *Border Crossings: Mexican and Mexican-American Workers* (1998). Cloth ISBN 0-8420-2716-5  Paper ISBN 0-8420-2717-3

Brian Loveman, *For* la Patria: *Politics and the Armed Forces in Latin America* (1999). Cloth ISBN 0-8420-2772-6 Paper ISBN 0-8420-2773-4

Guy P. C. Thomson, with David G. LaFrance, *Patriotism, Politics, and Popular Liberalism in Nineteenth-Century Mexico: Juan Francisco Lucas and the Puebla Sierra* (1999). ISBN 0-8420-2683-5

Robert Woodmansee Herr, in collaboration with Richard Herr, *An American Family in the Mexican Revolution* (1999). ISBN 0-8420-2724-6

Juan Pedro Viqueira Albán, trans. Sonya Lipsett-Rivera and Sergio Rivera Ayala, *Propriety and Permissiveness in Bourbon Mexico* (1999). Cloth ISBN 0-8420-2466-2 Paper ISBN 0-8420-2467-0

Stephen R. Niblo, *Mexico in the 1940s: Modernity, Politics, and Corruption* (1999). ISBN 0-8420-2794-7

David E. Lorey, *The U.S.-Mexican Border in the Twentieth Century* (1999). Cloth ISBN 0-8420-2755-6 Paper ISBN 0-8420-2756-4

Joanne Hershfield and David R. Maciel, eds., *Mexico's Cinema: A Century of Films and Filmmakers* (2000). Cloth ISBN 0-8420-2681-9 Paper ISBN 0-8420-2682-7

Peter V. N. Henderson, *In the Absence of Don Porfirio: Francisco León de la Barra and the Mexican Revolution* (2000). ISBN 0-8420-2774-2

Mark T. Gilderhus, *The Second Century: U.S.-Latin American Relations since 1889* (2000). Cloth ISBN 0-8420-2413-1 Paper ISBN 0-8420-2414-X

Catherine Moses, *Real Life in Castro's Cuba* (2000). Cloth ISBN 0-8420-2836-6 Paper ISBN 0-8420-2837-4

K. Lynn Stoner, ed./comp., with Luis Hipólito Serrano Pérez, *Cuban and Cuban-American Women: An Annotated Bibliography* (2000). ISBN 0-8420-2643-6

Thomas D. Schoonover, *The French in Central America: Culture and Commerce, 1820–1930* (2000). ISBN 0-8420-2792-0